ADVANCEMENT OF HUMAN RIGHTS IN INDIA

CONTEMPORARY AND EMERGING CHALLENGES

Edited by

DEBARATI HALDER

SHRUT S. BRAHMBHATT

ATLANTIC

PUBLISHERS & DISTRIBUTORS (P) LTD

ATLANTIC
PUBLISHERS & DISTRIBUTORS (P) LTD
7/22, Ansari Road, Darya Ganj, New Delhi
Tel.: +91-11-4077 5252, 2327 3880
E-mail: orders@atlanticbooks.com
Web: www.atlanticbooks.com

This edition published in 2024 by Atlantic Publishers & Distributors (P) Ltd.

Previous edition published by Sage Publications in 2021

Registered Office and Editorial Office
Atlantic Publishers & Distributors (P) Ltd.,
7/22, Ansari Road, Darya Ganj, New Delhi-110002, India

Library of Congress Cataloging-in-Publication applied for

ISBN 978-8-126-94306-7

For details of our editorial offices, customer service, and more information about Atlantic Publishers and Distributors (P) Ltd. products, visit us at www.atlanticbooks.com

Printed and bound in United States of America

Prof. (Dr) Debarati Halder dedicates this book to her daughter Mriganayani

Dr Shrut S. Brahmbhatt dedicates this book to his wife Kinjal Brahmbhatt

Contents

Section II: Child Rights and Human Rights

Section III: Contemporary Issues and Human Rights

List of Abbreviations

AFSPA	Armed Forces Special Powers Act
AIDS	Acquired Immunodeficiency Syndrome
BPA	The Beijing Platform for Action, 1995
CAP	Common Agricultural Policy
CBSE	Central Board of Secondary Education
CEC	Commission of the European Communities
CEDAW	Convention on the Elimination of All Forms of Discrimination Against Women, 1979
CEFC	Clean Energy Finance Corporation
CFF	Carbon Farming Futures
CGIAR	Consultative Group on International Agricultural Research
CICEF	Central Institute of Coastal Engineering for Fishery
CIFNET	Central Institute of Fisheries Nautical and Engineering Training
CRC	Convention on the Rights of the Child
CrPC	Criminal Procedure Code, 1973
CRPD	Convention on the Rights of Persons with Disabilities, 2006
CSA	Climate-Smart Agriculture
CSR	Corporate Social Responsibility
DAC&FW	Department of Agriculture Cooperation & Farmers Welfare
DPEP	District Primary Education Programme
DPSP	Directive Principles of State Policy
DRC	Democratic Republic of Congo
DV Act	Protection of Women from Domestic Violence Act, 2005
FAO	Food and Agriculture Organization

FRA	Scheduled Tribes and Other Traditional Forest Dwellers (Recognition of Forest Rights) Act
FSI	Fishery Survey of India
FSSAI	Food Safety and Standards Authority of India
GACSA	Global Alliance for Climate-Smart Agriculture
GDP	Gross Domestic Product
HAMA	Hindu Adoptions and Maintenance Act, 1956
HIV	Human Immunodeficiency Virus
HMA	Hindu Marriage Act, 1955
HSA	Hindu Succession Act, 1956
ICCPR	International Covenant on Civil and Political Rights, 1966
ICESCR	International Covenant on Economic, Social and Cultural Rights, 1966
ICF	International Classification of Functioning, Disability and Health
ICJ	International Court of Justice
ICMR	Indian Council of Medical Research
ILO	International Labour Organization
IOSGSSR	International Organization for Standardization's Guidance Standard on Social Responsibility
IPC	Indian Penal Code, 1860
IPSW	Indirect Primary Sex Workers
ISO	International Organization for Standardization
IT	Information Technology
ITPA	Immoral Traffic (Prevention) Act, 1956
JJA	Juvenile Justice (Care and Protection of Children) Act, 2015
JJB	Juvenile Justice Board
LA Act	Land Acquisition Act, 1894
LGBTQ	Lesbian, Gay, Bisexual, Transgender and Queer
LLP	Limited Liability Partnership
MFP	Minor Forest Produce
MoTA	Ministry of Tribal Affairs
NABARD	National Bank for Agriculture and Rural Development
NALSA	National Legal Services Authority

NCLP	National Policy on Child Labour, 1987
NCRB	National Crime Records Bureau
NGO	Non-Governmental Organization
NHRC	National Human Rights Commission of India
NICRA	National Initiative on Climate Resilient Agriculture
NIFPHATT	National Institute of Fisheries Post Harvest Technology and Training
NNSW	National Network of Sex Workers
NIFPHATT	National Institute of Fisheries Post Harvest Technology and Training
NTFPs	Non-Timber Forest Products
NWFPs	Non-Wood Forest Products
OHCHR	Office of the United Nations High Commissioner for Human Rights
PAs	Protected Areas
POCSO	Protection of Children from Sexual Offences Act, 2012
PUCL	People's Union for Civil Liberties
PVTGs	Particularly Vulnerable Tribal Groups
RFCTLARR	Right to Fair Compensation and Transparency in Land Acquisition, Rehabilitation and Resettlement Act, 2013
RPDA	Rights of Persons with Disabilities Act
RPwD	Rights of Persons with Disabilities Bill
RTE	Right of Children to Free and Compulsory Education Act, 2009
SHG	Self-Help Group
SSA	Sarva Shiksha Abhiyan
STD	Sexually Transmitted Disease
TB	Tuberculosis
UDHR	Universal Declaration of Human Rights, 1948
UN	United Nations
UN CRC	United Nations Convention on the Rights of the Child, 1989
UNCRPD	United Nations Conventions on the Rights of Persons with Disabilities

UNDRIP	United Nations Declaration on the Rights of Indigenous People
UNICEF	United Nations Children's Fund
UNIDO	United Nations Industrial Development Organization
WAAPP	West African Agricultural Productivity Program
WHO	World Health Organization
WLPA	Wild Life Protection Act
YCJA	Youth Criminal Justice Act

Foreword

Since the beginning of the era of globalization, issues of human rights have assumed great significance. The interface between the basic rights and the forces of liberalization heralded an unprecedented churning in the social and political lives of people. The spread of feminism has added new dimensions to issues of gender justice. Feminists are increasingly using the legal idioms of human rights. The grammar of human rights has helped develop a new language of gender rights. The processes of law are also adding to the efforts of feminists all over the world. The minuscule minority of almost-invisible lesbian, gay, bisexual, transgender, queer (LGBTQ) people regained their status of *Homo sapiens* through judicial interventions in India. The states and the people, though hesitatingly, are now recognizing their presence in society. People with disabilities got their rights of equal opportunities through legislative formulations. It has been possible because of the universalization of human rights that people with disabilities are occupying legal space and laws protecting their interests are being legislated. The rights of senior citizens were being ignored in the wake of rapid urbanization, as mass migration from rural areas to urban centres made them vulnerable to abuse and humiliation by their own children. A sublime interpretation of human rights has brought them under the protective umbrella of welfare legislations. Assisted reproductive technology has helped the womenfolk enjoy the right to choose and the fruits of motherhood, but it does impact the rights of surrogate mothers, which has recently prompted the government to make a law to provide a rights' framework in this area.

The corporate sector has spread its tentacles in all spheres of social life, including education and health too. The idea of corporate social responsibility has also brought new players to the hitherto uncharted domains in which the issues of human rights are bound to crop up. The sectors of education and health were not considered to be meant for the corporate sector in India. It is good for the private sector to enter the areas of education and health, but it needs to remain within the discipline of human rights. The poor must have equal access to quality education and health, which should be made available at affordable prices. Like universal primary education to all children and universal distribution of the COVID-19 vaccine are directly related to the human rights of people.

This edited book brings out several nuances and shades of human rights: child rights from different perspectives, rights of children of sex workers, women's rights for reproduction, surrogacy and related rights violations, marital rape, land rights, rights of the LGBTQ people, rights of the forest dwellers, discussions on access to justice by persons detained in foreign lands and rights of victims of army atrocities in conflict zones are some that have been elaborately discussed in this book. Discussions on corporate social responsibilities, which has created new dimensions in human rights laws and policies, have also been included in this book.

I congratulate the editors of this book, Prof. (Dr) Debarati and Dr Shrut S. Brahmbhatt, for their hard work. The book is well organized and offers an interesting read. I am sure this book will be helpful for readers as a whole in understanding the human rights and the policymakers will pay heed to the recommendations offered by this book.

Professor Subir K. Bhatnagar
Vice-Chancellor

Preface

The issue of human rights has always been a dynamic subject for research for legal researchers, practitioners, students and activists. In the present age, the concept of human rights cannot be trapped within the understanding of basic rights, such as the right to live with dignity, right to food and shelter, right to live and work in a healthy atmosphere, etc., which are associated with human beings because they are human beings. In this 21st century, the understanding about human rights is expanding in a rapid way: the right to communicate has been expanded to include the right to have an Internet connection; the right to marry has been construed to include the right to choose a life partner from homosexual communities; the right to gender orientation has been recognized as a novel and essential right; and the right to privacy has been expanded to include the right to be forgotten in cyberspace. Courts have also started recognizing rights of the elderly beyond the scope of mere monetary maintenance. Individuals from disabled and transgender communities have also secured their right to proper, user-friendly toilet facilities. Interestingly, the understanding about gender justice has been expanded to include the role of fathers in the upbringing of their children and mothers' right to work, leaving their children in day care or in the care of other caregivers. Child rights, again, are no more limited to the understanding of the right to protection against child labour, but they have expanded to cover the right to holistic development of children: this includes the right to education, right to protection against sexual violence, child marriage, marital rape, etc. Further, stakeholders are also showing concern over the right to food, land acquisition and its impact on human rights violations, etc. Above all, the courts have increasingly emphasized corporate social responsibilities towards ensuring all kinds of human rights.

This book presents 24 chapters addressing these different aspects of human rights. The 24 chapters adhere to three different themes: gender justice and human rights; child rights and human rights; and contemporary issues of human rights, which include discussions on the corporate sector and human rights, globalization and socio-economic rights, etc. The first theme, that is, gender justice and human rights, addresses issues of the need for gender-sensitive laws to protect the rights of women, the role of gender-biased laws in facilitating victimization of women, disabled women and their rights, rights of sex workers, forced sterilization of differently abled women and how it impacts reproduction, gender justice for third-gender people and marital rape. The second theme, that is, child rights and human rights, addresses different aspects of rights of children. For instance, it addresses the right to education and its role in the holistic development of children, the reformative aspect of the juvenile justice system in India, issues of child marriages and child marital rape, child labour and the role of forensic dentistry in detecting child sexual harassment. The third theme, that is, contemporary issues of human rights, further addresses different aspects of human rights, including surrogacy and how it violates certain human rights, rights in regard to agricultural revitalization, food security of indigenous people, human rights violations in regard to land acquisition, rights of transgenders, the right to consular assistance as a crucial human right for people arrested in a foreign land, issues of human rights violations by the armed forces in Jammu and Kashmir, corporate social responsibility, paternity leave, etc.

As this book addresses varied aspects of human rights from current perspectives, it promises to cater to the needs of human rights lawyers, practitioners, activists and researchers in the field of law, social sciences, including human rights, international relations, etc.

This book would not have been possible without the motivation from and active help of a few people. We deeply acknowledge their help. Foremost among them is Mr Ritesh Hada, President of Karnavati University, and Dr Deepak Shishoo, Hon'ble provost of Karnavati University, Gandhinagar, Gujarat. Without their motivation and blessings, this book would not have been possible. We thank Professors Shri Subir. K. Bhatnagar, Hon'ble Vice Chancellor, Dr Rammanohar

Lohia, National Law School, Uttar Pradesh, Dr Arvind Jasrotia, Professor of Law, Department of Law, Jammu University, Dr N. Vijaylakhsmi Brara, Manipur University, and Prof. (Dr) Akil Saiyed, Dean of Law, Parul University, for motivating us to make this book a reality. We deeply thank our reviewers and all contributors, without whom this book would not have been a reality. We also wish to thank Professor (Dr) Namrata Bajaj for helping us in editing this book. We also wish to thank all our colleagues at Unitedworld School of Law for rendering their support for this book.

This book would not have been possible without our respective families. Prof. (Dr) Debarati Halder acknowledges the support and motivation of her daughter, Mriganayani. Dr Shrut S. Brahmbhatt acknowledges the support and motivation of his wife, Mrs Kinjal Brahmbhatt, his son, Tryaksh Brahmbhatt, and his parents.

Introduction

Every individual, as a member of human society, possesses some unique rights that are universal in nature. These rights are essential for leading a dignified life. As the history of human rights suggests, certain civilizations had recognized the existence of basic human rights as early as 5,000 years ago: the Indian, Egyptian and Roman civilizations are the prime examples. Ancient Indian scriptures, including the Vedas, Manusmriti, Arthashastra, relics of Ashoka and Thirukkural from the Dravidian regions in southern India, may show that the king or the state was duty-bound to protect the basic rights of human beings. Simultaneously, every individual was duty-bound to respect the rights of others. However, the concept of rights was much narrower than that of the rights being enjoyed by human beings of the present era. Invasions in different ages in different countries suppressed several existing rights and introduced new rights. While this widened the concept of human rights violations, it also created a strong base for creating a universal concept of human rights. The devastating effects of the two World Wars showed the need to formulate a universally acceptable code of human rights. It was also felt that peaceful coexistence of nation states should be the key to maintaining human rights and developing new concepts in this regard. Immediately after international stakeholders met to develop the draft declaration of human rights in 1945, several countries established their 'independent nation state' status as colonial rulers withdrew their governance from these colonies. This phase created another unique situation that demanded further development of human rights, especially in relation to access to justice, right to good governance, right to vote, right against arbitrary actions by the government, equal distribution of public wealth and natural wealth, etc. The 1960s was the era of rights explosions in several jurisdictions, including India. This era saw the growth of discrimination based on colour, creed, race and gender, especially in the labour market.

The effect of economic recessions was still haunting the United States and European countries, and this further fuelled and also created several industries that flourished through exploiting human rights: these included flesh trade, running of illegal domestic and international cheap-labour supply agencies involving extremely poor migrant workers, etc. By the 1970s, several stakeholders, including the United Nations, realized the gross violation of women's rights, which resulted in the development of the Convention on the Elimination of All Forms of Discrimination Against Women (CEDAW). The CEDAW emphasized not only equal rights for women in society but also equal wages for equal work for women. Soon, the creation of the convention on child rights followed. However, none of these key conventions and declarations could prevent further human rights violations. The freedoms of speech, expression, press, etc., explored several other sorts of human right violation, which included right violation of disabled persons, children, civil citizens staying in the combat zones, aboriginals and tribal people living in the forest for generations, etc. These rights explosions heavily impacted the growth of judicial activism, pro bono lawyering and public interest litigations.

India was no exception. The Constitution of India was influenced by the Universal Declaration of Human Rights. The parliamentarians of newly independent India considered the need to frame statutes, rules and policies that would strengthen the human rights in India. However, the grievance explosions outweighed the laws. Justices Bhagawati and Krishna Iyer of the Supreme Court of India took the lead role in the 1970s to draft the aims of Articles 39A (which speaks about access to justice) and 32 and 226 (which speak about remedies to human rights violations through writs) of the Constitution of India. Even though India is not a leading country where citizens and aliens may enjoy absolute protection of human rights, India is not a leading country in the case of human rights violations either. Credit goes to the judicial activism and constant research on human rights by right activists, professors and researchers of law, sociology, criminology, political science, international relations, management, etc. This book is an attempt to further the research on human rights, gender rights, child rights, restoration of justice for violation of human rights, etc. The first section of the book deals with gender justice and human rights, which includes discussions on critical analyzes of the general rights of women, including people belonging to LGBTQ communities, and detailed discussions on the rights of disabled women from different perspectives, including the perspectives of sexual rights, marital rape and rights of sex workers. The second section of the book deals with child rights from various perspectives. This section carries detailed discussions on the general rights of children, the right to education, issues related to child marriage and child labour, the role of medico-legal services in analysing child sexual abuse and reformative aspects of the juvenile justice system. The third section deals with contemporary issues of human rights, which includes detailed discussions on corporate social responsibilities towards ensuring human rights, surrogacy and related rights, the right to food, rights of forest dwellers, rights related to agricultural land and products and equal distribution of food grains, the right to consular assistance, the right to protection against illegal search, arrest and detention by the army and related human violations, etc.

This book would help us realize where we stand when it comes to discussions on and evaluation of the implementation of human rights laws in India.

SECTION I

Gender Justice and Human Rights

Chapter 1

Victimization of Disabled Women in India

A Critical Analysis

Dipa Dube

INTRODUCTION

A large population of the world suffers from physical and mental disability. According to the World Health Organization (WHO) definition, 'Disabilities is an umbrella term, covering impairments, activity limitations, and participation restrictions'.[1] Physical and mental disability may occur in individuals either due to birth defects, genetic disorders or poor health conditions or due to physical injuries, etc.[2] As the WHO report shows, more than 15 per cent of the world population suffers from some form of disability.[3] The growth of population with

[1] See https://www.who.int/topics/disabilities/en/, accessed 1 May 2020.

[2] Centers for Disease Control and Prevention, 'Prevalence and Most Common Causes of Disability Among Adults--United States, 2005', *MMWR: Morbidity and Mortality Weekly Report* 58, no. 16 (2009): 421–26. https://www.safetylit.org/citations/index.php?fuseaction=citations.viewdetails&citationIds[]=citjournalarticle_99524_12, accessed 1 May 2020.

[3] For more, see Disability and Health: Key Facts. https://www.who.int/news-room/fact-sheets/detail/disability-and-health, accessed 1 May 2020.

disability over the years poses serious and pertinent questions of social well-being of disabled persons and their rehabilitation. However, the volume of research on rights of disabled women from human rights perspective is comparatively less.[4] Even though the United Nations (UN) Convention on the Rights of Persons with Disabilities was brought in by the international stakeholders in 2006,[5] this author argues that the said convention has not yielded much results in South Asian countries, including India, when it comes to ensuring rights of women with disability. Women with disabilities may suffer unique victimization patterns,[6] and India is no exception due to the social–legal–economic–cultural structure of the Indian society.

The present chapter is based on a cross-sectional study of disabled women in India, which was sponsored by the Ministry of Social Justice and Empowerment, Government of India. The said study revealed that there is a prominent connection between disability and victimization of women in all forms. The study included respondents from different states of India representing the geographic regions of northern, western, southern and eastern India. It may be noted that earlier studies have shown that worldwide, disabled women may be discriminated at home and at the workplace, may be sexually exploited by their own family members and may not access proper healthcare and hygienic living conditions, basic education, food, etc.[7] However, these studies did not

---

[4] Lina Abu Habib, '"Women and Disability Don't Mix!": Double Discrimination and Disabled Women's Rights', *Gender & Development* 3, no. 2 (1995): 49–53. https://www.jstor.org/stable/pdf/4030515.pdf?casa_token=qgahZi5yd1MAAAAA:DorR2czpVLy1otpsACS_lACpYtG-GSqeQOEr1H99n1rhoYfSgCGrVwTZnJAeeoRBXRb6fL-l0vfspzTaR_ssuHmZTqPndYX44jeYu_vJKtCuxHziA20, accessed 1 February 2020.

[5] See Frédéric Mégret, 'The Disabilities Convention: Human Rights of Persons with Disabilities or Disability Rights?' *Human Rights Quarterly* 30 (2008): 494–516. https://muse.jhu.edu/article/237738/pdf, accessed 1 May 2020.

[6] Sara-Beth Plummer and Patricia A. Findley, 'Women with Disabilities' Experience with Physical and Sexual Abuse: Review of the Literature and Implications for the Field', *Trauma Violence Abuse* 13 (2012): 15–29 (2012).

[7] See Anita Ghai, 'Disabled Women: An Excluded Agenda of Indian Feminism', *Hypatia* 17, no. 3 (2002): 49–66; Nasa Begum, 'Disabled Women and the Feminist Agenda', *Feminist Review* 40, no. 1 (1 March 1992): 70–84.

address the issue of disability of women from a geographic region–based approach in India. This study aims to fulfil this lacuna.

It was found that disabled women from all these regions uniformly suffer most of the patterns of victimization which have been observed by the earlier studies. However, they may suffer extreme levels of such domestic violence and discrimination in regard to childhood care, healthcare, basic education and food. It was also found that disabled women have extremely limited rights of movement outside their homes. They are also discriminated in the area of vocational training for a livelihood, as their families do not allow them to access such training. Such women are rather considered as a financial burden by their families. The study further found that women with disabilities may be denied their basic needs of existence by their own families, there are high possibilities of childhood abandonment for them and they also suffer social seclusion. The study further indicates that such disabled women may be married at an early age for reproduction purposes, and they may be deserted soon after childbirth. Such women and girls with disability may also be prone to sexual violation. This study also shows that some women also become disabled as a result of violent sexual violations, and most of such disabled women in the geographic regions mentioned in the study have to stay in homes and institutions run by the government and non-governmental organizations (NGOs) in poor, unhygienic conditions, facing serious financial challenges.

This chapter is divided into four parts, including introduction as the first part. The second part provides a general understanding about disability, with special reference to India. The third part analyses the empirical data on victimization of women and presents critical discussions on this very issue. The fourth part is the conclusion.

DISABILITY—A CONCEPTUAL FRAMEWORK

David John Thomas very accurately explained the term disability in the following words:

> Within the world of disabilities, one can find contradictory images of success and failure, optimism, and pessimism, tragedy and humour

> 'matter of fact' reactions and pathological responses, acceptance and stigma, recognition of individual differences and stereotyping, superb support services and inadequate ones, sensible and silly legislation, community support and social isolation, resignation and rebellion, successful careers and appalling job prospects, deeply satisfying personal relationships and loneliness, acceptance and rejection.[8]

As mentioned in the introduction, the term 'disability' has been briefly defined by WHO as an inclusive term: in the words of WHO, 'Disabilities is an umbrella term, covering impairments, activity limitations, and participation restrictions'.[9] In this definition, three specific concepts are seen, that is, impairment, activity limitations and participation limitations. Each of these terms implies stages of disability. The global report on disability, released by WHO in 2011,[10] explains these three terms as follows: impairment implies 'problems in body function or alteration in body structure'.[11] The report further explains the term with examples of paralysis or blindness.[12] It may be seen that the first sort of impairment may occur due to sudden physical injury and trauma, or it may also occur due to genetic disorder. The second sort of impairment may also be genetic or may occur due to birth defects. It may also occur due to poor health conditions. The report explains the term 'activity limitations' in the following words: 'activity limitations... are difficulties in executing activities'.[13] The examples provided for such activity limitations include difficulty in walking or eating.[14] Thus, it may be seen that impairment and activity limitations may be different issues, but they may be connected. The term 'participation restrictions' is further explained in the report as '...problems with involvement in any area of life'.[15] This indicates problems in connectivity with peers,

---

[8] David John Thomas, *The Experience of Handicap* (London: Methuen, 1982), 3. Also see Habib, 'Women and Disability Don't Mix!'

[9] See https://www.who.int/topics/disabilities/en/

[10] For more, see https://www.who.int/disabilities/world_report/2011/chapter1.pdf, accessed 1 May 2020.

[11] See Mégret, 'The Disabilities Convention'.

[12] Ibid.

[13] Ibid.

[14] Ibid.

[15] Ibid.

the environment, etc. The report explains this term by providing examples of discrimination at the workplace, in public places, including transport, etc.[16] As may be understood from the explanations above, the term disability may imply abnormal functioning of the body as a whole or of a sensory organ.[17]

Hence, as commonly understood, a disabled person means a person who is not capable of understanding things or carrying out any work assigned to him/her in a normal manner, on account of any defect afflicting the five sensory parts of the body, due to which he/she is not in a position to see or hear or perform any act with the help of his/her limbs in a requisite manner, which could be expected from a man/woman of normal prudence with an average intelligence and health.[18] The UN Declaration on the Rights of Disabled Persons defines the term as 'any person unable to ensure by himself or herself, wholly or partly, the necessities of a normal individual and/or social life, as a result of deficiency, either congenital or not, in his or her physical or mental capabilities'. [19]

WHO in 1976 drew a three-way distinction between 'impairment', 'disability' and 'handicap',[20] establishing that 'impairment' refers to organ-level functions or structures, 'disability' refers to person-level limitations in physical and psycho-cognitive activities, and 'handicap' to social abilities or relations between the individual and society.[21] Later, the International Classification of Functioning, Disability and Health, known more commonly as ICF, was officially endorsed by WHO as the international standard to describe and measure health and disability

---

[16] Ibid.

[17] See G. N. Karna, *United Nations and The Rights of Disabled Persons: A Study in Indian Perspective* (New Delhi: APH Publishing, 1999), 52–3.

[18] Gursharan Varandani, 'Law Relating to Disabled Persons and the Proposed Remedial Measures in the Context of Prospective Action Plan', In *Rights of Persons with Disabilities* (1st ed. 2002), 81.

[19] United Nations, *Declaration on Rights of Disabled Persons* (9 January 2018), http://www.ohchr.org/EN/ProfessionalInterest/Pages/RightsOfDisabledPersons.aspx.

[20] Karna, *United Nations and The Rights of Disabled Persons*, 52–3.

[21] World Health Organization, *International Classification of Functioning, Disability and Health: ICF* (5 January 2018), http://www.who.int/classifications/icf/en/.

[22] The ICF beginner's guide titled 'Towards a Common Language for Functioning, Disability and Health ICF'[23] clearly mentions the following:

> ICF puts the notions of 'health' and 'disability' in a new light. It acknowledges that every human being can experience a decrement in health and thereby experience some disability. This is not something that happens to only a minority of humanity. ICF thus 'mainstreams' the experience of disability and recognises it as a universal human experience.[24]

ICF has further clarified that the concept of disability may go beyond medical or biological abnormalities and may also include environmental factors that go a long way to deny basic human rights to disabled people.[25] The term 'disability' therefore includes several 'functional limitations': it may include physical disabilities, including hearing impairment, blindness, and impaired limbs. The term disability also necessarily includes mental disability.[26] Further, disability, whether caused due to accidental, physical or mental trauma or acquired due to genetic disorders, etc., affects human beings at large, irrespective of gender, age and race.[27]

Disability in India

India is a signatory to the UN Convention on the Rights of Persons with Disabilities. It has ratified the said treaty by introducing the Rights

---

[22] World Health Organization, 'International Classification of Functioning'.

[23] Available at https://www.who.int/classifications/icf/icfbeginnersguide.pdf, accessed 1 May 2020.

[24] Ibid., p. 4.

[25] WHO, *megret supra note* 5.

[26] United Nations Department of Public Information, *The Standard Rules on the Equalization of Opportunities for Persons with Disabilities* (1994). https://www.un.org/development/desa/disabilities/resources/general-assembly/standard-rules-on-the-equalization-of-opportunities-for-persons-with-disabilities-ares4896.html.

[27] Karna, *United Nations and The Rights of Disabled Persons.*

of Persons with Disabilities Act (RPDA), 2016, which came into force in 2017. The Rights of Persons with Disabilities (RPWD) Bill had included 21 types of disabilities within the definition of disability.[28] The list in the bill includes the following disabilities:

> Blindness, Low-vision, Leprosy Cured persons, Hearing Impairment (deaf and hard of hearing, Locomotor Disability, Dwarfism, Intellectual Disability, Mental Illness, Autism Spectrum Disorder, Cerebral Palsy, Muscular Dystrophy, Chronic Neurological conditions, Specific Learning Disabilities, Multiple Sclerosis, Speech and Language disability, Thalassemia, Hemophilia, Sickle Cell disease, Multiple Disabilities including deaf blindness, Acid Attack victim, Parkinson's disease.[29]

Based on this categorization, RPDA, 2016 has defined disability under three different categories. These are as follows:

'Person with benchmark disability': Section 2(r) of RPDA explains such disability as follows:

> Person with benchmark disability means a person with not less than forty per cent. of a specified disability where specified disability has not been defined in measurable terms and includes a person with disability where specified disability has been defined in measurable terms, as certified by the certifying authority.

'Person with disability': Section 2(s) of RPDA explains such disability by stating that 'Person with disability means a person with long term physical, mental, intellectual or sensory impairment which, in interaction with barriers, hinders his full and effective participation in society equally with others'.

Person with disability having high support needs: Section 2(t) of RPDA explains this term by stating that 'Person with disability having high support needs means a person with benchmark disability

---

[28] For more, see https://pib.gov.in/newsite/PrintRelease.aspx?relid=154862, accessed 1 May 2020.

[29] Ibid.

certified under clause (a) of sub-section (2) of Section 58 who needs high support'.

The other related disability legislations[30] define the term in its specific context to include people with different handicaps or conditions relating to autism, cerebral palsy, mental retardation or mental illness, etc.[31]

According to the Census 2011,[32] there were 26.8 million persons with disability in India, constituting 2.21 per cent of the total population. This includes persons with visual, hearing, speech, locomotor, mental and multiple disabilities. The census also showed that there had been a steep increase in the population with disabilities in both rural and urban areas over the last decade (2001–2010), though the proportion of those in rural areas was higher.[33] Further, it also showed that the proportion of disabled males (18.6 million) was higher than that of disabled females (8.2 million), though the increase in the percentage of persons with disabilities had been higher among females over the last decade (2001–2010).[34]

The Invisible Population: Disabled Women

Women with disabilities constitute more than 250 million of the world's population.[35] However, the majority of women with disabilities would claim that the barriers and human rights violations that they may have faced are due to male domination. Chenoweth (1993) correctly observed that '...Being relegated to a marginalised status by their disability, and further discriminated against through their gender, women with disabilities score "two strikes" One consequence of this is that they are rendered virtually invisible in both the disability and

[30] The Rehabilitation Council of India Act, 1992.

[31] Ibid.

[32] C. Chandramouli and Registrar General, *Census of India 2011* (Provisional Popul. Totals New Delhi: Gov. India, 2011).

[33] Ibid.

[34] Ibid.

[35] For example, see Disabled Person in India: A Statistical Profile 2016. http://mospi.nic.in/sites/default/files/publication_reports/Disabled_persons_in_India_2016.pdf, accessed 12 December 2018.

the women's movements'.[36] This dual marginalization exposes women with disabilities to grave risks of emotional, physical and sexual abuse, and when such abuse occurs, they are likely to be ignored by both the disability- and violence-related support systems. In other words, women find themselves up against double discrimination. In such a situation, disabled women may face grave violation of human rights, including denial of right to education, unemployment, denial of access to healthcare, etc., and this may push them to be violated physically and sexually by family members, as well as by unknown perpetrators.

Studies show that people with disabilities are more prone to be victimized by way of violent crimes.[37] Women with disabilities may also experience sexual assault or rape, robbery or aggravated assaults, as well as verbal–emotional abuse and neglect.[38] Women with disabilities in fact are more prone to be physically and sexually victimized than men with disabilities.[39]

One of the earliest studies by Sobsey and Doe[40] reported the patterns of sexual abuse and assault among children and adults with developmental disabilities. The sample included 82 per cent women and 70 per cent persons with intellectual impairments, and it covered a very wide age range (18 months to 57 years). In 96 per cent of the cases, the perpetrators were known to the victims; 44 per cent of the perpetrators were service providers. Of the individuals, 79 per cent

---

[36] Lesley Chenoweth, 'Invisible Acts: Violence Against Women with Disabilities', *Australian Disability Review* 2 (1993): 22–28.

[37] Erika Harrell, *Crimes Against Persons With Disabilities, 2009–2015–Statistical Tables 2017* (9 January 2018), https://www.bjs.gov/content/pub/pdf/capd0915st.pdf.

[38] NCVRW Resource Guide, Crimes Against Persons with Disabilities (15 January 2017), http://victimsofcrime.org/docs/default-source/ncvrw2015/2015ncvrw_stats_personswithdisabilities.pdf?sfvrsn=2.

[39] Laurie E. Powers et al., 'Interpersonal Violence and Women with Disabilities: Analysis of Safety Promoting Behaviours', *Violence Women* 15 (2009): 1040–1069; Sandra L. Martin et al., 'Physical and Sexual Assault of Women with Disabilities', *Violence Women* 12 (2006): 823–37; Douglas A. Brownridge, 'Partner Violence Against Women with Disabilities: Prevalence, Risk, and Explanations', *Violence Women* 12 (2006): 805–22.

[40] Dick Sobsey and Tanis Doe, 'Patterns of Sexual Abuse and Assault', *Sexuality and Disability* 9 (1991): 243–59.

were victimized more than once.[41] Furey (1994) showed that in 73 per cent of the cases, people with disabilities, including women, were denied treatment services, or such services were inadequate.[42] Another study, around the same time, found that about 83 per cent of women with disabilities were sexually assaulted throughout their life.[43] Further, several researchers have also observed that women with disabilities may not only suffer sexual, physical and emotional abuse, but they may also be denied basic health-related rights, including denial of access to medicines, mobility devices, and support system for personal care by family members. There may be extremely less chances for providing them paid services for personal care.[44]

The situation is no better in India, where women and girls with disabilities may suffer extreme physical and mental abuse, including sexual abuse, especially within homes and institutional care systems also.[45] In a study conducted in Odisha,[46] a sample of 729 women, 595 with physical disabilities and 134 with mental challenges, were compiled. The respondents were asked whether they had ever

[41] Ibid.

[42] Eileen M. Furey, 'Sexual Abuse of Adults with Mental Retardation: Who and Where', *Mental Retardation* 32 (1994): 173.

[43] L. Stimpson and E. Best, *Courage Above All: Sexual Assault and Women with Disabilities* (Toronto: DisAbled Women's Network-Toronto, 1991).

[44] Linda Carman Copel, 'Partner Abuse in Physically Disabled Women: A Proposed Model for Understanding Intimate Partner Violence', *Perspectives in Psychiatric Care* 42, no. 2 (2006): 114–29; Julianne S. Oktay and Catherine J. Tompkins, 'Personal Assistance Providers' Mistreatment of Disabled Adults', *Health & Social Work* 29 (2004): 177–88; Stephen French Gilson, Elizabeth Depoy, and Elizabeth P. Cramer, 'Linking the Assessment of Self-reported Functional Capacity with Abuse Experiences of Women with Disabilities', *Violence Women* 7 (2001): 418–31. J. Riddington, Beating the 'odds': Violence and women with disabilities, 2 POSITION PAP. (1989); Danuta M. Krotoski, Margaret Ann Nosek, and Margaret A. Turk, *Women With Physical Disabilities: Achieving and Maintaining Health and Well-Being* (Austin: Brookes Publishinh Co., 1996); D. Valenti-Hein and L. Schwartz, *The Sexual Abuse Interview for Those with Developmental Disabilities* (St. Barbara: James Stanfield Co. 1995).

[45] Indumathi Rao, *Equity to Women with Disabilities in India* (New Delhi: National Commission for Women, 2005).

[46] Sruti Mohapatra and Mihir Mohanty, *Abuse and activity limitation: a study on domestic violence against disabled women in Orissa, India* (Orissa: Swabhiman, 2005), 6–5.

experienced emotional, physical or sexual abuse. It was found that parents, husbands and close family members were the most common perpetrators of emotional or physical abuse for both groups. Deaf women were sexually abused by family members and close friends, as also were those who were mentally challenged. Women with physical disabilities appeared to be at risk of emotional, physical and sexual abuse to the same extent as women without physical disabilities.[47] Unique vulnerabilities to abuse, experienced by women with disabilities, included social stereotypes of asexuality and passivity, acceptance of abuse as normal behaviour, lack of adaptive equipment, inaccessible home and community environments, increased exposure to medical and institutional settings, dependence on perpetrators for personal assistance and lack of employment options.[48] Those with intellectual disabilities are further subject to prolonged periods of detention. Further, it was also found that lack of awareness about disability and disability-related rights, available community-based services, other available services and government policies, etc., may make women with disabilities even more prone to victimization by their own family.[49]

THE PRESENT STUDY

According to Lawson (2007), there has been an increase in the attention to the global marginalization of disabled people living in deplorable conditions, who are denied basic human rights.[50] This understanding made the national and international stakeholders create policies, conventions, etc., to end discriminatory practices against

---

[47] Ibid.

[48] Shampa Sengupta, *Violence Against Women with Disabilities* (Kolkata: Jadavpur University, 2003).

[49] Human Rights Watch, 'Treated Worse than Animals'—Abuses Against Women and Girls with Psychosocial or Intellectual Disabilities in Institutions in India (3 January 2017), https://www.hrw.org/sites/default/files/reports/india_forUpload.pdf.

[50] Anna Lawson, 'The United Nations Convention on the Rights of Persons with Disabilities: New Era or False Dawn?' *Syracuse Journal of International Law and Commerce* 34 (2006): 563.

disabled persons.[51] However, the issue of victimization of women with disabilities still needs attention, as women with disabilities may not even be allowed to speak about their pathetic conditions.[52] In this regard, comparatively less studies, including empirical studies, have been conducted in the Indian context to understand the plight of disabled women.

The present study[53] was a cross-sectional one conducted to explore the links between disability and victimization of women. The units of the study were disabled women and girls. The entire country was divided into four zones: North, South, East and West. From each zone, two states were selected randomly: West Bengal and Odisha (East), Maharashtra and Gujarat (West), Kerala and Karnataka (South) and New Delhi and Uttar Pradesh (North). In addition, two other states, namely Madhya Pradesh and Andhra Pradesh, were also included in the study. A comprehensive database of disability homes, schools and medical and research institutes was prepared. For this purpose, several sources, such as government departments, NGOs and websites, were referred to. Most of these homes and institutions were subsequently contacted over e-mail or telephoned to inform them about the study being conducted and the assistance needed for data collection. After their confirmation, researchers were sent to each of the places to collect data. Purposive sampling was used to identify the girls and women for the present study.

The data were collected mainly through unstructured interviews and observation. Researchers interacted with the respondents on various issues pertaining to their disability and experiences of victimization, if any. Group discussions among women and girls in schools or communities were conducted, and significant points concerning victimization by family and friends were raised in the course of these

---

[51] Ibid.

[52] Plummer and Findley, 'Women with Disabilities' Experience'.

[53] The present study was sponsored by the Ministry of Social Justice and Empowerment, Government of India. The author wants to express her gratitude to Dr Indrajit Dube, Dr S. K. Verma, Ms S. Sengupta for their support and cooperation.

discussions. Wherever required, assistance of experts and therapists was taken in order to understand the responses of the respondents.

The total sample of the study comprised 756 disabled women and girls. The researchers also interacted with the caregivers to verify and ascertain facts. About 100 officials, including doctors, superintendents, principals, teachers and therapists working in the area of disability and well aware of the conditions of these women and girls, were interviewed. On several instances, the researchers and the project director visited the homes and workplaces and also resided in the institutions to assess and understand the social dynamics.

Findings and Analysis

The disability profiles of the female respondents included physical disability, hearing, speech and visual impairment, mental retardation and mental illness as shown in Table 1.1. About 37 per cent of the total sample of 756 women constituted those who were intellectually disabled (including those with cerebral palsy and autism), while 21 per cent, 15 per cent and 12 per cent, respectively, constituted women with physical, visual and hearing impairment. Nearly 11 per cent of the respondents had more than one disability (multiple disabilities). Girls and women in the age group of 6–65 years were part of the study. Regarding the age profile of the respondents, 7 per cent of the respondents were girls below 12 years of age and 16 per cent were girls in the age group of 13–18 years. In the age groups of 19–21 and 22–35 years, there were 21 per cent and 30 per cent women, respectively. Another 26 per cent of the respondents were above 35 years of age. Thus, the sample was a well-distributed one with all age groups of women being represented therein.

Most of the women interviewed in the course of the study were unmarried, constituting about 71 per cent of the respondents. About 21 per cent of the women were married, while another 8 per cent were unable to state their marital position, owing to unknown past records or memory. No divorced or widowed women were found in the course of the study, though many women, not legally divorced, were deserted by their husbands or left at institutions without any family support or care.

Table 1.1 *Profile of Respondents*

		Percentage (*N* = 756)
Disability	Physical	21
	Visual	15
	Hearing	12
	Intellectual (retardation and illness)	37
	Multiple	11
Age	Below 12	7
	13–18	16
	19–21	21
	22–35	30
	36–50	16
	Above 50	10
Marital status	Never married	71
	Married	21
	Not known	8
Educational profile	Illiterate	38
	Till class VIII	32
	Secondary	12
	Higher secondary	6.5
	Graduation and above	11.5
Resident status	House resident/home maker	45
	Inmate (govt./NGO inst./hostel)	55
Profession/vocation, if any	None	72.5
	Vocational work/self-employment	25
	Govt. employment	2
	NGOs	.5
Income	None	72.5
	Below ₹1,000	12
	Above ₹1,000–₹5,000	10
	Above ₹5,000	5.5

Source: The author.

Regarding the education profile of the respondents, many of the respondents were illiterate (38%), whereas 32 per cent had completed education till about class VIII. Respondents with graduate or postgraduate degrees were primarily traced in the category of mental illness; the women had studied and even pursued some career before they were affected by the mental condition.

In the course of the study, we tried to find the residency status of the female respondents to understand to what extent they continued to be part of mainstream life and living. It was found that nearly 55 per cent of the women and girls were inmates of various governmental or non-governmental institutions or hostels, where they continued to live for years together, sometimes as long as life itself. Children as young as 3 years were found to be living in these institutions under the foster care of other disabled inmates, as their real families had abandoned them or left them for separate stay and education. Regarding the hostels were, though they are meant to be places for temporary stay for educational purposes, they substitute for homes for the disabled children for years; even during festival holidays, the parents express a general reluctance to take them back home. However, about 45 per cent of the women and girls were living with their families, either in their parental or marital home.

The respondents were questioned about their profession or vocation. A large percentage of the women were unemployed, with no work or vocation, though this also included young girls who were studying. About 25 per cent of the women were engaged in some vocational work or training or self-enterprise enabling them to earn some meagre income for their sustenance. Almost 2.5 per cent of the respondents were engaged in governmental and non-governmental employment, with Indian Railways being the largest employment source for the disabled women. Respondents reported lack of skill orientation and training facilities as the prime reasons for lack of engagement, as also the reluctance of private/governmental agencies in employing disabled people. Strangely, however, all women in the age group of 18 years and above displayed a unanimous attitude to learn different trades and earn their own living. Even married women expressed their willingness to earn and supplement the family earnings.

One of the reasons stated for this was the feeling of separateness from and disconnect with their families because of the disability. Adolescent young girls, especially the visually impaired and hearing impaired, expressed their fears of an uncertain future if they did not engage in some job after their education. While some had the option of joining family businesses like *zari* and embroidery work, most women did not have such options, except with governmental assistance. The income levels of the disabled women were abysmal. The monthly income range of the women interviewed varied from ₹0 to ₹1,000. Almost 5 per cent of the respondents had an earning of ₹5,000 and above.

Most of the women (almost 74%) were disabled since birth. Of the respondents, 7 per cent were disabled by the age of 5 years, and an equal percentage by the age of 18 years. About 12 per cent of the women were disabled later in life. Regarding the causes of disability, it was found, in the course of the interviews, from a search of the medical history of the respondents and from their doctors' views, that in 67 per cent of the cases, the reasons were congenital (inherent birth defects, hereditary or other unknown factors), while other cases involved medical negligence, accidents and diseases such as jaundice and *kala-azar* or visceral leishmaniasis. The last category for cause of disability was somewhat new and not generally recorded: disability as a result of an act of violence. In about 12 per cent of the cases, the woman or girl had become disabled as a result of an act of aggression by a person. About 59 instances involved acts of physical violence, such as beating, kicking, hitting with hard objects and setting on fire; 74 cases were the result of sexual assaults, including gang rapes, violent sexual molestation and sexual abuse by family members; 25 disabilities were caused due to emotional abuse and neglect by the family, which had a traumatic impact on the girl or woman, resulting, in most cases, in mental breakdown (mental illness). It may be mentioned herein that domestic violence figures very high as one of the causative factors of disability, but as it takes the form of either physical, sexual or emotional abuse or neglect, it has been intertwined with the above factors and not separately mentioned. Eight other cases of disability resulted from violence from mixed sources, such as explosions and political or local conflicts. The officials closely associated with and working on disability issues were asked whether they were aware of cases involving women being disabled because of acts of violence. Almost half of the respondents answered the question in the affirmative. What was apparent was that, though not frequent, cases of disability do occur due to violence in the family and outside. The officials enumerated several instances of rape, molestation, assault, acid throwing, abandonment, etc., which had been the cause of physical, visual, hearing and mental disability among women.

The focus of the study was victimization of disabled women. The concept of victimization was explained to them in simple language through various examples as inclusive of physical, sexual, emotional and financial abuse, as well as neglect. About 68 per cent of the respondents, constituting 514 women, agreed that they had been subject to victimization both at home and outside. Such victimizations included all forms of abuse, from aggressive acts of violence to subtle instances of neglect and discrimination in the family. While it was difficult to ascertain the exact number of victimizations faced by respondents for each category of abuse, given their disability, as well as the complexity in differentiating one form of abuse from another, an overwhelming 94 per cent of the officials seconded the views of the respondents. Rape figured as one of the prominent forms of victimization, out of all other types of sexual abuse. Molestation, eve-teasing and harassment on roads, in transport and at workplaces were common for disabled women. Unwanted sexual intimacies and intrusions from family members, including father, uncle, and brother, were also prominent. Officials opined that in the absence of proper training and education, the disabled girls failed to identify the 'good' touch from the bad touch and often became prey to fondling, caressing or oral or genital sex. The sexuality of young women, especially those who were intellectually disabled, sometimes led them to develop closeness with strangers, resulting in the latter taking advantage and exploiting them. Unwanted pregnancies in respondents were found; about 2 per cent had had an abortion or childbirth. The fear of sexual victimization was also the primary cause of forced sterilization of girls and women. About 10 per cent of the respondents had undergone such sterilization. Physical and emotional abuse was also a common feature among these women. Whether in the parental or marital home, being beaten, kicked, burnt, verbally abused, etc., were regular occurrences in the lives of the disabled women. Those who were employed faced the ire of the common people. Thus, degrading comments at the workplace, abuse by bus conductors and drivers, intolerance from pedestrians, etc., were routine affairs.

Discrimination in households was remarkably high—72 per cent—though, in many cases, the girls did not find that objectionable. The parents preferred not to educate disabled girls, as there was not much to expect from them. Malnourishment and ailments such as tuberculosis, asthma and skin disorders were commonly reported among women and girls with disabilities. Early marriage of young disabled girls, where possible, was quite common. In fact, in most cases of blindness, hearing and speech impairment and physical disability, the girls were married off by their families in their pre-teens and teens. Generally, the marriage was contracted with men of an advanced age and greater disability. Many times, these women were the second or third wife of their husbands. Most cases of ill-treatment resulted from failure to fulfil household duties, while in some cases, there was desertion after childbirth. Disinheritance from property, constituting a form of financial abuse, was also prevalent among the disabled women, especially the intellectually disabled ones. The researchers came across cases where, even though the parents were wealthy, either the parents had disowned the disabled girl or the sibling(s) fraudulently took over the shares of the disabled sister. In institutions for the disabled, it was found that after admitting the girl, the relatives severed all ties with her, and future expenditures were not met, leaving the girl at the mercy of the institution. Sometimes, the families were no longer traceable. Where a girl or woman was taken to her family, the latter refused to accept her. The same was especially true for mentally ill people who sometimes were able to overcome the condition of disability but, in the absence of family care and support, reverted to depression, schizophrenia, bipolar disorder, obsessive compulsive disorder, etc.

In the event of victimization, what become significant are the aftercare or support services that these women are accorded. One of the significant components of the same is healthcare or medical assistance. The female respondents were questioned about their access to healthcare and medical facilities, in general due to the disabled condition, as well as in the event of violent victimization. Most of the respondents, 77 per cent, reported that no medical assistance was afforded to them. In a few cases, preliminary medical aid had been provided to women in the event of abuse. However, the women firmly spoke of the reluctance of families to provide for regular medical check-ups, as well as necessary medical interventions (such as operations), for the female children. The women living in institutions also spoke of neglect of health issues, a matter supported by the officials because of insufficient funds.

The respondents were asked about their reactions to the victimization faced at home and outside. To this, 67 per cent of the women replied that they accepted the victimization, as they felt that it was futile to raise their voices, since disability hindered a decent and human existence; 11 per cent of the respondents protested against the victimization, while only 4 per cent took recourse to the law. However, these women were not aware of the legal developments and could not provide further information about the same.

Lastly, one of the questions posed was whether they viewed their disability and their gender as key factors behind their victimization, whether abuse or discrimination. An overwhelming 97 per cent of the respondents agreed that gender and disability hindered decent and dignified living as well as caused ill-treatment at the hands of family and strangers. They opined that they were at the mercy of their caregivers, whether families or institutions, even for their basic necessities and, hence, open to abuse and exploitation at all points of life. Even the officials confirmed, especially on behalf of those who were unable to interact themselves, that their disabilities coupled with their gender made their conditions worse.

Limitations of the Study

The study, comprising disabled girls and boys, was on a very sensitive topic. It was a challenge for the field workers to reach out to them, gain their confidence and make them speak about the issues of abuse and discrimination. In several cases, especially those involving intellectually challenged and ill women who were incapable of communicating themselves, strenuous efforts had to be made to observe and understand them, through the help of therapists and caregivers. In the process, the significant area of abuse by caregivers could not be highlighted. Several schools for the disabled and institutions run by the government and medical professionals refused to participate or part with information, even on assurance of confidentiality of the respondents. The institutes that agreed to participate were very reserved in their discussions concerning matters such as sterilizations, pregnancies, and sexual assaults. Even where

Table 1.2 *Disability and Victimization*

		Percentage (*N* = 576)
Age when disabled	Since birth	74
	Less than 5 years	12
	6–18 years	7
	After 19 years	7
Cause of disability	Congenital	67
	Disease	5
	Medical diagnosis and treatment	10
	Accident	6
	Acts of violence	12
Abuse faced	Yes	68
	No	32
Discriminatory practices	Yes	72
	No	28
Medical/healthcare assistance	Yes	20
	No	77
	Can't afford	3
Reactions to victimization	Silently accepted	67
	Protested	11
	Recourse to legal authorities	4
	None	18
Cause of abuse/discrimination	Yes, gender and disability	97
	Don't think so	3

Source: The author.

the field workers approached families of disabled girls/women, the families were mostly unreceptive and repeatedly emphasized increased financial assistance as well as jobs for the disabled or their family members.

Table 1.2 shows response of the participants regarding the age of disability and cause of disability; who faced abusive behaviors and discriminatory practices; who received medical assistance; the percentage of participants who accepted or retaliated to the victimization; whether they knew of cause or abuse, etc. It was challenging for the field workers to explain these points for the purpose of the collection of data.

More in-depth research using innovative techniques was felt to be necessary because of the category of respondents included in the study. The present study could only reveal the tip of the problem facing disabled women and girls in our country.

CONCLUSION

Disability poses multiple problems for individuals, ranging from functional limitations to negative societal perceptions. A woman finds herself at a double disadvantage, placed at the lowest rung of the otherwise-marginalized lot. This increases her vulnerability and risk of victimization from her family and society. From neglect and apathy to abusive relationships to violent rapes, a disabled woman has to face it all. Whether in the house or outside, her physical and mental impairments come in the way of her safety, security and dignified living. Coupled with the vulnerabilities is the problem of lack of education, employment and healthcare. A vicious circle is built, pushing the woman to a state of misery and utter helplessness.

The Convention on the Rights of Persons with Disabilities, 2006 marked a 'paradigm shift' in attitudes and approaches to persons with disabilities. It took to a new height the movement from viewing persons with disabilities as 'objects' of charity, medical treatment and social protection to viewing them as 'subjects' with rights, who were capable of claiming those rights and making decisions for their lives based on their free and informed consent as well as being active members of society. The convention marked 'a growing awareness of the extent to which disabled people throughout the world have been marginalised by their societies and denied access to what, in the case of non-disabled people, have generally been regarded as fundamental human rights'.[54] It emphasized the principles of equality, dignity, accessibility, effective participation and non-discrimination for the empowerment of persons with disabilities. In line with the same, RPDA, 2016, recently enacted in India, proclaims the rights and entitlements of disabled persons and calls upon the government to take appropriate steps towards their realization. Section 6 specifically mandates ensuring that measures are taken to protect disabled persons from being subjected to torture or cruel, inhuman or degrading treatment. Section 7 further takes note of the prevalent abuse, violence and exploitation of disabled persons and provides a mechanism to prevent it.[55] It may not be out of place to mention that the Criminal Law (Amendment) Act, 2013,[56] for the first time, included disability as one of the grounds for a strict sentence.[57] Thus, disability and the issues arising thereunder have caught the attention of the state, and necessary measures are being taken to produce changes in the situation. The concerns of women and girls, among the disabled, however, need specific attention, the problem being widespread, multidimensional and deep-rooted. It calls for more in-depth analysis of their situation—understanding the sexuality, absence of education, training and employment opportunities, discriminatory and derogatory practices, etc. Concerted and coordinated efforts on the part of the government, and the community as a whole, towards the assimilation of disabled women and girls into the mainstream as well as empowerment through education, skill building and awareness, may go a long way in improving the scenario.

---

[54] Lawson, 'The United Nations Convention on the Rights of Persons with Disabilities'.

[55] Choudhary Laxmi Narayan and Thomas John, 'The Rights of Persons with Disabilities Act, 2016: Does it Address the Needs of the Persons with Mental Illness and Their Families', *Indian Journal of Psychiatry* 59 (2017): 17.

[56] Section 376 (2) (l), Indian Penal Code, 1860.

[57] Rukmini Sen, 'Women with Disabilities: Cartographic Encounters with Legal Interstices', *Indian Anthropological* 46 (2016): 75–91.

Chapter 2

Rights of Women and Gender-biased Laws in India

A Critical Socio-legal Analysis

Janardhana Rao Killi

INTRODUCTION

Traditionally, on the basis of biological and physical differences, human society was divided into two groups, namely males and females. This classification is based on two concepts, that is, sex and gender. While the former is connected with biology, physiology, which is derived from birth, etc., the latter concept is generally associated with individual and social psychology, culture and legal understanding about 'achieved status' related to the gender identity of men and women.[1] The concept of sex in this understanding may remain static, but the concept of gender may be widened again on the basis of gender orientation: thus, an individual who is biologically a male may change his gender orientation to be included in the category of trans women or gay or bisexual people. Vice versa, a woman may also shift from the category of the female 'gender' to a trans male, lesbian or bisexual person, etc., through shifting her

[1] West Candace and Don H. Zimmerman, 'Doing Gender', *JSTOR Gender* 1 (1987): 125–51.

gender orientation.[2] Gender may therefore be divided into three groups, namely male, female and 'other', which may be inclusive of gay, lesbian, transgender, bisexual and queer people. It is interesting to note that gender and gender orientation play important roles in the formation of laws ensuring rights. Ironically, globally, women have been conferred the status of the second gender and men have been conferred the status of the first gender. Feminist researchers argue that this gender-based hierarchy has been created by sociological norms, wherein women have been considered less efficient as compared to men because of their physical shortcomings when compared with the physical characteristics of the latter.[3] As such, women have been traditionally prevented from enjoying certain rights that their male counterparts have enjoyed so far. Consider the cases of property rights in countries like India,[4] wage disparity among university faculties in the United States[5] and the robust literature on sexual assault on women, domestic violence against women, etc.: in almost all cases, it may be seen that women have been discriminated against, suppressed or even motivated to not report their victimization mainly because of the fear of social taboo. Thus, women have been categorically victimized due to gender discrimination and gender oppression. This is largely due to denial of equality, rights and opportunities and suppression of women by the society at large. Gender inequality, unlike other forms of inequality (i.e., economic, political, racial, cultural, etc.), has proved to be highly influential in determining

---

[2] For more, see Anne C. Mary Case, 'Disaggregating Gender from Sex and Sexual Orientation: The Effeminate Man in the Law and Feminist Jurisprudence', *The Yale Law Journal* 105, no. 1 (October 1995): 1–105, https://www.jstor.org/stable/797140, accessed 7 January 2020.

[3] For example, see K. Scott and D. Brown, 'Female Wrst, Leader Second? Gender Bias in the Encoding of Leadership Behavior', *Organizational Behavior and Human Decision Processes* 101 (2006): 230–33, https://ideas.wharton.upenn.edu/wp-content/uploads/2018/07/ScottandBrown2006.pdf, accessed 7 January 2020.

[4] D. Halder and K. Jaishankar, 'Property Rights of Hindu Women: A Critical Review of Succession Laws of Ancient, Medieval, and Modern India', *Journal of Law and Religion* XXIV, 25th Anniversary issue (2008): 101–22.

[5] For more, see Joyce J. Chen and Daniel Crown, 'The Gender Pay Gap in Academia: Evidence from the Ohio State University', *American Journal of Agricultural Economics* 101, no. 5 (October 2019): 1337–52, https://doi.org/10.1093/ajae/aaz017; https://academic.oup.com/ajae/article/101/5/1337/5532316, accessed 7 January 2020.

the social status of women. Compared to issues of general inequality in the economic or social context, or in the racial or linguistic context, gender inequality resulting in disparity between men and women in all fields was marginalized and kept invisible for centuries. To curtail this problem of gender discrimination that prevents recognition of the basic rights of women, their empowerment and development, adopting laws favourable to their uplift became a necessity. The Indian situation, in regard to the social–political–economic–legal suppression of women's rights, has been no better. An analysis of ancient religious scripts, medieval social history and colonial sociocultural norms in India would show that the issue of women's rights has never been given proper consideration.[6]

However, after the coming into effect of the Convention on the Elimination of All Forms of Discrimination Against Women (CEDAW) in 1979 and, further, the ratification of the CEDAW by India in 1993, several laws, policy guidelines, etc., were adopted by the government of India in support of Article 15(3) of the Constitution of India, which states that 'Nothing in this article shall prevent the State from making any special provision for women and children'.[7] India has adopted several laws and policy guidelines to ensure the rights of women; the noteworthiest among these are the Muslim Women (Protection of Rights on Divorce) Act, 1986, the Commission of Sati (Prevention) Act, 1987, Protection of Women from Domestic Violence Act, 2005, Indecent Representation of Women (Prohibition) Act, 1986, Sexual Harassment of Women at Workplace (Prevention, Prohibition and Redressal) Act, 2013, Criminal Law (Amendment) Act, 2013, etc.

Here, what the term 'gender-biased laws' actually connotes needs to be explained. The World Health Organization (WHO) explains gender as follows:

> Gender refers to the socially constructed characteristics of women and men—such as norms, roles and relationships between groups of women

[6] See Halder and Jaishankar, 'Property Rights of Hindu Women'.

[7] Article 15 of the constitution speaks about Prohibition of discrimination on grounds of religion, race, caste, sex or place of birth and in subclause (3) provides special exception for women and children to the general rule of equal rights and equal protection of laws.

> and men. It varies from society to society and can be changed. While most people are born either male or female, they are taught appropriate norms and behaviours including how they should interact with others of the same or opposite sex within households, communities and work places. When individuals or groups do not "fit" established gender norms they often face stigma, discriminatory practices or social exclusion—all of which adversely affect health.[8]

Thus, the term 'gender' carries with it the concept of social norms. Laws are made to fix the roles, responsibilities and rights of every individual in a society so that everyone may enjoy their own rights and may allow others to enjoy their respective rights as well. It may be interesting to note that societal norms have a deeper influence on law-making in certain cases, especially when a law affects the behaviours of males and females: in many geographic regions, society as a whole has not yet approved same-sex marriages and child custody rights for homosexual couples.[9] As a result, laws are yet to be made for legalizing same-sex marriages and the right of same-sex couples to have children. Again, in almost all jurisdictions, society has largely approved of laws providing for heavy punishment for perpetrators of sexual assault on women.[10] As a result, women have certain legal safeguards against sexual abuse. Laws thus created for safeguarding the interests of a specific category of human beings falling under the umbrella term of 'woman' may also be extended to individuals who may have a gender orientation akin to the female gender, even though by birth they are not female. These kinds of laws are extremely gender-sensitive, as victims must necessarily be women and perpetrators may or may not be women. Gender-biased laws necessarily make one gender a 'static victim', and in this case, the static victims are women. Such gender-biased laws emphasize the rights of the victim belonging to the specific gender and aim to achieve complete

---

[8] For more understanding, see https://www.who.int/gender-equity-rights/knowledge/glossary/en/

[9] For example, see Linda Silberman, 'Same-Sex Marriage: Refining the Conflict of Laws Analysis', *University of Pennsylvania Law Review* 153, no. 6 (2005): 2195–214.

[10] Kathleen Daly and Brigitte Bouhours, 'Rape and Attrition in the Legal Process: A Comparative Analysis of Five Countries', *Crime and Justice* 39, no. 1 (2010): 565–650.

justice for the benefit of that particular gender. These laws would fall within the exceptional categories of equality rights, and these may or may not be challenged on the basis of constitutionality. Gender-biased laws may necessarily be results of public interest litigations or social rights movements by concerned stakeholders.[11] Globally, gender-biased laws started developing especially after the Universal Declaration of Human Rights, through the International Covenant on Civil and Political Rights (ICCPR), 1966 and the International Covenant on Economic, Social and Cultural Rights (ICESCR), 1966, established specific rights for women. Later, CEDAW, 1979 and the Fourth World Conference on Women: Action for Equality, Development and Peace (popularly known as the Beijing conference), 1995 redefined rights of women and highlighted the need for women-centric laws for promoting women's rights and preventing violence against women.[12]

However, the gradual development of the jurisprudence of gender-biased laws has seen several objections raised by different stakeholders and rights activists, especially in India, in recent times: the laws and policies thus made have been criticized as being biased to one particular gender, giving rise to several accusations of violation of rights of men. Stakeholders have also raised the issue of misuse of such laws for getting undue benefits from the criminal justice administration. This chapter focuses on a critical analysis of such 'gender-biased laws' and their need to be discriminating for prioritizing the rights of women over those of the opposite sex.

This chapter is divided into three main parts, including the introduction. The second part carries a detailed critical discussion on the need for and development of gender-biased laws, with special reference to some existing laws made specifically for women. The third part contains the conclusion.

---

[11] A good example could be Vishakha v. State of Rajasthan, (1997) 6 SCC 241, AIR 1997 SC 3011, (1998) BHRC 261, (1997) 3 LRC 361, (1997), which paved the way for creating The Sexual Harassment of Women at Workplace (Prevention, Prohibition and Redressal) Act, 2013.

[12] Charlotte Bunch and Susana Fried, 'Beijing'95: Moving Women's Human Rights from Margin to Center', *Signs: Journal of Women in Culture and Society* 22, no. 1 (1996): 200–204.

DEVELOPMENT OF GENDER-BIASED LAWS IN INDIA

Regarding the ancient history of India, it is well known that a major part of it has expatiated upon the position of women, and their status has often been undetermined. Though daughters of the Vedic era were considered equal to their male counterparts with regard to certain basic rights,[13] the innumerable invasions on India led to the downfall of the sociocultural and legal status of women. Women were discriminated against in the inheritance of family property, both from the father's side and from the husband's side.[14] Similarly, women were also subjected to several barbaric practices, including *Sati Pratha* (immolating women in the pyre of their husbands),[15] abandonment of widows, female infanticide, child marriage, etc. In the colonial era, however, the colonial rulers brought in some preventive legislations that declared *Sati Pratha*, child marriage, etc., as penal offences. The Bengal Renaissance further uplifted the status of women first in Bengal and then across India.[16] However, in reality, these initiatives were not welcomed by society as a whole. Though a period of 70 years has passed since independence, India has still not accomplished the dream of an equalitarian society as envisaged in its constitution. Sexual and gender discrimination continued to escalate in society, and the evil practices of female infanticide, dowry harassment, sexual assault on women and girls are still rampant in the country. All the reforms made so far were possible only because of the various legislative schemes that were instrumental in the amplification of the position of women in India. The Constitution of India under Article 15(3) mandates the following: 'Nothing in this article shall prevent the State from making any special provision for women and children'. In other words, it requires the state to make special laws for safeguarding the rights of women and children. At this juncture, it is necessary to throw light on the inherent meaning of Article 14 of the constitution, which prohibits class legislation, that

[13] Padma Sharma, 'Status of Women in India' (PhD diss., Aligarh Muslim University, 1981).

[14] D. Halder and K. Jaishankar, 'Rights of Women Prisoners in India: A Legal Analysis', *International Journal of Cloud Computing* 28 (2007): 12–20.

[15] Halder and Jaishankar, 'Rights of Women Prisoners in India'.

[16] Goutam Neogi, 'Bengali Women in Politics: The Early Phase (1857–1905)', *Proceedings of the Indian History Congress* 46 (1985): 483–92.

is, it does not permit exclusive laws for individuals who are equal. But when read through, Article 14 shows that it does not prevent classification for the purpose of legislation either. Thus, if there is any reasonable basis for classification, the legislature would be required to make a different legislation for the cause of a particular group or unit of society. Interpreting the constitutional provisions, in *Sianik Motors (M/S) v. State of Rajasthan*,[17] the Supreme Court observed that where the constitution itself mandates a classification, such legislation and the lawmakers may not be levelled against for the charge of discrimination. Two cases may be mentioned in this regard: in the case of *Yousuf Abdul Aziz v. State of Bombay*,[18] the court placed emphasis on provisions related to adultery in the Indian Penal Code which punished only the male participant and not the female; and in the case of *Government of Andhra Pradesh v. P. B. Vijaykumar*,[19] the court took up the matter of 30 per cent reservations for women in state services—it was contended that the special provisions made for women were unconstitutional and discriminatory on the basis of sex and that they contradicted Article 14 and Article 15(1), which promote equality. The court in both cases upheld the supremacy of Article 15(3) over other constitutional provisions and validated the legislation. However, neither this provision nor the Directive Principles of State Policy under Part IV could ensure the full safety of women in society. Even though the Directive Principles mandated that women should be given an equal status as men in society (Article 39), they should be eligible for free legal aid (Article 39A), they should be given equal opportunities for employment (Article 39), etc., gender discrimination in property inheritance, underdevelopment of children, including girls, violence against women, etc., continued even post the ratification of the CEDAW by India in 1993.[20]

To address these issues, it was felt by the Parliament that a dedicated set of women-centric laws must be made whereby women are given priority as victims, and as beneficiaries, and that appropriate infrastructure

---

[17] Sianik Motors (M/S) v. State of Rajasthan. AIR 1961 SC 1480 (1486).

[18] Yousuf Abdul Aziz v. State of Bombay. AIR 1951 Bom 470.

[19] Government of Andhra Pradesh v. P. B. Vijaykumar. AIR (1995) SC 1648.

[20] NCRB Data, *Violence Against Women* (March 21, 2018), http://ncrb.gov.in/StatPublications/CII/CII2016/pdfs/NEWPDFs/Crime%20in%20India%20-%202016%20Complete%20PDF%20291117.pdf.

must be in place for proper execution of such laws and policies. In this course, various legislations were adopted for the welfare of women, including: the Dowry Prohibition Act, 1961, which penalizes the practice of dowry, demanding of dowry and harassment of women for dowry by their in-laws; the Equal Remuneration Act, 1986, which made it mandatory for employers to pay equal wages for men and women for equal work; the Hindu Succession Act, 1956 (amended in 2005), which expanded the scope of succession laws to include women as inheritors of properties with the same powers to enjoy or dispose of the property as their male counterparts; the Indecent Representation of Women (Prohibition) Act, 1986 to prohibit indecent representation of women in advertisements or through publications, writings, etc.; the Muslim Women (Protection of Rights on Divorce) Act, 1986, which protects the interest of divorced Muslim women; the Commission of Sati (Prevention) Act, 1987, which penalizes the barbaric act of immolation of widows in the pyre of their husbands or even instigation for the same; the Protection of Women from Domestic Violence Act, 2005, which has defined as domestic violence and penalized several harassing, cruel and inhuman acts against women, including married women; the Sexual Harassment of Women at Workplace (Prevention, Prohibition and Redressal) Act, 2013, which prohibits and penalizes sexual harassment of women at the workplace; and the Criminal Law (Amendment) Act, 2013, which amended the Indian Penal Code to penalize and also revise punishments for several offensive acts targeting women, including rape, sexual molestation, voyeurism, stalking, etc. Apart from these legislations, courts have also paid attention towards the causes of women. The recent decisions like that on 'triple talaq' in *Shayra Bano v. Union of India*[21] or those giving custody of children, including male children, to mothers instead of fathers[22] show that courts have finely used the principles of natural justice in decoding laws in a

---

[21] Shayra Bano v. Union of India. Writ Petition (C) No. 118 of 2016, (March 12, 2018), supremecourtofindia.nic.in/supremecourt/.../6716_2016_Judgement_22-Aug-2017.pdf.

[22] D. Halder, 'Who Wins the Battle for Custody? An Analysis of the Nature of Modern Judicial Understandings of Women's Rights in Cases of Custody of Minor Children in Matrimonial Disputes Under the Hindu Laws', in *Essays in Family Law in Memory of Professor B N Sampath: Gender, Human Rights and Law*, Vol. 2, ed. Sarasu Esther Thomas (Bangalore: National Law School of India University, 2013), 8–18.

manner that is gender-biased. As mentioned above, each of these laws has addressed exclusive rights of women and has extended its scope to prescribe punishment for violation of rights of women and girls in every sector. The effectiveness of these laws is reflected in the data of National Crime Records Bureau (NCRB), where it may be seen that such laws have been used by the police for arresting offenders in crimes related to women.[23] However, even though this move has been hugely supported by feminist researchers and feminist jurisprudence scholars, the gender-biased laws have also been hugely criticized for overemphasizing women as victims of crimes, patriarchal social structure, etc. These critics have emphasized 'gender-neutral laws', rather than gender-biased laws, which in their opinion would balance the rights of all genders and simultaneously would ensure the best safeguards for women's rights within their scope.[24]

Arguments for Gender-Neutral Laws

Researchers supporting the need for gender-neutral laws opine that the concept of equality is a dynamic phenomenon and needs to be re-looked at as the social conditions change. For example, consider the case of rape laws, especially in India, which are dealt with under Section 375 (defining rape) and Section 376 (prescribing punishment for rape) of the Indian Penal Code, which are gender-biased and see women as victims and men as perpetrators: several lawyers, social scientists and researchers have expressed concerns that the effects of rape on male victims may have gone unnoticed and male victimization by way of sexual assault may have been completely ignored by rape law jurisprudence for long.[25] Further, questions have also been raised for scrapping Section 377 of the Indian Penal Code, which prescribes punishment for sexual intercourse between people of the same sex and for carnal intercourse between a

---

[23] For more understanding, see http://ncrb.gov.in/, Accessed 7 January 2020.

[24] The Oxford Dictionary describes 'Gender Neutrality' as an adjective that is suitable for, applicable to, or common to, both male and female genders. It describes the idea that policies, language, and other social institutions should avoid distinguishing roles according to people's sex or gender, and emphasizes on the equal treatment of men and women legally with no discrimination.

[25] P. Rumney, 'In Defence of Gender Neutrality Within Rape', *Seattle Journal of Social Justice* 6 (2007): 481. http://ssrn.com/abstract=1316252

man and an animal, for an effective gender-neutral law.[26] One of the best examples against gender-biased laws in India could be the Justice Verma Committee Report,[27] which suggested forming a gender-neutral law for rape victims while retaining a gender-specific law for perpetrators. The 172nd Law Commission Report also recommended that rape law, for both the victim and the offender, must be gender-neutral.[28] The supporters of gender-neutral laws opine that Indian gender-biased laws may overlook the rights of male victims of sexual assault, stalking, adultery, voyeurism, rape, domestic violence, dowry death, harassment at workplace, etc., as these women-centric legislations are not framed on the basis of scientific and logical reasons as to why they are meant to favour only a single gender.

However, it needs to be noted that feminists and supporters of women-centric laws strongly opposed gender-neutral laws for such offences as rape, sexual assault and violence (including domestic violence) against women at home and at the workplace, because they felt that gender-neutral laws would take the focus off women, who were still victims of a number of offences committed against them. The NCRB Report of 2016 showed that in 2014–2015, 53.9 per cent women were victimized by crimes that are cognizable in nature in India.[29] This figure further increased to 55.2 per cent in 2016.[30] These statistics make it evident that the crime rate of cognizable offences against women is

---

[26] R. Kapur, 'The New Sexual Security Regime', *The Hindu*, 2013, http://www.thehindu.com/opinion/op-ed/the-new-sexual-security-regime/article4379317.ece.

[27] Report of the Committee on Amendments to Criminal Law January 23, 2013, http://www.prsindia.org/uploads/media/Justice%20verma%20committee/js%20verma%20committe%20report.pdf.

[28] Law Commission of India, '172nd Report on Review of Rape Laws' (March 2000), http://www.lawcommissionofindia.nic.in/rapelaws.htm.

[29] Crime in India 2015 Statistics, Crime Against Women, Chapter 5, Table 5.1, Cases Reported & Rate of Crime Committed Against Women During 2015, National Crime Records Bureau (Ministry of Home Affairs) Government of India (March 03, 2018), http://ncrb.gov.in/StatPublications/CII/CII2015/FILES/CrimeInIndia2015.pdf.

[30] Crime in India Statistics 2016, Crime Against Women (States & UT's), Chapter 3A, Table 3A.1 Crime against Women (IPC + SLL)—2014–2016, National Crime Records Bureau (Ministry of Home Affairs) Government of India, (March 03, 2018),

increasing despite the many legal provisions. Besides, these statistics do not include non-cognizable cases against women. These figures indicate that there should be stricter women-centric laws and that their execution and implementation should be flawless. Thus, creating gender-neutral laws would only harm and not serve the purpose of protecting women from becoming victims. Feminist advocate Flavia Agnes opined thus:

> gender neutrality lies on the presumption that by neutralizing the law to be victim and perpetrator neutral, the offence of rape will be desexualized and the stigma attached to the offence will vanish and if the reforms take place they will be injurious to women and that the basic and primary problems will not be highlighted.[31]

The very aim of gender-biased laws is to uplift the female gender. These laws strive to secure women from any inhuman treatment, cruelty or injustice, which they are often subjected to, and to punish the wrongdoers. Thus, these so-called 'gender-biased laws' may not be considered discriminatory prima facie. Even though Article 15(3) of the constitution enables the passing of many laws for the welfare and development of the status of women in India, it has not yet achieved its objective of completely eradicating certain evil practices from society. This is the main reason why legislators and women's rights activists feel the need to adopt more women-oriented legislations. For example, dowry deaths, including brutal treatment by in-laws and husbands, abetment to commit suicide, etc., still have not been eradicated completely from society. It may further be noted that the Dowry Prohibition Act[32] was passed to control and eradicate the menace of dowry rampant on a large scale. Later, it was replaced with the Dowry Prohibition (Amendment) Act, 1984.[33] Further, stringent provisions under the Indian Penal Code were included to deal with such problems: the noteworthiest of such laws are Section 304B of the Indian Penal

---

http://ncrb.gov.in/StatPublications/CII/CII2016/pdfs/NEWPDFs/Crime%20in%20India%20-%202016%20Complete%20PDF%20291117.pdf.

[31] F. Agnes, 'Law, Ideology and Female Sexuality: Gender Neutrality in Rape Law', *Economic and Political Weekly* 37, no. 9 (2002): 844–847.

[32] The Dowry Prohibition Act, 1961.

[33] The Dowry Prohibition (Amendment) Act, 1984.

Code, which prescribes punishment for the husband and in-laws in case a dowry death occurred within a period of 7 years of marriage, and Section 498A of the Indian Penal Code, which makes cruel treatment or harassment of a married woman punishable. Section 498A does not set any time period like Section 304B of the Indian Penal Code. Looking at their retributive, as well as restorative, effects, it may be understood that the Protection of Women from Domestic Violence Act, 2005 was but needed to be enacted, as it extended holistic protection to other women in the family who may be victimized by domestic violence but may not be connected with the perpetrator by way of marriage. A brief perusal of this Act also suggests that in spite of it being a gender-biased law, the judicial understandings and legislative amendments made to the Act have reduced the scope of its misuse, as it defines all the offences in detail and does not leave anything to the discretion of judges. The law therefore guarantees that it can be ensured that it is not misused in the form of fake cases against men.[34]

Let us now understand the impact of gender-biased laws on the status of women in a male-dominant society like India. These gender-biased laws may ensure a stronger and safer position for women in the male-dominant society. For example, consider the case of succession rights of women with regard to their ancestral properties which had been established by the 2005 amendment of the Hindu Succession Act, 1956.[35] Earlier, women had been denied this right. Further, the Commission of Sati (Prevention) Act, 1987 made *Sati Pratha* or burning women alive on the funeral pyre of their husbands a cognizable offence. This has come a long extent to create a deterrent effect in society regarding such inhuman traditional and cultural practices targeting women. The Equal Remuneration Act, 1986, on the other hand, ensured equal pay for equal work for women and men. While in reality, in the unorganized sector, women may not get equal wages as their

---

[34] For example, see Pallavi Mahajan, 'Critical Analysis of Domestic Violence Act, 2005' (13 May 2011), https://ssrn.com/abstract=1840628 or http://dx.doi.org/10.2139/ssrn.1840628.

[35] Dr. Justice AR. Lakshmanan, 'Let Us Amend the Law, It Is Only Fair to Women' (19 January 2018), http://www.thehindu.com/opinion/open-page/let-us-amend-the-law-it-is-only-fair-to-women/article2288188.ece.

male counterparts, in the organized labour sector, women are provided rights to claim equal wages and facilities as their male counterparts in India. Let us now examine the effects of the Medical Termination of Pregnancy Act, 1971 or Pre-Conception and Pre-Natal Diagnostic Techniques (Regulation and Prevention of Misuse) Act, 1994, which prescribe punishment for determination of the sex of a foetus and female feticide; these have come a long way to support women's rights against unwanted abortions and the rights of a child to be born, besides making the attempt of or commissioning of a sex determination test by either would-be parents or hospitals or clinics a criminal offence. Also consider the effects of the laws like the Indecent Representation of Women (Prohibition) Act, 1986 or Suppression of Immoral Traffic in Women and Girls Act, 1956 on society as a whole: these laws have not only made objectifying women as sex items or in pornographic content or representing them in a manner that is grossly offensive penal offences, but they have also prescribed stricter punishments for trafficking of women and girls in the name of marriage, job, etc. All these laws ensure effective implementation of the fundamental rights granted to all without any discrimination. The laws thus created also ensure prevention of atrocities against women. The case of *Vishakha v. State of Rajasthan*[36] is the noteworthiest example here, wherein Supreme Court guidelines were laid down about the measures to be taken by employers to ensure the safety of female employees at the workplace. The judgement also laid the path for the creation of the Sexual Harassment of Women at Workplace (Prevention, Prohibition and Redressal) Act, which enhanced the scope of equal rights at the workplace and rights against all sorts of victimization. Thus, the laws that carry the blame of being women-centric, as well as the laws that are considered as gender-neutral, and their interpretation by courts through landmark judgements empower women to fight against injustice and access justice in case of violation of rights. Such efforts by the courts and the legislature, instead of being obstructed, need to be admired and supported, so that they achieve their objectives.

[36] Vishakha v. State of Rajasthan. AIR 1997 SC 3011.

CONCLUSION

Laws, as well as the judiciary, have always stood up as the sentinels of the right and the needy, not of the wrong or the mighty. Laws stem out of the existing needs and circumstances of the social structure. Questioning the existence of gender-biased laws can be equated to doubting the very existence of the legislative and judicial structure. In this modern era, gender-biased laws have created a special impact on individuals and helped them understand the rights and dignity of women. However, this does not imply that such laws should be misused. If in the struggle for equality gender-biased laws act as shields and weapons for the protection of rights of women, then it is morally and socially inappropriate to ask them to be struck down.

Regarding the contention that gender-biased laws are discriminatory in nature as they violate the spirit of equality enshrined in Article 14, the article in question establishes 'equality among equals': it can be observed that at the present state women have not yet been given equal rights as their male counterparts. However, this author strongly opines that such gender-biased laws should not exist forever: the criminal justice administration as a whole must work towards a crime-free society where women feel safe. In conclusion, it can be said that the gender-biased laws have definitely improved the position of women, though not entirely. Society now accepts them as individuals capable of living a dignified life and taking part in worldly activities independently. Therefore, gender-biased laws have relevance and need to be endorsed till the journey towards an equalitarian society is successfully accomplished.

Chapter 3

Forced Sterilization of Differently Abled Women
A Critical Analysis

Priju Bhaskar T.

INTRODUCTION

Disabled persons are generally seen as 'abnormal', those not able to perform general motor functions of normal human beings and those who may need support for daily chores. Earlier, the term 'disability' was associated majorly with physical disabilities. It was largely due to the United Nations Convention on the Rights of Persons with Disabilities (UNCRPD), 2008 that the scope of the term disability was extended to the mental-health sector too. The concepts of disability and disability-related rights violations were considered by the UNCRPD, 2008 as evolving. The preamble to this convention explains the issue of disability rights from the perspectives of discrimination and negligence.[1] Disability, in a country like India, may attract various right violations,

[1] See Clause 5 of the Preamble to the UN Conventions on Right, *Rights of Persons with Disabilities* (2008). https://www.un.org/development/desa/disabilities/convention-on-the-rights-of-persons-with-disabilities/preamble.html, accessed 12 December 2019.

including discrimination in society and at the workplace, social taboos around women and social ostracization. Women with disabilities are also rejected in the marriage market in India, because such women may be considered as unfit for founding a family and bearing and bringing up a child. Thus, gender and physical and mental disability may go hand in hand in making differently abled women worse sufferers when compared with their male counterparts. Women with disability may also face violation of their reproductive rights. This chapter aims to explore forceful sterilization of women: the author argues that differently abled women may have to face forced sterilization as part of domestic violence and harassment in India, because it is infamously believed that disability might run in the blood and disabled mothers might never be able to produce and raise healthy children.[2] It has been observed by several researchers that wrongful stereotyping related to disability and gender may also affect the enjoyment of sexual and reproductive health and rights of the woman concerned,[3] and her right to found a family. Women with different abilities may also be subjected to barbaric practices of forced or coerced sterilization, administering of contraception against their will and abortion in case the woman had conceived.[4] Indian feminist researchers in the disability rights sector, including Anita Ghai, have further observed that women and girls with mental and physical disabilities may also be forcefully sterilized because they may not be able to maintain menstrual hygiene. Such sterilization may happen with the consent of the guardians who may or may not know the consequences of such sterilization on the health of the women concerned.[5] Several studies have also shown that while several stakeholders have raised their voices against forced sterilization

---

[2] Dr Sruti Mohapatra and Mr Mihir Mohanty, *Abuse and Activity Limitation: A Study on 15 Domestic Violence against Disabled Women in Orissa, India* 16 (2004). http://swabhiman.org/userfiles/file/Abuse%20and%20Activity%20Limitation%20Study.pdf, accessed 12 December 2019.

[3] Sruti and Mihir, *Abuse and Activity Limitation.*

[4] UN Special Rapporteur on Violence Against Women, 'Report of the Special Rapporteur on Violence Against Women, Its Causes and Consequences', U.N. Doc. A/67/227 (2012) 28, 36. www.ohchr.org/Documents/Issues/Women/A.67.227.pdf.

[5] For more, see: Anita Ghai, 'Disabled Women: An Excluded Agenda of Indian Feminism', *Hypatia* 17, no. 3 (Summer 2002), http://www.aifo.it/english/resources/onlIne/books/cbr/Disabled%20women%20india-AGhai.pdf.

of disabled women, such stakeholders have not considered initiating robust awareness campaigns about the right to menstrual hygiene of disabled women, because this may be considered as wastage of time.[6]

It may be pertinent to note that in India, forceful and non-consensual sterilization is considered as violative of government mandates[7]: as one government mandate suggests, sterilization may be allowed for family-planning purposes on adult males and females. Such sterilization may be done with proper consent of the parties and under the monitoring of registered medical practitioners. With a few exceptions, governmental and non-governmental data regarding forceful and non-consensual sterilization of women (including women with disabilities) are rare in India. However, the 2014 review of the Committee on the Elimination of Discrimination Against Women (CEDAW Committee) did mention that the practice of non-consensual sterilization of women with intellectual disabilities in India is prevalent.[8] The CEDAW Committee review observed that India has a coercive family-planning system that is extremely detrimental, especially to disabled women. Sterilization of disabled women is often non-consensual, forceful and violative of the bodily integrity, reproductive rights and privacy of such women. The United Nations (UN) Special Rapporteur on Violence Against Women also shared similar concerns, especially in regard to the responsibility of the state to take preventive measures to stop such coercive sterilization of disabled women.[9]

It is an unfortunate fact that both governmental and non-governmental sources are silent on data regarding forced sterilization of women with different abilities in India. There is a silence within the society that permeates many areas of disability and sexuality. The

---

[6] For example, see https://www.womenenabled.org/pdfs/WEI%20WWDIN%20India%20UPR%20Submission%20September%202016.pdf, accessed 12 December 2019.

[7] For more see Manual for Family Planning Insurance Scheme, https://mohfw.gov.in/sites/default/files/8067313868Manual%20Family%20Planning2009-99209825.pdf, accessed 12 December 2019.

[8] For more see https://tbinternet.ohchr.org/Treaties/CEDAW/Shared%20Documents/Ind/INT_CEDAW_NGO_Ind_17511_E.pdf, accessed 12 December 2019.

[9] Ibid.

message that is commonly conveyed is that women with different abilities have no place in the realm of sexuality. Their sexuality and reproductive rights have not gained significant visibility in research, policy and the activism discourse in India. The lack of academic research in this area has widened the lack of understanding regarding the relationships among coercive, non-consensual sterilization of differently abled women, discrimination against such women, violation of such women's right to reproduction, domestic abuse of such women and societal ignorance of the issue. This chapter aims to fulfil this lacuna.

The chapter aims to discuss the abusive practices of forced sterilization of women with different abilities and to highlight specific dimensions and the intensity of such practice in India, which often goes unaddressed. The chapter is divided into four parts, including the introduction. The second part discusses the discrimination that women with different abilities experience when it comes to sexual and reproductive rights, with a specific focus on forced sterilization. The third part discusses the international instruments that provide rights against forced sterilization of women with different abilities. This part also emphasizes the poor domestic legal framework that may have pushed women with disabilities to suffer and experience grave discrimination and denial of basic human rights. The fourth part offers a conclusion and suggestions.

FEMALE STERILIZATION AND TYPES OF HUMAN RIGHTS VIOLATIONS FACED BY WOMEN WITH DISABILITIES

In India, women with disabilities face several types of discrimination and oppression at the hands of family members as well as society. Mohanty and Mohapatra (2004) brought out an articulate profile of such sorts of victimization of women: their study showed that physically and mentally disabled women are beaten up by their family members for no reason; that they may not be regularly assisted in changing their clothes or cleaning themselves, including combing hair and cleaning and washing after using washrooms; that they may not be provided basic and proper education; that they may be locked up in a separate room when guests visit; and that they may neither be allowed to take food with the rest of the family nor be allowed to participate in family tours, visits to relatives' place etc.[10] At the societal level, the researchers mentioned that disabled women may face social ostracization. They may not be welcome at social and cultural ceremonies, including weddings and ceremonies related to childbirth. Mohanty and Mahapatra (2004) further showed that disabled women are vulnerable targets of rape, sexual assault, disrobing in public, inappropriate touching of the body for sexual pleasure, etc.[11] Ghai (2008), on the other hand, emphasized the discrimination against disabled women from the perspective of sexual and reproductive rights.[12] In her research, she showed that women with disability may be considered as hypersexual or not fit for any sort of sexual connection, because they might not have sexual feelings. In other words, they may be considered unfit for marriage.[13] Further, Ghai (2008) also showed that legislative efforts to create a special status for disabled people, including disabled women, may not always yield positive results, as disabled women might not be allowed to seek any benefits for themselves by their respective families.[14] While the discussion so far shows the profiling of rights violations against disabled women, it may also be noted that such women are also prone to be sexually violated. They may not be able to express their consent; they may not be able to express their victimization to their family members either, which may further push the family to experience embarrassment and shame. To control all this, families and guardians may consider sterilization as the best possible mechanism to prevent further embarrassment. Disabled women, as such, may be denied the right to bodily integrity and bodily autonomy, including the right to make their own reproductive choices, which follows directly from the Universal Declaration of Human Rights and the Convention on the Elimination of All Forms of Discrimination Against women.

---

[10] See S Mohapatra and M Mohanty, 'Abuse and Activity Limitation: A Study on Domestic Violence Against Disabled Women in Orissa, India', (2004), http://swabhiman.org/upload/images/file/Abuse%20and%20Activity%20Limitation%20Study.pdf, accessed 12 December 2019.

[11] Mohapatra and Mohanty, 'Abuse and Activity Limitation'.

[12] Ghai, 'Disabled Women', 49–46, https://www.jstor.org/stable/3810795.

[13] Ghai, 'Disabled Women'.

[14] Ghai, 'Disabled Women'.

It becomes necessary here to determine what is meant by sterilization and how Indian laws govern the same. Some studies have explained the concept of sterilization as a medical procedure to control fertility which might have immense physical and psychological side effects. It might be irreversible as well.[15] Even though the Convention on the Rights of Persons with Disability clearly states that forced sterilization of any individual, irrespective of gender, must be prohibited, in several parts of the world, especially in India, disabled women may have to go through forced sterilization, which involves medically disabling the reproductive system without proper consent of the disabled women.[16] Consent for such sterilization is however provided by the guardians/family members of the woman concerned. The said *consent* is not informed consent either, as such women would not be informed in this regard and they would not necessarily be given any chance to be heard as well. This is indeed an act of violation of human rights and women's rights. This is essentially so because the women who might undergo sterilization might not have any decision-making power over their bodies and their reproductive system. They might also go through varied forms of psychological stress when they understand that forced sterilization might be irrevocable. In the maximum cases of sterilization in married couples, it has been seen that women (and not men) have to undergo sterilization as a social-oppression mechanism.[17] In the case of a disabled woman, sterilization might be authorized by a third party without the consent of the woman concerned: this is nothing but an act of violence, a form of social control and a clear and documented violation of the right to be free from torture.[18] As discussed earlier, it must be noted that such forced sterilization may also be performed on disabled women

---

[15] For a better understanding, see: Committee on Ethics, 'Sterilization of Women: Ethical Issues and Considerations', Committee Opinion No. 695. American College of Obstetricians and Gynecologists. *Obstetrics & Gynecology* 129 (2017): e109–16, https://www.acog.org/Clinical-Guidance-and-Publications/Committee-Opinions/Committee-on-Ethics/Sterilization-of-Women-Ethical-Issues-and-Considerations?IsMobileSet=false, accessed 12 December 2019.

[16] Committee on Ethics, 'Sterilization of Women'.

[17] Committee on Ethics, 'Sterilization of Women'.

[18] Committee on Ethics, 'Sterilization of Women'. Also see Patel Priti, 'Forced Sterilization of Women as Discrimination', *Public Health Review* 38 (2017): 15, doi: 10.1186/s40985-017-0060-9, accessed 12 December 2019.

for different purposes, including population control, menstrual-hygiene management and prevention of unwanted pregnancy (especially that resulting from sexual abuse). Several research studies have also indicated that forced sterilization of girls and women with disabilities might have its roots in traditional practices, culture, religion or superstition.[19] Almost in all cases, researchers have unanimously agreed that in cases of forced sterilization of disabled women and girls, the perpetrators are rarely held accountable, and the victims might not even access justice due to social pressure and lack of awareness.

It may be seen that according to the 2011 census (updated in 2016), approximately, India has the maximum population of disabled women in the world.[20] They form one of the most marginalized groups of Indian society. As stated earlier, such women with disability are generally considered as sexually inactive and not suitable for the role of a wife or a mother. A disabled daughter is considered a long-term burden on her parents, as she is not considered a suitable candidate for the marriage market.[21] It must not be forgotten that sterilization may cover up the sexual abuse of disabled women, as it may prevent unwanted pregnancy. Hence, forced sterilization is considered as the best option for protecting such women against all possible odds, including sexual abuse and unwanted pregnancy, and also to reduce the burden of cleaning of the concerned woman by family members.[22]

India is party to a number of international human rights conventions that have relevance to forced sterilization of women with different

---

[19] For example, see: Women with Disabilities in Australia, 'Dehumanised: The Forced Sterilisation of Women and Girls with Disabilities in Australia', https://namati.org/resources/forced-sterilisation-of-women-and-girls-with-disabilities-in-australia/, accessed 12 December 2019.

[20] For more see https://enabled.in/wp/disabled-population-in-india-as-per-census-2011-2016-updated/, accessed 12 December 2019.

[21] Namrata Caleb, *For Women with Disabilities, It is a Life of Double Disadvantage*, Youth Ki Awaaz (2 July 2017), https://www.youthkiawaaz.com/2016/11/indian-women-with-disabilities-live-life-of-disadvantage/.

[22] See Shuaib Chalklen, 'Letter to UN Special Rapporteurs on Involuntary Sterilization of Women and Girls with Disabilities', (2012, March 9), https://www.hrw.org/news/2012/03/09/letter-un-special-rapporteurs-involuntary-sterilization-women-and-girls-disabilities.

abilities.[23] India is committed to the rights proclaimed by the Universal Declaration of Human Rights and has also signed and ratified the UNCRPD. As a signatory, it has the responsibility to ensure that persons with disabilities enjoy their human rights through enacting national legislations and adopting appropriate policies and programmes. However, the country had no legal provision prohibiting forced sterilization before the Rights of Persons with Disabilities Act, 2016[24] was enacted in accordance with the UNCRPD. The Act replaced the Persons with Disabilities Act, 1995, which was silent on the rights of women with different abilities. Even though no separate chapter is devoted in the present Act to ensure the rights of women with different abilities, there are some gender-specific clauses integrated in different chapters. The Act includes sections protecting women with disabilities from forced sterilization,[25] torture, cruel or degrading treatment,[26] abuse, violence and exploitation,[27] ensuring their access to human rights–based sexual and reproductive healthcare[28] and ensuring their access to justice.[29] However, this Act does not define the term 'forced sterilisation'. Article 10(2) of this Act directly goes on to prevent any medical procedure that may lead to infertility by stating that no person with disability shall be subject to any medical procedure that leads to infertility without his/her free and informed consent. However, the provision fails to mention how it would ensure that disabled women can make a choice based on free and informed consent. It is also silent on the treatment of those who had already been forcibly sterilized without being fully informed and without free consent. The provision does not mention about compensation and rehabilitation of such women either.

---

[23] India has signed and ratified several international conventions, such as the International Covenant on Civil and Political Rights, 1966, International Covenant on Economic, Social and Cultural Rights, 1966, Convention on the Elimination of All Forms of Discrimination Against Women, 1979, Convention on the Rights of the Child, 1989, etc.

[24] Act (No. 49 of 2016) of Parliament received the assent of the president on 27 December 2016.

[25] Section 10 (2), The Rights of Persons with Disabilities Act, 2016.

[26] Section 6 (1), The Rights of Persons with Disabilities Act, 2016.

[27] Section 7 (1), The Rights of Persons with Disabilities Act, 2016.

[28] Section 25 (2) (k), The Rights of Persons with Disabilities Act, 2016.

[29] Section 12, The Rights of Persons with Disabilities Act, 2016.

INTERNATIONAL INSTRUMENTS RELEVANT TO THE FORCED STERILIZATION OF WOMEN WITH DIFFERENT ABILITIES

There are a number of international human rights treaties and instruments that directly or indirectly prohibit forced sterilization of women with different abilities and ensure their right to bodily integrity and right to make their own reproductive choices. The Universal Declaration of Human Rights recognizes their right to protection against torture, cruel and degrading treatment[30] and their right to marry according to their own choice consensually and found a family.[31] Forced sterilization of girls and women with disabilities is also considered violative of Article 10 of the International Covenant on Economic, Social and Cultural Rights,[32] which recognizes the family as an essential unit of society and makes the state responsible for ensuring the protection of and social security to women, including working women, young persons and children without any discrimination, and Article 7 (which speaks about prohibiting torture and cruel, inhuman or degrading treatment), Article 17 (which speaks about ensuring the right to privacy) and Article 24 (which mandates special protection for children) of the International Covenant on Civil and Political Rights.[33] Further, the UN special rapporteur on disability has also observed forced sterilization to be violative of the inherent right of reproduction of women. The rapporteur emphasized the opinion and recommendation of the Committee Against Torture that stated:

> States take urgent measures to investigate promptly, impartially, thoroughly, and effectively all allegations of involuntary sterilization of women, prosecute and punish the perpetrators, and provide the victims with fair and adequate compensation.[34]

---

[30] Article 5, Universal Declaration of Human Rights.

[31] Article 12, Universal Declaration of Human Rights.

[32] Article 10 of the International Covenant on Civil and Political Rights.

[33] See also Sterilization of Women and Girls with Disabilities (A Briefing Paper), https://www.hrw.org/news/2011/11/10/sterilization-women-and-girls-disabilities, accessed 1 February 2020.

[34] For more see Chalklen, 'Letter to UN Special Rapporteurs'.

This rapporteur report also showed that forced sterilization of girls with disabilities has been identified as a form of violence.[35] It also recommended states party to the Convention on the Rights of the Child to make laws prohibiting forced sterilization of children with disabilities.[36]

Further, the CEDAW Committee has also considered forced sterilization to be a form of violation of a woman's right, as it might affect her right to human dignity and physical and mental integrity.[37] This committee also suggested making stringent domestic laws to prevent forced sterilization. However, the UNCRPD[38] offers the most comprehensive and authoritative set of standards on the rights of people with different abilities. The UNCRPD aims to ensure the equal rights, inherent dignity and fundamental freedoms of all disabled individuals, irrespective of the form of disablement. This convention also mandates its member states to ensure full participation of disabled people, including women, in relation to any decision related to their physical and mental health, bodily integrity, reproductive rights, etc.[39]

The UNCRPD mandates its member states to recognize that persons with disabilities enjoy the legal capacity to make decisions about their well-being on an equal basis as others.[40] While acknowledging forced sterilization of disabled women as a form of violence, it also mandates its member states to protect persons with disabilities from violence,

---

[35] The right of the child to freedom from all forms of violence (April 18, 2011), www2.ohchr.org/English/bodies/crc/docs/CRC.C.GC.13_en.pdf, accessed 25 June 2017.

[36] UN Committee on the Rights of the Child (February 27, 2007), www2.ohchr.org/English/bodies/crc/docs/GC9_en.doc, accessed 25 June 2017.

[37] CEDAW General Recommendation No. 24: Article 12 of the Convention (women and health), 1999 (June 25, 2017), www.refworld.org/docid/453882a73.html.

[38] Convention on the Rights of Persons with Disabilities (May 25, 2017), https://www.un.org/development/desa/disabilities/convention-on-the-rights-of-persons-with-disabilities.html.

[39] See Article 1 of the Convention on the Rights of Persons with Disabilities, https://www.un.org/esa/socdev/enable/rights/convtexte.htm.

[40] Convention on the Rights of Persons with Disabilities and Option Protocol, UN, Article 12.

cruelty, exploitation and abuse (including the gender-based aspects of such violations) and to ensure that persons with disabilities are not subjected to arbitrary or unlawful interference in their privacy and that the right to health and medical facilities of such persons is protected.[41]

CONCLUSION

As may be seen from the above discussions, forced sterilization is considered violative of rights of women, especially women with disabilities. It has been observed by different stakeholders that such sterilization of disabled women is mostly done with the consent of their family members, who might not treat such women with dignity. While acknowledging the existence of preventive laws in this regard in India, it is also seen that such laws have remained paper tigers in the majority of cases. Hardly any proper assessment has been done to determine the growth of forced sterilization of disabled women in India over the years. Such research reports may enable the government to reassess the effectiveness of the existing laws. This author further suggests that non-governmental organizations (NGOs) must be roped in for spreading large-scale awareness on the issue of rights of disabled women and the negative impact of forced sterilization of such women. It must be noted that there are several rescue and rehabilitation policies available for girls and women who may have been abandoned or sexually violated or who may need financial aid for supporting themselves and their children (if any). Several such rescue and rehabilitation mechanisms sponsored by the government, as well as non-governmental stakeholders, are also available for disabled women. However, information on such facilities is not widely shared with disabled women, especially women with mental disabilities. It becomes the duty of the government and non-governmental stakeholders to enable disabled women and their family members to access such information and utilize the same. This author further suggests that governmental stakeholders must also necessarily

[41] For more see WWDA, 'Dehumanised: The Forced Sterilisation of Women and Girls with Disabilities in Australia', https://tbinternet.ohchr.org/Treaties/CAT/Shared%20Documents/AUS/INT_CAT_NGO_AUS_18673_E.pdf, accessed 12 December 2019.

include such women in 'self-help groups', which may ensure vocational training and/or financial support for them for starting their own small-scale enterprises. Where such mechanisms already exist, the government must ensure proper, corruption-free implementation of the same. Further, the government must always audit the beneficiaries and ensure proper implementation of the relevant policies. Periodic assessment of the situation may go a long way in preventing any sort of violation of the rights of disabled women, including forced sterilization.

Chapter 4

Sex Workers and Right to Live with Dignity

A Critical Review

Mradul Mishra and Viralkumar B. Mandaliya

INTRODUCTION

> The obscenities of this country are not girls like you. It is the poverty which is obscene, and the criminal irresponsibility of the leaders who make this poverty a deadening reality. The obscenities in this country are the places of the rich, the new hotels made at the expense of the people, the hospitals where the poor die when they get sick because they don't have the money either for medicines or services. It is only in this light that the real definition of obscenity should be made.
>
> —F. Sionil José

Since time immemorial, certain professions in the human society have been seen as dangerous to the concepts of public health and morality: these professions may include manual scavenging, corpse burning, sex work, etc. While the government of India has taken several initiatives for ensuring the right to dignity for workers falling in the first two categories, the people belonging to the third category of profession are still looked at with disgrace, and their right to live with dignity is often violated. Sex-industry workers are majorly women, and they may not 'inherit' the profession by virtue of their caste, which may happen to other professions, like manual scavenging, corpse burning, etc., which may have attracted social disgrace for ages. Such women may have had to join the sex industry and prostitution due to poverty, trafficking, etc.[1] Several such women may have had to join the sex industry as teenagers due to trafficking, extreme poverty and also abandonment by their families because of their gender.[2] Such female sex workers may have to undergo extreme sexual violence that may be meted out by their clients, physical violence and emotional harassment by people (generally senior or retired female sex workers) who may host them and their agents and extreme harassment by society at large. The term 'prostitution', or sex work, itself carries with it a sense of immorality, illegality, obscenity and social harm. Female sex workers, irrespective of age, may not avail and enjoy the rights enshrined in the Universal Declaration of Human Rights (UDHR), 1948, International Covenant on Civil and Political Rights (ICCPR), 1966, International Covenant on Economic, Social and Cultural Rights (ICESCR), 1966, Convention on the Elimination of All Forms of Discrimination Against Women (CEDAW), 1979 (which deny discrimination on the basis of one's gender or occupation), etc. In the Indian context, they may also be denied basic fundamental rights, including the right to equality before the law and equal protection of laws, right to life, right to education, right to speech and expression, freedom of movement, etc. Historically, sex workers have existed since the Vedic period.[3] The history of social oppression, exclusion, disgrace and violence

---

[1] For more understanding, see Melissa Farley, 'Risks of Prostitution: When the Person Is the Product', *Journal of the Association for Consumer Research* 3, no. 1 (January 2018): 97–108, https://www.journals.uchicago.edu/doi/full/10.1086/695670?mobileUi=0&, accessed 14 December 2019.

[2] Molly Chattopadhyay, S. Bandyopadhyay, and C. Duttagupta, 'Biosocial Factors Influencing Women to Become Prostitutes in India', *Social Biology* 41, no. 3–4 (1994): 252–59, https://www.tandfonline.com/doi/abs/10.1080/19485565.1994.9988876, accessed 14 December 2019.

[3] Sukumari Bhattacharji, 'Prostitution in Ancient India', *Social Scientist* 15, no. 2 (1987): 32–61, https://www.jstor.org/stable/pdf/3520437.pdf?casa_token=3k8gV5FqLz4AAAAA:95Bwu0qsu0ipp3z7P3v_tkO6QJJHUjG_9shGjWQGclEJUbKFlKMyHtndu6_4vNJ49T7S1zhPuP500IssGxk4VMahHWXN-KvukJYF0_afji6MD29oU5Y, accessed 14 December 2019.

meted out to sex workers may also be traced back to the Vedic era. Prostitutes or sex workers, known as *Ganikas*, were considered crude, as well as cunning, immoral and indecent, because of their manners and ways of earning money.[4] This understanding has remained unchanged until now. The mediaeval age and modern age saw stricter rules and regulations for social isolation of prostitutes. The colonial era also saw the creation of rules supporting detention, fining and custodial torture, including custodial sexual violence, of prostitutes.[5] It was only the post 1980s that certain states in India developed certain rules and policies for the healthcare of sex workers and prostitutes: for example, West Bengal, India, developed several welfare measures for prevention of human immunodeficiency virus/acquired immunodeficiency syndrome (HIV/AIDS) in the red-light areas of Sonagachi and other places.[6] Soon, this step was also followed by stakeholders in other states as well. However, the main purpose of such measures was prevention of public health disorders. This chapter argues that, to a large extent, such moves by the government further pushed sex workers towards social exclusion, because they are seen as generators or carriers of sexually transmitted diseases. Several non-governmental organizations (NGOs) have also taken measures for the education of children of sex workers. The right to education also provides that children from socio-economically backward sectors should access quality education; however, this may not have achieved the expected results, because in several areas, elite schools may exclude children of sex workers from mainstream society.[7] Sex workers may not be entertained in any social functions either. This chapter argues that prostitutes are placed in such a

---

[4] Sukumari, 'Prostitution in Ancient India'.

[5] See Sukumari, 'Prostitution in Ancient India'.

[6] For more, see I. Basu, et al. 'HIV Prevention Among Sex Workers in India', *Journal of Acquired Immune Deficiency Syndromes (1999)* 36, no. 3 (2004): 845–52, https://doi.org/10.1097/00126334-200407010-00012, accessed 13 December 2019.

[7] Rashmi Diwan, 'School Leardership in the Wake of RTE Act 2009 Mapping Changes and Challenges', *Journal of Indian Education* XXXVII, no. 1 (May 2011): 97–111, https://www.researchgate.net/profile/Mahmood_Khan30/publication/326492944_An_Evaluative_Study_of_Sarva_Shiksha_Abhiyan_SSA_in_District_Anantnag/links/5b50c41545851507a7b1cda1/An-Evaluative-Study-of-Sarva-Shiksha-Abhiyan-SSA-in-District-Anantnag.pdf#page=99, accessed 13 December 2019.

disgraceful situation because the scope of the right to live with dignity, as has been enshrined in Article 21 of the Constitution of India, has not been fully explored from the perspectives of the rights of sex workers. This chapter aims to fill this gap.

In the second part, the chapter deals elaborately with the meaning of the right to live with dignity and the socio-legal scenario in India of the right to live with dignity of sex workers and prostitution. The third part contains the conclusion.

RIGHT TO LIVE WITH DIGNITY AND ITS EXPANDED UNDERSTANDING

With the introduction of the UDHR and other core instruments of human rights,[8] the meaning of the right to life has been expanded to include the right to equality, right to protection against discrimination, right to speech and expression, right to protection against slavery, right to choice of profession, right to food, shelter and health, right to form a family, right to education, right to life with privacy, right to life with dignity, etc. These rights have further been ensured by way of the ICCPR and ICESCR. Much later, in 1979, the international organizations also created the CEDAW, which deals exclusively with the rights of women and which declares that the state parties shall condemn discrimination against women in all its forms. Article 6 of the CEDAW declares that 'State parties shall take all appropriate measures, including legislation, to suppress all forms of traffic in women and exploitation of prostitution of women'. All these international instruments ensure that no human being lives a life of disgrace, shame and social exclusion. The right to live with dignity denotes the right to live a worthy life with honour. While the UDHR, ICCPR and ICESCR ensured that state parties ratified them to eradicate any socio-legal–political problems that may hamper enjoyment of life with dignity, women did not enjoy this right in its true sense till the CEDAW

[8] Universal Declaration of Human Rights (1948); International Covenant on Civil and Political Rights (1966); International Covenant on Economic, Social and Cultural Rights (1966); Convention on the Elimination of All Forms of Discrimination against Women (1979).

came into existence. Prior to the CEDAW, the rights of women were undermined worldwide. Education was restricted to male children, and as a result, women were considered not competent for decent jobs. Women were not provided the right to ancestral property either.[9] As a result, married women who were not financially independent could not afford to leave abusive relationships. Uneducated or less educated unmarried women, widows and deserted women had to face extreme poverty because the societal set-up would not permit them to take up jobs like their male colleagues did. This has been considered as one of the main reasons for the inflow of women into prostitution. India witnessed the growth of judicial activism, human rights explosions and more state parties' consideration of implementation of CEDAW principles for uplifting the status of women simultaneously.[10] Courts in India, especially the Supreme Court, explored the meaning of the right to life, as enshrined in Article 21 of the Indian Constitution, from various perspectives, including personal liberty through the case of *Maneka Gandhi v. Union of India*,[11] the right to life as inclusive of the right to equality, right to due process of law and right to speech and expression through the case of *A. K. Gopalan v. State of Madras*,[12] right to privacy through the case of *Kharak Singh v. State of UP*,[13] etc. In 1981, the Supreme Court finally explored the meaning of the right to live with dignity in a series of cases, including the case of *Francis Coralie v. Union Territory of Delhi*,[14] in which the court explained that the right to life, from the perspectives of the right to dignity, is a comprehensive right including the right to life with the bare necessities of life, adequate nutrition, clothing, shelter, the right to express one's opinion and acquire information, etc. Further, the concept of the right to live with

---

[9] D. Halder and K. Jaishankar, 'Property Rights of Hindu Women: A Critical Review of Succession Laws of Ancient, Medieval, and Modern India', *Journal of Law and Religion* XXIV, 25th Anniversary Issue (2008): 101–122.

[10] Jamie Cassels, 'Judicial Activism and Public Interest Litigation in India: Attempting the Impossible?' *The American Journal of Comparative Law* 37, no. 3 (Summer, 1989): 495–519, https://www.jstor.org/stable/840090, accessed 13 December 2019.

[11] Maneka Gandhi v. Union of India. AIR 1978SC 597.

[12] A. K. Gopalan v. State of Madras. AIR 1950 SC 27.

[13] Kharak Singh v. State of UP. 7.AIR 1963 SC 1295.

[14] Francis Coralie v. Union Territory of Delhi. SCC 608 (1981).

dignity was further expanded to cover the right to protection against exploitation, especially in regard to the right to work and earn a decent living, in the case of *Bandhu Mukti Morcha v. Union of India.*[15] Seen from the perspective of this very case, it becomes necessary to understand whether sex workers may fall within the category of employees or labourers or workers.

Several researchers have pointed out that prostitution is a kind of job. It involves sex workers who provide sexual solicitation for clients who 'buy' services. Prostitutes enter into contracts and agreements with their clients and with the owner of the place where they may provide their services.[16] In cases of online prostitution too, they may be involved in multiple agreements and contracts, which may include contracts with producers, directors, website owners, etc., who may facilitate uploading, sharing, etc., of the contents related to online prostitution. Several studies also indicate that there are different kinds of prostitution services available in the market in the category of offline prostitution: these may include brothel prostitution, where prostitutes may entertain their clients in brothels run by retired prostitutes or individuals engaged in flesh-trade rackets, call-girl systems, where women may offer their services independently at places chosen and/or designated by either the clients or by themselves, massage parlour services, where clients may avail sex work–related services from sex workers in the name of body massage,[17] escort services, which may or may not involve sexual penetration as may happen in other types of prostitution services,[18] etc. All such types of sex work services may include male, female and transgender sex workers who may have different types of demands

---

[15] Bandhu Mukti Morcha v. Union of India. (1989)4 SSC, 62

[16] D. Leidholdt, 'Prostitution: A Violation of Women's Human Rights', *Cardozo Women's Law Journal* 1 (1993–1994): 133, http://bibliobase.sermais.pt:8008/BiblioNET/upload/PDF2/01689_Leidholdt%20Prostitution%20Violation%20of%20Womens%20Human%20Rights.pdf, accessed 13 December 2019.

[17] For more understanding, see Tulsing Sonwani, 'Prostitution in Indian Society: Issues, Trends and Rehabilitation', https://www.ugc.ac.in/mrp/paper/MRP-MAJOR-SOCI-2013-25158-PAPER.pdf, accessed 13 December 2019.

[18] J. T. Parsons, J. A. Koken, and D. S. Bimbi, 'The Use of the Internet by Gay and Bisexual Male Escorts: Sex Workers as Sex Educators', *AIDS Care* 16, no. 8 (November, 2004): 1021–1035.

depending upon their customers' individual choices. In this course, sex workers, especially female sex workers, both offline and online, may face tremendous harassment and violence in the form of sexual slavery, discrimination and violation of rights. The following are some of the patterns of violence and violation of rights that sex workers of all categories might face.

Non-sexual Emotional Harassment and Physical Violence

The joint stakeholders' submission made in 2016 regarding violations faced by sex workers in India[19] pointed out that sex workers, irrespective of their gender and age, may receive abuses, physical beatings and threats from their clients, brothel owners and managers for various reasons, including refusing to provide sex to clients (especially in cases of newly trafficked victims), dissatisfaction in services offered, demand for better payment by the sex workers, denial of further sexual services because of health problems of the sex workers, etc. They may not be served proper food and may not have proper and hygienic washroom facilities, clean beds and sufficient time to rest either. They may also be severely bullied and mentally tortured for not obeying the brothel owners and managers. Sex workers thus harassed may not be able to share their victimization with the police or the criminal justice machinery, because then they may be considered as part of an illegal industry. Several NGOs have reached out to female sex workers for betterment of their living conditions. However, we are yet to receive any positive results from such outreach.

Sexual Violence within the Meaning of Prostitution

Researchers have defined sex work as 'the exchange of sexual services, performances, or products for material compensation'.[20] This essentially includes penetrative and non-penetrative sexual contacts between the

---

[19] See Joint Stakeholders Submission: Violations Faced by Sex Workers in India (September 20, 2016), https://www.upr-info.org/sites/default/files/document/india/session_27_-_may_2017/js9_upr27_ind_e_main.pdf.

[20] Alexandra Lutnick and Deborah Cohan, 'Criminalization, Legalization or Decriminalization of Sex Work: What Female Sex Workers Say in San Francisco,

service provider (the sex worker) and the client/customer. However, within this business relationship, prostitutes may undergo severe sexual violence. Female prostitutes may suffer severe squeezing of breasts and other softer body parts, ejaculation on face, aggravated penetrative sexual assault, which may include insertion of objects (other than body parts) inside the vagina, etc.[21] They may even be photographed while in a compromising position without their consent, and such images may be circulated widely to bring more harassment.[22] Such forced sexual violence may also result in sexually transmittable diseases, including gonorrhoea, syphilis, etc. Further, transwomen in sex work may also face severe sexual violence, as their genitals may be squeezed or slashed. They may be forced to perform oral sex, etc.[23] Sex workers who may contract a sexually transmittable disease or any other infected disease may not even be able to avail medical assistance in several cases due to poverty, blaming, ridiculing and secondary victimization at medical clinics, etc.

Violation of Rights at the Hands of the Police and Criminal Justice Machinery

In India, sex work or prostitution is not yet recognized as a legalized profession. Hence, brothels, hotel rooms and rented apartments used for prostitution and sexual slavery may not be considered as a legalized workplace for sex workers. As a result, sex workers, especially women, may never be able to lodge complaints with the police or with the criminal justice machinery for the abuses, physical beatings and threats they may receive from their clients, brothel owners and managers

USA', *Reproductive Health Matters* 17, no. 34(November 2009): 38–46, https://doi.org/10.1016/S0968-8080(09)34469-9, accessed 13 December 2019.

[21] Melissa Farley, 'Prostitution is Sexual Violence', https://resources.todaango.org.il/wp-content/uploads/2014/01/Farley.pdf, accessed 13 December 2019.

[22] For more understanding, see D. Halder and K. Jaishankar, *Cyber Crimes Against Women in India* (New Delhi: SAGE Publications, 2016).

[23] For more, see S. Y. Shaw et al., 'Factors Associated with Sexual Violence Against Men Who Have Sex with Men and Transgendered individuals in Karnataka, India', *PloS One* 7, no. 3 (2012): e31705, https://doi.org/10.1371/journal.pone.0031705, accessed 14 December 2019.

under the Sexual Harassment of Women at Workplace (Prevention Prohibition and Redressal) Act or any other penal laws if they wish to escape from 'work'. On the contrary, such sex workers may be victimized by the police during raids, in public places in the name of prevention of public nuisance, in police stations, as they may be brought to them on the charges of being associated with a brothel, damaging public health or performing immoral activities, or even false charges of committing theft, etc. A sex worker may also be charged with creating public nuisance[24] or for obscene conduct.[25] The reason may be traced back to the colonial-era policies that criminalized prostitution. In the colonial era in India, the Cantonment Act, 1864 regulated the sex industry. Later on, the Indian Contagious Diseases Act, 1868 was enacted, which prescribed the registration and inspection of sex workers. After independence, the rights of sex workers were covered under multiple laws, including the Immoral Traffic (Prevention) Act, 1956 (ITPA). According to the ITPA sex work in private is not illegal, but at the same time the ITPA prohibits running a brothel,[26] living on the earnings of prostitution,[27] procuring, inducing or detaining persons for the purpose of sex work with or without consent,[28] detaining a person in premises where prostitution is carried on[29] and seducing or soliciting for sex work in public.[30] The inhuman and degrading torture by the police may include beating prostitutes in public, pulling their hair aggressively, forcing them to bribe the police, forcing them to accept their guilt, putting them along with male criminals in police lock-ups and undertrial prisons, not arranging any medical tests for them, arresting their family members and treating them also on the same lines.[31] Such sex workers may not avail good legal assistance from the clinics offering free legal services either, as lawyers and paralegal

---

[24] Section 268, 290 of Indian Penal Code 1860.
[25] Section 294 of Indian Penal Code 1860.
[26] Section 3 of Immoral Traffic (Prevention) Act 1956.
[27] Section 4 of Immoral Traffic (Prevention) Act 1956.
[28] Section 5 of Immoral Traffic (Prevention) Act 1956.
[29] Section 6 of Immoral Traffic (Prevention) Act 1956.
[30] Section 8 of Immoral Traffic (Prevention) Act 1956.
[31] See 'Joint Stakeholders Submission: Violations Faced by Sex Workers in India'.

volunteers may also wish to maintain their distance from sex workers fearing taboo and social discrimination in their own social circles.

Discrimination and Social Ostracization

Prostitution as a profession attracts stigma. This is the main reason that may force sex workers to not disclose their identity for availing public facilities, including public health facilities. Prostitutes and sex workers face discrimination in all sectors, including availing banking facilities, medical facilities or essential-service supply facilities, and in accessing basic education as well. The very notion of Articles 14 (right to equality) and 21 (right to life) stands violated for them when they are discriminated against on the basis of their profession. During the census of 2011, sex workers raised a plea to differentiate themselves from 'beggars'.[32] This may indicate that prostitutes may not have been given even a fitting social category in the census reports made by governmental stakeholders. Sex workers may further be denied the basic fundamental rights, and various rights of sex workers are breached on a daily basis either by society or by law enforcement authorities. In general, sex workers do have the fundamental rights such as the right to peaceful association, right to privacy, right to be free from arbitrary interference, right to choose a profession of their own choice, right to have access to minimum education, right to have minimum wages, freedom of movement with dignity, etc. It may further be noted that in case a sex worker, including a minor sex worker, is rescued, it may become a Herculean task for NGOs and stakeholders to rehabilitate her and re-integrate her into mainstream society. The self-help group (SHG) scheme may provide some solace in this regard, but in such cases also, the problems of untouchability, disgrace and shameful curiosity exist.[33] This may further vitiate the philosophy of the Francis Corali case.

---

[32] TNN, 'Sex Workers Beg to Differ with Census Category', *The Times of India* (February 10, 2011), http://censusindia.gov.in/Ad_Campaign/press/News-%2011%20Feb%202011-ToI-Sex%20Workers%20beg%20to%20differ%20with%20census%20category.pdf, accessed 20 December 2019.

[33] For more, see https://shodhganga.inflibnet.ac.in/bitstream/10603/203382/5/chapter%204.pdf, accessed 14 December 2019.

Breach of Privacy

Sex workers may suffer privacy breach in several ways: while their privacy may be breached by their clients or even their managers by way of sharing of their phone number, location, data, photographs, including sexually explicit audiovisual content created with/without their consent and circulated without their knowledge, their privacy may further be breached during police raids. During the raids conducted by the police on any brothel, the entire operation may be aired on media channels, exposing the sex workers, which is a clear violation of the law, as well as their right to privacy. It may be deemed that the police and media may try to make the entire operation sensational. However, it may further make the sex workers more vulnerable and make their re-integration into mainstream society more problematic. Further, the health sector may also breach their privacy by way of tracking their data and leaking their sensitive personal data, causing further humiliation, because sex workers may not be aware of data privacy issues. They may themselves reveal a lot of sensitive, personal information that may be detrimental to their personal safety.[34]

The above discussion may suggest that the right to live with dignity is not ensured to the sex workers in India in spite of several attempts by stakeholders to uplift their status. Let us now look at some legislations that were created for the benefit of all individuals, including women and transgender people from socio-economically backward classes. Based on an understanding of the vicious connection between trafficking of women and children and violence against women by way of prostitution, the ITPA was brought into effect. A detailed reading of the same legislature leads to the finding that the Act does not directly prohibit sex work but rather mainly deals with immoral trafficking of women and children. The question that arises here is: when there is no specific law penalizing sex work, how is it made punishable? The ITPA prescribes punishment for some acts that are closely related to sex work; however, if some adult is engaged in sex work, he/she is doing it privately and the public is not affected by it, then the law cannot punish

[34] Catherine D. Perry, 'Right of Privacy Challenges to Prostitution Statutes', *Washington University Law Quarterly* 58 (1980): 439, https://openscholarship.wustl.edu/law_lawreview/vol58/iss2/8, accessed 13 December 2019.

him/her. The ITPA also mandates medical examination of persons removed from brothels.[35] The Act also provides for rehabilitation of sex workers.[36] Looking into the Constitution of India, it may be seen that there are sufficient provisions that can be used as an umbrella provision to address questions related to the rights of sex workers. The Preamble to the Indian Constitution speaks of 'dignity' of an individual. It states that all people in India have an invincible right to live their life with dignity. Thereafter, Article 14 provides that 'The State shall not deny to any person equality before the law or the equal protection of the laws within the territory of India'. It is clear from the language of Article 14 that sex workers have a fundamental right to be treated equally before the law. Thus, when any of their rights are violated, they must be given equal protection by law. The transformation of such a right into reality seldom materializes. Further, into the picture comes Article 19(1)(g), which states that 'All citizens shall have the right to practice any profession or to carry on any occupation, trade or business'. It is noteworthy here that this right is not absolute, as Article 19(6) places restrictions on the exercise of this right. This right can be restricted on the grounds of 'interests of general public'. Going by the language, sex work is also a profession; hence, it must also be covered under this article and sex workers must also be given the same freedom(s) as are people in other professions. Furthermore, Article 21 of the Constitution of India says that 'No person shall be deprived of his life or personal liberty except according to procedure established by law'. While interpreting the word 'life' under Article 21 in the case of *Maneka Gandhi v. Union of India*,[37] the Supreme Court held that the life should be a meaningful life. All the necessary requirements shall be covered under this article which make a person's life meaningful. The life of an individual should be a dignified life, which includes all the basic rights that make a life dignified. Further, it is imperative to read certain provisions under Part IV of the constitution, such as Article 39(a), which states that 'All the citizens, men and women equally, have the right to an adequate means of livelihood', and Article 39 (d), which provides that 'There shall be equal pay for equal work for

---

[35] Section 15 (5A) of Immoral Traffic (Prevention) Act 1956.
[36] Section 19, 21, 23 of Immoral Traffic (Prevention) Act 1956.
[37] Maneka Gandhi v. Union of India. (1978) SCR (2) 62.

both men and women'. These provisions collectively clarify that the constitution does not allow the state to differentiate the profession of sex work from any other work, and likewise, sex workers shall also not be discriminated against on the basis of their profession. However, in reality, these provisions have been paper tigers on many occasions.

The authors suggest that the right to live with dignity may be ensured for sex workers if the profession is legalized. In such a case, the standard labour laws would be applicable upon them, and they would get protections provided under the same. As a result, sex workers would get better work conditions and wages, in addition to their being able to freely choose their working hours. In the case of *Budhadev Karmaskar v. State of West Bengal*,[38] the Hon'ble Supreme Court acknowledged the rights of sex workers to live with dignity within the meaning of Article 21 and observed that it is the responsibility of the government to ensure the provision of all the fundamental rights and the right to rehabilitation to sex workers. In the case of *Tara v. State*,[39] the Delhi High Court overturned the forcible detention and transportation of 15 adult sex workers to Andhra Pradesh, because it was in violation of their right to live with dignity under the constitution. Reportedly, the Hon'ble Supreme Court also suggested to the central government to legalize sex work for preventing violation of rights of women, men and transgender people involved in the sex industry.[40] Further, legalizing sex work would also result in addressing the torture, harassment and discrimination that sex workers face on a daily basis. They would also be able to register cases of non-consensual, aggravated sexual violence with the police. The NGOs like Amnesty International also recommend full decriminalization of sex work and prostitution in order to protect the human rights of sex workers.[41]

---

[38] Budhadev Karmaskar v. State of West Bengal. (2011) 11 SCC 538.

[39] Tara v. State. W. P. (Criminal) 296/2012 before the High Court of Delhi.

[40] PTI, Legalize Prostitution If You Can't Curb It: SC to Govt (December 10, 2009), http://timesofindia.indiatimes.com/india/Legalize-prostitution-if-you-cant-curb-it-SC-to-govt/articleshow/5322127.cms, accessed 12 July 2017.

[41] Elgot Jessica, 'Amnesty Approves Policy to Decriminalize Sex Trade' (July 12, 2017), https://www.theguardian.com/world/2015/aug/11/amnesty-approves-policy-to-decriminalise-sex-trade.

CONCLUSION

The right to live with dignity for sex workers may not be effectively executed by the relevant stakeholders unless society as a whole changes its perception towards sex workers. Prostitution has carried with it social stigma for thousands of years in India. Legalizing prostitution may ensure certain rights to prostitutes, but unless society as a whole addresses the issue from the perspective of sexual victimization and exploitation of sex workers who may be engaged in this profession due to poverty, etc., the situation may remain the same forever. The authors suggests that awareness must be spread about the plight of sex workers due to discrimination, stigmatization and criminalization of their basic existence in society. Unless society as a whole accepts the legal norms and builds strong resistance against exploitation of individuals in the name of sex services, sex workers may not get any benefit from the judicial interpretations and directions regarding the right to live with dignity.

Chapter 5

Gender Equality and Human Rights in India

A Critical Review

Badri Sankar Das

INTRODUCTION

The term 'gender' has three basic understandings in the modern context—male, female and 'other', which implies choice of gender on the basis of gender orientation. However, the first two understandings are on the basis of sex, that is, male and female. As such, this understanding comes from the Rome Statute of the International Criminal Court that defined gender in the following lines: '…the term "gender" refers to the two sexes, male and female, within the context of society. The term "gender" does not indicate any meaning different from the above'.[1] The term 'gender' therefore includes the understandings of both biological and psychological aspects, especially when the said term expands its scope to include those who were born as biologically male or female but later developed an orientation towards the opposite gender.[2] The

[1] Article 7(3) of the Rome Statute of the International Criminal Court, 17 July 1998, 37 I.L.M. 999 (1998)

[2] S. J. Wendy, *Gender: An Enthnometholody Approach* (Chicago: University of Chicago Press, 1978).

concept of gender equality therefore does no longer only signify equality between two heterogeneous sexes but also extends its scope to all three gender aspects, namely, male, female and the third gender.[3] However, in practice, we do get to see that gender equality largely refers to equality between males and females, and both these terms may include transmen and transwomen. It is necessary to note that the international instruments, including the Universal Declaration of Human Rights (UDHR), International Covenant on Civil and Political Rights and International Covenant on Economic, Social and Cultural Rights have emphasized the rights of fundamental freedom, inherent dignity and equality for all irrespective of gender, sex, race, etc. These instruments also emphasize the equal right to be born, get parental care, get an education, work and choose a profession, own property, start a family, etc.[4] However, it has been noticed that gender disparity has existed, especially in India in cases of succession of property,[5] choice of children,[6] access to basic education for children,[7] access of nutritious food and holistic development for children irrespective of gender, etc. The concept of gender justice was further addressed by the Convention on the Elimination of All Forms of Discrimination Against Women (CEDAW), which was created in 1979. The CEDAW addresses issues of equality from the perspectives of the rights to life, work and equal wages, special protection against trafficking and illegal prostitution, protection against domestic and workplace violence against women, equal access to health and legal aid,

---

[3] Nalsa v. Union of India & others, WP (civil) no. 400 of 2012.

[4] See Universal Declaration of Human Rights, 'International Covenant on Civil and Political Rights and International Covenant on Socio-economic and Cultural Rights', https://www.ohchr.org/en/professionalinterest/pages/cescr.aspx.

[5] D. Halder and K. Jaishankar, 'Property Rights of Hindu Women: A Critical Review of Succession Laws of Ancient, Medieval, and Modern India', *Journal of Law and Religion* 24 (2008): 101–122.

[6] Sood Jyoti Dogra and K. N. Pillai Chandrashekhar, 'Female Foeticide in India', *NUALS Law Journal* 2 (2008): 1.

[7] Geeta Gandhi Kingdon, 'Does the Labour Market Explain Lower Female Schooling in India?' *The Journal of Development Studies* 35, no. 1 (2007): 39–65.

representation in the parliament, etc.[8] While the Indian Constitution has provided several provisions under Article 15(3) to ensure gender equality and special status to women and children, for whom special laws, policies, statutes, etc., may be created to protect their interest, it has been seen that such laws and policies are grossly neglected, abused and misused to suppress the rights of women and female children. The Parliament has enacted several laws, including the Immoral Traffic (Prevention) Act, 1956, Dowry Prohibition Act, 1961 (Act No. 28 of 1961) (amended in 1986), Indecent Representation of Women (Prohibition) Act, 1986, Commission of Sati (Prevention) Act, 1987 (Act No. 3 of 1988), Protection of Women from Domestic Violence Act, 2005, Sexual Harassment of Women at Workplace (Prevention, Prohibition and Redressal) Act, 2013, etc. In 2013, the government further amended the Indian Penal Code to accommodate gender-specific laws to protect women from sexual offences, including sexual assault, voyeurism, stalking, including cyberstalking, etc. However, in spite of all these efforts of the lawmakers, women continue to be suppressed in their homes, public places and workplaces. This author argues that gender discrimination and suppression of gender rights, especially those of women, happen because of sociocultural mindsets. The constitutional rights of women and female children are often eclipsed by the age-old social customs that may or may not have received legal support in India. This author aims to research on the social customs in India which hamper the successful execution of laws and rights provided for women and girls in the country.

This chapter is divided into four portions, including the introduction. The second part discusses prevalent sociocultural customs supporting gender disparity. It also discusses different forms of gender disparity prevalent in the Indian society. The third portion speaks about the constitutional efforts to protect the right to equality and human rights that further prohibit gender discrimination. This part also speaks about constitutional mandates for spreading awareness about gender equality and equality rights. The fourth part offers the conclusion. This chapter builds its arguments with the help of the doctrinal-research methodology.

---

[8] For more understanding, see Convention of Elimination of All Sorts of Discrimination Against Women (CEDAW), https://www.un.org/womenwatch/daw/cedaw/text/econvention.htm#article6.

PREVALENT SOCIOCULTURAL CUSTOMS IN INDIA SUPPORTING GENDER INEQUALITY

Since ages, India has seen gender disparity in several aspects, including issues around succession, administrative power at work, equal wages for equal work, safety of women at workplaces, child custody and guardianship, political leadership, etc. Women have been considered the *weaker sex* in handling such issues largely due to the patriarchal mindset. The above-mentioned aspects are discussed below:

Gender Disparity in Succession

The conventional Hindu in India emphasized that females can neither be the head of a family nor inherit ancestral properties superseding their male siblings. Two ancient succession laws, the *Dayabhaga* and *Meetakshara* laws, which assumed key roles in creating the present-day Hindu succession laws, rejected women as significant major shareholders of ancestral or marital properties.[9] Women were not considered fit inheritors of their husband's properties either. They were provided limited rights to reside in such properties till their death.[10] Young widows, childless widows and unmarried and disabled women were often abandoned. They were either sent to Vrindavan, where they may have had to live the life of beggars and die due to hunger, malnutrition or poverty[11] or be sold in the flesh market.[12] Researchers have observed that the main reason behind excluding women from inheritance rights may include the sociocultural understanding of lower maturity of women compared to that of men in handling property and

[9] See 'Convention of Elimination of All Sorts of Discrimination Against Women'.

[10] See 'Convention of Elimination of All Sorts of Discrimination Against Women'.

[11] Rekha Pande, 'The Forgotten Widows of Vrindavan in India', in *Religion and Theology: Breakthroughs in Research and Practice*, edited by Management Association and Information Resources, 61–77 (Hershey: IGI Global, 2020).

[12] Sarah Lamb, 'Being Single in India: Gendered Identities, Class Mobilities, and Personhoods in Flux', *Ethos* 46, no. 1 (2018): 49–69.

property-related issues and the intention by male folks to solely enjoy property and property-related profits, as it was understood that women must be satisfied with the jewellery received as *Stridhan,* etc. Such mindset may also include apprehension of financial loss and reduction of property and property-related financial gain share if women, including married women, take their share in the property.[13] Such patriarchal mindset has given rise to several offences targeting women and female children, including female foeticide, child marriage, bride burning, abandoning of women, including disabled women, etc.[14] However, the 2005 amendment to the Hindu Succession Act, 1956 brought some relief to women as successors and inheritors of ancestral property. The Act was revised to incorporate women as exclusive successors to both parental and marital property[15] However, this author observes that there is a lack of awareness about the new amendments to the succession right. Due to fear of social taboo and lack of economic independence, women still do not prefer to fight for their equal right to inheritance of ancestral and marital property.

Gagging Women's Right to Choose Their Life Partner

Quite along the lines of inheritance rights, women in India have been deprived of their right to choose their own life partner. It is interesting to note that women had not been allowed to stay in live-in relationships either until recently. While the latter was given partial social recognition due to the landmark judgement in the case of *S. Khushboo v. Kanniammal,*[16] where the court held that such choice of living falls within the broader understanding of Article 21 of the constitution, women living in live-in relationships are not yet accepted by the orthodox patriarchal society. In regard to their choice of their own life partner, it may be seen that while in Hindu mythology, the ritual of Swayamvar or selection of bridegroom by the bride was accepted as a regular norm, in reality, women may not be allowed to

[13] Lamb, 'Being Single in India'.

[14] Lamb, 'Being Single in India'.

[15] Lamb, 'Being Single in India'.

[16] S. Khushboo v. Kanniammal. (2010) 5 SCC 600.

choose their life partner according to their own wishes. Despite the fact that the UDHR and the covenants on civil and political rights and social, economic and cultural rights provide every individual, irrespective of race, gender, caste, creed, etc., the right to found a family as per their own choice and wishes, the majority of socio-religious communities in India would not allow women to choose their own life partner. Women may be forced to marry men, including older men, to satisfy the socio-economic–cultural needs of the families and society at large. For realizing such gains, underage girls may be given in marriage to men and underage boys by way of child marriage. Further, if a woman refuses to take part in such marriage or chooses her own life partner, who may or may not be from her caste or race, she may have to meet a fatal end by way of honour killing.[17] Women who may have to enter into wedlock without consent may also be subjected to domestic violence,[18] dowry harassment and death threats,[19] and also forceful abandonment or divorce without proper alimony.

Restricting the Right to Work

Indian sociocultural customs have restricted women to raising children, cooking and taking care of the domestic chores and family requirements. It may be seen that in several urban and rural societies in India, educated women may not be allowed join any profession or a workplace, because that may be considered a social taboo.[20] Male-dominated families may consider workplaces as risky for women.

---

[17] D. Halder and K. Jaishankar, 'Love Marriages, Inter-Caste Violence, and Therapeutic Jurisprudential Approach of the Courts in India', in *Therapeutic Jurisprudence and Overcoming Violence Against Women*, edited by D. Halder and K. Jaishankar (Hershey: IGI Global, 2017). doi:10.4018/978-1-5225-2472-4.ch003.

[18] See Corinne H. Rocca, et al. 'Challenging Assumptions About Women's Empowerment: Social and Economic Resources and Domestic Violence Among Young Married Women in Urban South India'. *International Journal of Epidemiology* 38, no. 2 (2009): 577–85.

[19] Linda Stone and Caroline James, 'Dowry, Bride-burning, and Female Power in India', *Women's Studies International Forum* 18, no. 2 (1995): 125–34.

[20] M. Bhattacharyya, A. S. Bedi, and A. Chhachhi, 'Marital Violence and Women's Employment and Property Status: Evidence from north Indian Villages', *World Development* 39, no. 9 (2011): 1676–89.

Further, women in such families may also be prevented from venturing out to public places alone, as the families and society may feel that women should be considered as 'properties' that should be *enjoyed* only by the owners, that is, the husbands or fathers. Researchers have observed that such orthodox mindsets have directly impacted the economic status of women, their right to custody of children in cases of divorce and separation, etc.[21] While this understanding may explain why women may not be allowed to be financially independent and join workplaces, we must also consider the aspect of gender disparity in labour markets in India.

Article 14 of the Constitution of India guarantees the right to equality irrespective of race, caste, sex, etc. Women are still considered as cheaper labourers in the labour market compared to men.[22] Researchers have indicated that such gender disparity in the labour market may be directly related to unequal treatment of female children in providing them basic and higher education and nutritious food and in their holistic development.[23]

CONSTITUTIONAL RIGHTS AGAINST GENDER DISPARITY IN INDIA

The colonial rulers were approached by social reformers to create penal laws for preventing gender disparity and oppression of women in British India.[24] However, the former carefully avoided touching upon socio-religious sentiments, which may affect the patriarchal social

---

[21] Debarati Halder, 'Who Wins the Battle for Custody? An Analysis of the Nature of Modern Judicial Understandings of Womens Rights in Cases of Custody of Minor Children in Matrimonial Disputes Under the Hindu Laws', in *Essays in Family Law in Memory of Professor B. N. Sampath: Gender, Human Rights and Law*, edited by Sarasu Esther Thomas, Vol. 2 (Bangalore: National Law School of India University, 2013).

[22] Geeta Gandhi Kingdon, 'Does the Labour Market Explain Lower Female Schooling in India?' *The Journal of Development Studies* (1998), http://eprints.lse.ac.uk/6715/1/Does_the_labour_market_explain_lower_female_schooling_in_India.pdf.

[23] Geeta, 'Does the Labour Market Explain Lower Female Schooling in India?'

[24] See 'Convention of Elimination of All Sorts of Discrimination Against Women'.

set-up. This resulted in zero amendments in the personal laws, including inheritance laws. The British government however considered the plea to penalize Sati Pratha and child marriage, considering the same to be social crimes.[25] Social reformers from Bengal, Maharashtra, Punjab, etc., tried to initiate education for women. However, such efforts did not meet with much success due to opposition from orthodox religious communities. Christian missionaries, however, started schools and colleges for women which had very few female students.[26] After independence, the framers of the constitution took care to include provisions to remove gender disparity. In doing this, India incorporated the UDHR in its constitution. Following the UDHR, the framers of the constitution inserted several provisions for ensuring gender rights which are noteworthy. These provisions and the statutes made on their basis are discussed further.

Article 14 of the Constitution of India speaks about the right to equality. This provision guarantees 'equality before the law' and 'equal protection of the laws'. The former suggests that no one should be denied equal treatment and no one should be given extra privilege on the basis of race, caste, creed, language, etc. The latter concept signifies equal protection of the laws to those who may not be equal with the rest due to their gender, age, maturity level, economic and social status, etc. Article 15(3) carries this significance further by providing special status to women and children, who should be protected by the state by way of creation of laws, policies and guidelines that would protect them from atrocities. Article 16 further enhances the scope of the right to equality through providing for equal opportunities in matters of public employment. Article 19 of the constitution, on the other hand, provides for the fundamental freedom of speech and expression, peaceful assembly, freedom of movement, freedom to reside and settle in any part or territory of India and the right to practise any profession. Article 21 of the Indian Constitution guarantees the right to life, which is considered as the heart of the constitution. The scope of the right to life extends to the right to a dignified life, right to privacy, right to protection against harassment and torture, including sexual slavery,

---

[25] See 'Convention of Elimination of All Sorts of Discrimination Against Women'.

[26] Srabashi Ghosh, '"Birds in a Cage": Changes in Bengali Social Life as Recorded in Autobiographies by Women', *Economic and Political Weekly* (1986): WS88–96.

etc. It also covers the right to health, right to legal aid, right to fair trial, etc. Article 23, on the other hand, prohibits trafficking of human beings, including sex trafficking and forced labour. This provision extends its scope to the right to protection against sex trafficking and illegal prostitution for women and girls. Article 24, which speaks about probation of child labour, must be read with Article 23 to understand the constitutional guarantees for a safe childhood and the right to protection against child abuse, including sexual abuse. It is interesting to note that the constitution mandates the state to implement several measures to remove gender disparity under the broad head of Directive Principles of State Policy, as provided in Part IV of the Constitution of India. Article 38 of the Constitution of India speaks about the state's responsibilities in securing social order for the promotion of the welfare of the people. Article 39, on the other hand, emphasizes the duty of the state to provide adequate means of livelihood to its citizens equally, irrespective of gender. It also includes the duty to ensure equal payment and the right to health. Article 39A emphasizes the responsibility of the state to secure equal justice and free legal aid. Article 42, on the other hand, addresses the responsibility of the state to provide for just and humane conditions of work and maternity relief. Article 46 emphasizes promotion of educational and economic aspects of the weaker sections of society and protection for all from injustice and exploitation. Article 47, on the other hand, directs the state to ensure the right to nutrition and proper standard of living for a dignified life.

The judicial interpretations of the above-mentioned constitutional provisions have further expanded the scopes of the provisions to address the right to work, right to financial independence, right to maternity benefits, etc. For instance, in the case of *Air India v. Nergesh Meerza*,[27] the court held that termination of the services of airhostesses because of pregnancy is against the constitutional guarantees and that such decision is unfair and unjust. Again, in the case of *Vishaka v. State of Rajasthan*,[28] the Supreme Court raised concerns over the workplace safety of women and issued specific guidelines, which later helped the legislature frame the Sexual Harassment of Women at Workplace (Prevention, Prohibition and Redressal) Act, 2013. In *Safin Jahan v. Ashokan K.*

[27] Air India v. Nergesh Meerza. (1981). AIR 1829.

[28] Vishaka v. State of Rajasthan. (1997). 6 (SCC) 241.

M., the Supreme Court, while upholding the extended scope of the right to life to cover the right to choose a life partner, held that the right to marry a spouse of one's own choice falls within the ambit of fundamental rights.[29] This understanding of the Supreme Court further strengthened the rights of women against domestic violence, the right to life and safety against honour killing. This case also further strengthened women's right to choose a religion as per their own choice. Further, in the landmark case of *Indian Young Lawyers Association v. The State of Kerala*,[30] the Supreme Court established that women should be given permission to enter religious places of worship, including the Sabarimala Temple, which had restricted access to only men.

The judicial interpretations of the earlier-mentioned provisions further motivated the legislature to create and amend the laws such as the Protection of Women from Domestic Violence Act, 2005, Indecent Representation of Women (Prohibition) Act, 1986, Maternity Benefit (Amendment) Act, 2017, Prohibition of Child Marriage Act, 2006, Equal Remuneration Act, 1976, Dowry Prohibition Act, 1961, Muslim Women (Protection of Rights on Marriage) Act, 2019, Criminal Law (Amendment) Act, 2013, etc. These constitutional provisions and statutes provide protection for women against various kinds of gender disparity, which would ensure gender equality.

CONCLUSION

The above discussion would show that in spite of the creation of gender-specific laws to protect the interests of women, sociocultural norms defy laws, including constitutional rights, human rights and fundamental rights. The Supreme Court, in the landmark cases of the Sabarimala Temple, Triple Talaq, Nirbhaya rape, etc., has observed that the judiciary, executive and legislature are working towards the protection of rights of women, but such attempts may be defied by the

---

[29] Apoorva Mandhani, *Right to Change of Faith is Fundamental Right of Choice, Supreme Court's Decision in The Hadiya Case* (May 21, 2018), http://www.livelaw.in/right-change-faith-part-fundamental-right-choice-read-reasons-scs-decision-hadiya-case/published on 10 April 2017.

[30] Indian Young Lawyers Association v. The State of Kerala. WRIT PETITION (CIVIL) NO. 373 OF 2006.

orthodox patriarchal societies even in the contemporary period. Even though the government has launched many schemes and policies for supporting women's rights, including Beti Bachao, Beti Padhao, which is a flagship policy for promoting the female sex ratio in country and encouraging parents to provide education to the girl child, the 24-hour toll-free Women Helpline to receive complaints of violence against women, National Creche Scheme (for the children of working mothers), Pradhan Mantri Ujjwala Yojana, (for providing liquefied petroleum gas [LPG] cylinders to women living below the poverty line), policies for supporting and training women for vocational training purposes, etc., not many women have been benefitted by these policies, because the male family members may not have supported the welfare and holistic growth of women. The social evils such as child marriages, dowry deaths, rapes, sexual assaults in public places or at workplaces, etc., are still rampant. India has not yet recognized marital rape either. This has made women who may not be financially independent more vulnerable to domestic violence. However, it must be noted that the national and state commissions for women's and children's protection, non-governmental organizations (NGOs) and the district legal services authorities have been conducting tremendous awareness campaigns to create awareness among everyone about women's rights, equality, legal consequences of domestic violence, practices discriminating between male and female children, etc. However, society needs to be more receptive to support the holistic realization of women's rights. This author suggests that the Indian states and the central government must take more initiatives to include women from different socio-economic strata to hear their voices. This would enable the stakeholders to understand how to proceed in achieving gender equality. This author further suggests that men should be sensitized more about gender rights. The government should take stricter measures to monitor treatment of women and girls at workplaces, public places and homes. The police must be sensitized to treat each case of violence against women, women's rights violation, etc., in proper manner. The police and society at large should restrain from victim blaming in cases of sexual harassment of and domestic violence against women. Police infrastructure must be amended to include more women-friendly reporting mechanisms. Complete gender equality may not be achieved unless all stakeholders join hands to support the holistic welfare of women.

Chapter 6

Marital Rape in India

A Critical Socio-legal Analysis

Zeel Raval, Heli Shah and Debarati Halder

Introduction

The right to form a family is one of the prime rights which has been accorded to human beings through Article 16 of the Universal Declaration of Human Rights (UDHR), which acknowledges this right in a threefold manner: The first 'fold' speaks about the equal rights of men and women to enter into marriage and form a family. Article 16(i) therefore says as follows:

> (1) Men and women of full age, without any limitation due to race, nationality or religion, have the right to marry and to found a family. They are entitled to equal rights as to marriage, during marriage and at its dissolution.

The second fold speaks about free consent of the prospective spouses, and Article 16(ii) says:

> (2) Marriage shall be entered into only with the free and full consent of the intending spouses.

The third fold speaks about the importance of the family as an essential unit of society and the responsibility of society and the state to provide protection to the same. Article 16(3) therefore says:

(3) The family is the natural and fundamental group unit of society and is entitled to protection by society and the State.[1]

The said right to form a family by way of marriage has also found support in the International Covenant on Civil and Political Rights in Article 23,[2] which says as follows:

1. The family is the natural and fundamental group unit of society and is entitled to protection by society and the State.2. The right of men and women of marriageable age to marry and to found a family shall be recognized.3. No marriage shall be entered into without the free and full consent of the intending spouses. 4. States Parties to the present Covenant shall take appropriate steps to ensure equality of rights and responsibilities of spouses as to marriage, during marriage and at its dissolution. In the case of dissolution, provision shall be made for the necessary protection of any children.[3]

Both the above-mentioned documents suggest that it is an inherent right of individuals to form a family by way of marriage, which must be entered into with free will and consent. Article 23 of the International Covenant on Civil and Political Rights further emphasizes the duty of the state to protect the family, as it is an inherent part of society. It may be clearly seen here that while, on the one hand, the article signifies the role of society as a whole in providing protection and support to individuals who start a family by way of the institution of marriage, the duties of the state are also highlighted, especially in cases where a particular society may demand the members of a family to perform illegal, unethical and inhuman activities to gain its support. However, with the broadening understanding of the rights of heterosexual or homosexual couples to stay as civil law partners or live-in partners,[4] or enter into the institution of marriage to form a family, states, as well as societies, all over the world

---

[1] See Article 16 of the Universal Declaration of Human Rights

[2] See Article 23 of International Covenant on Civil and Political Rights https://www.ohchr.org/en/professionalinterest/pages/ccpr.aspx, accessed 12 December 2019.

[3] Ibid.

[4] Celia Kitzinger and Sue Wilkinson, 'The Re-Branding of Marriage: Why We Got Married Instead of Registering a Civil Partnership', *Feminism & Psychology* 14, no. 1 (1 February 2004): 127–50, https://doi.org/10.1177/0959353504040308, Accessed 12 March 2020.

have accepted the changing norms of formation of a family by two individuals who may or may not belong to the same sex and who may or may not have registered their marriage or performed the rituals of marriage as have been laid down in the customary laws. The institution of marriage, however, has been considered the most accepted institution to form a family. In the words of Roscoe Pound (1916), 'marriage is a public community status and institution that serves both public and private purposes'.[5] As this definition suggests, marriage has two specific kinds of purposes, the first being the 'public purposes', which may imply recognition of the family as a social unit by society at large and the state. Such public purposes may also indicate legal recognition of spouses and children born out of such marriages, eligibility of the families to get state-sponsored financial benefits, etc.[6] The second kind is 'private purposes' of marriage, which may necessarily indicate legalized sexual union between two spouses and reproduction.[7] It may also include succession rights of property and the right to reside in the property of the spouse, parents and children to a certain extent. As such, marital sex creates an essential element of marriage laws in customary laws: this is understood from various studies on family laws and marriage laws which signify that intentional non-consummation of marriage that may have been entered into by two consenting people from different sexes may be considered as grounds for mental cruelty and divorce.[8] However, feminist scholars have tried to bring out different connotations of attaching legal responsibilities to refusal to marital sex, especially by female spouses. Marital sex may change into marital rape when the male spouse dominates over the female spouse for sadistic sexual pleasure.[9] The concept of marital rape is comparatively new, compared to the traditional understanding of rape.

---

[5] Roscoe Pound, 'Individual Interests in the Domestic Relations', *Michigan Law Review* 14(1919): 177.

[6] Maggie Gallagher, 'What is Marriage For? The Public Purposes of Marriage Law', *Louisiana Law Review* 62 (2001): 773.

[7] Gallagher, 'What is Marriage For?'

[8] For example, see Vidhya Vishanathan v. Kartik Balakrishnan CIVIL APPEAL NO. 9036 OF 2014 (Arising out of S.L.P.(c) No.25056 of 2012), http://rajasthanjudicialacademy.nic.in/docs/juds/41950.pdf.

[9] For more understanding, see David Finkelhor and Kersti Yllo, 'Rape in Marriage: A Sociological View', *Crime and the Family* (1983): 121–33, http://citeseerx.ist.psu.

In patriarchal societies like India, providing marital sex to the male spouse especially for reproduction has been considered as a sacrosanct duty of the female spouse, as ancient texts have suggested that marriages are entered into especially for reproduction. However, it must not be ignored that in India, marriage is considered as a precondition for sexual intercourse in many societies. It is for this reason that several Indian rural and urban societies still practise child marriage, majorly to prevent adolescent children and matured teens, especially girls, from entering into a sexual relationship with men without being married. The apex court took a strong note on this issue in the case of *Independent Thought v. Union of India*[10] and criminalized sexual intercourse with a minor wife, adding more weight to the Protection of Children from Sexual Offences Act (POCSO Act), 2012[11] over Sections 375 and 376 of the Indian Penal Code (IPC) which discuss rape and punishment for the same.

However, unlike considering marital sex between two spouses (one of whom is a child) as a criminal activity as per the POCSO Act, Indian courts have not been able to make any clear decision regarding marital rape. This is mainly because marital rape is not recognized as a criminal offence in India. This could be seen in the case of *Nimeshbhai Bharatbhai Desai v. State of Gujarat*,[12] where the Gujarat High court observed that the concept of marital rape does not exist in India for adult married couples.[13] However, marital sex should not be considered

---

edu/viewdoc/download?doi=10.1.1.417.8576&rep=rep1&type=pdf#page=209, accessed 12 March 2020; Lynne Henderson, 'Rape and Responsibility', *Law and Philosophy* 11, nos. 1–2 (1992): 127–78, https://www.jstor.org/stable/pdf/3504906.pdf?casa_token=dSZ-iKZRyegAAAAA:NHigkS7Vj69si79b-LmgBYpzw1uSif_wPAXo95nMW7fUJ7AfUuKj4rErVmYRmzVpBZT1eimUm6VAFOl_tEd5VePHJJR2fWLBtWX_XLmzqfF-WhAo_QI, accessed 12 March 2020.

[10] Independent Thought v. Union of India, W.P. (c) No. 382 of 2013 http://supremecourtofindia.nic.in/supremecourt/2013/17790/17790_2013_Judgement_11-Oct-2017.pdf, accessed 21 March 2018.

[11] For more, see Protection of Children from Sexual Offences Act, 2012 Act Number: 32

[12] Nimeshbhai Bharatbhai Desai v. State of Gujarat, CR.MA/26957/2017 (4 April 2018) http://164.100.58.190:8080/GujaratCaseStatus/#

[13] *Live Law Network*, Marital Rape Is Not A Husband's Privilege But A Violent Act And An Injustice That Must Be Criminalized: Gujarat HC (8 April 2019),

as the 'husband's privilege' either.[14] Clearly, the rape laws in India codified under Sections 375 (which deals with definition of rape) and 376 (which deals with punishment for rape) do not recognize marital rape within a marriage but recognize sexual intercourse with the woman by her husband as rape only when such couple were legally separate under the decree of separation when the sexual intercourse took place. However, this does not mean that Indian laws do not recognize sexual abuse of wives within marriage: it is interesting to note that the Protection of Women from Domestic Violence Act, 2005 includes the concept of 'sexual abuse'[15] meted out by the male 'respondent'[16] to the female aggrieved person[17] within the meaning of domestic violence.[18] The explanation of the term 'sexual abuse' under Section 3(b)(ii) of this statute emphasizes violation of the dignity of the woman concerned. However, courts have never entertained any plea for recognizing and criminalizing marital rape even when complaints may have been filed under this provision, coupled with Section 498A

---

http://www.livelaw.in/marital-rape-not-husbands-privilege-violent-act-injustice-must-criminalized-gujarat-hc-read-judgment/.

[14] *Live Law Network*, Marital Rape Is Not A Husband's Privilege.

[15] The term 'sexual abuse' has been explained under Section 3(b)(ii) of the Protection of Women from Domestic Violence Act, 2005 as 'sexual abuse which includes any conduct of a sexual nature that abuses, humiliates, degrades or otherwise violates the dignity of woman'.

[16] According to Section 2(q) of the Protection of Women from Domestic Violence Act, 2005, the term 'respondent' means 'any adult male person who is, or has been, in a domestic relationship with the aggrieved person and against whom the aggrieved person has sought any relief under this Act: Provided that an aggrieved wife or female living in a relationship in the nature of a marriage may also file a complaint against a relative of the husband or the male partner'.

[17] According to Section 2(a) of the Protection of Women from Domestic Violence Act, 2005, the term 'aggrieved person' means any woman who is, or has been, in a domestic relationship with the respondent and who alleges to have been subjected to any act of domestic violence by the respondent.

[18] Section 3(a) defines the concept of domestic violence as follows: 'For the purposes of this Act, any act, omission or commission or conduct of the respondent shall constitute domestic violence in case it—(a) harms or injures or endangers the health, safety, life, limb or well-being, whether mental or physical, of the aggrieved person or tends to do so and includes causing physical abuse, sexual abuse, verbal and emotional abuse and economic abuse'.

of the IPC, which speaks about punishment for cruelty meted out to a woman by her husband or a relative of her husband. Rather, the Supreme Court has very recently stipulated guidelines to restrict misuse of Section 498A of the IPC and the Domestic Violence Act.[19] In the *Nimeshbhai Desai* case, the Gujarat High Court addressed the issue not from the perspective of rape laws (i.e., Sections 375 and 376 of the IPC) but from the perspective of Section 354 of the IPC, which speaks about punishment for assault or criminal force to a woman with the intent to outrage her modesty. This indicates that the Gujarat High Court did not want to go overboard with Sections 375 and 376 of the IPC but wanted to address the issue from the perspective of violation of the woman's modesty within her marriage. The question that needs to be researched is whether violating women's modesty, including sexual modesty, within marriage by their husbands could really be considered as marital rape in India.[20] The Gujarat High Court, in Nimesh Deshai's case, did not rely on rape laws, that is, Sections 375 and 376 of the IPC, because these provisions have built up the rape-law jurisprudence on the basis of consent of the victim. In marriage, it is understood that consent of the wife for sexual intercourse is implied and that the wife is duty-bound to satisfy the sexual desire of the husband. This understanding flows from the implied-consent theory within marriage established by Sir Mathew Hale, Chief Justice in England, who stated that 'The husband cannot be guilty of a rape committed by himself upon his lawful wife, for by their mutual matrimonial consent and contract; the wife hath given herself in kind unto the husband, whom she cannot retract'.[21] This understanding has prevailed in many countries that had been British colonies and which had a common

[19] See Rajesh Sharma & Others v. State of UP & another, CRIMINAL APPEAL NO. 1265 OF 2017, Supreme Court of India, https://indiankanoon.org/doc/182220573/, accessed 12 December 2019.

[20] See discussion above regarding considering denial of sex for a long time by wife as grounds for divorce. Also see Vidhya Vishanathan v. Kartik Balakrishnan, CIVIL APPEAL NO. 9036 OF 2014 (Arising out of S.L.P. (c) No.25056 of 2012), http://rajasthanjudicialacademy.nic.in/docs/juds/41950.pdf.

[21] See Maria Pracher, 'The Marital Rape Exemption: A Violation of a Woman's Right of Privacy', *Golden Gate University Law Review* 11 (1981), http://digitalcommons.law.ggu.edu/ggulrev/vol11/iss3/, accessed 21 March 2018.

genre of colonial legal history. Marital rape by the husband essentially violates the marital privacy of a woman.[22] However, it must be noted that many countries have recognized marital rape as an offensive and penal behaviour against the female spouse. Indian legal understandings have not yet recognized martial rape between two adults as an offence, because this may directly impact the customary laws that still have not considered the rights of women against sexual abuse and sexual privacy within marriage. These authors argue that Indian laws have not matured in this regard.

As may be seen in the above paragraph, this chapter discusses marital rape in India from socio-legal perspectives. The second part of this chapter discusses the exemptions of Sections 375 and 376 of the IPC and their impact on the Indian society. The third part discusses marital privacy and how it may affect the criminalization of marital rape. The fourth part offers suggestions and conclusions.

MARITAL RAPE AS AN EXCEPTION TO INDIA'S RAPE LAWS

According to the traditional definitions, rape is understood as 'unlawful carnal knowledge of a woman by force against her will'.[23] Lyon (2004) has explained that the above definition of law indicates three elements of rape, that is, intercourse, force and lack of consent.[24] The above definition and its explanation have been the underlying principle for rape laws for many jurisdictions.[25] In almost all statutory provisions that criminalize sexual assault amounting to rape or rape in general,

---

[22] Robin L. West, 'Equality Theory, Marital Rape, and the Promise of the Fourteenth Amendment (19 May 2011)', *Florida Law Review* 42 (1990); Georgetown Public Law Research Paper No. 11-65. (12 February 2018), https://ssrn.com/abstract=1846819.

[23] See Catharine A. Mackinnon, *Sex Equality: Rape Law* 801 (2001) (quoting William Blackstone, commentaries on the laws of England) 210 (1765); 'e Definition of Rape', *Journal of Criminal Law & Criminology* 95 (2004–2005): 277.

[24] Matthew R. Lyon, 'No Means No: Withdrawal of Consent During Intercourse and the Continuing Evolution of the Definition of Rape', *Journal of Criminal Law & Criminology* 95 (2004–2005): 277.

[25] For more, see Constance Backhouse and Lorna Schoenroth, 'A Comparative Study of Canadian and American Rape Law (1984)', *Canada-US Law Journal* 7 (1984): 173–213, https://ssrn.com/abstract=2263413, accessed 11 January 2018.

married men are immune to any criminal liability in regard to raping their wife.[26] The common legal understanding states that men cannot rape their legally wedded wives, and women cannot be 'raped' by their husbands. The issue of consent for sexual intercourse by women has been immaterial in such cases.[27] In India, the term 'rape' is defined under Section 375 of the IPC through the following provisions:

1. When the man has penal–vaginal or penal–oral or penal–urethral or penal–anal penetration with a woman to any extent or makes her do so;
2. When he inserts any other object or part of the body (except the penis) into the vagina, mouth, urethra or anus of a woman or makes her do the same with him or with anyone else;
3. When he manipulates any part of the body of a woman to cause penetration;
4. When he applies his mouth to the vagina, mouth, urethra or anus of a woman or makes her do so;
5. When such acts are done against her will, without her consent, with her consent, when the consent has been obtained under threat or fraudulently, etc.[28]

As may be seen, the definition of rape in Section 375 also emphasizes sexual intercourse, force and lack of consent. Further, Section 375 excludes sexual intercourse done within certain relationships from the concept of 'rape'. These include medical procedures or interventions and sexual intercourse or sexual acts by a man with his own wife who is above 15 years of age.

As mentioned above, the second part of the second exception, that is, exception clause (b), was read down by the court in the case of *Independent Thought v. Union of India*,[29] whereby the court held that

---

[26] Backhouse and Schoenroth, 'A Comparative Study of Canadian and American Rape Law'.

[27] Matthew, *No Means No*.

[28] See Section 375 IPC.

[29] Independent Thought v. Union of India, W.P. (c) No. 382 of 2013, Supreme Court of India.

sexual intercourse with a married wife who is under 18 years of age would always be considered as 'rape'.

While this is the present understanding from the perspective of the IPC, we may need to understand the sociology of Indian marriages to understand why sexual intercourse in the nature of rape has never been recognized as an offence within the institution of marriage. The laws of marriages in India are guided by personal laws that emanate from ancient religious texts. The foreign invaders who went on to rule India for several decades and centuries may have influenced the penal or revenue laws of the land but did not disturb the personal laws governing marriage or inheritance to a great extent.[30] As a result, the laws of marriage from the ancient religious texts continued to govern the 'duties' of spouses even in the modern period through modern legal provisions. Consider the Hindu Marriage Act, 1955, for instance: these 'duties' are not explicitly mentioned in the provisions of the Hindu Marriage Act, but the grounds for divorce or grounds for cruelty, which were later built up on the basis of modern judicial understanding, may show the concept of 'duties'. For instance, consider the grounds for divorce under Section 13 of the Hindu Marriage Act, 1955,[31] which implies the duties of spouses to each other. Some of these duties are as follows:

1. To not enter into an adulterous relationship with a third party or commit sexual assault, including rape, on a third party;
2. To not desert the spouse;
3. To abstain from cruelty, including physical and mental torture, to the spouse;
4. To not hide mental disorder, leprosy, venereal disease from the spouse;
5. To not marry again during the existence of lawful marriage with the wedded spouse; and
6. To cohabit with the lawfully wedded spouse.[32]

---

[30] D. Halder and K. Jaishankar, 'Property Rights of Hindu Women: A Critical Review of Succession Laws of Ancient, Medieval, and Modern India', *Journal of Law and Religion* XXIV, no. 25th Anniversary issue (2008), 101–22.

[31] See for Grounds of Divorce in S.13 of the Hindu Marriage Act, 1955, https://indiankanoon.org/doc/932494/, accessed 12 December 2019.

[32] Ibid.

These implied duties were also considered by courts on several occasions; the Supreme Court of India, in the case of *Vidhya Viswanathan v. Karthik Balakrishnan* (2014), gave the broadest understanding about the consequences of denial of sexual intercourse by a wife for a long time without any proper reason, and it observed that such denial would amount to mental cruelty to the other spouse.[33] From this perspective, it may seem that the Indian socio-legal understanding makes it compulsory for spouses to consummate their marriage and cohabit for the continuation of the marriage. The above-mentioned case stands as a significant case that, in a way, passively supports marital rape of the wife by the husband. Now, we need to understand why the Indian judiciary has *not* considered cohabitation including sexual intercourse by husband with wife *without consent* as an offensive behaviour that may be criminalized. *Marital rape* itself is considered to be a concept originating from feminist ideologies. This is inherently related to sexual violence of women.[34] Feminist scholars have emphasized that marital rape could not be criminalized in many jurisdictions because in a marriage the consent of the wife for sexual intercourse is almost always thought to be implied.[35] This again relates to male dominance over women's body and mind. Several religious scriptures from which the modern family laws originate also show that a devoted wife should never be deserted: if, however, she is deserted because of adultery committed by her husband or because of a decision by the husband of renouncement from worldly affairs, etc., she should not only be compensated but also be protected through provision of residential rights over property. Several feminist researchers have opined that courts all over the world have on several occasions perceived women and girls as mothers of children

---

[33] Vidya Vishwanathan v. Karthik Balakrishnan, CIVIL APPEAL NO. 9036 OF 2014, Supreme Court of India; Samar Ghosh v. Jaya Ghosh (2007) 4 SCC 511.

[34] M. Goodwin, 'Marital Rape: The Long Arch of Sexual Violence Against Women and Girls', *American Journal of International Law Unbound* 109 (2015): 326–31, https://www.cambridge.org/core/journals/american-journal-of-international-law/article/div-classtitlemarital-rape-the-long-arch-of-sexual-violence-against-women-and-girlsdiv/29C78B4A3971F611B66AE838AC511EBE, accessed 12 March 2018.

[35] Catharine A. MacKinnon, 'Feminism, Marxism, Method, and the State: Toward Feminist Jurisprudence', *Chicago Journals* 8, no. 4 (Summer, 1983): 635–58.

conceived either by legitimate sexual intercourse that is legitimized by way of marriage or by rape.[36] Several courts, including courts in India, have not permitted abortion of the foetus even when the mother was physically and emotionally not ready to give birth.[37] However, this approach of the Indian courts goes directly against the international understanding about women's right to privacy even in marriage; for example, consider Article 2 of the Declaration on the Elimination of Violence against Women, which includes marital rape explicitly in the definition of violence against women by stating:

> Violence against women shall be understood to encompass, but not be limited to, the following: (a) Physical, sexual and psychological violence occurring in the family, including battering, sexual abuse of female children in the household, dowry-related violence, marital rape, female genital mutilation and other traditional practices harmful to women, non-spousal violence and violence related to exploitation.[38]

Several countries, including France, Sweden, Denmark, Norway, Poland, Canada and the United States (certain provinces), have considered penalizing marital sex on the basis of the above-mentioned declaration.

MARITAL PRIVACY AND IMPACT OF THE SAME ON THE CONCEPT OF CRIMINALIZING MARITAL RAPE

While marital rape is not considered as a criminal offence in India, the observation of the Gujarat High Court in the case of *Nimeshbhai Bharatbhai Desai v. State of Gujarat*[39] suggests that marital rape may be considered as an injustice, should not be considered as a privilege of the

---

[36] MacKinnon, 'Feminism, Marxism, Method, and the State'.

[37] For example, see *Live Law News Network*, SC Rejects Plea of 10 Yr Old Rape Victim's Plea to Abort, Orders Panels in States to Examine Such Cases (2017), http://www.livelaw.in/sc-rejects-plea-10-yr-old-rape-victims-plea-abort-orders-panels-states-examine-cases/, accessed 12 February 2018.

[38] Declaration on the Elimination of Violence Against Women (1 February 2018), http://www.un.org/documents/ga/res/48/a48r104.htm.

[39] Nimeshbhai Bharatbhai Desai v. State of Gujarat, CR.MA/26957/2017 (2 April 2018), http://164.100.58.190:8080/GujaratCaseStatus/#.

husband and should be statutorily abolished. The case involved marital dispute and sexual violence against the wife by the husband, both of whom were doctors. The court in this case observed that there may be three types of rape in marriage. It went on to explain the three types in the following language:

> Battering rape: In this type of marital rape, women experience both physical and sexual violence in the relationship and in many ways. Some instances are those where the wife is battered during the sexual violence, or the rape may follow a physical violent episode where the husband wants to make up and coerces his wife to have sex against her will. In most cases, the victims fall under this stated category.
>
> Force only rape: In this type of marital rape, husbands use only that amount of force, as it is necessary to coerce their wives. In such cases, battering may not be a characteristic and women who refuse sexual intercourse usually face such assaults.
>
> Obsessive rape: In obsessive rape, assaults involve brutal torture and/or perverse sexual acts and are most commonly violent in form.[40]

It may be seen that Nimeshbhai's case involved not only physical and mental torture within the meaning of Section 498A of the IPC (which prescribes punishment for cruelty to wife) but also pervasive sexual acts in public and in private. The court observed that the husband's offensive sexual acts included forcing the wife to perform such sexual activities in public which were not expected to be done in public and which may violate the concept of public decency. However, the court also observed that certain sexual activities done between married spouses in public, such as hugging, kissing, holding hands affectionately, etc., may not be considered as indecent activities in the context of the present age. However, at the same time, the court further opined that certain sexual activities that may harm the modesty of a woman in public, even when the concerned woman is the wife, cannot be permitted to be treated as regular, normal behaviour between a husband and wife. The court in this case emphasized the right to privacy of the wife over her own body. Keeping aside the question of whether

---

[40] Ibid.

marital rape can be criminalized, breaking the settled understanding in the earlier cases, the court observed that the case must be seen from the perspective of what the woman can prevent legally by virtue of Section 354 of the IPC, which speaks about assault on or criminal force upon a woman with the intent to outrage her modesty. Incidentally, feminist studies have indicated that marital rape also includes forceful infringement of the privacy of a woman by her husband. However, the court in Nimeshbhai's case carefully avoided mixing both the concepts within the meaning of an offensive marital sexual relationship in private. The court hence emphasized that the woman had been subjected to assault and criminal force that had been used with an intention to harm her modesty. Again, the court maintained that in this case, the protection of Section 354 of the IPC expanded to the wife against the sexual activities of the husband, because such activities were not done in private and nor did the wife provide consent for such activities that were executed in public. Thus, the court observed that marriage with a woman does not give a man the right to perform sexual activities against her wish anywhere and at any time and in a place that is not private. Clearly, the court indicated that exemption of marital rape from the statutory understanding of rape does not give a husband the privilege to sexually assault, torture and infringe the bodily privacy of his wife in places where such acts are prohibited by the moral standards of society.

While the court did not explicitly cover the present case within the meaning of marital rape only, it did however mention the necessity to amend Sections 375 and 376 of the IPC to include marital rape as a criminal activity. However, it was also pointed out by the court that if marital rape was criminalized, it might also open the floodgates to allegations of torture of women by male spouses, and it would further increase the misuse of the Protection of Women from Domestic Violence Act, 2005.[41] The analysis of *Nimeshbhai's* case therefore shows that while courts do recognize the need to criminalize marital rape in India, they are also concerned about the possible misuse of the criminalization. However, the concern of the Law Commission of India

[41] Ibid.

regarding criminalizing marital rape was also noticed by the Gujarat High Court in this very case.[42]

It is unfortunate to note that in spite of the efforts of the Gujarat High Court and the concern of the Law Commission of India, marital rape remains unrecognized as a crime in India. The effects of marital rape can be extremely traumatic on the victims: they may suffer from anxiety, shock, intense fear, depression, suicidal ideation and post-traumatic stress. Victimized wives may also suffer from eating and sleeping disorders, depression, sexual dysfunction, etc. Further, such abusive sexual relationship between a couple may also impact the upbringing of their children.

CONCLUSION AND SUGGESTIONS

As can be seen from the discussions, marital rape in India has not yet received legal recognition as a criminal offence when this manuscript was being prepared by the authors. The law is constantly evolving: the Law Commission of India has recognized the need for criminalizing rape within a relationship, including marital rape, and the Justice Verma Committee had also suggested that criminal law should be amended to include marital rape within the ambit of Section 376 of the IPC.[43] In this very light, the authors suggest that while the law

---

[42] For example, the court had quoted the 172nd Report of the Law Commission of India, which made the following recommendations for a substantial change in the law regarding marital rape: explanation (2) of Section 375 of IPC should be deleted; forced sexual intercourse by a husband with his wife should be treated equally as an offence, just as any physical violence by a husband against the wife is treated as an offence; and on the same reasoning, Section 376A should be deleted. In the light of *Sakshi v. Union of India and Others*, 'sexual assault on any part of the body should be construed as rape'.

[43] Justice Verma Committee, in their report for the Criminal Law (Amendment) Bill, 2013, suggested the following recommendations in regard to marital rape:

1. The exception for marital rape be removed.
2. The law ought to specify that: (a) marital or other relationship between the perpetrator or victim is not a valid defence against the crimes of rape or sexual violation. (b) The relationship between the accused and the complainant is not relevant to the inquiry into whether the complainant consented to the sexual activity; (c.) The fact that the accused and victim are married or in another intimate relationship may not be regarded as a mitigating factor justifying lower sentences for rape

should also consider the evolving nature of gender roles and afford men sufficient protection, the concept of marital rape should no more be left to be a 'privilege of husbands'. Several female victims of marital rape may find it extremely difficult to establish that rape occurred and that the same was non-consensual, especially when they had been in some kind of relationship with their 'rapist'. In marriage, it may be even harder to prove the same because of the Indian socio-legal understanding about a wife's duty towards her husband. The main reason for this is the concept of privacy believed to have existed for centuries between spouses in Indian marriages. The right to privacy is an exclusive right when it comes to individual human rights. At the same time, a family unit may also have privacy. However, this should in no way give way to an abusive relationship between a husband and wife. Thus, the law should be amended to criminalize marital rape, taking into consideration this understanding of spousal privacy and free consent of the wife. Simultaneously, the law should also legislate stiffer penalties for false allegations. Further, these authors strongly suggest that both men and women should be made aware of spousal rights and duties within marriage. It is interesting to note that the courts are slowly expanding the understanding of liabilities of partners and spouses in live-in relationships, as well as in marriages, through various social interest litigations and private interest litigations.[44] This trend is encouraging, as this is also breaking the glass ceiling of the socio-legal understanding of spousal relationships and male dominance in the same for socio-legal aspects, including decision-making in property issues, child upbringing and even allowing of women to report crimes to the police. It is the right time therefore for the judiciary and the legislature to consider marital rape as a criminal behaviour.

[44] *Live Law News Network*, Supreme Court Upholds Right of Live-in Partner to Claim Maintenance (6 May 2015), http://www.livelaw.in/supreme-court-upholds-right-of-live-in-partner-to-claim-maintenance/, accessed 1 February 2018.

Chapter 7

Human Rights of Sex Workers and Their Children

A Critical Analysis

Vihasi Shah

INTRODUCTION

Prostitution has been considered the most ancient profession that has necessarily pushed women towards more oppression. Studies on prostitution may show that women involved in it may be socially ostracized. Children of such women may also face discrimination, and their necessary rights, including essential child rights, may also be violated. With the coming into effect of the Convention on the Elimination of All Forms of Discrimination Against Women (CEDAW) in 1979 and the Convention on the Rights of the Child (CRC) in 1989, the basic rights of women and children, irrespective of their profession, race, country, creed, etc., were highlighted. However, these United Nations (UN) documents and mandates have not been able to make the situation better till date, especially for female sex workers and their children. The rights of such women and children in the Indian context still need to be uplifted. Prostitution being an ancient mechanism to oppress women, one must look into the ancient scripts that had a significant impact on Indian sociocultural ethics and policies that classified sex workers and prostitutes as 'dangerous' for the society, social norms and morals.[1] The Western documents on human rights in the mediaeval periods, including Magna Carta[2] and the French Declaration of the Rights of Man and the Citizen, 1789, [3] fail to mention any specific rights for female sex workers. Both the documents put women in the category of second-rate citizens and human beings. This impacted the post-Second World War 'rights explosions', and the Universal Declaration of Human Rights, 1948, recognized every person's right to life, liberty and security.[4] Later, these declarations were given a legal status through the international covenants on civil and political rights and social, economic and cultural rights in 1966, which emphasized the right to choose a profession, the right to protection against discrimination on the basis of gender, race, nationality, etc. Thus, these documents further highlighted several rights, including equality rights, child rights and the right to protection against oppression and discrimination. The rights of sex workers, however, did not get any focused attention. Much later, the CEDAW in 1979 and the CRC in 1989 laid down protocols to create new policies to prevent abuse of women, irrespective of their origin, profession, language, etc., and ensure holistic development of children, including preventive mechanisms against women and child trafficking.

Presently, almost all countries have ratified the above-mentioned conventions except a few. Such near-universal acceptance of responsibilities to protect the rights of human beings irrespective of gender, age, etc., has not only led to more 'human rights explosions', but it has also empowered women in various ways. The concept of women empowerment has been widened through expanding the scope

---

[1] For more, see Priya Darshini, 'Status of the Ganikas in the Gupta Period: Change or Continuity?' *Proceedings of the Indian History Congress* 64 (2003): 167–72, www.jstor.org/stable/44145457, accessed 13 December 2019.

[2] For better understanding, see Harris Carolyn, 'Magnacarta and Women's Rights', https://www.queensu.ca/gazette/alumnireview/stories/magna-carta-and-womens-rights, accessed 12 December 2019.

[3] For better understanding, see Sonali Gupta, 'Liberty for All? An Exploration of the Status of Women in Revolutionary France', http://www.indiana.edu/~psource/PDF/Current%20Articles/Fall2014/3%20Gupta%20Fall%2014.pdf, accessed 12 December 2019.

[4] In India, the Indian constitution enshrines Human rights through different constitutional provisions including Articles 12, 14, 15, 19, 21, 32, etc.

of women's right to choose a profession, right to seek protection at the workplace, right to equal wages for equal work, etc. This widening of the concept has also influenced child rights and childcare policies of working women. Several countries, including India, adopted welfare schemes for maternity healthcare, child healthcare, care of children of working women, etc. However, this chapter argues that in reality, female sex workers and their children remain in the dark in this regard. In a country like India, female sex workers have been considered as persons of loose moral and a pool of diseases.[5] Since ancient times, female sex workers have been socially ostracized. This has also impacted the rights of the children of sex workers. It may be noted that the modern Indian legal set-up has ensured certain rights of women in this regard: while, on the one hand, Articles 15 and 17 of the Indian Constitution establish the right to protection against discrimination and special status for women and children, Article 23 of the constitution, on the other, prohibits trafficking and forced labour, which are key elements of sex work. Based on these rights, including the fundamental rights enshrined in the Indian Constitution, the Immoral Trafficking (Prevention) Act (ITPA), was enacted in 1986 by the Indian Parliament. These laws not only punish trafficking but also lay down policies for rehabilitation of trafficked victims. However, in reality, the scenario is different for sex workers and their children. This chapter looks into the questions of what sort of rights violations happen to sex workers and their children, why implementation of laws has not been satisfactory in this regard in India and what could be the solution for the same. This chapter is divided into four parts, including the introduction. The second part discusses social and legal perspectives of female sex workers in the Indian society. The third part discusses the socio-legal position of children of sex workers in India, and the fourth part offers the conclusion.

SOCIO-LEGAL PERSPECTIVE OF FEMALE SEX WORKERS IN INDIA

As discussed in the above paragraph, female sex workers have been considered as ostracized from and *acchut* (untouchable) in mainstream

[5] See John O' Neila, et al., 'Dhandha, Dharma and Disease: Traditional Sex Work and HIV/AIDS in Rural India', *Social Science & Medicine* 59 (2004): 851–60.

society because of the nature of their profession.[6] In India, since ancient times, female sex workers have been considered as individuals with low morals who may affect the social hygiene and moral standards of society because they earn money through unethical ways, that is, by way of sexually entertaining 'customers' irrespective of the latter's marital status or age, which may have a devastating effect on mainstream societal understanding of family, marriage and legal reproduction. The ancient scripts including the Manusmriti and Dharma Shastra emphasize that women who earned by way of prostitution may be severely punished by the king: they were also restricted from participating in social functions, and food served by them was considered prohibited for mainstream society members. The ancient scripts also emphasize that children born out of and/or raised by such women may also be dealt with in a similar manner and they may not be considered fit to claim any social benefits and rights, including accessing knowledge and livelihood in mainstream society.[7] However, the feminist perspectives argue that every woman engaged in sex work is forced and coerced to do such work for maintenance of herself and for her dependents.[8] Thus, no woman can choose to do 'sex work' according to her free will. The literature on feminism and sex trade may show that women were pushed into sex trade due to war, recession, famine, etc., when the menfolk could not provide money for daily survival and food for them and their children. Such women may not be educated enough to support themselves in a decent way. Even if they were, the patriarchal set-up at the job market may not have allowed them to make an earning in a decent way.[9]

---

[6] See Priya Darshini, 'Status of the Ganikas in the Gupta Period'.

[7] ibid.

[8] Scouler Jane, 'The "Subject" of Prostitution Interpreting the Discursive, Symbolic and Material Position of Sex/work in Feminist Theory', *Feminist Theory* 2004 (12 February 2018), https://s3.amazonaws.com/academia.edu.documents/5511794/the_subject_of_prostitution_in_feminist_theory_scoular_fem_theor_5_3__2004_343.pdf?AWSAccessKeyId=AKIAIWOWYYGZ2Y53UL3A&Expires=1522146077&Signature=tunT2XwpwJ8aXyxD%2F4f08Ita4Ok%3D&response-content-disposition=inline%3B%20filename%3DThe_Subject_of_Prostitution.pdf, accessed 13 December 2019.

[9] Lacey Sloan and Stephanie Wahab, 'Feminist Voices on Sex Work: Implications for Social Work', *Affilia* 15 (2000): 457, https://www.researchgate.net/profile/Lacey_Sloan/publication/314100334_Feminist_Voices_on_Sex_Work_

In the modern sociocultural set-up, female sex workers are not only victimized by way of violation of basic rights, but they may also be trafficked. Given this understanding, there may be three basic patterns of victimization of female sex workers, which are as follows:

1. Victimization of women and girls by way of commercial prostitution that may involve sex trafficking: Commercial prostitution falls in the grey area of prohibitive laws in many jurisdictions. While several countries have provided several legal rights to sex workers, including prostitutes, the Indian scenario is different in this regard.[10] Commercial prostitution may involve sex trafficking,[11] and India is no exception in this regard. In commercial prostitution, sex workers may entertain their 'clients' or 'customers' for a particular amount of money either in their own apartments or in the brothels where such sex workers may be accommodated by older, retired sex workers who may run a flourishing business of commercial prostitution. Such commercial sex workers may have agents or pimps to get more customers.[12] In general, this may be part of a vicious racket of sex trafficking which may target not only adults but also children for the 'sex

Implications_for_Social_Work/links/5deb364a4585159aa468a043/Feminist-Voices-on-Sex-Work-Implications-for-Social-Work.pdf, accessed 13 December 2019.

[10] Magaly Rodríguez García, 'Ideas and Practices of Prostitution Around the World', in *The Oxford Handbook of the History of Crime and Criminal Justice*, eds. Paul Knepper and Anja Johansen, 132–53, https://s3.amazonaws.com/academia.edu.documents/57223411/Rodriguez_Prostitution_OxfordHB.pdf?response-content-disposition=inline%3B%20filename%3DIdeas_and_practices_of_prostitution_arou.pdf&X-Amz-Algorithm=AWS4-HMAC-SHA256&X-Amz-Credential=AKIAIWOWYYGZ2Y53UL3A%2F20200316%2Fus-east-1%2Fs3%2Faws4_request&X-Amz-Date=20200316T071106Z&X-Amz-Expires=3600&X-Amz-SignedHeaders=host&X-Amz-Signature=2fb819ea0c18b4c95b3c941463067255bf3e79381a9b1d402c37729499c4aa47, accessed 13 December 2019.

[11] Ronald Weitzer, 'Sex Trafficking and the Sex Industry: The Need for Evidence-Based Theory and Legislation', *Journal of Criminal Law & Criminology* 101 (2013): 1337.

[12] Sharon Cowan, *To Buy or Not to Buy? Vulnerability and the Criminalization of Commercial BDSM* (25 October 2013). Edinburgh School of Law Research Paper No. 2013/37, https://ssrn.com/abstract=2345245 or http://dx.doi.org/10.2139/ssrn.2345245.

market'. Commercial prostitution may necessarily involve both penetrative and non-penetrative sexual contact for money. Sex workers falling in this category may reside in a particular brothel for life and may even beget children from different customers who may or may not be brought back to prostitution as a way of survival.[13]

2. Victimization of female bar dancers as sex workers: The presence of female bar dancers in bars and restaurants selling hard liquor is not an unusual phenomenon. Traditionally, these women are used to allure customers, whereby such women may be used as a 'sexual spectacle' to entice customers to buy and consume more products from the bars.[14] They may be considered as indirect primary sex workers (IPSWs)[15] who may not necessarily be similar to brothel-bred prostitutes. Such IPSWs may have wider options for earning money, that is, by way of dancing in bars, as well as by providing sex to the customers of the bars or other customers as well.[16] However, this may not mean that they are never trafficked. Further, they may or may not join regular prostitution in later life. However, they may also be socially blamed and ostracized because of their association with the dance-bar and sex industry. The recent case of the ban on dance bars in Mumbai, India, may be a glaring example: the Maharashtra government imposed a ban on dance bars because it was contended that the women may do obscene performances to attract customers and also sexually solicit them. The Supreme Court, while upholding laws and guidelines for cancelling the licenses of several dance bars, maintained that

---

[13] Prabha Kotiswaran, *Born Unto Brothels—Towards a Legal Ethnography of Sonagachi's Sex Industry* (18 May 2011), https://ssrn.com/abstract=1845663 or http://dx.doi.org/10.2139/ssrn.1845663.

[14] For more, see Sonal Makhija, 'Bar Dancers', *Morality and the Indian Law Economic and Political Weekly* 45, no. 39 (25 September to 1 October 2010): 19–23, https://www.jstor.org/stable/25742114, accessed 13 December 2019.

[15] Abhay Nirgude, et al., 'Study of Sexual Behaviour of Bar-girls Residing in an Urban Slum Area of Mumbai', *Indian Journal of Community Medicine* 36, no. 1(January–March 2011): 31–35, https://www.ncbi.nlm.nih.gov/pmc/articles/PMC3104705/, accessed 21 March 2018.

[16] Nirgude et al., 'Study of Sexual Behaviour'.

making the dance-bar women jobless would bring more distress to them.[17] However, in spite of the clarification of the Supreme Court, the dance-bar women have been considered as sex workers.

3. Online prostitution and victimization of women: Online prostitution is a thriving stream of the sex market where actors (who may or may not be sex workers in real life) offer non-physical sexual gratification to clients of porn content. In the course of online prostitution, the 'seller' may also provide information about her contact details, may get paid for each session of 'sex chat' or showing of sexual activities through an audiovisual mechanism and may also entertain customers for a fee at a physical place that may have been decided upon over an online chat.[18] Online prostitution may also involve online sex trafficking of adults and children.

It may be noted that the female sex workers falling in the three categories above may be victimized by social ostracism. Presently, in India, the issues of keeping a brothel, procuring persons for prostitution, trafficking persons, including children, and living on the earnings gained from prostitution are regulated by the ITPA, 1956, which was amended in 1986. Interestingly, the ITPA does not penalize acts of prostitution but penalizes the act of keeping a brothel or allowing the use of one's premises as a brothel under Section 3. Similarly, Section 4 of the ITPA penalizes any person above the age of 18 years living on the earnings of prostitution. This indirectly means that prostitutes or sex workers may not be punished for acts of prostitution and nor may they or their children under the age of 18 years be prosecuted if they are not involved in maintaining a brothel, sex trafficking or procuring or inducing others for prostitution or carrying out prostitution in the

---

[17] For more, see Indian Hotel and Restaurant Association (ahar) & Anr. v. The State of Maharashtra & Ors. Writ Petition (civil) no. 576 of 2016 in the Supreme Court of India Civil Original Jurisdiction, https://www.jurist.org/news/wp-content/uploads/sites/4/2019/01/2019-Dance-Bar-judgment-.pdf, accessed 12 December 2019.

[18] Michael Pittaro, 'Pornography and Global Sex Trafficking: A Proposal for Therapeutic Jurisprudence as Court Innovation in the United States', in *Therapeutic Jurisprudence and Overcoming Violence against Women*, eds. D. Halder and K. Jaishankar (Hershey: IGI Global, 2017), 121–35.

vicinity of public places, etc., as has been specified under Section 7. However, while the ITPA mentions about the rescue of persons who may have been engaged in prostitution from a brothel or a place of prostitution under Section 16, social acceptance of such rescued women or female children is very less.[19] In the process of rescue operations of sex workers, these women and girls may be socially shamed, beaten and put through further traumas. They may also lack basic rehabilitation facilities because of social ostracism and may also be tangled up in the legal understanding about criminalization of prostitution.

Apart from physical violence, social oppression and legal confusion may also cripple the life of sex workers. For instance, consider the financial condition of the majority of sex workers in India: sex workers, especially those who may have been trafficked into this profession or who may have been forcefully made to engage with this profession at a much younger age, and who may not have received basic education due to poverty, may never retain their earnings with them. Most of their earnings may be seized by their 'managers' or brothel owners, and what is left is an amount that is not even sufficient for one meal a day. In some areas of Sonagachi, the red-light district of Kolkata, it has been observed that sex workers were made to give their entire income to brothel owners, a situation similar to slavery.[20] Further, research shows that people involved in sex work are also at a much higher risk of sexually transmitted infections, including human immunodeficiency virus/acquired immunodeficiency syndrome (HIV/AIDS) not because of their unprotected sexual contact with customers but because they may lack proper medical facilities due to their profession and social status.[21] Such discriminatory practices are noticed by several researchers; for

[19] G. Gangoli, *Silence, Hurt and Choice: Attitudes to Prostitution in India and the West* (21 March 2018), http://www.lse.ac.uk/asiaresearchcentre/_files/arcwp06-gangoli.pdf.

[20] Christine Joffres, et al., 'Sexual Slavery Without Borders: Trafficking for Commercial Sexual Exploitation in India', *International Journal for Equity in Health* 7 (2008): 22.

[21] S. Gruskin and D. Tarantola, 'HIV/AIDS, Health and Human Rights', in *HIV/AIDS Prevention and Care Programs in Resource-Constrained Settings: A Handbook for the Design and Management of Programs*, eds. P. Lamptey, H. Gayle, and P. Mane (Arlington: Family Health International, 2001), 661–78.

instance, in a hospital, an HIV test is prescribed for a general person only if he/she is suffering from tuberculosis, a sexually transmitted disease or diarrhoea, but in the case of a sex worker, HIV tests are mandatory even if they want to get themselves treated for a common cold. Such happenings not only are entirely discriminatory in nature, but they also result in the further stigmatization and marginalization of sex workers.[22] Again, researchers have also noted that in some metro cities like Kolkata, it is part of the process for health workers and medical practitioners to take a blood sample of every woman visiting a hospital for treatment, if she happens to be a sex worker. There is no justification provided for the nature and purpose of such a test. This amounts to a clear violation of sex workers' right to information and right to privacy.[23]

The author further argues that the situation may be extremely difficult for adult female and mature teenage sex workers who may have begotten children due to unprotected sexual contact. Prostitution involving matured teenagers and young adults may necessarily involve rape and penetrative sexual assault. These women and girls may hardly be aware of sexual hygiene and pregnancy-related information because of lack of education and poverty. As a result, they may not be expected to be aware of the legal period for termination of a pregnancy either. In the majority of cases, sex workers may also be forced to give birth to children in unhygienic conditions due to lack of access to government healthcare mechanisms.[24] Sex workers thus become 'unwed' mothers unintentionally or intentionally and may further undergo several rights violations, including violations of their right to start a proper family, right to work with dignity and right to equality and equal protection of

---

[22] S. Bharat, *HIV/AIDS Related Discrimination, Stigmatization and Denial in India* (Mumbai: Tata Institute of Social Sciences, 1999), 89.

[23] Stephen Bindman, 'Prostitute Murders Hard to Solve, and No One Cares'. Ottawa Citizen [Canada], 29 July 1996.

[24] Hena John-Fisk, 'Uncovering the Realities of Prostitutes and their Children in a Cross National Comparative Study Between India and The U.S.' (Diss. submitted to the faculty of The University of Utah in partial fulfilment of the requirements for the degree of Doctor of Philosophy College of Social Work The University of Utah, August 2013) (21 March 2018), https://www.mensenhandelweb.nl/system/files/documents/17%20dec%202014/2543.pdf.

laws. Motherhood may in several ways hamper their profession of sex work. Single motherhood may also be a bar for getting a decent job or even financial and social assistance to start small-scale entrepreneurship, because the new customers or banks or society at large may not be willing to do business or support an erstwhile prostitute.[25] As a result, many female sex workers who may have begotten unwanted children may have to abandon their children in hazardous conditions immediately after birth[26] or may also be motivated to kill the newborn child.

RIGHTS VIOLATION OF THE CHILDREN OF SEX WORKERS

While sex workers may be victimized due to several reasons and by several means, as mentioned earlier, children of sex workers may face multiple rights violations since even before their birth. Such sorts of violations are discussed further.

BASIC RIGHT TO NUTRITION AND MEDICAL CARE

As mentioned earlier, sex workers may not always be aware about pregnancy hygiene–related health information; as a result, expecting mothers may severely lack in prenatal nutrition and rest. Babies born in such a situation may not get basic medical help.[27] Further, the babies may not get basic neonatal care either, in case the mother is HIV-infected. Even though several government schemes on family welfare promise ensuring child healthcare even if the mother is a single mother, a sex worker, who may also be categorized as a single mother, may not get proper treatment for her child due to her profession and social status.

SOCIAL OSTRACISM

The children of sex workers are kept far away from mainstream society and denied even their most elementary human rights, such as housing,

---

[25] John-Fisk, 'Uncovering the Realities of Prostitutes and their Children'.

[26] D. Halder, 'Rights of Unwed Mothers to Abandon the Children Versus Rights of Unwanted Children for Mother's Love and Care in India: A Critical Legal Analysis', in *Society and Law*, A. Hazra (England: Cambridge Scholars Publishing, 2017).

[27] John-Fisk, 'Uncovering the Realities of Prostitutes and their Children'.

health, education, etc., due to various factors, such as their position in a 'legal vacuum', absence of political commitment and the conservative nature of the society in which they are born and live.[28] They may be forced to socialize with other trafficked children who may be sex workers themselves or other social goons who may be agents of the sex market. They may also be deprived of socialization with their relatives, including distant relatives, as their mothers may not be accepted in the family. Due to the absence of parental identity (especially that of the father), such children may also be deprived from the right to property that would naturally be inherited by them if their parents were legally married.

DEPRIVATION OF THE RIGHT TO EDUCATION

Education empowers and provides choices and a voice to disadvantaged children and young people. It also promotes well-being through teaching them about good health practices and active citizenship through development of skills for life and for a sustainable future. In these ways, it helps socio-economically disadvantaged children break the poverty cycle. Education also ensures a better future. It is with this understanding that the Constitution of India amended Article 21 to expand the meaning of the right to life and inserted Article 21A to guarantee the right to education for all children, irrespective of their social or financial background, place of birth, race, language, etc. Apart from the right to education, the Juvenile Justice (Care and Protection of Children) Act (as amended in 2015) and the Protection of Children from Sexual Offences Act, 2012 also offer help in this regard. Children born in a brothel or forced to stay in a brothel due to their mother's profession may be rehabilitated to open shelters or children's homes, or they may even be placed under foster care till they attain the age of majority. However, in spite of such welfare provision, children of sex workers may not be benefitted because of social taboo, unaware parent or guardians and poor treatment of such children by the criminal justice machinery. Several children may not want to leave their mothers; several sex workers may want their children to get proper education but not in a shelter home or children's home, because they may fear

[28] John-Fisk, 'Uncovering the Realities of Prostitutes and their Children'.

aggravated sexual harassment in such homes. Possibilities of post-rescue discrimination in shelter homes or children homes or in schools due to the mother's profession may also not be waived off.

The above discussions may suggest that the present situation may not proceed towards realizing the goal set by the International Covenant on Civil and Political Rights and the International Covenant on Economic, Social and Cultural Rights, which India has ratified. While several provisions have been created, as mentioned earlier, the present situation may not be improved unless there is proper implementation of the existing laws. It becomes necessary here to examine certain socio-legal possibilities that may help improve the situation.

RESCUE AND REHABILITATION METHOD

It is essential that the state explore all the ways and means by which the rights of sex workers can be effectively protected and their economic and social status be elevated. This author suggests that more emphasis may be placed on Sections 16 and 17 of the ITPA, which speak about rescue and rehabilitation of sex workers. Proper planning for rescue and rehabilitation of such victims may further need proper implementation by the juvenile police unit and engagement of more special courts that may deal with effective justice delivery for victims of child sexual abuse and trafficking. It is also necessary that non-governmental organizations (NGOs) working in the field of prevention, protection and rehabilitation of female and child flesh trade be engaged in aftercare in the justice delivery process. State participation is also needed for proper implementation of family welfare plans for pregnant sex workers, rehabilitation of adult sex workers and financial help to bring them back to mainstream society through helping them get decent jobs. The state must also ensure that the sex workers thus rescued should not be violated again by way of public shaming or blaming when they are taken for medical examination or when they are produced before the court. The police must also be sensitized about the right of sex workers to protection against custodial physical violence in case such women are rescued in the course of arrest of brothel owners.

REDEFINING PROSTITUTION

This author strongly opines that the socio-legal position of sex workers and their children can be improved if prostitution is legalized in India. The first step in the process of legalizing prostitution would be to *redefine* 'prostitution' as 'sex work'. Sex workers have been referred to as prostitutes ever since the concept of sex work originated in the West. Prostitutes are considered to be a category of women who are looked down upon and alienated from the 'mainstream society' because of their mannerisms, commodification sex and morale.[29] Classifying prostitutes as a vulnerable group or considering special rights for them would in itself be a violation of their rights, as this may distinguish prostitutes from the mainstream labour force where women also constitute a unit.[30] It may be noted that the concept of sex work or prostitution has attracted several negative ideologies because of the association of the concept of forced sexual violence over a woman and lack of consent in the engagement of sexual activity while 'selling' sex.[31] However, it is essential that commercial sex work be considered a legalized service and that the same be detached from the concepts of sex trafficking, sexual slavery and sexual violence.[32]

'Sex work' is a term that the sex workers have themselves come up with. Instead of attaching social and psychological connotations to it, one should simply see it as just another income-generating activity for women and men.[33] The International Labour Organization (ILO) has taken a protectionist approach in this regard. In 1996, the

---

[29] Sharon Cowan, 'To Buy or Not to Buy? Vulnerability and the Criminalization of Commercial BDSM (October 25, 2013)', Edinburgh School of Law Research Paper No. 2013/37 (21 March 2018), https://ssrn.com/abstract=2345245 or http://dx.doi.org/10.2139/ssrn.2345245.

[30] Cowan, 'To Buy or Not to Buy?'

[31] Cowan, 'To Buy or Not to Buy?'

[32] See *Recommendation on UN Women's Approach to Sex Work, Sex Trade and Prostitution* (22 March 2018), http://www.nswp.org/sites/nswp.org/files/UN%20Women%20Submission%20on%20Sex%20Work%2C%20AINSW%20-%202016.pdf.

[33] Human Rights Watch, *A Modern Form of Slavery, Trafficking of Women and Girls into Brothels in Thailand* (New York, 1993), 25, 54, 59.

Global Alliance Against Traffic in Women launched an international investigation of 'Trafficking in Women'.[34] The report examined the process of recruitment of sex workers and the living and working conditions that they were subjected to. It also stressed upon the issues such as lack of accountability in this unorganized and informal sector, lack of recourse to authorities and the extremely high levels of violence and abuse that prevailed in the sex industry. This research was groundbreaking in terms of realizing the need for recognition of the human rights and labour rights of sex workers and establishing the minimum standards for working conditions in the sex industry.

Furthering economic and societal benefits could be expected through legalizing sex work. However, the legalization of sex work should not go without proper guidelines that need to be set, in terms of workplace security and safety for workers and labourers, with special attention to female workers. Legalizing sex work would also result in significantly improving the working conditions of sex workers. Since the sex industry would become a regulated industry and minimum standards for work could be established, sex workers would not be subjected to exploitation and abuse. Brothel owners and moneylenders would be accountable to law enforcement agencies and would be governed by a statutory framework of laws. Sex workers would be entitled to labour rights, as well as regular earnings in exchange for their services. Also, there would be a reduction in the discriminatory treatment that is meted out to sex workers in the areas of healthcare and education.[35] However, this may not mean that societal response towards female sex workers may be immediately and effectively changed. However, legalizing sex work would result in a general reduction in the level of violence and crime against female sex workers which prevails in the society. The Indian sex industry would no longer be required to remain underground. Stricter legal sanctions on the trafficking of women for the purpose of prostitution may reduce the chances of victimization of

---

[34] GAATW, *Handbook for Human Rights Action in the Context of Traffic in Women* (Bangkok, Thailand: Global Alliance Against Trafficking in Women [GAATW], 1997).

[35] *Redefining Prostitution as Sex Work on the International Agenda* (11 July 2017), http://www.walnet.org/csis/papers/redefining.html.

women from poor socio-economic backgrounds, and this may also help in regulating job scams that may involve using women fraudulently for online prostitution. Further, conflicts between brothel owners and sex workers would not go unnoticed, and sex workers would no longer be at the vulnerable edge. Along with legalizing sex work or prostitution, the government should also consider removing the penalty imposed on prostitution that is not illegal. This action of decriminalizing sex work would allow sex workers to live with more freedom and exercise their rights against oppression, discrimination and arbitrary arrests and their right to equality. Regularization and decriminalization of sex work may also ensure their right to form an association for positive purposes, right to get old-age pension benefits, right to enjoy free medical benefits, etc. Such regularization and decriminalization would also ensure equal rights for the children of sex workers.

However, legalization and decriminalization of sex work may also have their vices. They may result in the practice of excessive state control. This, coupled with the stigmatization of sex work as immoral, might make achievement of the desired result unlikely. It is imperative that the state strikes a balance and understands the context and constraints under which sex workers operate. Along with it, the government and other stakeholders, including NGOs working for the rights of sex workers, their children, etc., must take up the responsibilities of spreading awareness among sex workers and educating them. Such education and awareness programmes should include implementation of adult-education schemes, the right to education, awareness about basic sexual hygiene, the rights to protection against discrimination and oppression, the right to information, child rights and women's rights, etc. The stakeholders must also sensitize sex workers about other self-help employment schemes to improve their financial conditions.

CONCLUSION

The sex industry in India is plagued with problems, such as sexual slavery, sex trafficking, including child sex trafficking, lack of access to healthcare and education and violence, abuse and exploitation at the hands of brothel owners, local moneylenders and law enforcement agencies. Even though the Indian Constitution and existing legal provisions provide various welfare measures for the benefit of sex workers and their children and several commissions have been set up to tackle issues of human rights violation, they have been ineffective in guaranteeing the fundamental rights to sex workers. Methods of rescue and rehabilitation have failed due to the existence of social taboo and corrupt practices within the government. This must be revised completely in order to achieve the objectives of human rights. Further, the popular imagery of a woman engaging in sex work needs to be re-engineered to the extent that the stakeholders such as politicians, the media and law enforcement agencies stop visualizing and portraying sex workers through a binary lens and in a stereotypical manner.

Enacting newer legislations to restrict sex work would not prove to be effective unless there is a clear understanding of the sorts of constraints that coerce women to inadvertently become part of the sex industry, be it their low status in society, marginal earnings or domestic abuse. NGOs play a vital role in bridging the gap between mainstream society and sex workers. Their non-judgemental and unbiased approach and the credibility they enjoy enable them to aid sex workers with better access to healthcare and education and provide them information and other technical support.

Awareness and sensitization about the human rights would go a long way in ensuring better treatment of sex workers. Sonagachi has set up a self-regulatory body that comprises members of the district and officials from the National Human Rights Commission of India and the Bar Council of India. Such establishments must be set up in other parts of India as well.

Chapter 8

Gender Justice

A Pathway to Human Rights

Shrut S. Brahmbhatt and Anamika Tyagi

INTRODUCTION

Human rights, rights available to a human being by virtue of his/her being human, include gender equality. Gender equality is necessary not only for men and women but also for those persons who do not fall within these two gender categories. Such persons are generally known as persons belonging to the LGBTQ (lesbian, gay, bisexual, transgender, queer) community; they can be homosexual, bisexual, lesbian, transsexual or queer. Transsexual or transgender persons are known as *Hijras* or *Kinnars* in India. Kinnars residing in western Indian states are mostly devotees of Goddess Bahuchara, and mostly they earn their living through offerings received from their blessing newborn babies and newly wedded couples. During the British Raj, Britishers introduced Section 377 of the Indian Penal Code (IPC) of 1860. Due to this, persons from the LGBTQ community do not have the legal right to marry. International and national non-governmental organizations, through various LGBTQ rights movements, have prompted Indian courts to provide gender justice. Inception of the doctrine of gender justice was pronounced by the Delhi High Court in 2009. The court declared that Section 377 is unconstitutional.[1] In 2013,[2] the Supreme Court ruled that Section 377 does not criminalize a person of a particular identity or orientation but only identifies certain unnatural acts that if committed would constitute an offence. During ancient period, they had the right to personal liberty, privacy, expression, equality in the eyes of law and society. In the landmark judgement of the National Legal Services Authority (NALSA) case,[3] the Hon'ble Supreme Court gave legal recognition to eunuchs, *Hijras* or *Kinnars* as the 'third gender'.[4] Reservation for them in the education and employment sectors was declared. The Transgender Persons (Protection of Rights) Bill, 2016 was introduced in the Lok Sabha in 2016.

THE LGBT RIGHTS MOVEMENT

In ancient times, LGBTQ people had the rights to personal liberty, privacy, expression and equality in the eyes of law and society. However, the colonization and imposition of rules by British rulers started the discrimination-based approach towards this community. Numerous international and national non-governmental organizations, such as Amnesty International, Naz Foundation, Ford foundation, etc., through their LGBTQ rights movement and statements have prompted Indian courts to provide gender justice.

GAY RIGHTS AS HUMAN RIGHTS

Protests arose across the entire world against the Indian Supreme Court ruling that re-criminalized homosexuality. A number of massive gatherings took place in Indian cities—Delhi, Mumbai, Chennai, Kolkata, etc.—as well as abroad—outside the Indian embassy on Massachusetts Avenue in Northwest, Washington D.C. and in New York, London, Toronto, etc. On 13 December 2013, three dozen

---

[1] Naz Foundation v. Government of NCT of New Delhi and Others, (2009) WP(C) No. 7455/2001.

[2] Suresh Kumar Kaushal v. Naz Foundation, (2014) 1 SCC 1.

[3] National Legal Services Authority v. Union of India and Ors, (2014) 5 SCC 438.

[4] Shrut Brahmbhatt, 'Transgender Identity: Socio-Legal Position in the District of Gandhinagar' (April–June 2017), ISBN: 978-81-936348-2-0.

activists participated in the protest outside the Indian embassy near Dupont Circle. The United Nations (UN) High Commissioner for Human Rights Navi Pillay declared the decision as a 'significant step backwards' and urged the Indian government to review the ruling.

ANCIENT LEGAL AND SOCIAL STATUS

Sexual diversity has existed in India since the ancient times.[5] Indian temples have carvings that portray homosexuals. Homosexuality was already present in our Indian society and law. Our ancestors of ancient times have maintained records of Indian homosexuality and Indian customary law on homosexuality in their sacramental rituals and monuments, legal documents, religious texts, literary works and artworks. Further, the presence of *Kinnars* at a place was considered sacred. In the common words of that time: 'Since, Kinnars placed their legs on the land, the land became pure'. The four popular varnas of Hinduism—Brahmins, Kshatriyas, Vaishyas and Sudras—gave great respect to *Kinnars*. Brahmins taught their students about the importance of *Kinnars* in Hinduism. Different emperors of India also gave great respect to *Kinnars*. The best example is the Mughal emperor Jalal-ud-din Muhammad Akbar. Akbar had many servants who were *Kinnars*, and Nimat was one among them. Kshatriyas, especially, were the biggest worshippers of *Kinnars*. They had great faith in Goddess Bahuchara. Kinnars were the biggest disciples of Goddess Bahuchara. Except the Kinnars, nobody was ever listed as or considered to be direct disciples of Goddess Bahuchara. It did not matter how devoted a person was to Goddess Bahuchara; the only thing that mattered was the gender of the person. Only if a person was a *Kinnar* would they be widely recognized or religiously established as a disciple of Goddess Bahuchara. A well-known incident from the life of Goddess Bahuchara is that when she was young and passing through a forest in Gujarat, a few thieves arrived on the spot; they inflicted a fear on her mind that they would rape her. Bahuchara at that moment cut off her breasts with a dagger. Thus, she committed an act of self-denial of her actual sex.

---

[5] Empirical Study on Transgender Identity, *supra* note 4.

Kinnars were very popular among local artists, poets and kings. There was a deep understanding about the psychology of *Kinnars*. 'How they used to feel, what they like, what they expect from society' were very commonly known by the people of that time. *Hijras* were recognized as a community or society, instead of as individuals. They never visited any house alone and only visited as a group. There was hardly any age in history when they did not share a common identity.

CURRENT LEGAL AND SOCIAL STATUS

In India, homosexuality has been considered a sin that is unnatural and shameful. Homosexuals are not considered to be part of society, and morally they are not permitted to display their inner selves.[6] There are many issues that create imbalances in the concept of gender equality in the context of society, and in legality as well. Persons from the LGBTQ community do not have the legal right to marry another person of a gender of their desire. They also do not have the right to be in a civil or domestic partnership. Hinduism, the religion that is widely practised in India, is actually respectful of LGBTQ people. Transgender persons have been given the utmost respect, at par with Lord Rama, in society; their blessings have been considered as those of lords. Homosexual art, culture, lifestyle, dance, customs, beliefs, thoughts, expressions, etc., are all rooted in Hindu culture.

LEGAL APPROACH TO PERSONS FROM THE LGBTQ COMMUNITY

Colonial Era[7]

Under the British Raj, the sacramental ceremonies and practices of worshipping of Hijras were taken away through Section 377 of IPC, 1860. The British introduced this section because:

1. They had a belief that this was against public order, morality and decency; and

---

[6] Shrut Brahmbhatt, 'Homosexuality: The Scuffle Between Morality and Law', *Unitedworld Law Journal* 1 (January–June 2017). ISSN No.: 2457-0427.

[7] See https://www.bing.com/images/search?q=lgbt+and+ancient+india+images&FORM=HDRSC2.

2. They had great faith in the Lord Jesus Christ and Christianity's holy book, the Bible.

Due to these gender-biased laws, Indian juveniles are pushed towards juvenile delinquency. As LGBTQ people, including *Hijras*, have been facing social exclusion since childhood from their parents and relatives, juveniles are generally very hostile towards them because of their sex.

Modern Era

The roles of the judiciary, executive and legislature have been vital in deciding various cases relating to persons from the LGBTQ community. In the landmark judgement in the case of *ADM Jabalpur v. Shivkant Shukla*,[8] the Hon'ble Supreme Court of India observed that 'the object of making general aspects of rights fundamental is to guarantee them against illegal invasion of these rights by executive, legislative, or judicial organ of the State'.[9] These organs can play an exploratory role on the doctrine of gender justice. Gender justice is a doctrine that brings equality before the law, public order, morality, decency and equal treatment of LGBTQ persons within societal customs and religions. Gender equality is one of the major human rights, enshrined under Article 14 of the Indian Constitution and Article 1 of the Universal Declaration of Human Rights (UDHR). Thus, it can be concluded that gender justice is a pathway to human rights. The Delhi High Court in 2009[10] observed that fundamental rights shall not be violated by any provision and, due to the anti-therapeutic effect of Section 377, decriminalized homosexuality in its jurisdiction. However, the Hon'ble Supreme Court in 2013[11] reversed the decision of the Delhi High Court and observed that Section 377 does not criminalize people of a particular identity or orientation and only identifies certain acts that if committed would constitute an offence. Further, it was observed that 'No court can alter or, amend section 377 of Indian Penal Code. But,

---

[8] ADM Jabalpur v. Shivkant Shukla, (1976) AIR 1976 SC 1207.

[9] ADM Jabalpur v. Shivkant Shukla, (1976).

[10] National Legal Services Authority v. Union of India and Ors, (2014).

[11] Shrut Brahmbhatt, 'Transgender Identity: Socio-Legal Position in the District of Gandhinagar' (April–June 2017).

parliament has the power to amend or alter section 377 of IPC under Article 368 of Indian constitution'.

All fundamental rights are human rights, but all human rights are not fundamental rights. Mrs Hillary Clinton stated that gay rights are human rights and human rights are gay rights.[12] After the NALSA judgement,[13] the Transgender Persons (Protection of Rights) Bill, 2016 was introduced in the Lok Sabha by the minister for Social Justice and Empowerment and was set to be reintroduced in the Parliament.

CONSTITUTIONAL INTERPRETATION

The Indian Constitution is the supreme law of the land, and hence India is bound to follow its provisions. Anything that is against the constitutional provisions is termed as ultra vires.

The Preamble of Indian Constitution states:

> WE, THE PEOPLE OF INDIA, having solemnly resolved to constitute India into a SOVEREIGN SOCIALIST SECULAR DEMOCRATIC REPUBLIC and to secure to all its citizens:
>
> JUSTICE, social, economic and political; LIBERTY of thought, expression, belief, faith and worship; EQUALITY of status and of opportunity; and to promote among them all FRATERNITY assuring the dignity of the individual and the unity and integrity of the Nation; IN OUR CONSTITUENT ASSEMBLY this 26th day of November, 1949, do HEREBY ADOPT, ENACT AND GIVE TO OURSELVES THIS CONSTITUTION.[14]

Here: 'We, the people of India' means all citizens of India; 'Citizens' includes all persons from the LGBTQ Community; 'Justice' includes all kinds of justice, whether social, economic or political, and also Gender Justice; 'Liberty' includes liberty of thought, expression, belief, faith and worship, popularly known as personal liberty, provided under

---

[12] See https://www.hillaryclinton.com/issues/lgbt-equality/.

[13] NALSA Judgment, *supra* note 5.

[14] Preamble, Constitution of India, 1950.

Article 21 of the Indian Constitution; 'Equality' includes equality of status and opportunity, which is enshrined under Article 14 of the Indian Constitution, including gender equality; and 'Fraternity' includes assuring the dignity of individuals and unity and integrity of the nation. The right to a life with dignity is enshrined under Article 21 of the Indian Constitution.

Articles 14, 19 and 21 of the Indian Constitution are interrelated with and interdependent on each other. The literal interpretation of Article 14 of the Indian Constitution implies that even persons from the LGBTQ community have the right to equality before the law and equal protection of the laws; they cannot be ignored merely on the basis of their distinct gender. Article 15 of the Indian Constitution forbids discrimination on the basis of sex, implying thereby that all people are equal and everyone holds equal rights, and therefore everyone has the equal right to choose their loved ones; this includes also the right to love equals or people of the same gender. Hence, if this provision is adopted in totality, it can protect even same-sex marriages. Article 19 of the Indian Constitution provides for freedom of speech and expression, which means everyone has the right to speak and express themselves. Persons from the LGBTQ community also have this freedom, and they can express their love, habits and lifestyle the way they feel like, and this can absolutely not be questioned or criminalized. Further, the right to life and personal liberty enshrined under Article 21 of the Indian Constitution and conferred on Indian citizens provides that persons from the LGBTQ community have personal liberty in thought, expression, belief, faith and worship. They cannot be held liable for merely committing the act of marriage, as the right to life includes the right to marriage. Personal liberty even includes carnal intercourse that shall not be considered as a criminal act.

UNIVERSAL DECLARATION OF HUMAN RIGHTS

The UDHR, the mother of modern human rights, recognizes the inherent dignity and equal and inalienable rights of all members of the human family as the foundation of freedom, justice and peace in the world.[15] Despite the strong preamble of the UDHR which calls for freedom, justice and peace in the world, the world community has failed to adhere to it to some extent.[16]

As far as the binding articles of the UDHR are concerned, human rights are universal rights, instead of international rights. Article 1 of the UDHR provides that all human beings are born free and equal in dignity and rights. In the case of India, Articles 14, 19 and 21 of the Indian Constitution can be read with Article 1 of the UDHR. It is crystal clear that the right to equality is a broader concept. The Hon'ble Supreme Court has also observed that 'Equals must be treated alike, in like circumstances and conditions'.[17] This way of treating likes alike might have become one of the causes for the unequal treatment of LGBTQ people. However, there has been no clarification on the appropriate reasons for favouring the colonial sodomy laws. The right to dignity of an individual is paramount, as earlier discussed, and is also enshrined in Article 21 of the Indian Constitution. All humans are born free, and hence it can be said that LGBTQ people have the freedom of speech and expression. The British, who brought the law criminalizing homosexuality to India during the year 1860, are also now criticizing the same. The former Secretary of the UN Ban Ki-Moon took the great initiative of decriminalizing homosexuality. He urged the international community to continue working for equal rights for and fair treatment of lesbian, gay, bisexual and transgender (LGBT) people, reiterating the UN's commitment to securing their human rights.[18]

Further, Article 2 of the UDHR states that no discrimination should be done on the basis of race, colour, ethnicity, gender, age, language, sexual orientation, religion, political or other opinion, national, social or geographical origin, disability, property, birth or other status. Article 15 of the Indian Constitution adopts this provision. Considering the adoption of this provision, it can be said that India has failed to

---

[15] Preamble, The Universal Declaration of Human Rights, 1948.

[16] Shrut Brahmbhatt, 'Homosexuality: The Scuffle Between Morality and Law'.

[17] Parvej Aktar and Ors v. Union of India and Ors (2009), 1993 SCC (2) 221.

[18] Sustainable Developmental Growth, https://www.un.org/sustainabledevelopment/blog/2016/09/ban-calls -for-efforts-to-secure-equal-rights-for-lgbt-community.

adopt it in totality, as persons from the LGBTQ community have yet not received equal rights as have other citizens. Considering Article 16 of the UDHR, which talks about the right to marry a person of one's own choice, and reading it with Articles 14 and 21 of the Indian Constitution, it can be understood that this provision of the UDHR has also not been interpreted and adopted in totality.

OUTCOME OF A PILOT STUDY

The co-authors of this chapter conducted a pilot study among a few young people, precisely 35 samples, of their residential region. The study revealed that 31 per cent of the sample respondents were of the opinion that persons from the LGBTQ community were living a free life in society; however based on a question on Section 377 of the IPC, it was found that nearly 46 per cent of the respondents were unaware about the provision and were surprised to know that the human rights of such persons have not been safeguarded.

Further, it was observed that 82.85 per cent of the respondents were unaware of extremely skewed X-chromosome inactivation among pregnant women, which has been considered a process that results in homosexual babies, but nevertheless, the majorly practised religion of India, Hinduism, considers persons from the LGBTQ community as an essential part of society, which was agreed to by nearly 46 per cent of the sample population. The respect given to such persons and the political, social and religious stands offered regarding them since ancient times prove that their presence in society has always been embraced; however, their family members, due to the extreme desire for continuation of the bloodline, have not always embraced such children. Modernization of society has affected sacramental value of such persons but persuaded their acceptance as normal social members. They are now accepted as regular members of society, and hence the special status conferred upon them by religion has been reduced. Approximately 72 per cent of the respondents accepted that they did not like taking blessings from *Kinnars*, who are otherwise considered at par with gods, since they consider them as equal to heterosexuals. This is a conflicting response as the population size and region is such which might have been the reasons for such opinions. As another study[19] carried out by one of the authors at the district level revealed, nearly 85 per cent of the population of Gandhinagar district appreciate the presence of *Kinnars* in public places for blessings. Further, 80 per cent of the sample population agreed that human rights should be ensured to such persons and that the provisions criminalizing their activities should be removed.

CONCLUSION

Human rights, rights available to a human being by virtue of his/her being human, include gender equality. Gender equality is necessary not only for men and women but also for those persons who do not fall within these two gender categories. This includes those who fall within one of the LGBTQ categories—persons with a sexual orientation and/or gender identity different from straight and cisgender persons. It is a traumatic situation for the soul of such people, as their actual desires due to their sexual orientation contradict their body. Such people are not the outcomes of modern society; they have been existing in society since time immemorial. However, their existence could not ensure their legal rights due to the orthodox nature of society and their minority status, as social norms affect their chances of being socially connected. Modern technology has connected these persons with each other, and hence they are able to voice their rights. Being humans, they do have the right to be considered as equal to others. There have been several attempts to provide one or the other right to any category of persons belonging to the LGBTQ community.

Gender justice denotes the meaning of providing 'human rights for females'; however, the concept shall now be expanded to include a largely weak section of the global society—'transgender' people. The term is not novel, but their treatment shall be novel in the modern world. The period of their struggle for basic rights has now ended with the introduction of one or the other legislation recognizing their presence across the globe. Human rights, being rights for human beings,

---

[19] Empirical Study on Transgender Identity, *supra* note 6.

can be extended to transgender persons, which has been proved and is evident from the development of policies for their community. India, being a developing country, has begun to pay heed to the issues and concerns of transgender persons. The NALSA judgement[20] was a victory for transgender persons in India, and the recognition of the third gender raises hope for preservation of their rights by virtue of their being human. Though the fundamental rights are ensured by the Indian Constitution, transgender persons could not be endowed with them due to the social stigma attached to them. Reforms are still required in India for the betterment of this section, but the developments so far in India are worthy of appreciation. The modern society and younger generations have shown a positive response and do embrace the choice of gender of other members of society, and this is the way to balance the inequality faced by them. Gender justice is the only pathway to achieve human rights for the transgender community of India.

[20] NALSA Judgment, *supra* note 5.

SECTION II

Child Rights and Human Rights

Chapter 9

Child Sexual Abuse and Forensic Dentistry

A Critical Medico-legal Analysis

Pallavi Dey and Dhwani Patel

INTRODUCTION

Child sexual abuse is considered as the most aggressive form of violation of child rights. Such form of abuse may include physical and psychological abuse, traumatization of children and usage of children for illegal and unethical gain by way of trafficking for sex trade. Children who may suffer such kinds of abuses may show extremely devastating effects: they may permanently bear physical trauma, may show withdrawal tendency or may even turn into sexual abusers themselves.[1] While the Universal Declaration of Human Rights (UDHR), 1948 codified the basic rights of human beings, it did not specifically mention about violation of child rights, including the right of children to protection against sexual abuse. This was however codified first in the International Covenant on Economic, Social and Cultural Rights and the International Covenant on Civil and Political Rights, in 1966, and then in the Convention

[1] David Finkelhor, et al., 'The Lifetime Prevalence of Child Sexual Abuse and Sexual Assault Assessed in Late Adolescence', *Journal of Adolescent Health* 2013 (January 10, 2018): 1–5, http://www.unh.edu/ccrc/pdf/9248.pdf.

on the Elimination of All Forms of Discrimination Against Women (CEDAW) in 1979 and finally in the Convention on the Rights of the Child (CRC) in 1980. The last convention specifically focused on the holistic development of children in an abuse-free environment. It encouraged state parties to enact legislations for the protection of child rights, prevention of child abuse and the right to participation of children in justice delivery systems. India is no exception to this: after ratification of this convention, India enacted the Juvenile Justice (Care and Protection) Act[2] and the Protection of Children from Sexual Offences Act (POCSO Act), 2012, which are considered as primary provisions for dealing with child sexual abuse and rescue and rehabilitation of sexually abused victims. It may be noted that prior to the coming into effect of the POCSO Act, the cases of child abuse including child sexual abuse were being dealt with through the various provisions in the Indian Penal Code, Immoral Traffic (Prevention) Act, 1956, Prohibition of Child Marriage Act, etc. However, it was through the POCSO Act, 2012 that the issues of child sexual abuse received specific focus in the Indian criminal justice administration. The POCSO Act, 2012 specifically focuses on the types of sexual abuse of children, the possible effects of such abuse and the role of courts and the criminal justice machinery in effective justice delivery to child victims, which may also include medico-legal rescue and rehabilitation of the victims.[3] According to this legislature, sexual abuse may happen to any child under the age of 18 irrespective of gender.[4] The uniqueness of the POCSO Act lies in the fact that it recognizes penetrative sexual assault in the form of non-consensual, forceful mouth-to-penal or mouth-to-vaginal sexual activities, sexual assaults that may take place due to biting with intention for sexual assault and gratification, etc. While the POCSO Act and the Juvenile Justice (Care and Protection) Act mandate that victims

---

[2] The present version of the Juvenile Justice (Care and Protection) Act came into existence in 2015. The earliest version of the said Act came into existence in 1980 and was repealed when the millennium amendment came into effect by way of the Juvenile Justice (Care and Protection) Act, 2000. Later, it was further amended in 2006 and then again in 2015.

[3] For more, see D. Halder, *Child Sexual Abuse and Protection Laws in India* (New Delhi: SAGE Publications, 2018). ISBN: 9789352806843.

[4] This is evident from the definition of 'child' under Section 2d, which says that 'child' means any person below the age of 18 years.

of child sexual abuse must be forthwith given medical aid, the Ministry of Women and Child Development Model Guidelines under Section 39 of the POCSO Act[5] suggest proper procedures for administration of medical aid for and psychological counselling and rehabilitation of such children by frontline professionals, including medical professionals. It has been noted by several researchers and practitioners that child sexual abuse including sexual assaults involving biting may happen in the head and neck regions and softer parts of the body, including the chest, stomach, upper arms, thigh areas, buttocks, etc.[6] Medical and legal professionals who may be aware of forensic dentistry may help the prosecution in effectively tracing the perpetrator/s beside providing medical care to the victim. This chapter, which is exploratory in nature, argues that in several cases of child sexual abuse in India, the prosecution may not seek the help of forensic dentistry. In cases where medical professionals may provide assistance, the reports may not be effective because the doctors, especially junior doctors, may not be aware about forms of child sexual abuse that have been recognized by the POCSO Act. It has been observed by researchers that while dentists play a major role in child healthcare, several dentists, including those who having less than 10 years of practice experience, might not keep proper records of dental check-ups of children. They might also not be aware of the relationship between dental hygiene of adults and children and child sexual abuse.[7] Nor might several dentists know why it is important to check bite marks in children, whether it is essential to include the same in the dental check-up and if included what may be inferred from this.[8] Dentists and

[5] Ministry of Women and Child Development Model Guidelines under Section 39 of The Protection of Children from Sexual Offences Act, 2012; Guidelines for the Use of Professionals and Experts under the POCSO Act, 2012 (September 2013), https://wcd.nic.in/sites/default/files/POCSO-ModelGuidelines.pdf, accessed 14 December 2019.

[6] N. G. Kumar and G. Anuradha, 'Child Abuse: An Orodental Perspective', *International Journal of Forensic Odontology* 2016, no. 1 (July 20, 2016): 43, http://www.ijofo.org/text.asp?2016/1/2/43/195056.

[7] S. Sengupta et al., 'Forensic Odontology as a Victim Identification Tool in Mass Disasters: A Feasibility Study in the Indian Scenario', *Journal of Forensic Dental Sciences* 6 (2014): 58–61.

[8] N. N. Singh, et al., 'Exploring Trends in Forensic Odontology', *Journal of Clinical and Diagnostic Research* 8, no. 12 (2014): ZC28–30, https://www.jcdr.net/article_fulltext.asp?id=5273, accessed 19 December 2019.

paramedics might also not be aware that not checking dental hygiene and bite marks in children from the perspective of child sexual abuse possibilities may also land them in legal trouble.[9]

It may be noted that the Central Board of Secondary Education (CBSE) has mandated that all schools must keep a health manual of students and schools may arrange for a health check-up, including a dental health check-up, which must be inserted into the health manual of the schools.[10] This chapter argues that dentists must be made aware about the forms of child sexual abuse so that they may provide vital information to the police, courts and childcare stakeholders regarding any sexual abuse that a child may have gone through. It must be understood that lack of awareness among dentists regarding this very issue may vitiate the evidentiary value of the forensic reports that may be provided to the prosecution in child sexual abuse cases. It is therefore essential to analyse the forms of child sexual abuse in the light of the POCSO Act to identify which sorts of offences may involve the use of mouth and teeth by the perpetrator/s. Further, it is also necessary to understand how dentists and dental clinics may play significant roles in ascertaining sexual abuse of children and how they may assist the prosecution. Not much literature is available on the relationship of forensic dentistry and child sexual abuse, and this chapter aims to fill this lacuna. This chapter aims to answer two main questions: (a) what forms of child sexual abuse may involve the use of mouth, teeth etc; and (b) how forensic dentistry may help in identifying cases of child sexual abuse and help the prosecution. This chapter is divided into four parts, including the introduction. The second part deals with the first question, that is, the forms of child abuse that may involve the use of mouth and teeth as have been recognized under the POCSO Act. The third part deals with the second question, that is, how forensic dentistry may help in identifying and preventing further escalation of child sexual abuse cases. The fourth part offers the conclusion.

---

[9] For a better understanding, see Section 21 of the POCSO Act, which prescribes punishment for failure to report or record child sexual abuse cases.

[10] For more, see Revised School Health Manual, http://cbseacademic.nic.in/web_material/HealthManual/HEALTH%20MANUAL%20VOL%201.pdf, accessed 2 February 2020.

FORMS OF CHILD SEXUAL ABUSE AS PER THE POCSO ACT

A brief analysis of the POCSO Act may show that this legislation has divided child sexual abuse into four basic forms, which are as below:

1. Penetrative sexual assault, which may turn aggravated by way of gang rape, institutional penetrative sexual assault, penetrative sexual assault through insertion of sharp object in the private parts of a child etc.;
2. Non-penetrative sexual assault, which may turn aggravated by way of gang sexual assault, institutional sexual assault, assault by police, etc.;
3. Sexual harassment; and
4. Using children for pornographic purposes.

Each of these forms is discussed in detail below.

Penetrative Sexual Assault

Section 3 of the POCSO Act defines penetrative sexual assault in the following words:

> A person is said to commit "penetrative sexual assault" if (a) he penetrates his penis, to any extent, into the vagina, mouth, urethra or anus of a child or makes the child to do so with him or any other person; or (b) he inserts, to any extent, any object or a part of the body, not being the penis, into the vagina, the urethra or anus of the child or makes the child to do so with him or any other person; or (c) he manipulates any part of the body of the child so as to cause penetration into the vagina, urethra, anus or any part of body of the child or makes the child to do so with him or any other person; or (d) he applies his mouth to the penis, vagina, anus, urethra of the child or makes the child to do so to such person or any other person.

Section 4 provides punishment for penetrative sexual assault which shall not be less than 7 years of imprisonment or with a fine. The provision further states that the maximum sentence can be life imprisonment, which may also be accompanied by a fine. Section 5 of the POCSO Act further provides the definition for aggravated sexual assault, whereby it is stated that if the penetrative sexual assault is committed by any police officer within his/her local limit, any army or security officer, any public servant, any staff and management of any institutional care home, including remand home, children's home, jail, etc., or that of hospitals, educational institutions, religious institutions, etc., and/or where the penetrative sexual assault may have been committed by way of gang rape, by administering any life-threatening drugs, penetrating and infecting the child with disease or inserting any sharp object in the body parts of the child, such penetrative sexual assault may be considered as aggravated penetrative sexual assault.

Section 5 of the POCSO Act states as follows:

Aggravated penetrative sexual assault.-

a. Whoever, being a police officer, commits penetrative sexual assault on a child-
    i. within the limits of the police station or premises at which he is appointed; or
    ii. in the premises of any station house, whether or not situated in the police station, to which he is appointed; or
    iii. in the course of his duties or otherwise; or
    iv. where he is known as, or identified as, a police officer; or
b. whoever being a member of the armed forces or security forces commits penetrative sexual assault on a child-
    i. within the limits of the area to which the person is deployed; or
    ii. in any areas under the command of the forces or armed forces; or
    iii. in the course of his duties or otherwise; or
    iv. where the said person is known or identified as a member of the security or armed forces; or
c. whoever being a public servant commits penetrative sexual assault on a child; or
d. whoever being on the management or on the staff of a jail, remand home, protection home, observation home, or other place of custody or care and protection established by or under any law for the time being in force, commits penetrative sexual assault on a child, being inmate of such jail, remand home, protection home, observation home, or other place of custody or care and protection; or
e. whoever being on the management or staff of a hospital, whether Government or private, commits penetrative sexual assault on a child in that hospital; or
f. whoever being on the management or staff of an educational institution or religious institution, commits penetrative sexual assault on a child in that institution; or

g. whoever commits gang penetrative sexual assault on a child. Explanation.- When a child is subjected to sexual assault by one or more persons of a group in furtherance of their common intention, each of such persons shall be deemed to have committed gang penetrative sexual assault within the meaning of this clause and each of such person shall be liable for that act in the same manner as if it were done by him alone; or
h. whoever commits penetrative sexual assault on a child using deadly weapons, fire, heated substance or corrosive substance; or
i. whoever commits penetrative sexual assault causing grievous hurt or causing bodily harm and injury or injury to the sexual organs of the child; or
j. whoever commits penetrative sexual assault on a child, which-
    i. physically incapacitates the child or causes the child to become mentally ill as defined under clause (l) of section 2 of the Mental Health Act, 1987 or causes impairment of any kind so as to render the child unable to perform regular tasks, temporarily or permanently; or
    ii. in the case of female child, makes the child pregnant as a consequence of sexual assault;
    iii. inflicts the child with Human Immunodeficiency Virus or any other life threatening disease or infection which may either temporarily or permanently impair the child by rendering him physically incapacitated, or mentally ill to perform regular tasks; or
k. whoever, taking advantage of a child's mental or physical disability, commits penetrative sexual assault on the child; or
l. whoever commits penetrative sexual assault on the child more than once or repeatedly; or
m. whoever commits penetrative sexual assault on a child below twelve years; or
n. whoever being a relative of the child through blood or adoption or marriage or guardianship or in foster care or having a domestic relationship with a parent of the child or who is living in the same or shared household with the child, commits penetrative sexual assault on such child; or
o. whoever being, in the ownership, or management, or staff, of any institution providing services to the child, commits penetrative sexual assault on the child; or
p. whoever being in a position of trust or authority of a child commits penetrative sexual assault on the child in an institution or home of the child or anywhere else; or
q. whoever commits penetrative sexual assault on a child knowing the child is pregnant; or

r. whoever commits penetrative sexual assault on a child and attempts to murder the child; or
s. whoever commits penetrative sexual assault on a child in the course of communal or sectarian violence; or
t. whoever commits penetrative sexual assault on a child and who has been previously convicted of having committed any offence under this Act or any sexual offence punishable under any other law for the time being in force; or
u. whoever commits penetrative sexual assault on a child and makes the child to or parade naked in public, is said to commit aggravated penetrative sexual assault.

Section 6 of the POCSO Act provides punishment for aggravated sexual assault which includes rigorous imprisonment for a term which shall not be less than 10 years. The section further provides that such sentence may also extend to life imprisonment in specific cases and such sentence may also include liability to pay a fine.

The above discussion on the profiling of penetrative and aggravated penetrative sexual assault may imply that such types of sexual assault may include the use of mouth and teeth, as the above-mentioned provisions have indicated that penetrative sexual assault may also be done by way of oral sex, applying mouth to the penis or vagina of the child or making the child to do so. In the case of aggravated sexual assault, the use of mouth and teeth may necessarily exist and the child may also suffer bites in private body parts and/or in softer parts of the body.

Non-penetrative Sexual Assault

Section 7 of the POCSO Act defines such assaults in the following lines:

> Whoever, with sexual intent touches the vagina, penis, anus or breast of the child or makes the child touch the vagina, penis, anus or breast of such person or any other person, or does any other act with sexual intent which involves physical contact without penetration is said to commit sexual assault.

Section 9 further speaks about aggravated sexual assault that may be committed by any police officer within his/her local limit, any army or security officer, any public servant, any staff or management of any institutional care home, including remand home, children's home, jail, etc., or that of hospitals, educational institutions, religious institutions, etc., and/or groping of the body parts of a child by multiple persons, causing injury on the body of a child with sexual intention, etc.[11] In such cases too, possibilities of using the mouth and teeth or biting soft body parts with sexual intention may exist. Further, such sexual conducts may also include forceful kissing, biting inner parts of the mouth, lips, etc.

Sexual Harassment

Section 11 of the POCSO Act defines sexual harassment in the following lines:

> A person is said to commit sexual harassment upon a child when such person with sexual intent,- i. utters any word or makes any sound, or makes any gesture or exhibits any object or part of body with the intention that such word or sound shall be heard, or such gesture or object or part of body shall be seen by the child; or ii. makes a child exhibit his body or any part of his body so as it is seen by such person or any other person; or iii. shows any object to a child in any form or media for pornographic purposes; or iv. repeatedly or constantly follows or watches or contacts a child either directly or through electronic, digital or any other means; or v. threatens to use, in any form of media, a real or fabricated depiction through electronic, film or digital or any other mode, of any part of the body of the child or the involvement of the child in a sexual act; or vi. entices a child for pornographic purposes or gives gratification therefore.[12]

The explanation added to this section states that 'any question which involves "sexual intent" shall be a question of fact'.[13] As may be seen, in this form of abuse, the mouth and teeth may not be directly used by the perpetrator for conducting offensive sexual behaviour, but the child victim might feel traumatized. This may result in not taking personal care, including not cleaning the inner side of the mouth or brushing the teeth, etc.[14]

---

[11] For more, see Sections 6 and 7 of the POCSO Act.

[12] See Section 11 of the POCSO Act

[13] ibid.

[14] For a better understanding on this, see pp. 43–46 in C. L. Schachter, et al., *Handbook on Sensitive Practice for Health Care Practitioner: Lessons from Adult Survivors*

Child Online Abuse

This form of abuse may include usage of children for pornographic purposes and storing of child sexual abuse materials in devices, cloud storages, etc. The former is dealt with under Section 13 of the POCSO Act, and the latter is dealt with under Section 15 of the said Act. While storage of child porn materials may not involve forensic dentistry much, let us analyse Section 13 from the perspective of child sexual abuse here. Section 13 states:

> Whoever, uses a child in any form of media (including programme or advertisement telecast by television channels or internet or any other electronic form or printed form, whether or not such programme or advertisement is intended for personal use or for distribution), for the purposes of sexual gratification, which includes-(a). representation of the sexual organs of a child; (b).usage of a child engaged in real or simulated sexual acts (with or without penetration); (c). the indecent or obscene representation of a child, shall be guilty of the offence of using a child for pornographic purposes.[15]

The explanation added to this section says '...for the purposes of this section, the expression "use a child" shall include involving a child through any medium like print, electronic, computer or any other technology for preparation, production, offering, transmitting, publishing, facilitation and distribution of the pornographic material'.[16]

It may be seen that this provision also speaks about using a child in real or simulated sexual acts: this further attracts the attention of the authors, since such activities may also involve oral sex, biting, etc. From the above discussion, it may be seen that the POCSO Act deals with two main forms of child sexual abuse, that is, contact abuse and non-contact abuse. Contact abuse, which is generally known as physical abuse, is a form of abuse in which the victim is harassed by physical touch. This may

---

of Childhood Sexual Abuse (Ottawa: Public Health Agency of Canada, 2008), https://www.integration.samhsa.gov/clinical-practice/handbook-sensitivve-practices4healthcare.pdf, accessed 13 February 2020.

[15] See Section 13 of the POCSO Act.

[16] ibid.

include sexual penetration, touching of any private part of the body of the victim with sexual intent and/or making the victim to do the same thing for the sexual gratification of the perpetrator, masturbation, rape or penetration by putting an object or body part inside a child's mouth, vagina or anus, making a child take his/her clothes off, etc. In the case of non-contact abuse, or non-physical abuse, a victim is harassed or abused without physical contact. However, the impact of the same may be grave: the child may be dragged to perform or view sexual acts, he/she may be constantly monitored, groomed or made to hear or see sexually enticing content for sexual gratification of the perpetrator, etc.

The forms of abuse assist courts in determining the punishment for the wrongdoer. However, it may not make any difference to the after-effects and mental agony that the child faces throughout the life. The trauma of sexual abuse, if not healed with therapeutic treatment, leads to psychological disorders that a child may not be able to overcome ever.[17] The effects of such abuse may include stress, lack of sleep, fear, depression, eating disorders, phobias, etc. In a few cases, such children may also face psychological disorders throughout their life and become violent with other children and make them face what they faced in their childhood. Child sexual abuse may also lead to permanent trauma or death of a child. It is associated with a number of other child welfare problems, such as running away from the residence, teen pregnancy and suicidal behaviour.[18] Previously, certain other provisions were used to deal with child sexual abuse, which include Sections 375 and 376 of the Indian Penal Code, which deal with rape and punishment for rape, Section 354 of the Indian Penal Code, which deals with sexually assaulting women and outraging the modesty of a woman, Section 320 of the Indian Penal Code, which deals with grievous hurt, Section 377 of the Indian Penal Code, which deals with non-consensual homosexuality, unnatural offences and carnal intercourse, Section 509 of the Indian Penal Code,

---

[17] David K. Carson, Jennifer M. Foster, and Nishi Tripathi, 'Child Sexual Abuse in India: Current Issues and Research', *Psychological Studies* 58, no. 3 (2013): 318–25.

[18] D. Finkelhor and L. Jones, *Have Sexual Abuse and Physical Abuse Declined Since the 1990s?* (Durham: Crimes Against Children Research Center, 2012), http://www.unh.edu/ccrc/pdf/CV267_Have%20SA%20%20PA%20Decline_FACT%20SHEET_11-7-12.pdf, accessed 15 July 2017.

which deals with offensive word/s or gesture/s to insult the modesty of women, etc. However, with the introduction of the POCSO Act, more emphasis has been placed on child sexual abuse than is placed by provisions from other legislations, including the Indian Penal Code.[19] Further, apart from the POCSO Act, Section 67B of the Information Technology Act (which prescribes punishment for creating, producing or circulating child pornographic content) is also used in cases of child online sexual abuse.[20]

ROLE OF FORENSIC DENTISTRY IN JUSTICE DELIVERY

Articles 14 (which deals with the right to equality) and 15(3) (which deals with the state's power to make special provisions for women and children) of the Indian Constitution mandate that children may be provided extra care and protection for their holistic development. Section 21 of the POCSO Act also mandates that whoever comes to know about any case of child sexual abuse must report the matter to the concerned stakeholders, including the police, Child Welfare Committee or even the magistrate. Dentists play an important role in child healthcare. As mentioned in the introductory portion of this chapter, schools are mandated to arrange for a health check-up of children, including oral- and dental-health check-up.[21] Such oral-health check-up may be performed every 5 or 6 months. Dentists may observe child abuse injuries during the course of dental treatment.[22] They may also identify sexual abuse victims, including penetrative sexual abuse victims, through observing the outer facial skin, including bruises on lips, cheeks, neck, etc.[23] Dentists may also engage children in communication once they identify any bite marks or bruises on the face, neck, hands, chest area, inner thighs, etc., and may then investigate any other bite mark, signs of oral sex, etc. They may also identify signs

[19] For more understanding, see Halder, *Child Sexual Abuse and Protection Laws in India.*

[20] Halder, *Child Sexual Abuse and Protection Laws in India.*

[21] See Section 5 of the POCSO Act.

[22] See Singh, 'Exploring Trends in Forensic Odontology'; Section 21 of the POCSO Act.

[23] Ibid.

of child sexual abuse through examining the oral cavity in the mouth of children. Practitioners and researchers have further observed that unexplained oral injuries, including broken teeth, injury in the tissues in the inner parts of gums, the tongue, etc., may also indicate sexual abuse. According to Costacurta et al., '...Oro-facial manifestations of physical abuse include bruising, abrasions or lacerations of tongue, lips, oral mucosa, hard and soft palate, gingiva, alveolar mucosa, frenum; dental fractures, dental dislocations, dental avulsions; maxilla and mandible fractures'.[24] It has also been observed that victims of child sexual abuse may also have gonorrhoea, which is a common sexually transmitted disease found in child abuse victims.[25] As the Ministry of Women And Child Development Model Guidelines for the Use of Professionals and Experts under Section 39 of the POCSO Act, 2012 suggests, in all cases where a medical professional finds out about any indication of child sexual abuse, the same should not be aggravated through opening the wound further. Before administering medicine, the said wound or injury must be documented. The victim and the parents must be asked to provide accurate information as to where and by whom the injury had been inflicted, when it happened, etc. The medical professionals, including dentists, are duty-bound to report such matters to the concerned stakeholders, including the police, to provide immediate justice to the victims. The information gathered from the direct victims and their caregivers and parents and the medical records of oral injuries, if any, formation of cavity, bite marks in other parts of the body and forensic analysis of the said marks, etc., must be provided to the police and to the prosecution for corroboration of the statements and information.[26] Such forensic reports of bite marks or presence of saliva, etc., may also help identify the accused. It must be remembered that the child victim and his/her parents or guardians may not consent for medical examination for fear of social taboos. In such

---

[24] For a better understanding, see M. Costacurta et al., 'Oral and Dental Signs of Child Abuse and Neglect', *Oral & Implantology* 8, no. 2–3 (2016): 68–73, https://doi.org/10.11138/orl/2015.8.2.068.

[25] For a better understanding, see Costacurta et al., 'Oral and Dental Signs of Child Abuse and Neglect', A. C. Percinoto et al., 'Condyloma Acuminata in the Tongue and Palate of a Sexually Abused Child: A Case Report', *BMC Research Notes* 7 (2014): 467.

[26] See Ministry of Women and Child Development Model Guidelines.

cases, the doctors must record the statements of the victims and their caregivers for refusing such medical check-up.[27] However, caregivers may not know about the evidentiary value of forensic dentistry. In cases where a parent or family member or an institutional staff who may have committed the penetrative or non-penetrative sexual abuse on a child or abetted or instigated such offence or participated in online child abuse, they may force the child to not undergo medical examination, and dental check-up and reports of such check-up may provide admissible evidence in such cases.

CONCLUSION

Forensic odontologists play a significant role in the detection and evaluation of child sexual abuse cases. However, there exists lack of awareness of the role of forensic dentistry in providing effective justice to victims of child sexual abuse cases. Parents and schools may avail the services of dentists as mandated by governmental stakeholders for the overall health improvement of their children. However, such check-ups may also be used to identify old or current physical and emotional trauma that may or may not be connected with child sexual abuse. It is noteworthy that while the POCSO Act places special emphasis on sexual abuses performed with the help of the mouth, teeth, tongue, etc., not much awareness has been created, even among dentists, regarding their role in identifying child sexual abuse victims and perpetrators. It is also important for the police and prosecution to refer to the oral health records during the preparation of the charge sheet, during examination and arguments, etc. In other jurisdictions, like the United Kingdom, oral health records are given prime importance in ascertaining the existence of child sexual abuse. It is necessary that in India dentists and dentistry students be made aware about forms of child sexual abuse and their roles in bringing out such issues that may be hidden by parents and children due to various types of fears and anticipation of embarrassment. If medical professionals, including junior dentists, are made aware of the provisions of the POCSO Act, it may be expected that cases of child sexual abuse be detected early and effectively.

---

[27] Ministry of Women and Child Development Model Guidelines.

Chapter 10

Child Labour and Human Rights

A Critical Analysis

Smit Hingu

INTRODUCTION

> Child slavery is a crime against humanity. Humanity itself is at stake here. A lot of work still remains but I will see the end of child labor in my lifetime.
>
> —Kailash Satyarthi

The concept of child labour can be multifaceted. It may be hazardous or non-hazardous, may or may not be beneficial for children, may be a way of engaging children in learning and earning or may be extremely detrimental for the physical and mental health of children. The United Nations (UN) Convention on the Rights of the Child, 1989 (CRC) mandates that each state party must make provisions for the holistic development of children. It also mandates that state parties make proper policies to differentiate between hazardous and non-hazardous work[1]

[1] See Article 32 of the United Nations (UN) Convention on the Rights of the Child (CRC), which states as follows: '1. States Parties recognize the right of the child to be protected from economic exploitation and from performing any work that is likely to be hazardous or to interfere with the child's education, or to be harmful to the child's health or physical, mental, spiritual, moral or social

and create policies that may help children learn through performing certain works that would not hamper their basic rights, including the right to a safe environment, right to nutritious food, right to education, right to protection against exploitation, etc.[2] It may be noted that in a country like India, several families living below the poverty line or in socio-legally–politically backward regions, parents, stakeholders and family members may not be aware of the effective child development norms that have been enshrined in the domestic laws based not only on UNCRC but also on other international instruments, including the Universal Declaration of Human Rights (UDHR), International Covenant on Economic, Social and Cultural Rights (ICESCR), International Covenant on Civil and Political Rights (ICCPR), Conventions 138 and 182 of the International Labour Organization (ILO), etc. The United Nations Children's Fund (UNICEF) 2016

---

development. 2. States Parties shall take legislative, administrative, social and educational measures to ensure the implementation of the present article. To this end, and having regard to the relevant provisions of other international instruments, States Parties shall in particular: (a) Provide for a minimum age or minimum ages for admission to employment; (b) Provide for appropriate regulation of the hours and conditions of employment; (c) Provide for appropriate penalties or other sanctions to ensure the effective enforcement of the present article'.

[2] For more, see Article 28 of the UN CRC, which states as follows: '1. States Parties recognize the right of the child to education, and with a view to achieving this right progressively and on the basis of equal opportunity, they shall, in particular: (a) Make primary education compulsory and available free to all; (b) Encourage the development of different forms of secondary education, including general and vocational education, make them available and accessible to every child, and take appropriate measures such as the introduction of free education and offering financial assistance in case of need; (c) Make higher education accessible to all on the basis of capacity by every appropriate means; (d) Make educational and vocational information and guidance available and accessible to all children; (e) Take measures to encourage regular attendance at schools and the reduction of drop-out rates. 2. States Parties shall take all appropriate measures to ensure that school discipline is administered in a manner consistent with the child's human dignity and in conformity with the present Convention. 3. States Parties shall promote and encourage international cooperation in matters relating to education, in particular with a view to contributing to the elimination of ignorance and illiteracy throughout the world and facilitating access to scientific and technical knowledge and modern teaching methods. In this regard, particular account shall be taken of the needs of developing countries'.

database shows that worldwide (including India), more than 150 million children are engaged in child labour, including hazardous work.[3] It is thus a global problem, and law and justice enforcement agencies may also not be aware about all international norms that may protect the rights of children, especially from the perspective of child labour, which may or may not have been included in the respective domestic laws of countries. Several researches have spoken about child labour and its impact on child rights, the necessity to develop laws, etc.[4] However, there is not much research analysing various international covenants and protocol documents, statistical data available with UNICEF, etc., to provide functional suggestions to recognize issues of child labour that exploit children, possible ways to stop child labour and improvement of the juvenile justice organizational structure at national and international levels to unify the efforts to completely eradicate child labour. This chapter aims to fill this lacuna by way of an analytical research method. The author takes up various international instruments to analyse the inherent meaning of the right to holistic development of children free from exploitation; the author then explores how these instruments, including provisions from ILO, emphasize issues of child labour from different perspectives and what solutions are offered in cases of rescue and rehabilitation of child labourers. The author also analyses Indian constitutional provisions to understand how the issue has been addressed from Indian perspectives.

This chapter is divided into four segments, including the introduction. The second part discusses the general meaning of child labour and also speaks about various types of child labour as have been

---

[3] UNICEF Global Databases, 2016, Based on DHS, MICS and Other Nationally Representative Surveys, 2009–2015 (15 June 2016), https://data.unicef.org/topic/child-protection/child-labour/.

[4] Ravinder Rena, 'The Child Labour in Developing Countries—A Challenge to Millennium Development Goals', (February 10, 2017), https://mpra.ub.uni-muenchen.de/15162/2/MPRA_paper_15162.pdf, accessed 10 October 2017; also see O. O'Donnell, Eddy van Doorslaer, and Furio C. Rosati, 'Child Labour and Health: Evidence and Research Issues (January 2002)', Understanding Children's Work Programme Working Paper, SSRN, (February 12, 2017), https://ssrn.com/abstract=1780320 or http://dx.doi.org/10.2139/ssrn.1780320, accessed 12 February 2017.

described in different international documents and covenants. The third part discusses the role of fundamental rights and directive principles in eradication of child labour. This part also discusses the impact of different Indian statutes on prohibition of child labour. The fourth part offers conclusions and suggestions.

UNDERSTANDING CHILD LABOUR FROM THE PERSPECTIVE OF VARIOUS INTERNATIONAL DOCUMENTS

It is interesting to note that there is no uniformity about the definition of the term 'child'. Various international instruments, including international covenants, declarations and domestic laws of different countries, provide different explanations for the term 'child'. Further, the definition of 'child' has also been influenced by the concepts of child labour, considering the age and maturity level of the child. For instance, Article 1 of the UN CRC defines the term 'child' in the following way: '...every human being below the age of eighteen years unless under the law applicable to the child, majority is attained earlier'.[5] This provision therefore leaves it to the discretion of member states to determine who may be called a 'child'. From Indian legal perspectives, the Child Labour (Prohibition and Regulation) Act, 1986 defines the term 'child' in the following terms: a child is 'a person who has not completed his fourteen years of age'.[6] Noticeably, universally, there is no comprehensive definition of the term 'child labour' as well.[7] Hence, researchers usually explain it by indicating to different forms of conduct or acts done by children which may or may not be hazardous for the physical and mental health of the children and which may be directed to be done by adults: this may include children working in factories, mines, the sex market, the carpet weaving industry, domestic services, etc. ILO's Forced Labour Convention, 1930 (No. 29) is one of the oldest international

[5] Article 1 of the UN CRC, 1989.

[6] Section 2(ii), The Child Labour (Prohibition and Regulation) Act 1986.

[7] For more, see Mark Lansky, 'Perspectives Child Labour: How the Challenge is Being Met', *International Labour Review* 136, no. 2 (Summer 1997), https://www.ilo.org/public/english/revue/download/pdf/pers2-97.pdf, accessed 14 December 2019.

instruments available in modern times which attempted to address the issue of child labour from the perspectives of exploitation of children,[8] especially through the Minimum Age (Agriculture) Convention, 1921. This convention to a large extent aimed to protect children's right to education and to prevent child labour that would prejudice the children's school attendance. Article 1 of this convention states:

> Children under the age of fourteen years may not be employed or work in any public or private agricultural undertaking, or in any branch thereof, save outside the hours fixed for school attendance, the employment shall not be such as to prejudice their attendance at school.[9]

Later, in 1924, the League of Nations adopted the Geneva Declaration of the Rights of the Child, 1924, which addressed rights of children from the perspective of holistic development of children largely against the background of the First World War. This convention addressed the rights of children to normal development, food, medical assistance and healthcare, shelter, including for orphaned children, and protection from exploitation.[10] However, this declaration was silent about the age of children which should be taken into consideration for the purpose of engagement in work, etc. It was also silent about the implementation mechanism and process. After the formation of the UN, the UDHR was brought into effect in 1948. The UDHR provides a compendium of basic rights of human beings and does not specifically focus on the rights of children against forced labour or any kind of work that may deprive them of the natural enjoyments of childhood. However, special focus may be given to Article 4 of the UDHR, which states: 'No one shall be held in slavery or servitude; slavery and the slave trade shall be prohibited in all their forms'. Here, the terms 'slavery' and 'servitude' may be interpreted as inclusive terminology towards prohibiting exploitation of children by way of child labour. Article 5, on the other hand, states, 'No one shall be subjected to torture or to cruel, inhuman

[8] Lansky, 'Perspectives Child Labour'.

[9] See Article 1, Minimum Age (Agriculture) Convention, International Labour Organization (ILO), 1921.

[10] See Geneva Declaration of the Rights of the Child, 1924.

or degrading treatment or punishment'. This may also be construed in the language of Article 4 providing for the prevention of torture or cruel or degrading treatment of any child in the name of any job or employment. Subclauses (1) and (3) of Article 23 of the UDHR are also noteworthy in this context. These subclauses state:

> (1) Everyone has the right to work, to free choice of employment, to just and favourable conditions of work and to protection against unemployment.
>
> (3) Everyone who works has the right to just and favourable remuneration ensuring for himself and his family an existence worthy of human dignity, and supplemented, if necessary, by other means of social protection.[11]

Now, let us concentrate on Article 25, which states:

> (1) Everyone has the right to a standard of living adequate for the health and well-being of himself and of his family, including food, clothing, housing and medical care and necessary social services, and the right to security in the event of unemployment, sickness, disability, widowhood, old age or other lack of livelihood in circumstances beyond his control. (2) Motherhood and childhood are entitled to special care and assistance. All children, whether born in or out of wedlock, shall enjoy the same social protection.[12]

Article 26 further states:

> (1) Everyone has the right to education. Education shall be free, at least in the elementary and fundamental stages. Elementary education shall be compulsory. Technical and professional education shall be made generally available and higher education shall be equally accessible to all on the basis of merit.... (2) Education shall be directed to the full development of the human personality and to the strengthening of respect for human rights and fundamental freedoms. It shall promote understanding, tolerance and friendship among all nations, racial or religious groups, and shall further the activities of the United Nations for the maintenance of peace. (3) Parents have a prior right to choose the kind of education that shall be given to their children.[13]

---

[11] See Article 23 of the Universal Declaration of Human Rights (UDHR).
[12] See Article 25 of the UDHR.
[13] See Article 26 of the UDHR.

The three provisions of the UDHR mentioned above may indicate the collective rights of children to safe childhood, decent upbringing without any sort of exploitation and learning through various mechanisms, including vocational courses. These provisions may also indicate that a child of appropriate physical and mental maturity level may also chose to earn by way of non-hazardous jobs that would not hamper his/her right to education and right to protection against exploitation.

Unlike the UDHR, however, ICCPR, 1966 in Article 24 clearly mentions children's right to protection and identity. The provision states as follows:

> 1. Every child shall have, without any discrimination as to race, color, sex, language, religion, national or social origin, property or birth, the right to such measures of protection as are required by his status as a minor, on the part of his family, society and the State. 2. Every child shall be registered immediately after birth and shall have a name. 3. Every child has the right to acquire a nationality.[14]

ICESCR, 1966 in Article 10(3) further provides clear guidance on the right of children to protection against any discrimination and especially on child labour issues; it states:

> (3) Special measures of protection and assistance should be taken on behalf of all children and young persons without any discrimination for reasons of parentage or other conditions. Children and young persons should be protected from economic and social exploitation. Their employment in work harmful to their morals or health or dangerous to life or likely to hamper their normal development should be punishable by law.[15]

As may be seen from the extracts from these two covenants, they directly deal with the right of children to protection against child labour or any other similar form of child exploitation. However, still

---

[14] See Article 24 of the International Covenant on Civil and Political Rights (ICCPR).

[15] See Article 10(3) of the International Covenant on Economic, Social, and Cultural Rights (ICESCR), 1966.

there was a need for some effective actions and specific codification of the rights of children, because these two provisions were not enough to address the whole aspect of child labour and other related rights of children. Further, the two covenants could not effectively influence the state parties to implement stronger mechanisms to deal with the issue.

The issues of child rights were holistically covered in the CRC that was created in 1989. It is the first legally binding international instrument to ensure a wide range of human rights, such as civil, cultural, economic, political and social rights, for children. The CRC has been ratified by 195 states in the world, and it enunciates four core rights: the rights to survival, protection, development and participation. This very convention shows a dedicated focus towards the issue of child labour in Article 23, which states: 'all states should work to end such child labor practices and see how the conditions and circumstances of children in legitimate employment can be protected to provide adequate opportunity for their healthy upbringing and development'.[16]

Further, in Article 32, the CRC urges the state parties to recognize children's right to be protected from economic exploitation and against employment in hazardous jobs that may hamper their right to education and be harmful to their physical and mental health.[17] Two more important provisions in this regard are Article 6 and Article 28: the former articulates the inherent right to life and survival of children, and the latter emphasizes the right to education for the development of children, their inner talents and their unique personality. These two provisions, read with the other provisions mentioned above, may suggest that a child may take up a job for earning money, but the job should not overburden the child, should not be exploitative in nature and should not withdraw the natural tenets of childhood from the child.

Almost 10 years later, on 17 June 1999, ILO adopted Convention 182, the Worst Forms of Child Labour Convention, which provided

[16] See Article 23 of the UN CRC, 1989.

[17] See Article 32 of the UN CRC, 1989.

more refined policies on the prevention of child labour. Some of the most noteworthy features of this convention include the classification of child labour as hazardous, intolerable, illicit, etc.[18] This convention emphasizes the use of children for slavery and servitude in most modern forms, including child prostitution and pornography, trafficking of children for the said purposes, drug trafficking through using children, etc.[19] This convention also mandates establishment of appropriate mechanisms for monitoring implementation of the policies. The other unique feature of this convention is restricting employment of children below the age of 12 in any profession, including non-hazardous jobs. Further, this convention also mandates that engaging children under the age of 15 in any job that may prevent their school attendance and continuous learning may also be considered as a form of child labour. It also mandates that any employment of children under the age of 18 which may prove detrimental to their physical and mental health should be considered as a hazardous job and a form of child labour.[20]

However, the above-mentioned international instruments are only prescriptive in nature. Hence, unless the state parties ratify the instruments and implement them in their own legal framework, prohibitive measures for child labour may remain only paper tigers.

---

[18] For more, see Article 3 of the Worst Forms of Child Labour Convention, which states:

'For the purposes of this Convention, the term the worst forms of child labour comprise:

(a) all forms of slavery or practices similar to slavery, such as the sale and trafficking of children, debt bondage and serfdom and forced or compulsory labour, including forced or compulsory recruitment of children for use in armed conflict;

(b) the use, procuring or offering of a child for prostitution, for the production of pornography or for pornographic performances;

(c) the use, procuring or offering of a child for illicit activities, in particular for the production and trafficking of drugs as defined in the relevant international treaties;

(d) work which, by its nature or the circumstances in which it is carried out, is likely to harm the health, safety or morals of children'.

[19] ibid.

[20] See Article 1 of the UN CRC, 1989.

CONSTITUTIONAL PROVISIONS, FUNDAMENTAL RIGHTS, DIRECTIVE PRINCIPLES, SPECIFIC STATUTES AND THEIR ROLE IN ADDRESSING THE ISSUE OF CHILD LABOUR

India recently ratified Convention 138[21] and Convention 182.[22] India has also ratified many other international covenants, such as the UDHR, ICCPR, ICESCR, CRC and various other ILO conventions. This signifies that India is now committed to preventing child labour, especially in the hazardous-work sector, providing equal remuneration for equal work, ensuring better execution of laws for safeguarding various human rights, etc. In 2016, in order to comply with two core ILO conventions—182 and 138—India amended the Child Labour (Prohibition and Protection) Act, 1986, which prohibits and penalizes engagement of younger children in all sorts of work, irrespective of the hazardous or non-hazardous nature of the work. It also prohibits and penalizes engagement of adolescent children in hazardous work, like work in the fireworks industry, mining, etc. It may be observed that apart from these laws, the Constitution of India itself has several provisions for individuals, including children, which ensure the right to safe childhood and right to basic education. The constitution further mandates that the state is duty-bound to ensure proper implementation of these rights. These rights and duties are enshrined in Articles 21, 14, 19, 23, 24, 39, 45, etc. Let us now analyse the role of these provisions in addressing the issue of child labour.

While Article 14 of the constitution speaks about the right to equality and equal treatment of all, Article 15(3) speaks about special treatment by the state for women and children, since they are considered as belonging to the most vulnerable groups. The latter provision indicates

---

[21] Convention 138 Minimum Age Convention, 1973 Sets the Minimum Age for Admission to Employment. For more, see https://www.ilo.org/dyn/normlex/en/f?p=NORMLEXPUB:12100:0::NO::P12100_ILO_CODE:C138.

[22] Convention 182 Worst Form of Child Labour Convention, 1999, which penalises and prohibits the worst form of child labour. For more, see https://www.ilo.org/dyn/normlex/en/f?p=NORMLEXPUB:12100:0::NO::P12100_ILO_CODE:C182.

creation of special laws to prohibit exploitation of children, and this includes issues of child labour as well. Article 21 speaks about the right to life and liberty and guarantees unfettered rights to all, irrespective of age and gender. This ensures the right to protection against exploitation by way of trafficking for the purpose of prostitution, begging, etc., which have been considered the worst forms of child labour. Further, Article 24 very specifically prohibits employment of children under the age of 14 in factories and in hazardous jobs. Articles 38, 39 and 45 are also noteworthy here, as these provisions contain Directive Principles of State Policy. While Article 38 speaks about the duty of the state to promote a social order in which justice, social, economic and political, shall be ensured, Article 39, especially subclause (E), speaks about the duty of the state to promote the general health of individuals, with special reference to young children. It also emphasizes prohibition of forced labour wherein individuals, especially children, may be forced by economic necessity to be engaged in jobs that may not be suitable for their physical and mental health. Article 45 of the constitution ensures free and compulsory education for all children until they complete the age of 14 years.

The above-mentioned constitutional provisions strengthen the aims and objectives of the Child Labour (Protection and Prohibition) Amendment Act, 2016. It is important to note that prohibition of labour of children below the age of 7 years had already been enacted through the Factory Act of 1881. However, this Act did not throw light on engagement of older children in work. Later, the Factory Act was amended in 1911 to prohibit employment of children in dangerous occupations and work during night hours.[23] Presently, Factories Act, 1948 is considered the leading provision for setting 14 years as the minimum age for employment in factories. Further, the Mines Act of 1952 is also noteworthy here due to its prohibition of employment of children below 18 years of age in mines. This indeed is a crucial legislature to prevent fatal accidents in mines which may cause long-standing or permanent physical and mental trauma in children. Presently, the Child labor (Prohibition and

[23] C. K. Shukla and S. Ali, *Child Labour and the Law* (Sarup and Sons, 2006), 42.

Regulation) Amendment Act, 2016 is considered the main legislation for prohibition and regulation of child labour in India. This Act has influenced various recommendations made by several committees, including Report of the National Commission on Labour, 1969, the Committee on Child Labour report in 1979, etc. This legislation not only lays down principles for engaging children in non-hazardous work for them to gain vocational training and/or help their family due to economic necessities, but it also prescribes punishment for engaging children in hazardous work.[24]

These constitutional and statutory provisions are presently implemented and executed through various policies in India, including the National Policy on Child Labour, which provides policies for rescue and rehabilitation of child labourers in mainstream society, etc. Further, courts have also emphasized prevention of child labour and protection and rehabilitation of its victims. For example, in the case of *M. C. Mehta v. State of Tamil Nadu & others*,[25] the Supreme Court allowed children to work in the fireworks industry provided they were employed in the packaging sector only, which is less hazardous than manufacturing. This judicial understanding is noteworthy, as the court adopted a very unique way to tackle issues of child labour through providing certain guidelines to the central and state government: this included engaging only adults in hazardous jobs and slapping fines on employers for violating the relevant guidelines and statues, relocating child labourers to a safer place, counselling the parents who may have sent their child for hazardous work, etc. Courts have taken welfare steps towards prohibiting child labour in hazardous conditions in several other cases as well, including *People's Union for Democratic Rights v. Union of India*,[26] *Bandua Mukti Morcha v. Union of India & Others*,[27] etc.

---

[24] Rudra Srivastava, *India: Child Labour (Prohibition and Regulation) Amendment Act, 2016* (June 15, 2017), http://www.mondaq.com/india/x/602434/employee+rights+labour+relations/Child+Labour+Prohibition+And+Regulation+Amendment+Act+2016+Of+India.

[25] M. C. Mehta v. State of Tamil Nadu & others, (1996) AIR 1991 SC 283.

[26] People's Union for Democratic Rights v. Union of India, (1982) AIR 1473.

[27] Bandua Mukti Morcha v. Union of India & Others, (1997) 10 SCC 549.

CONCLUSION AND SUGGESTIONS

One of the major international concerns with regard to child labour is identification of child labour in various occupations and industries, as employers do not necessarily maintain proper records of children employed in their workplace as it may lead to legal consequences. There are confusions regarding the uniform definition of 'child' and 'child labour'. This has created several lacunae in the execution of domestic laws; this has also restricted several countries from ratifying international conventions addressing child labour. This author suggests that there should be a uniform definition of the terms 'child' and 'child labour'. Further, along with the governmental stakeholders, the role of non-governmental organizations (NGOs) should also be considered in this regard. The role of UNICEF in this regard must not be forgotten. UNICEF has introduced 10 principles in its booklet 'Children's Rights in Policies and Codes of Conduct—a tool for companies', which speaks about employers' liability towards child labourers.[28] Such information may be spread not only by state mechanisms but also by NGOs, which may play a very important role in ensuring proper execution of human rights and spreading awareness in this regard. A number of NGOs have already taken up the issues of child labour and bonded labour and carried out programmes to throw light on these issues. As may be seen, there are various NGOs working in this field. It is expected that if states and NGOs work together, the menace of child labour may be reduced.

---

[28] See https://www.unicef.org/csr/css/Children_s_Rights_in_Policies_26112013_Web.pdf.

Chapter 11

Issues of Child Marriages and Marital Rape in India

A Critical Legal Analysis

Vishwa Patel

INTRODUCTION

Marriage is one of the most important social institutions, through which human beings establish families and through which society exists. However, the institution of marriage is not as sacred as it promises to be, especially if we see it from the perspective of child marriage. Several studies have shown that India has the highest number of child marriages, especially involving girls who are forced to get married before completion of the age of 18.[1] Even though in India The Prohibition of Child Marriage Act, 2006 prescribes the minimum age for marriage as 18 for women and 21 for men,[2] various issues, including poverty and lack of awareness about child health, risks of teen pregnancy, impact of marriage on adolescent minds, etc., have

[1] Girls Not Brides, Child Marriage Around the World—India (20 February 2018), http://www.girlsnotbrides.org/child-marriage/india/.

[2] This is apparent from the definition of 'child' under Section 2(a) of this act, which states: (a) 'child' means a person who, if a male, has not completed twenty-one years of age, and if a female, has not completed eighteen years of age'.

been primary motivating factors for supporting child marriages, which may essentially involve marital rape of children. Young girls may not be physically fit to withstand the trauma of sexual intercourse, and this may lead to lifelong physical and mental trauma. Young boys, who may be forced into marriage, may, on the other hand, face similar trauma not only from the perspective of sexual activities but also from the perspective of sudden change in their social position; they may even be forced to leave school in order to financially support the newly formed family. Researchers have shown that the existing prohibitive provisions against child marriage may be continuously violated because of religious beliefs, customary traditions and cultural norms of specific societies.[3] This author argues that while provisions have been made to restrict child marriages, they may not be fruitful in reality not only because of the above-mentioned factors but also because of the legal understanding of marital rape under the Indian Penal Code. For instance, Section 375 of the Indian Penal Code, which penalizes rape, exempts marital intercourse with brides above the age of 16 but under the age of 18 from the definition of rape.[4] This has given extra socio-legal power to parents and families who force young girls to get married to men who may not be children, that is, under 18 years of age. This lacuna has motivated several families to make young girls get married to older men, defying the crucial understanding that such girls may not be physically fit to withstand sexual intercourse and pregnancy as a consequence of such sexual intercourse. Very recently, the Supreme Court of India took a unique step in *Independent Thought v. Union of India & Others*[5] to include child marital rape within the meaning of rape. However, this decision of the Supreme Court may remain mere lip

---

[3] Satnam Singh Deol, *Human Rights in India—Theory and Practice*, 291 (New Delhi: Serials Publications, 2011).

[4] See, for example, the explanation of rape under Section 375(6) of the Indian Penal Code (IPC), which states: '375. Rape.—A man is said to commit 'rape' who, except in the case hereinafter excepted, has sexual intercourse with a woman under circumstances falling under any of the six following descriptions:—.... Sixthly,— With or without her consent, when she is under sixteen years of age. Explanation.—Penetration is sufficient to constitute the sexual intercourse necessary to the offence of rape'.

[5] Writ Petition (Civil) No. 382 of 2013. http://supremecourtofindia.nic.in/supremecourt/2013/17790/17790_2013_Judgement_11-Oct-2017.pdf

service until there is proper implementation of laws prohibiting child marriages. This chapter therefore emphasizes the need for revamping the rape law in the light of child rights from the perspectives of child marriage and marital rape. This chapter is divided into four parts, including the introduction. The second part speaks about the history and development of child marriage–restraining provisions in India in the light of marital rape. The third part throws light on the need for a new law for prohibiting marital rape of children, and the fourth part offers the conclusion.

HISTORY AND DEVELOPMENT OF LAWS RESTRAINING CHILD MARRIAGE AND MARITAL RAPE IN INDIA

Marital rape has remained unrecognized as an offence in India for long.[6] It is nonetheless a form of non-consensual sexual relationship wherein the female spouse may have to undergo physical and mental torture because of the 'sexual demands' of the male spouse. Marital sexual intercourse without consent could not be categorized as an offence because the Indian social understanding has for centuries rejected the concept of non-consensual cohabitation by a wife with her husband. It has been observed by researchers that since ages, if wives refuse to sexually cohabit, they may be ostracized, beaten or even raped by male members of the family. Such women may also be restricted in their access to parents, relatives or friends by their in-laws. In several cases, the parents may also not extend any help for such victims, because they may not be willing to accommodate daughters who may have been 'abandoned' by their husbands.[7] In India, the colonial rulers for the first time recognized the practice of child marriage as a customary practice against the law.[8] However, the British government remained reluctant to intervene in the traditional customary laws governing the institution

[6] Priyanka Rath, 'Marital Rape and the Indian Legal Scenario', *Indian Law Journal* (20 February 2018), http://www.indialawjournal.org/archives/volume2/issue_2/article_by_priyanka.html.

[7] Ibid.

[8] Geraldine H. Forbes, 'Women and Modernity: The Issue of Child Marriage in India', Women's Studies International Quarterly 2 (1979): 407–419, https://doi.org/10.1016/S0148-0685(79)90455-X, accessed 12 December 2019.

of marriage, as such a move could fuel a nationalist movement in India. It rather concentrated on raising alarms against early consummation by young children and related pregnancy that might create health hazards. However, they did not want to touch the issue of long-range consequences on the child brides and grooms and the society at large. It was only in 1891 that the British rulers took legal steps to set a minimum age for consummation of marriage,[9] skirting all other issues around child marriage. However, this could not stop child marriages in India. Neither the Hindu nor the Muslim community accepted British-made rules for governing marriages, including child marriages, which remained more a social and communal issue.[10] It was with the Child Marriage Restraint Act, 1929[11] that the colonial rulers for the first time tried to regulate marriage-related customs in India. The main aim of this Act being prevention of child marriages, it set the minimum age for marriage as 14 for girls and 18 for boys. This colonial-era law was amended in the year 1978 to increase the minimum age for marriage to 18 for girls and 21 for boys. Presently, The Prohibition of Child Marriage Act, 2006[12] is considered to be one of the main regulating provisions for regulating child marriages, but this Act is not free from loopholes either, as it makes child marriage voidable and not void in itself. As such, child marriages are still conducted in India, violating the laws restricting the same.

As discussed earlier, child marriages may essentially involve marital rape. However, unfortunately, while the colonial rulers and later the Indian Parliament did look into prohibition of child marriage from a very limited perspective, that is, only from the perspectives of age and health and later from a holistic perspective of child development, neither the colonial rulers nor the Indian Parliament or the courts in

---

[9] The Age of Consent Act, 1891 (Act X of 1891), enacted by the colonial rulers, set the minimum age for the consummation of marriage. For more information on this, see https://update.revolvy.com/topic/Age%20of%20Consent%20Act,%20 1891, accessed 20 February 2018.

[10] Nirantar Trust, 'Early and Child Marriage in India: A Landscape Analysis', American Jewish World Service 9 (April 2015).

[11] Also known as Sarda Act, passed on 28 September 1929 in British India Legislature of India.

[12] Act No. 6 of 2007. For more understanding, see https://legislative.gov.in/sites/default/files/A2007-06.pdf, accessed 12 December 2018.

independent India looked into the issue from the perspective of marital rape. In India, marital rape is not criminalized. The 42nd report of the Law Commission of India (1972) suggested that marital rape should be criminalized. However, this suggestion was later overturned, as the 84th report (1980) was not in favour of criminalization.[13] Nevertheless, in 1983, Section 376A of the Indian Penal Code extended its scope to criminalize rape on a judicially separated wife. The Supreme Court in the case of *Bodhisattwa Gautam v. Subhra Chakroborty*[14] also expressed its concern over the issue of marital rape by stating:

> [R]ape is a crime against basic human rights and a violation of the victim's most cherished of fundamental rights, namely, the right to life enshrined in Article 21 of the Constitution. Yet it negates this very pronouncement by not recognizing marital rape.[15]

The same issues were again taken up by the Law Commission of India in the year 2000, but no concrete decision was taken regarding the same.

Later, the Justice Verma Committee also emphasized criminalizing marital rape: the committee in its report on 23 January 2013 observed as follows:

> The IPC differentiates between rape within marriage and outside marriage. Under the IPC sexual intercourse without consent is prohibited. However, an exception to the offence of rape exists in relation to un-consented sexual intercourse by a husband upon a wife. The Committee recommended that the exception to marital rape should be removed. Marriage should not be considered as an irrevocable consent to sexual acts. Therefore, with regard to an inquiry about whether the complainant consented to the sexual activity, the relationship between the victim and the accused should not be relevant.[16]

---

[13] Anjali Shivastava et al., 'Marital Rape: A Legalised Sin', *Indian Journal of Applied Research* 3 (2013): 249–51.

[14] Bodhisattwa Gautam v. Subhra Chakroborty, (1996) AIR 922.

[15] Ibid.

[16] Justice Verma Committee Report Summary, PRS Legislative Research (21 February 2018), http://www.prsindia.org/parliamenttrack/report-summaries/justice-verma-committee-report-summary-2628/.

Recommendations made by the Justice Verma Committee thus included that the exception for marital rape should be removed.[17] However, despite such recommendation, no steps have been taken by the legislature regarding the same. Lawmakers in India did not agree to apply the international understanding of criminality of marital rape, because according to the larger understanding in India, marriage is a sacrosanct institution and the concept of marital rape may be misused because of socio-economic reasons among the parties to the marriage.[18]

LEGAL SCENARIO: ISSUES REGARDING CHILD MARRIAGE AND MARITAL RAPE—JUSTIFICATION FOR THE NECESSITY FOR LAWS

Worldwide, women have faced discrimination in society, at workplaces and at home. Girls have been denied the equal right to education and right to nutritious food. Compared to boys, girls face bigger risks of being trafficked for flesh trade due to poverty as well. India is no exception. Women in India regularly face domestic violence. Issues of bride burning, abandonment of widows and old women, etc., are rampant in Indian society. Child marriage is also one of the major problems that most female children have to face due to several sociocultural–economic reasons. We cannot but accept that poverty, weak enforcement of laws and sociocultural norms are the most important factors that increase the risk of underage girls being married off. Girls from poor families are married off to reduce the number of family members so that the family can economically survive. Further, several families from lower-middle-class strata try to get girls married off when their older siblings get married, to reduce the cost of marriage.[19] Several studies have also shown that child marriages of girls take place

---

[17] Anjali et al., 'Marital Rape'.

[18] The Swaddle Team, 'A Brief History of Stupid: Marital Rape in India Edition', *The Swaddle* (12 July 2017), https://theswaddle.com/marital-rape-in-india-history-stupid/.

[19] UNICEF, *Why 'NOT' Child Marriage* (21 February 2018), http://unicef.in/Whatwedo/30/Child-Marriage.

especially to avoid sharing of ancestral property with girls.[20] While these are the general sociocultural–economic reasons behind child marriages, it is essential to throw light on the legal lacuna as well. The Hindu Marriage Act, 1956 does not say much about prohibition of child marriages. While stipulating the conditions of marriage, Section 5 of the Hindu Marriage Act states that the bridegroom should have completed the age of 18 years and the bride should have completed the age of 15 years.[21] Again, according to Section 3 of The Prohibition of Child Marriage Act, 2006, child marriages are not illegal, but every child marriage has been made voidable by a contracting party who was a child at the time of solemnization of the marriage. This section in its proviso clause further mentions:

> ...a petition for annulling a child marriage by a decree of nullity may be filed in the district court only by a contracting party to the marriage who was a child at the time of the marriage.

This indicates that only the parties to the marriage may have locus standi in filing a petition for annulling a child marriage.[22] Section 12 further states that a marriage to a minor child shall be declared as void under three specific conditions. These are as follows:

> ...Child being a minor (a) is taken or enticed out of the keeping of the lawful guardian; or (b) by force compelled, or by any deceitful means induced to go from any place; or
>
> (c) is sold for the purpose of marriage; and made to go through a form of marriage or if the minor is married after which the minor is sold or trafficked or used for immoral purposes.[23]

The Prohibition of Child Marriage Act, 2006 also prescribes punishment under Sections 9 and 10 for marriage with a minor girl by an adult male and for solemnization of a child marriage. A brief reading of Section 10 would further suggest that anyone who may perform,

---

[20] B Suresh Lal, 'Child Marriage in India: Factors and Problems', *International Journal of Science and Research* 4 (2013): 2993–98.

[21] See Section 5(iii) of the Hindu Marriage Act, 1956.

[22] Prohibition of Child Marriage Act (2006), Section 3 (India).

[23] See Section 12 of the Prohibition of Child Marriage Act, 2006.

conduct, direct or abet a marriage involving children shall be liable to be punished with rigorous imprisonment for a term that may extend to 2 years and a fine up to ₹1 lakh. This implies that the 'whoever' may include a priest or a marriage broker or anyone who may direct or abet such marriage. However, Section 10 shifts the burden on such person to prove that he/she was not aware that the marriage involved children. Further, Section 11 of this Act is also noteworthy. The first subclause of the provision states:

> (1) Where a child contracts a child marriage, any person having charge of the child, whether as parent or guardian or any other person or in any other capacity, lawful or unlawful, including any member of an organisation or association of persons who does any act to promote the marriage or permits it to be solemnised, or negligently fails to prevent it from being solemnised, including attending or participating in a child marriage, shall be punishable with rigorous imprisonment which may extend to two years and shall also be liable to fine which may extend up to one lakh rupees.

A clear perusal of the above lines may show that this provision aims to rectify the act of a minor entering into a marriage contract through placing the onus on the legal guardian who may have failed to prevent the said child from entering into such marriage contract. Further, it also extends its scope to include any other person who may not be the legal guardian of the minor child but who may be a member of civil society or any other organization and who may wilfully or negligently encourage such marriage. In other words, this section places the onus on all civil society members to prevent child marriages.

However, this legislation also created several confusions, especially when read with the customary laws like the Hindu Marriage Act, 1956, which has not yet been amended in the light of The Prohibition of Child Marriage Act. It may be seen that defying these laws, many girls and women have been married off when they were under 18 either to adult men or to men who were also minors.[24]

---

[24] Sagnik Chowdhury, '30% Women Married Under the Age of 18', *The Indian Express* (31 May 2016), https://indianexpress.com/article/explained/child-marriage-women-india-census-data-2011-2826398/.

It must be noted that international instruments also provide clear mandates against child marriages: a clear reading of Article 16(2) of the Universal Declaration of Human Rights[25] would also suggest that a marriage shall be entered into only with the free and full consent of the intending spouses, and this indicates that child marriages are violative of this provision. Child marriages also violate the principles of the Convention on the Elimination of All Forms of Discrimination Against Women (CEDAW).[26] For instance, Article 16 (2) of the CEDAW states:

> The betrothal and the marriage of a child shall have no legal effect, and all necessary action, including legislation, shall be taken to specify a minimum age for marriage and to make the registration of marriages in an official registry compulsory.[27]

The United Nations (UN) Convention on the Rights of the Child (CRC) also emphasizes this fact. Articles 3 and 19 of the UN CRC are particularly noteworthy here; Article 3 states:

> ...in all actions concerning children, whether undertaken by public or private social welfare institutions, courts of law, administrative authorities or legislative bodies, the best interests of the child shall be a primary consideration.

Article 19, on the other hand, requires states to take all measures to prevent any form of child abuse. India ratified the UN CRC in 1992. However, in reality, the problem of child marriage still exists in India. This was observed by the Delhi High Court, which held that the 2006 Act overrides the personal laws, in the case of *Lajja v. State* (2012). However, laws have not been implemented in this regard in reality. This gap led to a disturbing judgement in May 2012 wherein the Delhi

---

[25] Universal Declaration of Human Rights, 1948 (22 February 2018), http://www.claiminghumanrights.org/udhr_article_16.html.

[26] Convention on the Elimination of All Forms of Discrimination Against Women (CEDAW), 1979, which came into effect on September 1981, (22 February 2018) http://www.un.org/womenwatch/daw/cedaw/text/econvention.htm#article16.

[27] See Article 16(2) of the CEDAW.

High Court, in the case of *Mrs. Tahra Begum v State of Delhi & Others*,[28] held that a 15-year-old girl, under Muslim personal law, has the right to marry without the consent of her parents as long as she has attained the age of puberty. Such loopholes allow child marriages to continue to be legally and socially valid, in violation of the CEDAW.[29]

In this regard, discussions on the issues of child marriages, marital rape and Indian legal understandings are essential. As the statutes and provisions discussed above show that child marriage is not completely prohibited in India, it is presumable that where a marriage between two children or between a child bride and an adult groom had taken place, some sort of sexual connection may have occurred between the bride and the groom irrespective of whether the marriage was fully consummated or not. Further, as India has not decriminalized marital rape, there is not much awareness about marital rape either between adult spouses or in marriages involving children. Thus, the parents and guardians of minor spouses may allow and force child brides and grooms to enter into sexual connection that may not necessarily be penal–vaginal penetration. Child brides and grooms may be exposed to sexual content on digital communication devices because of curiosity, and they may also be forced to touch each other with sexual intent without consent. This author argues that this situation has resulted mainly due to lack of awareness about the key concepts of The Prohibition of Child Marriage Act and myths about child marriages among people which may have been created due to prevalent customary laws.

The contradiction between customary laws and preventive statutes was put to rest to a great extent through the enactment of the Protection of Children from Sexual Offences Act (POCSO Act), 2012, which states that any sexual act with a child who is below the age of 18 is an offence.[30] Further, the Immoral Traffic (Prevention) Act, 1956 has also been considered to support the POCSO Act and The Prohibition of

[28] Mrs. Tahra Begum v State of Delhi & Others (2012) W.P. (CRL) 446/2012, Crl. M.A. 3701/2012.

[29] Akhilakolisetty, 'Child Marriage in India: Loopholes in the Law', *INTLAWGRRLS* (2 July 2015), https://ilg2.org/2015/07/02/child-marriage-in-india-loopholes-in-the-law/.

[30] See Protection of Children from Sexual Offences Act, 2012.

Child Marriage Act by way of preventing and penalizing trafficking of girls and rehabilitating them to protect them from child marriage. However, it must be noted that The Prohibition of Child Marriage Act, 2006 has not yet made child marriages completely void. This statute still leaves an option to make such marriages valid once they are consummated. However, the Supreme Court, in the case of *Independent Thought of India v. Union of India & Others*,[31] brought uniformity in this regard by stating that all marriages in which children are involved as the bride or as the groom would be considered invalid, because it may necessarily be presumed that such marriages may come within the scope of the POCSO Act. In this case, the court held that such cohabitation between child spouses or between a child spouse and an adult spouse and their probable sexual relationship violate the fundamental rights enshrined in Article 14 and Article 21 of the Constitution of India.[32] The court in this case threw light on certain basic issues that are included within the concept of marital rape. These included the following:

1. The question of right to sexual privacy must be considered within the broader purview of the right to privacy and right to life under Article 21.[33]
2. The right to bodily self-determination, which includes the rights to consent to sex and bodily privacy, is not expressed in clear terms under Article 21. However, it still exists within the spirit of the right to life and personal liberty under Article 21. Marital rape necessarily violates the right to bodily self-determination and therefore may be considered as violative of Article 21.[34]

---

[31] Independent Thought of India v. Union of India & Others, (2013) Writ Petition (Civil) No. 382.

[32] Shradhha Chaudhary, 'Independent Thought v. Union of India and the Unconstitutionality of Marital Rape', *Socio-Legal Review*, National School of India University (6 November 2017), http://www.sociolegalreview.com/independent-thought-v-union-of-india-and-the-unconstitutionality-of-marital-rape/.

[33] Kharak Singh v. State of UP AIR 1963 SC 1295; Govind v. state of Madhya Pradesh AIR 1975 SC 1378.

[34] Bhavesh Gupta and Meenu Gupta, 'Marital Rape: Current Legal Framework in India and Need for the Change', *Galgotias Journal of Legal Studies* 1 (2013): 16–32.

Further, in the discussion on legal loopholes in the issues of child marriages and marital rape, we should not neglect the role of the Protection of Women from Domestic Violence Act, 2005 (Domestic Violence Act, 2005). This Act provides protection to women against domestic violence and sexual abuse and offers civil remedies for crimes against women, including marital rape. Researchers argue that if the issue of marital rape is considered a criminal offence, then there could be more chances of prosecution and less chances of the same being committed by a husband on his wife.[35]

However, it is further observed by researchers that while the POCSO Act offers protection to children from sexual offences, it had not been used properly to restrain child marriages from the perspective of marital rape till the court considered the plea in the case of *Independent Thought of India v. Union of India*. It is expected that a proper law made on the basis of the judgement of the court in the Independent Thought case may help in total eradication of child marriage and proper implementation of The Prohibition of Child Marriage Act, 2006.[36] In a country that has many misconceptions about rape and deeply rooted cultural and religious stereotypes, criminalization of marital rape by the Supreme Court would go a long way in curbing the ill practice of child marriage prevalent in society.[37] It should also be noted that in preventing child marriages, consideration should be given to the rights of children of both genders, as several societies marry off not only underage girls but also underage boys, which violates the latter's right to holistic development too.[38]

---

[35] Neerja Malik, 'Marital Rape Laws and Women Security in India: A Critical Analysis', *Global Journal for Research Analysis* 4 (2015): 131–32.

[36] 'Challenge to Child Marriage Exception to Rape in SC: Petitioner-NGO Relies on the Recent Triple Talaq Judgment', *Live Law* (31 August 2017), http://www.livelaw.in/challenge-child-marriage-exception-rape-sc-petitioner-ngo-relies-recent-triple-talaq-judgment/.

[37] Arima Pankaj, 'Independent Thought v. Union of India: An Evaluation of the Judgment and Its Repercussion in the Field of Marital Laws', *IOSR Journal of Humanities and Social Science* 22, no. 11 (2017), http://www.iosrjournals.org/iosr-jhss/papers/Vol.%2022%20Issue11/Version-4/L2211047985.pdf.

[38] Vipul Vivek, 'Child Marriages Rising in Urban India, Declining in Rural', *The Wire* (June 2017), https://thewire.in/gender/child-marriage-urban-india.

CONCLUSION

Child marriages can be successfully prevented and made void only when marital rapes get criminalized by the legislature; such criminalization must be supported by the criminal justice machinery, including the police. This can be achieved through an individual rights–based approach to violations against women. Governmental and non-governmental stakeholders must take responsibility in spreading awareness about criminalization of child marriages, which may include penetrative or non-penetrative sexual connection between the spouses and which may fall within the broader meaning of marital rape. It is interesting to note that while the Supreme Court has taken strong note of marital rape within the meaning of child marriages, the Gujarat High Court has very recently noted the need for criminalizing marital rape for adults as well.[39] Such initiatives may go a long way in the formation of focused laws to criminalize marital rape. It is essential for the holistic development of children that child marriage–restraining provisions be seen from marital-rape perspectives as well. Hence, the Child Marriage Restraint Act should be amended to include the issue of marital rape to prescribe total prohibition of child marriages.

---

[39] A. K. Aditya, 'Marital Rape Ought to be a Crime: Justice Pardiwala of Gujarat HC', *Indian Legal News*, Bar and Bench (9 April 2018), https://barandbench.com/marital-rape-crime-justice-pardiwala-gujarat-hc/.

Chapter 12

Juvenile Justice System in India from the Perspective of Reformative Justice

A Critical Assessment

Gauri Singh and Namita Yadav

> A child is a person who is going to carry on what you started. He's going to sit where you are sitting and when you are gone, attend to those things you are think are important. You may adopt all the policies you please, but how they are carried out depends on him. He is going to move in and take over your crutches, Schools, Universities and Corporations. The fate of humanity in his hand.
>
> —Abraham Lincoln[1]

INTRODUCTION

With the introduction of the Convention on the Rights of the Child (CRC) by the United Nations (UN) in 1989, the treatment of children by the criminal justice machinery has undergone a sea change

[1] S. L. Goel, *School Health Education* (New Delhi: Deep and Deep Publication, 2008).

worldwide. According to Article 1 of the UN CRC, all individuals under the age of 18 are children. Considering their age and physical and mental immaturity and incapacity compared with adults, children may be victimized to a greater extent than their adult counterparts due to various factors, including poverty, illiteracy among parents and guardians, broken homes, violent and abusive parents and guardians, peer influences, faulty educational system, war, natural calamity, etc. Such factors may lead to juvenile delinquencies or may also cause withdrawal symptoms or traumatization of children which may hamper their natural growth. India ratified the CRC in 1993,[2] but before the ratification, India had enacted several statutes, including the Juvenile Justice Act, 1986 (which was amended several times) for the protection of interests of children who may have committed any offence or who may have been victimized by any offence.[3] The Juvenile Justice (Care and Protection of Children) Act (JJ Act), 2015, the present version of the said Juvenile Justice Act, 1986, includes several features of juvenile justice administration which are mandated and supported by the UN CRC. One such feature is inclusion of the term 'Children in conflict with law', which has a broader scope than any other term, including 'juvenile delinquency', which may mean committing of unlawful activities by minors.[4] The JJ Act, 2015 bifurcates 'children' into two classes, namely children in need of care and protection and children in conflict with the law. While the latter deals with children who have committed unlawful activities,[5] the former deals with several categories of children who may have been abandoned, who may be engaged in begging, child labour or sexual abuse, who may be in imminent

[2] M. Mehra, 'India's CEDAW Story', in *Women's Human Rights: CEDAW in International, Regional and National Law*, eds. A. Hellum & H. Aasen (Studies on Human Rights Conventions) (Cambridge: Cambridge University Press, 2013): 385–409, doi:10.1017/CBO9781139540841.018, accessed 12 January 2020.

[3] Ved Kumari, *The Juvenile Justice System in India*, 2nd edition (The Oxford University Press). ISBN-10: 0198065779.

[4] Larry J. Siegel and Brandon Welsh, *Juvenile Delinquency: The Core*, 4th edition (Belmont: Wadsworth/Cengage Learning, 2011). ISBN 978-0534519322.

[5] Section 2(13) of the Juvenile Justice (Care and Protection of Children) Act (JJ Act), 2015 defines 'child in conflict with law' as '...a child who is alleged or found to have committed an offence and who has not completed eighteen years of age on the date of commission of such offence'.

danger of getting married, who may be forced to live with abusive and/or offending parents and guardians, etc.[6] A minute analysis of the definition of the term 'child in need of care and protection' may suggest that it may loosely include the concept of child in conflict with the law, because such children may be in imminent danger of being abused by adult perpetrators. They may also need to be treated with more compassion by the criminal justice machinery, because the reasons for causation of crime by children may not be similar to those of that by adult offenders.[7] The treatment of children in conflict with the law must be carried out not with the aim of punishment but with the aim of reformation of the children. This understanding flows from the UN CRC, especially from Article 6 providing for the inherent right to life, survival and development of children, Article 37, which speaks about the right of children to protection against any sort of punishment, torture or reformative treatment in case of deprivation of liberty and Article 40, which deals with rights of children who may be accused of any offence. The UN CRC makes the right to life, right to education and right to holistic development of children its prime purposes. Treatment of children in conflict with the law must therefore adhere to the said principles. However, it is interesting to note that the UN CRC is not the only document to lay down principles for dealing with children in conflict with the law in a reformative way. The history of juvenile justice system may suggest that in 1704, Pope Clement XI first introduced the idea of 'the correction and instruction of profligate youth' in institutional systems,[8] and later the Reformatory Schools Act and Industrial Schools Act were enacted in Britain.[9] In the 17th, 18th and 19th centuries, several countries in Europe introduced a juvenile penological system that was more educative and

---

[6] See Section 2(14) of the JJ Act, 2015.

[7] D. Halder, *Child Sexual Abuse and Protection Laws in India* (New Delhi: SAGE Publications, 2018). ISBN: 9789352806843.

[8] See Thorsten Sellin, 'House of Correction for Boys in the Hospice of Saint Michael in Rome', 20 *American Institute of Criminal Law and Criminology* 533 (1929–1930), https://scholarlycommons.law.northwestern.edu/cgi/viewcontent.cgi?article=2161&context=jclc, accessed 12 December 2020.

[9] Gillian Carol Gear, *Industrial Schools in England, 1857–1933* (University of London, Institute of Education, 1999).

reformative in nature. The children who had been found violating the law were included in the industrial training sector to detach them from negative environments that may have pushed them to violate laws.[10] Later, the United States and the United Kingdom, followed by other countries, including Australia, New Zealand, etc., also set up a modern reformative penal system for juvenile offenders.

The above discussion suggests that the reformative theory of punishment has been considered as an integral part of the juvenile justice administration system in many jurisdictions, especially for the purpose of dealing with children in conflict with the law. The reformative theory of punishment suggests that the main aim of punishment should be to reform the offender, make him/her refrain from committing further crimes and rehabilitate him/her to a positive environment so that he/she does not commit any more crimes.[11] The reformative theory of punishment gets its strongest support from the principles of restorative justice. According to Howard Zehr, 'Restorative justice is a process to involve, to the extent possible, those who have a stake in a specific offense to collectively identify and address harms, needs and obligations in order to heal and put things as right as possible'.[12] The principles of restorative justice include three main understandings: existence of harm, obligation to repair the harm and engagement of stakeholders for restoring justice.[13] In cases of child offenders, reformative punishment may be the best way to bring them back to mainstream society. In such cases, harm may occur right from the time when a child is forced to commit an offence for any reason. The stakeholders, that is, governmental and non-governmental agencies, are duty-bound to not only achieve restorative justice for the victim/s but also provide benefits of restorative justice for the child in conflict with the law so

[10] Gear, *Industrial Schools in England*.

[11] For more, see Thom Brooks, 'T.H. Green's Theory of Punishment', *History of Political Thought* 24, no. 4 (Winter 2003): 685–701, https://www.jstor.org/stable/26220012, accessed 12 December 2019.

[12] For more, see Zehr Howard and Gohar Ali, *The Little Book of Restorative Justice* (2002), https://www.unicef.org/tdad/littlebookrjpakaf.pdf, accessed 12 December 2019.

[13] Howard and Ali, *The Little Book of Restorative Justice*.

that he/she does not commit the same mistake again.[14] The JJ Act, 2015 promises dedicated focus on children in conflict with the law. This chapter analyses whether the statute adheres to the principles of reformative justice for cases of children in conflict with the law. In the second part, the authors explore how the reformative theory of punishment has been incorporated in the criminal justice mechanism in different countries and whether relying on the reformative theory may produce better results for dealing with children in conflict with the law. This portion then analyses how far the provisions of the JJ Act, 2015 have incorporated reformative theories of punishment and whether the Act has provided any effective result. The third portion offers the conclusion and suggestions.

The research for this chapter was done in various stages. Primarily, we reviewed prior studies that have been conducted on the juvenile justice system in India with special reference to the reformative approach. To elaborate on various lacunae in the present juvenile justice system in India, primarily we expand on the statute, its recent amendments and its impact on the system. Emphasis is also placed on the precedents set by the Supreme Court of India and various High Courts. The chapter also examines the mechanisms employed by the administrative bodies of this country to provide a reformative and restorative juvenile justice system.

To supplement the comparative analysis of policies and infrastructure in India and those in other developed nations, namely the United States, Canada, the United Kingdom and Sweden, reports, foreign case laws and statues were reviewed. The ideas and opinions that have been put forward by leading experts in the field and how those ideas can help fill the crevices were also analysed. To accustom ourselves with the realities on the ground, we conducted surprise visits to nearby 'observation homes'. We interviewed many detained juvenile offenders, administrative authorities and judicial officers. These interviews have provided us with accounts of the abuse, atrocities and oppression that the juveniles have been undergoing daily. Using their depositions, we highlight the various lacunae present in the implementation of paper policies of India.

---

[14] Howard and Ali, *The Little Book of Restorative Justice*.

ROLE OF THE REFORMATIVE THEORY OF PUNISHMENT IN JUVENILE JUSTICE ADMINISTRATION

The reformative theory of punishment emphasizes moral laws and the wrongdoer's voluntary willingness through a well-planned restrictive process supported by the state.[15] Children may commit criminal activities for various reasons that may differ grossly from the crime causation factors for adults. These may include lack of parental control, supervision and monitoring, psycho-social–biological urge to survive, especially in cases where the child is put in a condition where he/she is deprived of food, peer influence, impulse to end dominance of violent, abusive or nagging parents, guardians, peer group, etc., influence of violence in media, etc.[16] Plainly, child offenders may not have heavy *mens rea* to attract heavier punishment. As the discussions in the above paragraph show, since the mediaeval period, European churches, educators and criminologists and penologists have applied reformative principles to 'purify' the thought process of child offenders and engage them in vocational training within properly supervised detention systems.[17] The result of this could be standard reformation of offending children who may not be violating laws for the reasons they did the same earlier. There are several UN guidelines, including the UN Standard Minimum Rules for the Administration of Juvenile Justice, 'the Beijing Rules', 1985, General Assembly resolution 40/33 of 29 November 1985, the UN Guidelines for the Prevention of Juvenile Delinquency, 'the Riyadh Guidelines', 1988, etc., that suggest that juvenile delinquency and children in conflict with the law must

---

[15] For more, see Brooks, 'T.H. Green's Theory of Punishment'.

[16] Bradley r. Entner Wright Avshalom Caspi Terrie e. Moffitt Phil a. Silva. 'Low Self-control, Social Bonds, and Crime: Social Causation, Social Selection, or Both?' *Criminology* 37, no. 3 (August 1999): 447–702, https://onlinelibrary.wiley.com/doi/10.1111/j.1745-9125.1999.tb00493.x, accessed 23 January 2020; Kevin D. Brownie and Cathernie Hamilton-Giachirstis, 'The Influence of Violent Media on Children and Adolescents: A Public-health Approach', *The Lancet* 371, no. 9619 (5–11 April 2008): 1137, http://bernard.pitzer.edu/~hfairchi/pdf/psychology/Social&Diversity/Browne(2005)ViolentMediaChildren.pdf, accessed o23 January 2020.

[17] See: Sellin, 'House of Correction for Boys'.

not be dealt with in the same manner as are adult offenders.[18] These guidelines further suggest that restorative justice must be used as the main supporting tool for reforming children in conflict with the law. According to these suggestions, restorative circles created with the help of social activists, teachers, properly trained police officers who may be able to handle child-related matters, parents, doctors and pro bono lawyers may be engaged to reform children in conflict with the law and re-integrate them into mainstream society.[19]

India has traditionally followed restorative justice methods and practices at the grassroots levels in dispute resolution: village panchayats are the best examples in this regard.[20] This has reflected in the modern understanding of juvenile justice administration too. The existing JJ Act, 2015 discusses about the administration of justice for children in conflict with the law in Chapters III and IV, which speak about establishing Juvenile Justice Boards (JJBs) to deal with children in conflict with the law, usage of the most-lenient-punishment theories for reforming such children, etc. As may be seen from Chapter III, each JJB is mandated to have a judicial magistrate of the first class, who should be assisted by two social workers, one of whom should be a woman.[21] This Act also mandates that treatment of a child in conflict with the law must be in accordance with the classification of the offence as a heinous crime,[22] serious offence[23] or petty offence,[24]

---

[18] See Promoting Restorative Justice for Children, https://sustainabledevelopment.un.org/content/documents/2599Promoting_restorative_justice.pdf, accessed 23 January 2020.

[19] Promoting Restorative Justice for Children.

[20] See Howard and Ali, *The Little Book of Restorative Justice.*

[21] See Section 4 of the JJ Act, 2015.

[22] Section 2(33) of the JJ Act, 2015 defines heinous offences as 'the offences for which the minimum punishment under the Indian Penal Code or any other law for the time being in force is imprisonment for seven years or more'.

[23] Section 2(54) of the JJ Act 2015 states that 'serious offences' include the offences for which the punishment under the Indian Penal Code or any other law for the time being in force is imprisonment for between 3 and 7 years.

[24] Section 2(45) of the JJ Act states that 'petty offences' include the offences for which the maximum punishment under the Indian Penal Code or any other law for the time being in force is imprisonment up to 3 years.

classification of the age of the child in conflict with the law, (it has been stated that those children above 16 years of age who may have committed heinous offences may be treated like adult offenders) and the intellectual maturity of the child in conflict with the law.[25] Chapter IV of the JJ Act, 2015 further mandates that there should be a special juvenile police unit to apprehend children in conflict in as child-friendly a way as possible. The child so apprehended must not be put in any police lock-up and must be produced before a JJB as soon as possible, within a maximum time limit of 24 hours. The JJ Act further mandates that the JJB must immediately apply its cognizance in such cases and may release such children under bail, after admonition, etc. However, this does not mean that such children would be completely acquitted within the meaning of the Criminal Procedure Code. They would need to attend counselling sessions as mandated by the orders of the JJB, and such counselling sessions must include the caregivers, fit guardians and parents as well. However, only in cases where releasing such children under bail may jeopardize their safety may the JJB order them to be put up in Observation Homes for a maximum period of 3 years, ensuring maximum rights to the concerned child which would enable him/her to access legal assistance, access his/her family and exercise rights necessary for his/her holistic development, the right to education, the right to express opinions, etc. The JJB must also ensure that the confidentiality and privacy of the child may be secured and there should be no stigmatization during his/her detention in an Observation Home. Further, the JJ Act, 2015 strictly forbids using any corporal punishment method even with children in conflict with the law staying under any institutional care. It further suggests mechanisms to deal with children in conflict who may not be released from their punitive institutional care even after they reach 18 years of age due to time-consuming investigation, inquiry and trial procedures. In such situations, the JJ Act, 2015 suggests shifting such children to special homes, under the care of specialized non-governmental organizations (NGOs), etc., who would be responsible for rehabilitating such children and bringing them back to mainstream society.[26] Chapter IV further

[25] See Section 15 of the JJ Act, 2015.

[26] For a better understanding, see Chapter IV of the JJ Act.

provides that proper inquiry should be made for the assessment of the age of any adult offender whenever such offender brings a plea of committing crime before completion of the age of 18 but being apprehended when an adult.[27] Thus, the JJ Act, 2015 in certain circumstances extends its scope with retrospective effect.[28]

The above discussion may suggest that India seems to tackle any problem of juvenile delinquency based on the three below-mentioned assumptions:

1. Such minors should not be tried, and they should rather be corrected.
2. Such minors should not be punished but be reformed.
3. If need be, such minors should be held in institutional homes, such as Observation Homes,[29] special homes, and [30] borstals, for reformation and correctional purposes.

However, the JJ Act, 2015 may not be without any lacuna. The earlier versions of this Act had provided opportunities to misuse its provisions, and the Act has been misunderstood and misinterpreted as well. Chapter IV of the present version of the JJ Act mandates that in case of plea of juvenility by any offender, including adult offenders, the magistrate before whom the said offender has been produced is duty-bound to make an enquiry in this regard.[31] However, the Act is silent about the proper process of verification of the age. The Supreme Court, in *Ramdeo alias Rajnath Chauhan v. State of Assam*, observed as follows: '...for the determination of the age of the juvenile for the purpose of his trial under the Juvenile Justice Act, his date of birth as recorded in the school register may be accepted provided it is entered by a competent authority'.[32] However, there are umpteen hurdles in such process: the school may not have the proper birth date, and if it has the same, it

[27] Ibid.

[28] Ibid.

[29] Section 8 of the JJ Act, 2015.

[30] Section 9 of the JJ Act, 2015.

[31] See Section 9(2) of the JJ Act, 2015.

[32] See Ramdeo alias Rajnath Chauhan v. State of Assam, AIR 2001 SC 2231.

might not match the data maintained by the birth and death registration office of the place where the offender may have been born. Again, such dates entered into the birth registration file may not match with the hospital records: this may be due to lack of awareness and education of the parents or even due to corrupt practices of the above-mentioned authorities. There is also much confusion as to on which date the age has to be taken into account. In *Umesh Chandra v. State of Rajasthan* (1982 (1) SCALE 335 (SC)), it was held that it must be the date of bringing the juvenile to the court. It was then corrected in *Arnit Das v. State of Bihar* (AIR 2000 SC 2264) as the date of bringing the accused to the court. However, again it was revised in *Pratap Singh v. State of Jharkhand*.[33] Further, when a child is apprehended, the JJ Act mandates that the apprehension must be done by a properly trained child-friendly police officer.[34] However, in reality, a special juvenile police unit may not always exist in every local police station. In the absence of a special juvenile police unit, other police officers may proceed to apprehend a concerned child. In such cases, it may be seen that the child may not be apprehended in a child-friendly manner, because the parents and guardians may prevent the child from being apprehended, may create unnecessary hassles and may attract curiosity in the neighbourhood, which may jeopardize the right to confidentiality of the child. The child and his/her family may be stigmatized even before the official proceedings in the court start. Further, there are issues related to keeping children in detention as well. Whereas the Beijing Rules and the JJ Act, 2015[35] clearly mandate that under no circumstances may a child in conflict with the law be tried and kept with an adult offender, even in cases where both the adult and the child offender had played parts in the causation of crime, it may be seen that juvenile offenders may still continue to exist in the premises of prisons meant for adults, defying the guidelines of the Supreme Court in the case of *Sheela Barse v. Union of India* (AIR 1986SC 1773). Further, the conditions of Observation Homes and special homes may also be analysed in the light of the JJ Act, 2015 and the Beijing Rules. Several Observation Homes and special

---

[33] Pratap Singh v. State of Jharkhand, (2005) Appeal (crl.) 210.

[34] See Chapter IV of the JJ Act, 2015.

[35] Ibid.

homes may lack proper infrastructure for reformation of children in conflict with the law. They may not be located within the campus of a JJB, which may make it difficult to produce the children before the board or carry out regular inspection. Such homes may also lack proper tutoring facilities for children. Further, such children may also not be able to attend regular school, because of lack of infrastructure and facilities, uninterested teachers and fear of stigmatization.[36] Nor may Observation Homes and special homes be free from sexual activities and sexual bullying of junior inmates by senior inmates or even supervisors. Several observation homes may not have the facilities to separate children who may suffer from hypersexual behaviour from other children. As a result, there might be every possibility of children in conflict with the law becoming children in need of care and protection within protection homes.[37] Counselling facilities for children in conflict with the law who may have been released under bail, bond or security are also questionable. In several cases, proper, trained child psychiatrists and counsellors might not be available to counsel children in conflict with the law. There might also be lack of family counselling, which might have extremely adverse results, like moving a child in conflict with the law to another jurisdiction, suspending the child from school, etc.[38] Further, the JJ Act, 2015 could not ensure proper implementation of the provisions related to the important roles of probation officers in social inquiry, supervision and rehabilitation of children and their re-integration into mainstream society. Probation officers might find themselves in an extremely helpless position when the local police and influential families refuse to accept their services.[39] It is also unfortunate to note that in spite of clear directions of the JJ Act, 2015 to not violate the inherent right of life and dignity of

[36] See Meghna Dasgupta, 'Rehabilitation Through Education for Juveniles in Conflict with Law', Working Paper No 238 CCS Researching Reality Internship 2010, accessed 21 January 2020.

[37] For more, see D. Halder, *Child Sexual Abuse and Protection Laws in India* (New Delhi: SAGE Publications, 2018). ISBN: 9789352806843.

[38] For more, see D. Halder and Jaishankar, 'Revenge Porn by Teens in the United States and India: A Socio-legal Analysis', *International Annals of Criminology* 51, no. 1–2 (2013): 85–111. ISSN: 00034452.

[39] See *supra*@40.

children in conflict with the law, the police might use its arbitrary powers to wrongly implicate minors with a previous record.[40]

At this point, it becomes important to look at the comparative analysis of the juvenile court systems of some countries, including India, the United Kingdom, the United States, Sweden and Canada.

Table 12.1 identifies the status of a few essential factors in the juvenile justice system of various countries. They are in contrast to the facilities India provides to its juvenile offenders. At a cursory glance, it would be appropriate to say that the Indian juvenile justice system is of an equivalent order to that of the other countries. As discussed earlier, in India, children in conflict with the law who are refused bail for their own safety are kept in Observation Homes. The reason for this is to separate the young offenders from seasoned criminals and put them on a reformative path. However, as the earlier discussions suggest, on several occasions, due to overcrowding and lack of infrastructure, Observation Homes end up damaging the process rather than rescuing the children. The United States, the United Kingdom and Sweden use juvenile police units and homes supported by social services which are specifically made for detaining children in conflict with the law. Canada prohibits detaining young offenders as per the Youth Criminal Justice Act, 2002. This option aids in reducing the burden in detainee homes. However, this Act is considered to be too lenient in its approach. India, the United States and the United Kingdom have special courts dedicated to the judicial process for juveniles. This set-up is essential for providing confidentiality and child-friendly justice to child offenders. However, Sweden has no special courts dedicated for the same. Canada has provisions for Youth Justice Committees and involves responsible stakeholders from within the community in ensuring the holistic development of juvenile offenders. In some communities in Canada, minor violent offences, such as assaults in schools, are dealt with by extrajudicial sanctions programmes. Such system may include family counselling, victim–offender reconciliation, personal services to the

---

[40] Poonam Agarwal, 'The New Juvenile Justice Act is Ripe for Misuse', *The Quint* (23 December 2015), https://www.thequint.com/news/india/the-new-juvenile-justice-act-is-ripe-for-misuse-experts, accessed 15 February 2018.

Table 12.1 Comparative Analysis of Juvenile Court System with Other Countries

S. No.		India	USA	UK	Sweden	Canada
1.	Speciality courts	Juvenile Justice Board[a]	Juvenile Courts/ Juvenile Review Court[b]	The Youth Court[c]	No special courts[d]	No special court[e] but Section 18(1) of the Youth Justice Committees (YJCs) helps in the administering of the YCJA by devolving power to the community
2.	Temporary detention	Observation Homes[f]	In custody of police officer/social worker/ child welfare	In custody of juvenile police unit in child friendly home run by social services	Social services and judicial system	Prohibited and considered unnecessary[g]
3.	Leniency in sentencing	Perceived as lenient[h]	Too lenient[i]	A British crime survey reveals that 'three out of four respondents [think] that the police and courts are too lenient in their treatment of juvenile offenders', and that 40% think that they are 'much too lenient'[j]	Believe in leniency[k]	Too lenient[l]
4.	Average number of parole days	No data	2 Days[m]	No data	No data	No data
5.	Open prisons for juveniles	Detained in borstal schools	Yes	Community based alternatives[n]	Yes[o]	Correctional centre

(Continued)

(Continued)

S. No.		India	USA	UK	Sweden	Canada
6.	Number of rehabilitation homes	Between 2001 and 2011, the four largest states of India[p] have a total of 175 child welfare committees	In 2006, more than 2,000 residential juvenile justice facilities in the United States housed more than 90,000 juvenile offenders[q]	2,392 Homes[r]	No data	No data

Source: The authors.

Notes: [a] Section 4 of the Juvenile Justice (Care and Protection) Act, 2000.

[b] Since USA has a federal structure, different states have different special courts. In the state of Connecticut, the Juvenile Courts are Juvenile Review Board. See http://www.cga.ct.gov/2004/rpt/2004-r-0941.html

[c] Section 45, Children and Young Persons Act, 1933.

[d] See https://www.ncjrs.gov/App/Publications/abstract.aspx?ID=154201

[e] The Youth Criminal Justice Act, 2002.

[f] Section 8 of the Juvenile Justice (Care and Protection) Act, 2000.

[g] Section 29, The Youth Criminal Justice Act, 2002.

[h] Editorial, Justice and the Juvenile, *The Hindu*, 6 September 2013.

[i] See Dawson (1990) and Feld (1997).

[j] Virk, Navpreet, *Juvenile Offenders: A Different Approach Needed?—Part I.* Criminal Law and Justice Weekly, July 25, 2014.

[k] See https://www.cairn.info/revue-internationale-de-droit-penal-2004-1-page-511.html

[l] Corrado, R. R. Introduction. In *Juvenile Justice in Canada: A Theoretical and Analytical Assessment*, edited by R. R. Corrada, N. Bala, R. Linden, & M. Le Blanc. Toronto, ON: Buttersworth; 1992:1–22.

[m] Chapter 7, *Juvenile Crime, Juvenile Justice (2001)*, The National Academics Press.

[n] Soler (2001, p. 32).

[o] Ward, David A., Inmate rights and prison reform in Sweden and Denmark. *Journal of Criminal Law and Criminology* 1972; 63(2):240–255.

[p] India's Hell Holes: Child Sexual Assault in Juvenile Justice Homes, Asian Centre for Human Rights (ACHR), 2013.

[q] Juvenile Residential Facility Census, 2006.

[r] Youth justice annual statistics: 2013–2014.

victim, paying of damages and compensation, restitution, etc., and community services by the offending child to make him/her understand the issue of moral wrong and also the importance of preventive criminal sanctions. The system may include apology by the victim to the offender only when all conditions are fulfilled.[41] Section 10 of Canada's Youth Criminal Justice Act (YCJA) provides that extrajudicial sanctions may be used only if a youth 'accepts responsibility' for the offence that is alleged to have been committed and consents to the imposition of the sanction.[42] In India, on the other hand, compensatory jurisprudence may be applied. The JJ Act, 2015 mandates that parents pay a fine for the misdeeds of their children. However, in many cases, it has been seen that affluent parents may actually encourage their children to do more offences, indicating that they can save their children through paying the fines.[43] Further, it may be seen that even though India has open prison institutions, which can be traced back to the first Indian Jails Committee in 1919–1920, they might not be completely functional in many regions, especially for dealing with children in conflict with the law. Simultaneously, other developed nations have experimented with open prisons (the United States and Sweden) or some other forms of progressive confinement.

The above comparative discussion may suggest that while the JJ Act, 2015, has included several reformative provisions in it, the 'Living Conditions In Institutions For Children In Conflict With Law Manual, 2017' prepared by the Ministry of Women and Child Development[44] also suggests several ways for reformation and rehabilitation of children in conflict with the law within the institutional system. However, due to many factors, including lack of funding facilities, lack of proper infrastructure and properly trained officials, the JJ Act, 2015

---

[41] J. Junger-Tas and S. H. Decker, *International Handbook of Juvenile Justice* (Springer, 2006): 37–64.

[42] Junger-Tas and Decker, *International Handbook of Juvenile Justice.*

[43] Halder Debarati and A. Shetty, 'Regulating Road Traffic Violation by Youth in India: A Therapeutic Jurisprudential Approach', in *Restorative Justice in Educational Settings and Policies: Bridging the East and West*, eds. D. S. W. Wong and T. Gavrielides (London: RJAll Publications, 2019). ISBN 978-1-911634-07-2.

[44] For more, see https://wcd.nic.in/sites/default/files/Final%20Manual%20 24%20April%202017_5.pdf, accessed 23 January 2020.

may not have achieved the goals of reformative justice till now. The noteworthiest point in this regard is lack of infrastructure for dealing with physically and mentally disabled children in conflict with the law in many regions. It may be apt to note the following observation of Professor Ved Kumari in this regard:

> It appears that Juvenile Justice System in India has not been a continuous process resulting from an uninterrupted concern for children. The timing and content of various developments related to Juvenile Justice System have close relationship with reforms taking place elsewhere in the world rather than with the demands of children in the country.[45]

Conclusion and Suggestions

The above discussions may suggest India's juvenile justice administration system needs more administrative efforts to achieve the goals of reformative justice and restorative justice. While the JJ Act mandates the formation of specialized courts and a reformative system, reporting of offences, especially those against women and children and online offences committed by children, is still less. Schools may also not have proper counsellors and a reporting mechanism for dealing with cases of sexual offences and physical bullying and online bullying that may not be categorized as ragging but which may be even more devastating than ragging for young minds. It is necessary to evaluate the entire juvenile justice system in the light of its efficient applicability, approachability of the system by the beneficiaries and the impact of the justice delivery mechanism on society as a whole. This chapter suggests that the present law and the juvenile justice system as a whole should adopt positive practical aspects of juvenile justice systems of other countries and develop more therapeutic approaches for better achievement of the objectives of the JJ Act.

---

[45] Ved Kumari, *The Juvenile Justice System in India: From Welfare to Rights*, 2nd edition (New Delhi: Oxford University Press, 2010).

Chapter 13

Child Labour in India

A Critical Legal Analysis

Rubel Bareja and Vishwajeet Singh Shekhawat

INTRODUCTION

With a population of more than 1 billion, India has the highest number of children in the world. However, at the same time, India still has not been able to provide satisfactory economic infrastructure to engage all children in learning, allow them to enjoy childhood and keep children aware of the vicious cycle of child labour. The International Labour Organization (ILO) has provided a holistic explanation of the concept of child labour in the following words: '"Child Labour" is often defined as a work that deprives children of their childhood, their potential and their dignity, and that is harmful to physical and mental development'.[1] Children may be forced to work against their will in hazardous conditions. They may be used in the labour market with or without pay, at less than minimum wages in the former case, and they may also be considered as additional labourers along with their parents. Such children may not be paid for the work they do; the payments may directly go to their parents or guardians, who may or may not provide basic meals to their children out of the meagre salary

[1] See http://libguides.ilo.org/child-labour-en, accessed 20 February 2018.

that the children may earn. The World Report on Child Labour, 2015 prepared by ILO suggests that the majority of children in India who may be engaged in child labour may be concentrated in some specific states, including Bihar, Uttar Pradesh, Rajasthan, Madhya Pradesh and Maharashtra.[2] There may be different and varied reasons for engaging children in child labour. Irrespective of the reasons, as Basu and Van (1998) observed, 'child labour is often characterized as pernicious and evil, something that has to be unequivocally rejected'.[3] According to a United Nations Children's Fund (UNICEF) report, India has 10.1 million child laborers.[4] International instruments, including conventions, declarations, treaties, etc., suggest that largely there can be socio-economic–cultural reasons for the growth of the child-labourer population in India. Among socio-economic reasons, poverty is considered to be the main reason for pushing children into the labour market. According to the report Poverty and Shared Prosperity 2016 published by the World Bank,[5] India has the highest number of people living below the poverty line.[6] Children from such families may be engaged in labour either by their parents or by themselves. The majority of such children may be engaged in the unorganized sector, including in the brick kiln industry, garment manufacturing industry, agricultural work, and street-side eateries.[7] Child labourers may also be found working as porters in large vegetable markets, in family enterprises, especially in the stone polishing industry, in the bookbinding industry and also in match- and firework-manufacturing industry. Apart from these apparently positive job sectors, children may also be used in the garbage picking and segregating sector for collecting recyclable materials

---

[2] International Labour Organization's World Report on Child Labour, 2015.

[3] K. Basu and P. Van, 'The Economics of Child Labor', *The American Economic Review* 88, no. 3 (1998): 412–27.

[4] For more, see Child Labor and Exploitation, https://www.unicef.org/india/what-we-do/child-labour-exploitation, accessed 21 January 2020.

[5] See http://www.worldbank.org/en/publication/poverty-and-shared-prosperity, 21 March 2018.

[6] Ibid.

[7] For more, see 5 sectors where Child labour can be found majorly in India (19 September 2017), https://www.savethechildren.in/resource-centre/articles/5-sectors-where-child-labour-can-be-found-majorly, accessed 21 February 2020.

from waste. The opportunities of earning in such sectors are huge. Children may be lured into such jobs by the promise of a midday meal, the quality of which may not be good, and a meagre wage. In several cases where children may be engaged in family enterprises, the parents may justify such engagement on the basis of high cost of labourers, low earnings, extreme poverty, etc. There are multiple reasons for the ever-growing population of child labourers in India: there may be lack of inspection and reporting facilities, especially in rural areas, the families of child labourers may not be educated or literate and may have unknowingly entered into bonded labour wherein they may be forced to engage their children, etc. Lack of government-aided or private open school facilities to provide quality education to children could also be another factor for demotivating families and children from attending schools. Families living below the poverty line may need more earning members: in this case, if the children are engaged in schools, they may not be able to earn and contribute to running the family. The existing schools, on the other hand, may not prepare children for the job market immediately. Lack of vocational training institutes in rural and semi-urban areas may also play a key role in the growth of child labour. Further, many families having their own enterprises of poultry, animal husbandry, agriculture, crafts making, small-scale garment manufacturing, sewing, stone polishing and jewellery making, eateries, etc., may consider training their children in their traditional family enterprise to be more useful than sending them to school for formal education, which may take more than 11 years to be complete. The researchers Bachman (2000) observed:

> ...in many developing countries, it is popular notion and socially accepted norm that child labour, child work and other economic related issues do not contribute negatively in the development of a child. Instead, it has valuable contributions towards child growth and professional grooming, making them a responsible citizen.[8]

Such understanding may justify why families may encourage more children to be engaged in the labour market rather than in the formal

[8] S. L. Bachman, 'A New Economics of Child Labour: Searching for Answers Behind the Headlines', *Journal of International Affairs* 53, no. 2: 545–72.

school system. It is also unfortunate to note that unorganized sectors, including small-scale family enterprises, may not have a strong labour union to support labourers, including child labourers, in cases of exploitation by employers, moneylenders and industry owners, who take huge advantage of the plight of poverty and illiteracy or lack of education of poor people.

International organizations, including ILO and UNICEF, have repeatedly prepared policies, reports and surveys on child labour and the negative impacts of child labour on the holistic development of children. These organizations have also extended help to state machineries and non-governmental organizations (NGOs) working to eradicate child labour and rescue and rehabilitate child labourers. India has also made several laws and policies for prohibiting child labour and rescuing and rehabilitating child labourers. However, in spite of such efforts, the population of child labourers is growing. This chapter therefore aims to carry on an exploratory study on the international instruments, domestic laws, etc., addressing child labour to search for lacunae and suggest possible solutions in this regard. It carries out discussions in four parts, including the introduction. The second part deals with the international instruments addressing child labour, and the third part discusses the domestic laws and policies regarding child labour. The fourth part offers the conclusion.

INTERNATIONAL INSTRUMENTS FOR PROHIBITION OF CHILD LABOUR

The Universal Declaration of Human Rights (UDHR), 1948 in its first eight articles lays down the right to protection against exploitation in any form. Articles 1 and 2 deal with the right to life and right to protection against discrimination based on age, gender, class, nationality, etc. The latter right is further reflected in Articles 6, 7 and 8, which discuss the right to universal recognition as a person before the law, right to equality and equal protection of laws and right to effective remedy for any violation of human rights by competent tribunals. Article 3 highlights the right to life, liberty and security of persons, which must also be supported by other rights for proper realization by every human being. Articles 4 and 5 discuss the right to protection against slavery and servitude and right to protection against torture and cruel, inhuman or degrading treatment.[9] Child labourers may be subjected to violation of all such rights, because neither they nor their parents may be aware of their basic rights. In order to make the state parties responsible for the protection of rights, especially the right to protection against economic and social exploitation of human beings irrespective of gender and age, the International Covenant on Economic, Social and Cultural Rights was created in 1966, which mandates the state parties to ensure the right to protection against exploitation in the labour market, job market and society as a whole.[10] This international instrument also mentions the right of children to holistic development, including the right to education for all. To further guarantee the rights mentioned in the above instrument, ILO and the United Nations (UN) Convention on the Rights of the Child (CRC) also laid down several principles for ensuring the rights of children to protection against degrading treatment, child labour, etc. As one of the oldest and integral agencies of the UN, ILO is engaged in taking legislative and administrative measures to protect human beings from being exploited in the labour sectors and to create better job opportunities for the welfare and benefit of society as a whole. The International Labour Conference, the main organ of ILO, through its multiple reports, policies, etc., has shown that several countries, including India, have a huge problem of child labour, which may be considered as the worst form of abuse.[11] In order to address

---

[9] For more, see Universal Declaration of Human Rights, https://www.un.org/en/universal-declaration-human-rights/, accessed 12 December 2019.

[10] For more, see International Covenant on Economic, Social and Cultural Rights, https://www.ohchr.org/en/professionalinterest/pages/cescr.aspx, accessed 11 December 2019.

[11] For more, see Mary Gray Davidson, 'The International Labour Organization's Latest Campaign to End Child Labor: Will it Succeed Where Others Have Failed', *Transnational Law & Contemporary Problems* 11 (2001): 203, https://heinonline.org/HOL/Page?handle=hein.journals/tlcp11&div=16&g_sent=1&casa_token=dwsv83Oz_eEAAAAA:ID7bZyxl_d8becd45kVLhIF9-iv-

the problems of child labour, ILO created two core conventions, namely Convention 138—Minimum Age Convention, 1973—and Convention 182—Worst Forms of Child Labour Convention. The former convention deals with the minimum age of employees: it sets the standard age limit for employment at 15 years, below which no human being would be permitted to enter the employment sector even if the same is a home enterprise. This age limit is set specifically to facilitate children to finish their basic compulsory education.[12] Further, the convention also mandates that no one below the age of 18 would be eligible to take up any employment in a hazardous work environment that may be detrimental to the physical and mental health of children. The second convention, that is, Convention 182, deals with the worst forms of child labour and states that using children for slavery and servitude, child prostitution, pornographic purposes or any other illegal and illicit work that may involve physical and sexual exploitation of children may be considered as the worst forms of child labour, and the same must be prohibited by the state parties through their own mechanisms.[13] The ILO conventions and principles for the prevention of child labour and child exploitation mandate that each state party ratify the conventions and provide periodic reports to ILO for further review of the situation. Paragraph 5(e) of the ILO Constitution reflects this, which runs thus:

> …Member except that it shall report to the Director-General of the International Labour Office, at appropriate intervals as requested by the Governing Body, the position of its law and practice in regard to the matters dealt with in the Convention, showing the extent to which effect has been given, or is proposed to be given, to any of the provisions of the Convention by legislation, administrative action, collective agreement or otherwise and stating the difficulties which prevent or delay the ratification of such Convention.[14]

M-b0itVzFZ5pwP3eXv_UX3cepKQtPQ_p2DH9iSoyW0R5Ww&collection=journals, accessed 12 December 2019.

[12] Article 2(3), C. No. 138, The Minimum Age Convention, 1973.

[13] Worst Forms of Child Labour Convention (1999), Article 3, C. No. 182.

[14] Article 19, Constitution of ILO.

The UN CRC, on the other hand, lays down rights for children for their holistic development. According to this convention, any person who is under 18 must be considered as a child.[15] However, at the same time, it also expands the scope to include any other age group to be considered for attaining majority by stating in Article 1: '...unless under the law applicable to the child, majority is attained earlier'.[16] This would indicate that the minimum-age ceiling by ILO of age 14 for joining employment may be accepted as legal, provided such employment is not hazardous, does not fall within the category of worst forms of labour and does not hamper the holistic growth of children. However, the UN CRC also mandates that for the proper enjoyment of childhood, children must be guaranteed the right to life and right to survival,[17] right to proper parental care, love and affection for complete enjoyment of the right to life,[18] right to protection against exploitation of any form,[19] etc. The convention also indicates that the welfare of children should be given prime importance during the preparation of any policy, laws, etc., by the state parties.[20] The UN CRC, through two of its optional protocols, namely Optional Protocol on the Sale of Children, Child Prostitution and Child Pornography and Optional Protocol on the Involvement of Children in Armed Conflict, also mandates that no children may be used and engaged in a job that may include child prostitution, child online sexual abuse, usage of children as soldiers in armed conflicts, terrorism, etc.

India has ratified conventions of ILO, as well as those of the UN CRC and its optional protocols, to create domestic laws, policies and guidelines for prohibition of child labour and rescue and rehabilitation of child labourers. However, even after such steps, the problem of child

---

[15] See Article 1 of the United Nations (UN) Convention on the Rights of the Child (CRC).

[16] Ibid.

[17] Article 6 of the UN CRC.

[18] Article 3 of the UN CRC.

[19] Article 19 of the UN CRC.

[20] For a better understanding, see https://www.ohchr.org/en/professionalinterest/pages/crc.aspx, accessed 21 January 2020.

labour has not been reduced as expected. It is therefore necessary to analyse the domestic laws of India in this regard.[21]

INDIAN LEGAL UNDERSTANDING OF CHILD LABOUR

The regulations prohibiting child labour in India may be traced back to the colonial era, to the introduction of the Factory Act of 1881 (which was also the first factories legislation), which prescribed minimum age criteria for workers and prohibited engagement of child workers in two factories on a single day. The Act subsequently got amended in 1891 to increase the minimum age for employment in factories from 7 to 9 years. In 1911, the said Act was further amended to categorize certain jobs as dangerous for children. The amendment also included the concept of 'certificate of fitness', which can be found in the provisions of the Factories Act, 1948.[22] This certificate of fitness would indicate whether the prospective employee would be physically and mentally matured to be engaged in the work. With the introduction of ILO Convention 5, which deals with the minimum age for engagement in industries, the Indian provision also increased the minimum age for employment in industries to 14 years. The ILO convention indicated that the concept of industry may include mines, quarries, etc., that may be hazardous and dangerous for children below 14 years of age. The Factories Act also restricted the working hours of child workers to 6 hours. Later, several other provisions, including the Indian Ports (Amendment) Act, 1931, Indian Mines (Amendment) Act, 1935, etc., also followed the amendments in the Factories Act and restricted the age limit and working hours of children accordingly. However, it was only with the Children (Pledging of Labour) Act of 1933 that the problem of 'child bondage' was acknowledged for the first time in India under the British rule. Section 2 of Children (Pledging of Labour) Act, 1933, clearly mandated in this regard the following:

[21] Article 3(1), C. No. 138, The Minimum Age Convention, 1973.
[22] Section 69(2) (a), The Factories Act, 1948.

> It is expedient to prohibit the making of agreements to pledge the labour of children, and the employment of children whose labour has been pledged.[23]

Further, the Employment of Children Act, 1938 also needs to be mentioned in this regard, which for the first time addressed the issue of child labour in colonial India. This legislation finds its root in the 23rd session of the International Labour Conference, 1937. Article 9[24] of the said convention requires special mention, as it recommended that employment of children below 13 years of age should be prohibited, especially in certain categories of employment which may be extremely hazardous for children. It further indicated that children below the age of 14 should not be engaged in the work of transportation of goods on docks and wharves.

After India's independence, the Constitution of India also included several articles to safeguard the interests of children, especially by way of Article 24, which deals with employment of children below the age of 14 in any factory or mine. Article 24 states: 'no child below the age of fourteen years shall be employed to work in any factory or mine or engaged in any other hazardous employment'. This provision indicates that the right to protection against child labour in hazardous employment sectors is an inherent part of the right to life under Article 21. Article 23 of the constitution further mandates that no person should be made to work as a beggar and that any sort of exploitation in the workplace must be prohibited and be made a penal offence. This provision also indicates that trafficking for the purpose of begging or prostitution, including child prostitution, must be prohibited in all forms.

Further, Article 39(e) of the constitution also addresses the issue of child labour, which may result due to economic necessities for survival. It states: 'the tender age of children are not abused and that citizens are not forced by economic necessity to enter avocations unsuited to

[23] Section 2, Children (Pledging of Labour) Act, 1933.

[24] ILO (12 January 2018), http://www.ilo.org/dyn/normlex/en/f?p=NORMLEXPUB:12100:0::NO::P12100_ILO_CODE:C060.

their age or strength'.[25] Article 39(f) further mentions that 'children are given opportunities and facilities to develop in a healthy manner and in conditions of freedom and dignity and that childhood and youth are protected against exploitation and against moral and material abandonment'.[26] As a Directive Principle, this provision mandates that the state should make laws and policies to ensure safe childhood and protection against all sorts of socio-economic exploitation. In line with these provisions, the Supreme Court, in the landmark decision in the case of *J. R. Unnikrishnan v. State of Andhra Pradesh*,[27] declared that the right to free education until the age of 14 should be considered as a fundamental right. The court also mandated that no child should be employed in any work that may deprive the said child from his/her fundamental rights. As a result, the Parliament, through the 86th amendment in 2002, added Article 21A, substituted Article 45 and amended Article 51A to make the 'right to education' part of the constitution. However, until the 1980s, there were not many provisions to deal with the problem of child labour except some, including the Factories Act, 1948, Plantations Labour Act, 1951, Mines Act, 1952, Motor Transport Workers Act of 1961, Beedi and Cigar Workers (Conditions of Employment) Act, 1966, etc., which majorly addressed the minimum age of employment of workers. These provisions however did not necessarily prescribe any heavy penalties for engaging children in hazardous, exploitative work, and nor did they throw much light on rescue and rehabilitation of child labourers. The courts, on the other hand, continued to develop child labour jurisprudence through public interest litigations during this time.

It was only in 1979 with the Gurupadaswamy Committee report on the status of child labour in India that the existing apathy towards child labour in India was acknowledged.[28] The committee noted grave violations of the laws, difficulties in regulation and the inadequately prescribed penalties. As per the suggestions of the committee, the Child

---

[25] Article 39 (e), The Constitution of India, 1950.

[26] Article 39(f), The Constitution of India, 1950.

[27] J. R. Unnikrishnan v. State of Andhra Pradesh, (1993) 1 SCC 645.

[28] For more, see https://labour.gov.in/childlabour/about-child-labour, accessed 12 December 2019.

Labour (Prohibition and Regulation) Act, 1986 was enacted, which was the first umbrella legislation in independent India to holistically address the problem of child labour. This Act, which has undergone several amendments since its inception, prohibits employment of children in certain specified hazardous occupations and provides clear mandates for safe working conditions which every employer must follow. In 1987, with the introduction of the National Policy on Child Labour, the issues of child labour and rescue and rehabilitation of child labourers were acknowledged and frameworks for surveying child labourers, working conditions, etc., were planned. This policy also prescribes measures for rescue and rehabilitation of child labourers and their admission into special schools for enabling them to join the mainstream formal schooling system.[29] The 1986 Act and the Employment of Children Act, 1938 address the issue of banning child labour quite in the same manner. However, the former differs from the latter in terms of mandating the formation of a child labour technical advisory committee to carry out investigations and advise on the issue of hazardous work environments for children.[30] The 1986 Act was further amended a few times so as to add and repeal certain provisions. The government of India through a resolution in 2003 adopted a National Charter for Children that included a clause concerning protection of children from economic exploitation and from performing tasks hazardous to their well-being. Later, in the year 2005, the Commissions for Protection of Child Rights Act were enacted. However, the most significant amendment that took place was the Child Labour (Prohibition and Regulation) Amendment Act, 2016.

The amendment brought in significant changes to address prohibition of engagement of children in all sorts of occupations and engagement of adolescent children in the age group of 14–18 years in hazardous environments.[31] The short title of the 1986 Act was amended to 'Child and Adolescent Labour (Prohibition and

[29] For more, see National Child Labour Policy (12 February 2018), http://ncpcr.gov.in/showfile.php?lid=129.

[30] N. Burra, *Born to Work: Child Labour in India* (Delhi: Oxford University Press, 1995).

[31] Child and Adolescent Labour (Amendment) Act, 2016.

Regulation) Act'.[32] The amended Act imposed a penalty of ₹50,000 on first-time offenders engaging children, violating the provisions. Further, it also increased the imprisonment term from 6 months to 2 years, made the offences cognizable and increased imprisonment from 1 to 3 years for repeat offenders. In the case of offences by parents through sending their children for employment, the provision prescribed a fine of ₹10,000, especially in cases of repeated offenders. However, on a close examination of the amended Act, it may be seen that the provision suffers from numerous flaws. For example, the number of hazardous occupations for children was brought down to three from an exhaustive list of 83. The new list included only mining, explosives and occupations mentioned in the Factories Act. Therefore, with the said change in the list, jobs in chemicals mixing units, brick kilns and battery recycling units (to name a few) got erased so as not to be considered hazardous occupations. Also, even the occupations listed as hazardous can be removed, which can be seen from a plain reading of Section 4, which states that the occupations on the list can be altered not by the Parliament but by government authorities at their own discretion. Further, the Act does not prescribe penalties for bad working conditions. The second provision that got amended was Section 3(5), and it allowed child labour in 'family or family enterprises' and allowed children to be 'an artist in an audio-visual entertainment industry'. The law prohibits employment of children below the age of 14. However, the proviso attached to the provision allows children to aid their families in business after school hours, and in this way it allows children to work in family enterprises without any constraint or fixed number of hours. Also, it allows adolescents (aged 14–18) to work in non-hazardous occupations. Presently, there may be about 32.3 million children in the age group of 15–19 who may be engaged in such occupations, according to the 2011 census. The legitimization of such engagements has made it possible for children from debt-ridden families to get engaged in work, in some cases sacrificing their education. Most such children get engaged in the family enterprise, including beedi rolling, *bindi* making, *papad* making, embroidery work, packing, handicrafts and the manufacturing of several other products,

[32] Ibid.

which has been camouflaged as minimum work for helping parents or adult siblings. This set-up also hides several forms of oppression and exploitation of children.

Thus, the 2016 Act contradicts the Juvenile Justice (Care and Protection) of Children Act of 2000, which prescribes punishment for engaging children in any sort of hazardous work as has been indicated by international and domestic legal documents.

However, the situation took a positive turn in 2017 when the negative aspects of the 2016 Act were acknowledged to a certain extent and the Ministry of Labour and Employment introduced the Child Labour (Prohibition and Regulation) Amendment Rules, 2017. These rules clarify that children should not be engaged in a non-hazardous family enterprise during school hours. They also mandate that children cannot be engaged in any work during natural hours of rest, school study hours, etc. It must be noted that while the 2016 Act widened the lacuna in regard to engagement of children in work, the 2017 Rules tried to repair the damages through fixing school hours and rest hours that are necessary for the holistic development of children.

The situation was best explained by Nobel Peace Prize winner Kailash Satyarthi, who commented: 'The Child Labour (Prohibition and Regulation Amendment) Act, 2016, had some lacunae when it was enacted, but the rules notified recently by the government have addressed the weaknesses'.[33]

CONCLUSION

After analysing the statistics and the standards that India follows in comparison to the international instruments and practices, it is certain that there is still a long way to go in finding solutions for the child labour problem in India. Though the efforts have been marvellous so far, there is a need for renewed action and hard work to eradicate this evil. Skill development has been an important step taken by the Indian government, and it is seen that many people are involved in their

[33] S. Jha, 'Satyarthi Backs New Child Labour Law', *The Hindu* (11 June 2017).

family business. Since there are a number of occupations that include family enterprise and traditional craft, it is suggested that children be provided vocational training for improving their skills. In many cases, it is seen that working directly for a business for the purpose of earning resources can be harmful to the physical and mental capacities of a child, because then the goal would not be learning but it would be working or earning. There is no denying the fact that in the globalized world of today there is a need to preserve and support traditional arts and crafts of such family-based units, but this should not act as a hindrance to children's right to avail quality education as enshrined under the Right to Education Act, 2009. This problem can be resolved if the school curriculum introduces such courses along with other subjects. Consequently, this would lead to inclusion of training with education in the curriculum.

Child labour is not only the result of poverty, but it may also cause poverty, as child labourers may take up the job opportunities of adults because the former are considered cheap labourers. Hence, the state should concentrate on improving the living conditions of parents to prevent their children from getting engaged in work.

The state must also ensure a decent work environment for working children in the age group of 15–18 years, which further needs to be strictly regulated. Household poverty is the prime cause of child labour, and thus a decent work environment, social protection and minimum wages should be ensured by the authorities in order to support poor families' livelihood. Finally, a strict and robust mechanism should be formulated to assign the accountability of all the relevant stakeholders in society, and larger budgets must be allotted towards eradicating the problem of child labour, as it concerns the future of the country. Rights can be declared and policies can be formulated, but unless the lives of children in their families and communities are improved, all such efforts shall be futile.

Chapter 14

Right to Education
A Critical Analysis

Anshuman Mohit Chaturvedi and Dhriti Gupta

INTRODUCTION

While drafting the Constitution of India after the country's independence, the framers of the constitution decided to emphasize the right to equality (as enshrined in Article 14), freedom of speech and expression, formation of opinions, etc. (as enshrined in Article 19), and right to life (as enshrined in Article 21) to arrive at a broader understanding of the right to education, which is a basic necessity for survival. The Universal Declaration of Human Rights (UDHR), 1948 and the Convention on the Rights of the Child (CRC) provide that every individual, especially children, has the right to education and that the same must be realized for enjoying the right to life, right to protection against socio-economic exploitation and right to holistic development (specifically for children).[1] The right to education has been considered as a sacred right that must be provided to all, irrespective of gender, nationality, ethnicity, etc. Both the UDHR and

---

[1] For more, see C. Raj Kumar, 'International Human Rights Perspectives on the Fundamental Right to Education—Integration of Human Rights and Human Development in the Indian Constitution', *Tulane Journal of International and Comparative Law* 12 (2004): 237.

the United Nations (UN) CRC mandate that state parties must provide mechanisms to ensure such right.[2] Article 28 of the UN CRC, 1989 must be analysed in this regard. It states as follows:

> 1. States Parties recognize the right of the child to education, and with a view to achieving this right progressively and on the basis of equal opportunity, they shall, in particular:(a) Make primary education compulsory and available free to all;(b) Encourage the development of different forms of secondary education, including general and vocational education, make them available and accessible to every child, and take appropriate measures such as the introduction of free education and offering financial assistance in case of need;(c) Make higher education accessible to all on the basis of capacity by every appropriate means;(d) Make educational and vocational information and guidance available and accessible to all children;(e) Take measures to encourage regular attendance at schools and the reduction of drop-out rates. 2. States Parties shall take all appropriate measures to ensure that school discipline is administered in a manner consistent with the child's human dignity and in conformity with the present Convention.3. States Parties shall promote and encourage international cooperation in matters relating to education, in particular with a view to contributing to the elimination of ignorance and illiteracy throughout the world and facilitating access to scientific and technical knowledge and modern teaching methods. In this regard, particular account shall be taken of the needs of developing countries.[3]

The Constitution of India through its Directive Principles of State Policy under Article 45 ensures guarantees for such rights by guaranteeing to provide free and compulsory education to all children below the age of 14 years. However, the right to education could not be recognized as a fundamental right before 2002 when the Parliament amended the constitution for introducing the right to life as a fundamental right under Article 21A, acknowledging free and compulsory education as a basic right for children in the age group of 6–14 years. The amendment was made possible largely because

---

[2] For more, see the Universal Declaration of Human Rights.

[3] See Article 28 of the United Nations (UN) Convention on the Rights of the Child (CRC) @ https://www.ohchr.org/en/professionalinterest/pages/crc.aspx.

of the case of *Mohini Jain v. State of Karnataka*[4] in which the Supreme Court considered the right to education as a fundamental right that must exist beyond the meaning of the right to life as guaranteed under Article 21. However, it was much later—in 2009—that the Right of Children to Free and Compulsory Education Act, 2009 (RTE) was introduced so that children in the age group of 6–14 years may get free and compulsory basic education, and the Act mandated that such education must also be quality education. The RTE casts an obligation on the appropriate government and local authorities to provide and ensure admission, attendance and completion of elementary education by all children in the 6–14 age group. While Article 21A guarantees the right to education for children in the age group of 6–14 years, the RTE lays down principles and mandates realization of such rights. It may be noted that prior to the recognition of the right to education as a fundamental right for every individual and the enactment of the RTE, several attempts were made by the government to formalize the procedure of imparting education. The earliest such government policy was the National Policy on Education, 1968, which emphasized imparting education on the basis of a three-language formula so that children may be trained in English, Hindi and the regional language. The policy also emphasized engagement of qualified teachers for elementary education.[5] Later, on the basis of a recommendation of the National Policy on Education, 1986, the District Primary Education Programme (DPEP) was launched in the year 1993, which aimed at achieving universal primary education. The DPEP was launched over several phases and covered 272 districts of the country. However, in spite of the vigorous efforts, the DPEP could not yield positive results, especially for education for girls. The programme to a large extent failed to motivate parents to send their children, especially girls, to complete their elementary education. As a result, children were found in labour markets and in home enterprises, and several children were also forced to get married even before they attained the age of 16.[6] The DPEP was

---

[4] Mohini Jain v. State of Karnataka, (1992) AIR 1858.

[5] For more, see http://www.ncert.nic.in/oth_anoun/npe86.pdf, accessed 21 January 2020.

[6] See Raj Kumar, 'International Human Rights Perspectives'.

however successful in terms of enrolment of minority children, and it introduced a new approach to educational policy in India.[7] Soon, the government introduced Sarva Shiksha Abhiyan (SSA) in 2001, which aimed at universalization of elementary education in a time-bound manner, as mandated by the 86th Amendment to the constitution for providing free and compulsory education to all children between 6 and 14 years of age. The uniqueness of the programme lay in its outreach, as it aimed at enrolling the maximum children in elementary education funded by the government. The campaigning for SSA was made vigorous to reach out to the maximum parents and children.[8] However, it was on the basis of Mohini Jain's case[9] that a need was felt to expand the scope of free and compulsory education to other elite schools, including government and private schools that may have better pedagogy and facilities for school education but which may not provide admission to children coming from socio-economically poor backgrounds due to their huge fee structures. It was with this mission that in October 2003 the first draft of the Right to Education Bill, 2003 was prepared, which finally got presidential assent in 2009 to become a full-fledged Act.[10]

This chapter aims to analyse the RTE to understand how far children from socio-economically poor backgrounds and children with special needs may be benefitted in terms of actual realization of the right to free and compulsory basic education. This chapter is divided into three parts, including the introduction. The second part carries out a detailed analysis of the RTE from the perspective of the basic and fundamental rights guaranteed by the constitution, and the third part offers the conclusion.

---

[7] District Primary Education Programme (DPEP) Twenty Second Joint Review Mission State Report: West Bengal (January 12–20, 2006).

[8] Gursharan Singh Kainth, 'A Mission Approach to Sarva Shiksha Abhiyan', *Economic and Political Weekly* 41, no. 30 (July 29–August 4, 2006): 3288–91, https://www.jstor.org/stable/4418492?casa_token=5ZoKUFSuLlsAAAAA:_BakqwKIpiq8WBHLcw2_69_a3sqbyPPnpODYx9-xK_K2E58IoFMgIwjqRFfZgN4lBaH0z0wSaCVc7qN9GI61KNEAnw0Sc2DynsUDAikzGe-M39dP158&seq=1#metadata_info_tab_contents, accessed12 December 2019.

[9] See *Mohini Jain v. State of Karnataka.*

[10] For more, see http://righttoeducation.in/know-your-rte/about, accessed 6 July 2017.

RIGHT OF CHILDREN TO FREE AND COMPULSORY EDUCATION ACT, 2009: A CRITICAL ANALYSIS

The RTE is a detailed and comprehensive piece of legislation that includes provisions related to schools, teachers, curriculum, evaluation, access and specific division of duties and responsibilities among different stakeholders for ensuring the right to elementary education for all children. However, in the preliminary portion, it may be seen that the RTE has excluded institutions imparting religious instructions, including Vedic Pathshalas, madrasas, etc., from its scope. Such exclusion is in accordance with the right to freedom of religion enshrined in Article 25, which speaks about the freedom of conscience and free profession, practice and propagation of religion, Article 26, which speaks about the freedom to manage religious affairs, and Article 28, which speaks about the freedom to attend any institution for religious instructions.[11] The RTE, while bringing under its scope all children in the age group of 6–14, also mentions under Section 2 about bringing children with physical and mental disability, children from socio-economically poor backgrounds, etc., within its definition of children.[12] This has extended the scope of the RTE to all children who may or may not be provided school admission due to their physical incapacity or mental maturity level. The definition of school, on the other hand, has been extended to cover government-aided, unaided and specified categories of schools with distinctive features.[13] Such expansion of the scope of the definition of school has been made necessarily to ensure that children need not travel far distances to attend school, which may deprive children of their right to leisure, rest and basic childhood rights.[14] For ensuring such facilities to children, the RTE however places the burden on the appropriate government and

---

[11] For a better understanding, see Chapter 1 of the Right of Children to Free and Compulsory Education Act (RTE).

[12] See Section 2 of the RTE.

[13] See Section 2(n) of the RTE.

[14] See Section 3 of the RTE, which states: 'Right of child to free and compulsory education.—1[(1) Every child of the age of six to fourteen years, including a child referred to in clause (d) or clause (e) of section 2, shall have the right to free and compulsory education in a neighbourhood school till the completion of his or her elementary education'.

local authorities to establish schools within their neighbourhood as well.[15] Chapter II of the RTE further provides that for completion of elementary education, no child would need to pay any fees, including any donation, which would jeopardize the basic aim of the RTE.[16] This provision further mentions that if in case any child could not be admitted to a school earlier for any specific reason, no school shall deny admission if the said child wishes to join any school in the locality, and such child should be put in the standard according to his/her intellectual maturity level.[17] The provision also gives the liberty to the child and his/her parents to seek transfer from one school to another and makes it mandatory for the head teacher to provide a proper transfer certificate so that his/her admission into the new school may not be hampered. Chapter III, on the other hand, emphasizes the responsibility of the appropriate state government and local authorities to build more schools with child-friendly infrastructure and provide financial assistance to the schools that may be aided, and also to children so that they do not drop out due to economic limitations of their families. Further, this chapter also puts the onus on the parents to compulsorily admit their children for elementary education.[18] Section 11 is noteworthy in this regard, which speaks about the government's liability to ensure preschool education and early childhood care; it states:

> With a view to prepare children above the age of three years for elementary education and to provide early childhood care and education for all children until they complete the age of six years, the appropriate Government may make necessary arrangement for providing free pre-school education for such children.[19]

Also see Section 6 of the RTE, which states: 'Duty of appropriate Government and local authority to establish school.—For carrying out the provisions of this Act, the appropriate Government and the local authority shall establish, within such area or limits of neighbourhood, as may be prescribed, a school, where it is not so established, within a period of three years from the commencement of this Act'.

[15] Ibid.

[16] For more, see Section 3 of the RTE.

[17] See Section 4 of the RTE.

[18] See Sections 6, 7, 8, 9 and 10 of the RTE.

[19] See Section 11 of the RTE.

This particular section is extremely significant for the realization of the right to early childhood care for children, and this has also been indicated in the international covenants of civil and political rights and social, economic and cultural rights,[20] the UN CRC and the Juvenile Justice (Care and Protection of Children) Act, 2015. Chapter IV discusses the responsibilities of schools and teachers towards children for their realization of their right to basic elementary education. The RTE mandates that the government, local authorities and schools must ensure that the children receive education from compassionate and trained teachers. While unaided private schools may afford to have well-trained teachers, aided schools situated in rural areas or in municipal areas may not have proper infrastructure and qualified teachers, due to corrupt practices in selecting teachers and building infrastructure.[21] Section 23 of the RTE is noteworthy in this regard, which states:

> (1) Any person possessing such minimum qualifications, as laid down by an academic authority, authorised by the Central Government, by notification, shall be eligible for appointment as a teacher.(2) Where a State does not have adequate institutions offering courses or training in teacher education, or teachers possessing minimum qualifications as laid down under sub-section (1) are not available in sufficient numbers, the Central Government may, if it deems necessary, by notification, relax the minimum qualifications required for appointment as a teacher, for such period, not exceeding five years, as may be specified in that notification: Provided that a teacher who, at the commencement of this Act, does not possess minimum qualifications as laid down under sub-section (1), shall acquire such minimum qualifications within a period of five years.(3) The salary and allowances payable to, and the terms and conditions of service of, teachers shall be such as may be prescribed.[22]

The RTE further mandates that the appointment of teachers should be corruption-free and that teachers must be engaged only in teaching activities, unless there are specific needs that may require the

---

[20] For more, see https://www.ohchr.org/en/professionalinterest/pages/ccpr.aspx and https://www.ohchr.org/en/professionalinterest/pages/cescr.aspx, accessed 12 December 2019.

[21] See Raj Kumar, 'International Human Rights Perspectives'.

[22] See Section 23 of the RTE.

government to engage teachers in other work.[23] Section 25 of this Act, on the other hand, indicates the duties of teachers, stating that teachers must be dedicated to completion of the curriculum, must not discriminate between students, must maintain punctuality and must provide proper and fare assessment reports of each child to the school authorities, who in turn should provide the same to the government stakeholders constituted specifically for the same purpose. The statute further prohibits any act of favouritism by teachers, especially stating that teachers appointed by schools for this purpose are prohibited from taking private tuitions, which may also motivate the teachers to provide better training to the children who may be able to pay him/her better than the children engaged in schools under the RTE.[24] This section further mentions about taking disciplinary action in a fair way in case a teacher fails to perform his/her duties in the proper way, stating:

> ...A teacher committing default in performance of duties specified in sub-section (1), shall be liable to disciplinary action under the service rules applicable to him or her:
>
> Provided that before taking such disciplinary action, reasonable opportunity of being heard shall be afforded to such teacher.[25]

As may be seen, Chapter IV makes it mandatory for the stakeholders to remove all sorts of difficulties in achieving the goals of the RTE, Article 21A and Chapter IV of the Constitution of India, which speaks about Directive Principles of the state. It mandates that no school should demand capitation fees for the purpose of elementary education and that all admissions should be made on the basis of age proof, which must be ascertained through the birth certificate provided by appropriate municipal authorities. However, it also provides that if a child cannot produce any birth certificate, the said child should not be denied admission.[26] It may be noted that this particular welfare measure would go a long way to benefit children from nomadic families and

---

[23] See Section 27 of the RTE.
[24] See Section 28 of the RTE.
[25] See Section 24 of the RTE.
[26] See Sections 14 and 15 of the RTE.

those from socio-economically backward societies where, due to lack of awareness of parents or due to lack of municipal offices, the parents may not have registered the birth of the child. This further corroborates the Juvenile Justice (Care and Protection of Children) Act, which mandates that children in conflict with the law should be given special, child-friendly treatment by specified courts and that their age verification may be done on the basis of school certificates in case of absence of the birth certificate.[27] Further, it also mandates that no child should be failed in any class, and nor should any child undergo expulsion from the class for any reason till the final year of elementary education.[28] This understanding corresponds with Section 17 of the RTE, which goes ahead to prohibit administration of corporal punishment on any student by teachers. It may be seen that the Juvenile Justice (Care and Protection of Children) Act, 2015 also mentions prohibition of corporal punishment that may violate the basic understanding of child rights as guaranteed in the UN CRC.

The RTE strictly adheres to the safety norms for children as have been mandated in the UN CRC, Juvenile Justice (Care and Protection of Children) Act, 2015 and the Constitution of India. For instance, this statute mandates that parents and representatives of local authorities must be engaged in monitoring the functioning of schools. Section 21 must be read in this regard, which states:

> A school, other than a school specified in sub-clause (iv) of clause (n) of section 2, shall constitute a School Management Committee consisting of the elected representatives of the local authority, parents or guardians of children admitted in such school and teachers: Provided that at least three-fourth of members of such Committee shall be parents or guardians: Provided further that proportionate representation shall be given to the parents or guardians of children belonging to disadvantaged group and weaker section: Provided also that fifty per cent. of Members of such Committee shall be women.(2) The School Management Committee shall perform the following functions, namely:—(a) monitor the working of the school; (b) prepare and recommend school

[27] See Section 14 of the RTE and Chapter IV of the Juvenile Justice (Care and Protection of Children) Act, 2015.

[28] See Section 16 of the RTE.

> development plan; (c) monitor the utilisation of the grants received from the appropriate Government or local authority or any other source; and (d) perform such other functions as may be prescribed.[29]

This clearly indicates that the RTE uses the checks-and-balances provision for managing the functioning of schools. Such engagement of parents and local authority members also ensures that the right of children to protection against any institutional abuse, including child sexual abuse by teachers or school authorities, may be prevented.[30] Further, the RTE also emphasizes the quality of infrastructure of schools. As it mandates, not only should schools have child-friendly infrastructure in terms of the building or playground, barrier-free access, etc., but the appropriate government must also establish schools in all localities so that children need not travel long distances.[31] The statue also mandates that schools should also provide nutritious midday meals to children so that they may have both physical and intellectual development in a holistic sense.[32] Further, Chapter V of the statute discusses proper curriculum for students. Section 29, which speaks about curriculum and the evaluation process, is noteworthy here, which reads:

> (1) The curriculum and the evaluation procedure for elementary education shall be laid down by an academic authority to be specified by the appropriate Government, by notification. (2) The academic authority, while laying down the curriculum and the evaluation procedure under sub-section (1), shall take into consideration the following, namely (a) conformity with the values enshrined in the Constitution; (b) all round development of the child; (c) building up child's knowledge, potentiality and talent; (d) development of physical and mental abilities to the fullest extent; (e) learning through activities, discovery and exploration in a child friendly and child-centered manner; (f) medium of instructions shall, as far as practicable, be in child's mother tongue; (g) making the

---

[29] See Section 21 of the RTE.

[30] For more, see D. Halder, *Child Sexual Abuse and Protection Laws in India* (New Delhi: SAGE Publications, 2018). ISBN: 9789352806843.

[31] For more, see Section 8 of the RTE.

[32] For a better understanding, see Schedule for norms and standards for a school under the RTE Act.

child free of fear, trauma and anxiety and helping the child to express views freely; (h) comprehensive and continuous evaluation of child's understanding of knowledge and his or her ability to apply the same.[33]

As it may be seen, the statute mandates that the curriculum should be in accordance with the constitutional values and should be designed in such a manner that may help in the overall development of children. This also includes curriculum development for children with special needs. Further, the RTE also mandates that all schools should be affiliated and recognized as per the government's norms. The Act also prescribes disciplinary actions against schools that may not be recognized, yet imparting education. This prescription is specifically to prevent students from being deprived of the final school-leaving certificates that may be distributed by the authorized secondary education boards through the affiliated and recognized schools.[34]

However, in spite of the robust and stringent provisions, the RTE could not achieve its goals fully. Several corruption issues related to appointment of qualified teachers under the RTE were reported by stakeholders.[35] Most teachers are reported to not be trained to provide quality elementary education to students.[36] There are reports of discrimination in admission of students in schools based on caste and religion as well.[37] Further, in many cases, the school infrastructure might not be child-friendly. In this regard, a mention may be made of the Kumbakonam school fire case, wherein several children were burnt to death due to the poor building infrastructure of the school.[38]

---

[33] See Section 29 of the RTE.

[34] For more, see Section 18 of the RTE.

[35] See Kiran Bhatty, 'Review of Elementary Education Policy in India: Has It Upheld the Constitutional Objective of Equality?' *Economic and Political Weekly* 49, no. 43/44 (November 1, 2014): 100–107.

[36] For more, see Kritika Sharma, In Elementary Govt Schools, A Third of Teachers Don't Have the Required Teaching Degree (June 8, 2018), https://theprint.in/india/governance/in-elementary-govt-schools-a-third-of-teachers-dont-have-the-required-teaching-degree/67805/, accessed 21 January 2020.

[37] See supra@37.

[38] See TNM Staff, '"What Justice Is This?": Madras HC Frees 10 in Kumbakonam School Fire that Killed 94 Kids', *News Mint*, August 10, 2017, https://www.thenewsminute.com/article/

Even though this incident was an eye-opener for stakeholders and also motivated the drafters of the RTE to emphasize safe building infrastructure for children, not much was practically done by school authorities, or by appropriate government authorities either, for stopping mushrooming of private tuition centres, or for taking actions against unsafe school building infrastructures.[39] Further, defying the norms of the RTE, several cases of child sexual abuse and corporal punishment of children as young as 8 or 9 have also taken place in several aided and unaided schools in India.[40] There are also reports of distribution of low-quality midday meals in government elementary schools in many parts of India, which may have motivated parents to take their children out of schools as well.[41] Further, several stakeholders have also reported that such aided schools might also not have proper toilet facilities for male and female children, making the entire infrastructure extremely unhygienic for children at large.

CONCLUSION AND SUGGESTIONS

Even after the RTE has been established and implemented, satisfactory results are still awaited. SSA, which has now been merged with the Samagra Shiksha programme,[42] is now being closely monitored by the government, as well as by international stakeholders, including the

what-justice-madras-hc-acquits-10-kumbakonam-school-fire-killed-94-kids-66601, accessed 21 January 2020.

[39] Consider the case of the coaching centre fire incident in Surat, Gujarat, in 2019, which took the life of 16 teenagers. For more, see India Tuition Center Fire Kills Many Teenage Students, https://www.dw.com/en/india-tuition-center-fire-kills-many-teenage-students/a-48871784#:~:text=Several%20students%20were%20seen%20jumping,Surat%20after%20it%20caught%20fire.&text=At%20least%2019%20students%20died,complex%20caught%20fire%20on%20Friday, accessed 21 January 2020.

[40] See Schedule for norms and standards for a school under the RTE Act.

[41] For more, see TNN, '60 Students of 2 Schools Fall Ill After Mid-day Meal', (December 21, 2018), http://timesofindia.indiatimes.com/articleshow/67183746.cms?utm_source=contentofinterest&utm_medium=text&utm_campaign=cppst, accessed 12 December 2019.

[42] See http://samagra.mhrd.gov.in/about.html, accessed 21 January 2020.

United Nations Children's Fund (UNICEF).[43] In such situation, it has become necessary to further emphasize the proper implementation of the RTE through the appropriate governments and local authorities. These authors suggest that school infrastructures and quality of education therein must be more frequently reviewed by senior-ranking officials who may have the authority to take immediate disciplinary actions against school authorities and local authorities, avoiding any red-tapism. Appropriate authorities must also take measures to transfer the children from one school to another on an urgent basis in case the former is de-recognized or suddenly closed due to any disciplinary issue. There should also be vigorous monitoring of teachers and school authorities to check issues of discrimination on the basis of caste, gender, physical and mental disabilities in children, etc. Further, teachers must also be mandatorily sent for training and refresher courses to be updated on their subjects, child psychology, safety issues, etc. School authorities must also ensure that surveillance cameras are installed in every possible room, passage, etc., and the generation of data from such surveillance cameras must be properly verified, considered and stored for ensuring the highest standard of safety for students. It is suggested that if the stakeholders show more vigilance for the proper implementation of the RTE, the said Act may make the goals of Articles 21 and 21A of the constitution a reality.

[43] For more, see State of the Education Report, India (2019), http://digitallibrary.in.one.un.org/TempPdfFiles/3793_1.pdf, accessed 21 January 2020.

SECTION III

Contemporary Issues and Human Rights

Chapter 15

Outblooming Human Rights Violations in Surrogacy

Thorns Beneath the Rose

M. B. Pavithra and V. Kolappan

INTRODUCTION

Reproduction and motherhood are biological functions. Their significance has been perceived in all the social and cultural beliefs, patterns and practices. Infertility is therefore widely experienced as a personal and familial tragedy. Childlessness is stigmatized, becomes a source of personal suffering and also leads to social exclusion. In India, 10–15 per cent of incidences of infertility are observed at any given time. In a population of 1,000 million Indians, approximately 13–19 million couples are likely to be infertile.[1] Recent advances in scientific, technological and medical sciences offer a wide range of reproductive choices to childless couples.[2] Equal rights to procreate and to benefit from medical and technological development are protected directly

[1] For more, see Guidelines for ART Clinics in India (2005). https://icmr.nic.in/art/art_clinics.htm, accessed 21 April 2017.

[2] Imrana Qadeer, 'Social and Ethical Basis of Legislation on Surrogacy: Need for Debate', *Indian Journal of Medical Ethics* 6, no. 1 (January–March 2009): 28–31. http://www.issuesinmedicalethics.org/171co28, accessed 12 June 2017.

and indirectly by human rights laws, be they international, regional or national. Despite the safeguards and assurances, the potential users do not have access to the correct knowledge, proper medical expertise, or the materials required for assisted procreation. Information is neither widely dispersed nor easily obtainable. The technology becomes a scarce resource for such a gullible population. When the resource becomes scarce, then the possession of such a resource confers power. Power tends to corrupt, and absolute power tends to corrupt absolutely. Here is a situation where such an anomaly is developing slowly. Persons with problems in procreation find that surrogacy is a better choice, as it involves a lesser degree of suffering for the commissioning parents. From a very marginal form of medically assisted reproduction, which was less than 1 per cent of the babies born, surrogacy is now yielding nearly 25,000 newborn babies per year.[3] Half of these babies are born to foreign parents. The demand for such services increases with the increasing number of seekers of the services. The service providers then become a centre of control, wielding power, which is exercised over a variety of stakeholders. This is where the fundamental human interest gets scarred. This is where the significance of human rights, its implications and legitimacy issues regarding surrogacy gets highlighted. A human rights perspective of surrogacy is articulated and applied in this study, and a critique of conventional legal approaches to surrogacy is also made.

SURROGACY POLICIES IN INDIA: AN OUTLINE

At any time, the centre of gravity of legal development lies not in legislation, nor in juristic science, nor in judicial decision, but in society itself. Policy statement is a proclamation of intent and position, which society hopes to strive for and achieve over a period of time. Ideally, any policy should precede law. In India, unfortunately, laws begin to exist without an articulated policy statement to accompany them. Policies in India have always remained a farce and a mere legalistic paradigm. In India, commercial surrogacy was actually initiated in 2002, probably with an intention to help childless couples have progeny. However,

[3] Virginie Rozee, et al., 'Gestational Surrogacy in India', *Population and Societies* 537, no. 9 (October 2016): 1–4.

this slowly paved the way for the creation of baby bazaars, egg markets, sperm markets, oocyte sales, uterus rentals, etc. Even the tourism sector has special packages for their foreign clientele in the name of fertility tourism, medical tourism, reproduction tourism, etc. Due to the severe exploitative procedures and practices adopted in surrogacy, especially after Baby Manji's case[4] and the case of Balaz,[5] we do have stringent legislations proposed to curb the problems. However, there are many slips between the cup and the lip. There are shortfalls and constraints reducing the effectiveness of such legal measures. Primarily, we do not have a policy that strikes at the source to prevent the evil exploitative practices in surrogacy. In 2010, the Indian Council of Medical Research (ICMR) provided guidelines and rules for regulating assisted reproductive technology.[6] These regulations concentrated on various issues pertaining to assisted reproduction and the possible misuse of the procedures used therein. The Law Commission of India submitted the 228th report on assisted reproductive technology procedures[7] discussing the importance and need for surrogacy and the steps taken to control surrogacy arrangements. The following observations were made by the Law Commission of India:

1. A surrogacy arrangement should be made through a contract among parties, which would require:
   a. consent of the surrogate mother to bear the child;
   b. agreement of her husband and other family members;
   c. medical procedures of artificial insemination; and
   d. reimbursement of expenses for carrying the child to full term.
2. Such an arrangement should not be for commercial purposes.

---

[4] Baby Manji Yamada v. Union of India and Another, (2008) 13 SCC 518.

[5] Union of India and Another v. Jan Balaz and Ors, SLP (Civil) No. 31639/2009, [From Jan Balaz v. Union of India, L.P.A. No. 2151 of 2009, High Court of Gujarat].

[6] The Assisted Reproductive Technologies (Regulation) Bill, 2010, Indian Council of Medical Research (ICMR), Ministry of Health and Family Welfare, Govt. of India.

[7] Law Commission of India (report no. 228) Need for Legislation to Regulate Assisted Reproductive Technology Clinics as well as Rights and Obligations of Parties to Surrogacy, 2009.

3. A surrogacy arrangement should provide for the event of death of the commissioning couple or individual before delivery of the child, or divorce between the intended parents and subsequent willingness of none to take delivery of the child.
4. A surrogacy contract should necessarily take care of life insurance cover for the surrogate mother.
5. One of the intended parents should be a donor as well.
6. In case the intended parent is single, he/she should be a donor to be able to have a surrogate child. Otherwise, adoption is the way to have a child, which must be resorted to if the biological (natural) parents and adoptive parents are different.
7. Legislation itself should recognize a surrogate child to be the legitimate child of the commissioning parent(s) without there being any need for adoption or even declaration of a guardian.
8. The birth certificate of the surrogate child should contain the name(s) of the commissioning parent(s) only.
9. The right to privacy of the donor, as well as the surrogate mother, should be protected.
10. Sex-selective surrogacy should be prohibited.
11. Cases of abortions should be governed by the Medical Termination of Pregnancy Act 1971 only.

These are a few points that can be identified in the guidelines framed by ICMR. The proposed Surrogacy (Regulation) Bill, 2016 ensures effective regulation of surrogacy, prohibits commercial surrogacy and allows ethical surrogacy to needy infertile Indian couples. It proposes to regulate surrogacy in India by establishing a National Surrogacy Board at the central level and State Surrogacy Boards and appropriate authorities in the states and union territories. The main aim of the proposed bill is to allow altruistic ethical surrogacy to intending infertile couples between the ages of 23 and 50 years and 26 and 55 years for females and males, respectively. This bill has several features, including the following.

The bill places certain restrictions and liabilities on the intending couple, which include that the intending couple should be legally married for at least 5 years and should be Indian citizens. They should not have not had any surviving child biologically or through adoption or through surrogacy earlier, except in the case they have a child who is mentally or physically challenged or suffers from a life-threatening disorder with no permanent cure. They shall not abandon the child born out of a surrogacy procedure under any condition. The child born through surrogacy would have the same rights as are available for a biological child.

The bill further provides for certain features regarding the surrogate mother, stating that the surrogate mother should be a close relative of the intending couple and should be between the age of 25 and 35 years. She can act as a surrogate mother only once. Such a surrogate mother would carry a child that is genetically related to the intending couple.

Further, the bill also states that an order concerning the parentage and custody of the child to be born through surrogacy is to be passed by a court of a magistrate of the first class. An insurance coverage of a reasonable and adequate amount shall also be ensured in favour of the surrogate mother.

The bill further provides certain preventive mechanisms, which include registration of surrogacy clinics, etc. It thus states that surrogacy clinics shall be registered under this act after the appropriate authority is satisfied that such clinics are in a position to provide facilities and can maintain equipment and standards, including specialized manpower, physical infrastructure and diagnostic facilities, as may be prescribed in the rules and regulations. It also states that no person, surrogacy clinic, laboratory or clinical establishment of any kind shall undertake commercial surrogacy, abandon the child, exploit the surrogate mother, sell human embryo or import embryo for the purpose of surrogacy. It makes violation to the said provision a criminal offence punishable with imprisonment for a term that shall not be less than 10 years and with fine that may extend to ₹10 lakhs. It also states that the surrogacy clinics shall have to maintain all records for a period of 25 years.

These are some of the features present in the drafts of proposed laws that are on the anvil to regularize surrogacy. There have been extensive discussions and debates on the practicality of these regulations in recent days. Of course, the bill would help in preventing exploitation of women, ensure better life and health of the surrogate mother and punish any violation with imprisonment for 10 years and with penalty up to ₹10 lakhs. However, there are shadows of the legislations which make the entire scene very gloomy and might lead to underground surrogacy, corruption and unethical practices. Not all medical clinics adhere to all laws. Even now, there are several unqualified personnel handling medical equipment and patients in operation theatres and labour rooms in reputed hospitals. Many medical professionals prefer to work in developed countries due to higher salary offers and other perks. Sometimes, they also feel that the working conditions are also much more organized and safer that way. This leaves us with mediocre medical doctors in clinics most unprofessionally set up to handle childbirth and pregnant women. The legal barriers are not that formidable for such medical crooks to have their way with commercializing surrogacy as ever. This paves the way for the surrogacy industry to flourish underground, as is happening with many other issues. The situation will continue to remain the same if legislations are just drafted and passed as a mere legislative duty rather than as a strong tool of social welfare. It may be noted that a clause in the bill states that a couple should be married for at least 5 years to have a surrogate child. However, in the case of people who get married late in life, waiting for another 5 years might lead to various other complications. Further, most of the women who willingly enter surrogacy do so for monetary benefits in India. Even if they are closely related to the intending parents, they take up childbearing for others only when they see some benefits attached to it. This is a very pragmatic view of the reality. However, if only altruistic surrogacy is possible, then probably most potential surrogate mothers would not be interested in the task or might be forced into it. The scenario might become either exploitative or antisocial. Women who have been in this trade may look for other ways of staying in it. They might get involved in an underground job of surrogacy, or even worse, they might commodify themselves in other ways. We further argue that our society being patriarchal, if only a close relative can opt for altruistic surrogacy, then a woman related to the male partner might not be a right choice to be a donor or a surrogate mother. Because of scientific reasons, hereditary diseases might be carried on genetically to the child. Then, a close relative of the female partner might be forced by the family to become a surrogate mother without her wish/consent, and sometimes there would be no way for her to complain about it, as she would be told that she should do it for the family. Sometimes, there arises a tricky situation wherein the intending couple do not have close relatives, and even if they do, the close relative might not be willing to be a surrogate. In this situation, if there is commercial surrogacy, then that would help the couple get a child. It only requires a contractual settlement, which is not very greedy of or demanding on either contracting party. Considering a child born to a closely related surrogate mother, socio-psychological problems can crop up as the child grows up. The issue of true identity would surface as frequent meetups happen in the family. Further, bringing in the insurance issue, the bill insists on providing an insurance coverage to the surrogate mother. However, as of now, we do not have any comprehensive medical insurance policy in our country which would take care of all the medical expenditures incurred. Even if insurance is provided, it might not be of much use to the surrogate mother in compensating for the expenditures she has to take up before, during and after the childbirth, leave alone any medical mishaps that might occur during the course of pregnancy.

Overall, the effectiveness of such legislation is questioned, because this legislation may face the same fate as faced by other piecemeal legislations drafted in similar fashion. For example, laws that prohibit dowry, environmental pollution, eve teasing, etc., have not been a success. If only they were, the country would be a much better place to live in. The laws bring down the curtains on certain activities and prohibit them, but they also sweep under the carpet certain subtle deviations of norms.

HUMAN RIGHTS VIOLATIONS FACED BY SURROGATE MOTHERS

In some places, 'baby farms' exist. Several women are abused in such systems. They are exploited as baby carriers. These women hail from remote villages and deep rural pockets of our country. They do not have much awareness regarding the medical conditions of pregnancy, as they usually adopt countryside medications and medical treatment practices during pregnancy and childbirth. As long as the child delivery is trouble-free, every other thing remains normal. These women believe that giving birth to a child is a very normal and easy task. Further, the current economic conditions of our country have relegated the agricultural sector to take a back seat. People who relied on agriculture for their family income are now economically troubled. They do not have any alternative source of income to manage the financial burden. The men who work as 'brokers' in fertility centres are paid to identify, convince and bring such women to the centre. The women are brought to the fertility centres and kept in dormitories. A visit to such a dormitory shows many women in various stages of pregnancies living there. They are selected based on their health status and age. Normally, the women who hail from villages do have better health than those in cities. They sustain for long even without food. Very meagre amounts of food are given to them for their maintenance every day in such a shelter home. They are not allowed to go out, and the place is heavily guarded. It is literally like a prison where these women are kept. They are escorted to the fertility centres every month for a medical examination. They are not allowed to contact anybody from their family during this period. After the delivery, according to the contract signed, the child should be handed over to the parents, and the woman can then return to her hometown. For this, the woman is paid \$50 every month and \$500 every trimester. After the delivery of the baby, a final settlement of \$1,000 is given to her. Mostly, the money is deposited in a bank account. All these payments total up to \$3,000, which is approximately equal to ₹200,000 (whereas the actual amount obtained from the commissioning parents would be around \$10,000). This money is more than sufficient for the poor lady to repay her debts and get things for her household. Definitely, the temptation to come back for more such tasks would be there, and the women do come back. Every time, they are treated badly, without the necessary care, good food and medical attention deserved by a pregnant lady.

Further, the standard of service and treatment often correspond to the social and economic status and the geographic location of these women. In some cases, membership in a specific caste or community also determines the treatment and standard of care offered. In certain jurisdictions heavy discriminatory practices prevail, which mirror racial and ethnic divisions. Being held captive in such a regime with discretionary restrictions and unregulated services, the women face greater risk to their overall health, and their well-being becomes a question in each case. In the future, they are sure to face severe health problems due to the very minimal medical attention they received during their term of pregnancy and afterwards. It should not be simply assumed that state regulation invariably ensures safer and more appropriate standards and options in all services. Anxiety and hardship can result for these individuals and their families. Here, as is the case, whenever the state fails to recognize or refuses to take positive steps to meet the fundamental needs of its citizens, human rights may be violated.

THE CRIES OF THE CHILD BORN IN SURROGACY

The most painful aspect is to hear the cry of a baby in pain and insecurity. Any child seeks its parents' affection whenever the wave of insecurity rises over it. However, if there is confusion over the parenting issue, nobody for sure knows to tackle it. A child born out of a surrogacy agreement may have up to six adults claiming parent's rights over him/her: the genetic mother (egg donor), the gestational mother (surrogate), the commissioning mother, the genetic father (sperm donor), the husband of the gestational mother (presumption of paternity) and the commissioning father. The gametes of one of or both the commissioning parents may have been used. The gestational mother may be the genetic mother; this is the case when she is artificially inseminated. Such manipulations are contrary to the genetic truth, which is paradoxically sought more and more, especially in fatherhood determination. They also violate the child's right to know his/her origin and identity, as ensured in Article 7 of the Convention on the Rights of the Child.[8]

[8] Katherine Wade, *The Regulation of Surrogacy: A children's Rights perspective*, CFLQ 29, no. 2 (2017): 113–31.

EXPLOITATIVE TACTICS OF MIDDLEMEN AND MEDICAL FRATERNITY

In this surrogacy industry, middlemen play a large role and take huge slices of the amounts paid by the parents, and only about 25 per cent ends up with the actual surrogate mothers. The agencies matching the intending parents and surrogates are largely unregulated. As a result, eager couples longing for a baby and poor surrogates seeking money can be preyed upon by the unscrupulous or incompetent. Among the abuses, the agencies' not paying the surrogate, failing to cover medical needs, overcharging intending parents and drawing up unenforceable contracts are the most frequently heard complaints.

ISSUES OF PROSPECTIVE PARENTS

Surrogacy is indeed a boon for childless couples. It is a scientific innovation through which the gametes of a fertile couple are used to create progeny for a childless couple. However, the boon becomes a curse when the scientific advancement is misused by some people. Since the surrogacy procedures are expensive, many are not able to afford them. However, for the rich and wealthy, surrogacy is easily available. This play of money in this evolving 'industry' makes the procedures very exploitative. Not only do the rich use these procedures due to infertility issues, but unfortunately many also feel that going through the turmoil of pregnancy is quite tiresome and interferes with their career prospects, and that it is unnecessary to go through all that when somebody else can carry their baby for them. Moreover, when they can have a surrogate baby at a throwaway price in India, where is the need to suffer for 280 days to have a baby. Many advertisements of fertility clinics in the Western world have mentioned this. It would take them just a couple of visits to India, and the contracting agent would arrange for all their travel requirements, stay and medical formalities in India. They would have to come to India once to provide the gametes, and after 9 months they can come again to take the baby back with them without any hassles. All the legalities are taken care of by the brokers here. Of course, with the rampant practices of corruption being omnipresent and omnipotent, anything can be done here for a price.

CONCLUDING SUGGESTIONS

A mere passing of laws does not really suffice to control the issue of surrogacy becoming an antisocial activity. The laws should be practical, and proper enforcement is essential. When corrupt practices exist, establishment of an authority or commission becomes meaningless. The laws should prove to be truly functional and curb violating practices strongly. There is a lot of money involved in surrogacy; several crores are transacted between the intending parents and the contracting agency. In case of any violation being detected, a penalty of ₹10 lakhs is to be paid. It is not a big amount for the people concerned, and there is a possibility of this fine being redefined as fees. Soon, this fine would become surrogacy fees to be paid to follow violative procedures. The forthcoming legislation on surrogacy should take these issues into consideration before the passing of the Act. The laws need to be looked at again so that they actually benefit surrogate mothers, prospective parents and children born from surrogacy.

Chapter 16

Forest, Food Security and Indigenous People

A Critical Analysis from Human Rights Perspective

Nadisha N. Vazirani

INTRODUCTION

In the contemporary world where forests are fast becoming government properties, indigenous people who live in forest areas, depending on forest properties for food and basic living, are finding themselves in an insecure position. Traditionally, indigenous people are known to have had long encounters with settlers, colonial rulers and modern democratic governments who may have created modern forest laws and environment protection laws for the benefit of the modern societies, whereby the former's rights were largely neglected.[1] In this set-up, governments may penalize them for using forests as their regular habitat; they may be penalized for hunting, as it might violate the animal rights laws, and they may not be allowed to use the land in forests and

[1] For more, see André Béteille, 'The Idea of Indigenous People', *Current Anthropology* 39, no. 2 (April 1998): 187–92. The University of Chicago Press on behalf of Wenner-Gren Foundation for Anthropological Research. https://www.jstor.org/stable/10.1086/204717, accessed 12 January 2020.

adjacent areas for cultivation, as they may be considered as encroachers of government lands. This occurs mainly because indigenous people may not have been recognized as members of civilized society by settlers, colonial rulers and then the modern democratic governments of independent sovereign countries.[2] There is no uniform definition of the term 'indigenous people'. However, in some documents, the United Nations (UN) has tried to explain the term from various perspectives: for example, in the webpage of the UN Department of Economic and Social Affairs on indigenous peoples, available at https://www.un.org/development/desa/indigenouspeoples/about-us.html, the term 'indigenous people' is explained as below:

> Indigenous peoples are inheritors and practitioners of unique cultures and ways of relating to people and the environment. They have retained social, cultural, economic and political characteristics that are distinct from those of the dominant societies in which they live. Despite their cultural differences, indigenous peoples from around the world share common problems related to the protection of their rights as distinct peoples.... Indigenous peoples have sought recognition of their identities, way of life and their right to traditional lands, territories and natural resources for years, yet throughout history, their rights have always been violated. Indigenous peoples today, are arguably among the most disadvantaged and vulnerable groups of people in the world. The international community now recognizes that special measures are required to protect their rights and maintain their distinct cultures and way of life.[3]

After independence, Indian lawmakers and the government have included indigenous people in the mainstream society by grouping them under Scheduled Tribes, and in some cases under Scheduled Castes.[4] However, such classification has created more chaos in several cases, as each 'tribe' may have its distinct sociocultural ways of life. Further, clubbing indigenous people with several other Scheduled Castes has also raised

---

[2] Ibid.

[3] For more, see UN Department of Economic and Social Affairs Indigenous Peoples. https://www.un.org/development/desa/indigenouspeoples/about-us.html, accessed 12 January 2020.

[4] André Béteille, 'The Idea of Indigenous People'.

a question mark over their socio-economic status.[5] Indigenous people, irrespective of their classification as Scheduled Tribes or Scheduled Castes, are usually among the poorest sections of society and suffer a high incidence of hunger and malnutrition. Indigenous peoples' traditional practices such as hunting, gathering and shifting cultivation are not only their means of obtaining food/livelihood but also part of their cultural identity. Uniquely, indigenous people view their right to food as a collective one.

This chapter seeks to analyse the 'right to food' from indigenous peoples' perspective. Given their symbiotic relation with forests, this chapter emphasizes the potential of 'forest produce' as a source of food, especially for indigenous people, and addresses the main issue, that is, access to forest produce/resources, that influences their food security.[6] For the purpose of this chapter, the author has adopted the doctrinal research method, primarily relying on databases and secondary sources of information available in libraries, such as books, journals, articles, reports and government/official publications. The study is organized in four parts, including the introduction. The second part discusses the right to food from the perspective of the basic rights guaranteed to every human being, including the indigenous people in India. This part also outlines concepts of food sovereignty and state obligations towards indigenous people. The third part discusses the interrelation between forests and indigenous people, the plight of forest dwellers and relevant legal developments in India. The fourth part contains the conclusion.

CRITICAL ANALYSIS OF THE RIGHT TO FOOD

Food and water are essential for living for every living being on earth. Considering this, the Universal Declaration of Human Rights (UDHR) expressly recognizes the right to food as one of the basic human rights in Article 25, which states:

> Everyone has the right to a standard of living adequate for the health and well-being of himself and of his family, including food, clothing,

[5] For more, see Virginius Xaxa, 'Tribes as Indigenous People of India', *Economic and Political Weekly* 34, no. 51 (18–24 December 1999): 3589–95. https://www.jstor.org/stable/4408738, accessed 12 January 2020.

[6] Lidija Knuth, *The Right to Adequate Food and Indigenous People: How Can the Right to Food Benefit Indigenous People?* (Rome: Right to Food Unit, FAO, 2009).

> housing and medical care and necessary social services, and the right to security in the event of unemployment, sickness, disability, widowhood, old age or other lack of livelihood in circumstances beyond his control.[7]

This basic right has also been enshrined in the preamble to the UDHR, which explains the concept of human rights in the very first line as inclusive of 'the inherent dignity and the equal and inalienable rights of all members of the human family'.[8] The preamble further states that the recognition and respect for this inherent dignity and equal and inalienable rights form 'the foundation of freedom, justice and peace in the world'.[9] Thus, 'equality' and 'non-discrimination' are inherent in the recognition and exercise of human rights. Keeping this principle in mind, the UN Special Rapporteur on the Right to Food explains the concept of right to food as follows:

> For the special rapporteur, the right to food is the right to have regular, permanent and unrestricted access, either directly or by means of financial purchases, to quantitatively and qualitatively adequate and sufficient food corresponding to the cultural traditions of the people to which the consumer belongs, and which ensure a physical and mental, individual and collective, fulfilling and dignified life free of fear.[10]

Over a period of time, the scope of the right to food has expanded, and this right has been codified into several international legal instruments, such as the International Covenant on Economic, Social and Cultural Rights (ICESCR), which expressly recognizes the 'right to food' as essential to an adequate standard of living and that it is the fundamental right of everyone to be hunger-free.[11] As such, the right to food has become an inherent and integral element in realizing the right to life as has been enshrined in Article 3 of the UDHR, which states, 'everyone

---

[7] See Article 25, UDHR.

[8] See the Preamble to the Universal Declaration of Human Rights. https://www.un.org/en/universal-declaration-human-rights/, accessed 12 January 2020.

[9] ibid.

[10] For more understanding on this, see UN Special Rapporteur on the Right to food. http://www.ohchr.org/EN/Issues/Food/Pages/FoodIndex.aspx, accessed 12 January 2020.

[11] ICESCR, Article 11.

has right to life, liberty and security of person'.[12] Presently, several countries have included the right to food within the broader meaning of the right to life in their constitutions,[13] and India is no exception.

The international regime on human rights resonates with the Indian Constitution, especially the right to life guaranteed under Article 21 in consonance with Article 3 of the UDHR and relevant articles of other international conventions as discussed earlier. The right to food is inherent to a life with dignity. The Hon'ble Supreme Court of India has established the same in a number of landmark cases.[14] Though 'Fundamental Rights' under Part III of the Constitution of India, 1950 does not expressly mention 'Right to Food', the same is addressed in Part IV of the Constitution, namely Articles 39(a) and 47, which are Directive Principles of State Policy (DPSP). Article 39(a) requires the state to direct its policy towards securing the rights of adequate means to livelihood for all. Article 47, on the other hand, speaks about the duty of the state to raise the level of nutrition and the standard of living of its people. The Supreme Court of India has finely executed this mandate through creative interpretation of Article 21, in the light of Articles 39(a) and 47, to include 'Right to Food' within its ambit in several cases, including *Francis Coralie v. Administrator, Union Territory of Delhi and Ors.*[15]; *Shantistar Builders v. Narayan Khimalal Totame*[16] and *PUCL v. Union of India and Others*,[17] etc.

---

[12] See Article 3 of UDHR.

[13] For example, countries in Africa have followed the principles laid down by UN Food and Agricultural organisation especially to address food security for everyone for all times including the periods of extreme summer when countries may be affected by draught and food insecurity. For more information on this, see http://www.fao.org/3/ca3518en/CA3518EN.pdf, accessed 12 January 2020.

[14] *Francis Coralie v. Administrator, Union Territory of Delhi and Ors.* (1981) 1 SCC 608; *Sunil Batra v Delhi Administration*, AIR 1980; *Maneka Gandhi v U.O.I*, AIR 1978.

[15] In Francis Coralie v. Administrator, Union Territory of Delhi and Ors., (1981) 1 SCC 608. The Supreme Court stated 'We think that the right to life includes the right to live with human dignity and all that goes along with it, namely, the bare necessaries of life such as adequate nutrition, clothing and shelter...'.

[16] In Shantistar Builders v. Narayan Khimalal Totame, (1990) 1 SCC 520. The Supreme Court stated 'The right to life is guaranteed in any civilized society. That would take within its sweep the right to food...'.

[17] In PUCL v. Union of India and Others, (2001) Writ Petition (Civil) 196. The Supreme Court, in its Orders stated 'prevention of "hunger and starvation" is "one of the prime responsibilities of the Government—whether Central or State"'.

RIGHT TO FOOD AND FOREST ACCESSORIES FOR TRIBAL PEOPLE AND INDIAN LEGAL UNDERSTANDING

As mentioned in the earlier paragraphs, researchers have observed that indigenous people had been involved in encounters with settlers and consequently with modern governments because they had been perceived as encroachers of government properties,[18] that is, the forests, even though they had been dwelling in the same since time immemorial and their rights over the said lands and forest properties had remained unrecognized.[19] The hard truth is, unlike the other socio-economically backward people living in villages and cities, who may have been affected by wars, poverty, famine, etc., and who may have received government recognition as socio-economically backward classes and government support for adequate living, indigenous people living in forest areas may not claim their right to life, including the right to food, in easy ways. The reason lies in the fact that there is no universally accepted definition of indigenous people that captures their diversity. The International Labour Organization (ILO) 'Indigenous and Tribal People Convention, C.169' (hereinafter referred to as 'ILO Convention No. 169') uses the terms 'indigenous and tribal people', and Article 1.2 of this convention states: 'self-identification as indigenous or tribal shall be regarded as a fundamental criterion for determining the groups to which the provisions of this Convention apply'.[20] It must be noted that according to the UDHR provisions, indigenous people also have an equal right to life, right to equality, rights against discrimination, etc. They live in varied landscapes, including inaccessible terrains, hills and dense forests, and they are dependent on their habitat for survival. Thus, access to land and productive resources (forest, fishing, water, etc.) are prerequisites for indigenous people's right to food. The cultural identity and heritage of indigenous people are inseparable from their traditional lands. Indigenous people obtain food directly from their lands by hunting, gathering or cultivating. They may also acquire food indirectly by marketing their

---

[18] See Béteille, 'The Idea of Indigenous People'.

[19] Ibid.

[20] For more, see Article 1 of C169—Indigenous and Tribal Peoples Convention, 1989 (No. 169).

products.[21] It is important to note that the United Nations Declaration on the Rights of Indigenous People (UNDRIP) is an important legal instrument for the recognition, promotion and protection of the rights and freedom of indigenous people. Even though the declaration does not contain specific provisions on the right to food, it includes provisions concerning land, territories, natural resources and subsistence activities in Article 26, which states: 'indigenous people have the right to the lands, territories and resources which they have traditionally owned, occupied or otherwise used or acquired and States shall give legal recognition and protection to them'. Such rights are relevant for the realization of the right to food for indigenous people. Further, ILO Convention No. 169, through its Article 15(1) and (2), also suggests: 'the rights of indigenous people to the natural resources pertaining to their lands shall be specially safeguarded'.[22]

Agenda 21, Chapter 26, Recognizing And Strengthening The Role Of Indigenous People And Their Communities, United Nations Conference on Environment & Development Rio de Janerio, Brazil, 1992, also mandates the protection of indigenous peoples' rights to access to and utilization of resources for ensuring food security for them.[23] This indicates that the international instruments in this regard suggest that states should respect and recognize indigenous people's right to land and territories, as both a collective and an individual right. Such right is inclusive of their right to access natural resources, and cultural rights as well.[24] Such right also extends to the forest areas

---

[21] FAO, Right to Food and Indigenous People. https://www.unscn.org/web/archives_resources/files/Focus_Right_to_food_and_Indigenous__566.pdf, accessed 8 May 2017.

[22] ILO Convention No.169, Article 15(1) and (2).

[23] Agenda 21, Chapter 26, *Recognizing and Strengthening The Role of Indigenous People and their Communities*, United Nations Conference on Environment & Development Rio de Janerio, Brazil, 3–14 June (1992) https://sustainabledevelopment.un.org/content/documents/Agenda21.pdf.

[24] For more, see Indigenous People' Consultation on the Right to Food: A Global Consultation, Atitlán, and Sololá, Guatemala (17–19 April 2002), http://www.un.org/esa/socdev/unpfii/documents/Right_to_food.pdf; African Commission on Human and Peoples' Rights (ACHPR), 155/96 Social and Economic Rights Action Center (SERAC); and *the Center for Economic and Social Rights (CESR) v. Nigeria*. http://www.achpr.org/files/sessions/30th/comunications/155.96/achpr30_155_96_eng.pdf, 12 accessed January 2020.

where they live and forest products, including fruits, roots, leaves, tubers, seeds, nuts, mushrooms, wildlife—including rabbits, etc.—fish and non-timber/non-wood forest products (NTFPs/NWFPs).[25] Researchers also opine that the rights of indigenous people to access forests and food should also be expanded to traditional medicines and construction materials, complementing crop production, forest vegetables, etc., which are important elements in the diet of indigenous people and their communities.[26]

There is growing recognition that forests and tree-based systems complement farmland agriculture in providing food security and nutrition. Indigenous people have been an inherent part of the history of India. The term 'indigenous' has come to be associated with the tribes of India.[27] Tribespeople are also popularly known as 'autochthons', 'adivasi' or 'adimjati', which means original settlers of India.[28] According to the data of Census 2011, Scheduled Tribes comprise 8.6 per cent of India's total population, many of which are forest-dwelling tribes. The communities recognized as Scheduled Tribes according to the mandates of Article 342 of the Indian Constitution live in about 15 per cent of the country's geographical areas in various ecological and geo-climatic conditions ranging from plains and forests to hills and other inaccessible areas. According to the 2015–2016 annual report of the Ministry of Tribal Affairs (MOTA), Government of India, there are 75 types of Scheduled Tribes which are collectively known as Particularly Vulnerable Tribal Groups (PVTGs) (earlier termed as Primitive Tribal Groups), which are characterized by the following features:

1. Pre-agriculture level of technology;
2. Stagnant or declining population;

---

[25] Bhaskar Vira, Christoph Wildburger, and Stephanie Mansourian, eds., *Forest, Trees and Landscape for Food Security and Nutrition: A Global Assessment Report*, Vol. 33, IUFRO World Series, Vienna. 172 p. (2015). http://www.un.org/en/zerohunger/pdfs/gfep-forests-and-food-security-policy-brief_.pdf, accessed 11 May 2017.

[26] Knuth, *The Right to Adequate Food and Indigenous People.*

[27] See Béteille, *The Idea of Indigenous People.*

[28] V. Xaxa, *State, Society and Tribes: Issues in Post-Colinial India*, 1st ed. (New Delhi: Pearson Education India, 2008).

3. Extremely low literacy; and
4. Subsistence level of economy.[29]

It has been observed by researchers that the first feature, that is, the pre-agriculture level of technology, may be an inherent characteristic of indigenous tribal communities, which may also use the techniques of shifting cultivation and hunting for regular supply of food.[30] The MOTA annual report further indicates that out of 58 districts of different states, including those of Madhya Pradesh, Odisha, Bihar, Chhattisgarh, etc., 51 have a majority tribal population, who can be categorized as indigenous tribespeople. They live in extreme poverty and rely on forest resources for food. They also rely on shifting cultivation, hunting, honey harvesting, hunting, etc., and make a living by selling forest products.[31] However, their health and immunity levels may be extremely poor and fragile, as they may not receive proper quantities and quality of good food. They may not access medical facilities either, because of their remoteness.[32]

As may be seen from the above discussion, the indigenous tribal communities in India have faced large-scale discrimination for ages. Historically, they have suffered a gradual loss of their customary forest rights and consequently their access to food in the process of consolidation of 'forests' as 'state property'. In the late-medieval and Mughal periods, the systems of community property resources were largely intact. However, in the colonial period, there was a complete erosion of common property rights, and forests became 'state property' with the passing of various statutes, including the Indian Forest Act, 1927, which continued to be in force in independent India. This provision created 'reserved', 'protected' and 'village' forest categories, and it severely curtailed the rights of the forest-dwelling tribes to collect forest products and practices such as shifting cultivation. The reservation of the forests resulted in considerable hardships to the indigenous communities.

---

[29] Ministry of Tribal Affairs (MoTA), *Annual Report, 2015–16*. http://tribal.nic.in/Content/AnnualReportsOtherLinks.aspx, accessed 10 May 2017.

[30] M. Radhakrishnan, Th*ought for Food: Starvation Among Forest-dependent Communities*, in Dev Nathan and Virginius Xaxa (Eds.) Social Exclusion and Adverse Inclusion: Development and Deprivation of Adivasis in India (New Delhi: Oxford University Press, 2012).

[31] See *supra* @51.

[32] For more, see UNICEF, *Nourishing India's Tribal Children: The Nutrition Situation of Children of India's Scheduled Tribes* (New Delhi, 2014).

The colonial forest policy was extended with renewed vigour by the state in independent India. The Forest Policy, 1952 (which was based on its predecessor, the colonial policy of 1894) largely ignored the rights of forest dwellers and tribespeople to forests. Further, the Wild Life Protection Act (WLPA), 1972 allowed the government to notify 'protected areas' (PAs) for wildlife protection and restricted human activities within them. At the same time, the forest-dwelling tribes living in some PAs, who once had access to forest resources, lost access to them. Hunting is prohibited under the WLPA, 1972.[33] Establishment of national parks and sanctuaries meant that these communities could be evicted in the name of wildlife conservation and had very limited access to forest produce within the declared PAs.[34] Some of the worst-affected indigenous tribes included the Sahariya tribe from Madhav National Park[35] and then from the Kuno wildlife sanctuary. This resulted in large-scale starvation deaths among the Sahariyas.[36]

However, noticing such pathetic conditions of the indigenous tribes, in February 2000, the Supreme Court of India, in the case of *T. N. Godavarman v. Union of India & Others*,[37] passed an order restraining state governments and their agencies from removing dead, dying or wind-fallen trees and grass from any national park or sanctuary in the country. This judgement was one of the first judgements to restore the rights of the indigenous tribes to food security in their own indigenous ways. In 2006, the Scheduled Tribes and Other Traditional Forest Dwellers (Recognition of Forest Rights) Act (FRA) was brought into force by the Indian Parliament, which promised to redress the injustices that tribal and forest-dwelling communities had faced since the colonial era.[38] This historic legislation recognizes individual and community rights over forest lands of forest-dwelling Scheduled Tribes and other traditional forest dwellers as well as their rights to use, manage and protect forest resources.[39] This provision

---

[33] Section 9 of the WLPA, 1972.

[34] *Supra* note 31.

[35] A. Zaidi, 'Death by Hunger', *Frontline*, 2005.

[36] A. Zaidi, 'State of Misery', *Frontline*, 2005.

[37] T. N. Godavarman v. Union of India & Others, (1995) Writ Petition (Civil) No. 202.

[38] Statement of Objects & Reasons of the FRA, 2006.

[39] Section 3 (1) (a)–(m), FRA, 2006.

conferred right to ownership over the minor forest products that they have been relying upon since time immemorial, collect such minor products and dispose them for living.[40] Minor forest produce (MFP) being a significant source of food and livelihood, Section 2(i) of this provision defines the term 'MFP' as follows: MFP are productions 'including all non-timber forest produce of plant origin including bamboo, brush wood, stumps, cane, tussar, cocoons, honey, wax, lac, tendu or kendu leaves, medicinal plants and herbs, roots, tubers, and the like'.[41] Noticeably, this provision seeks to not only secure the right to food and forest resources but also thereby implicitly secure the health of India's indigenous people, that is, the forest-dwelling Scheduled Tribes and other traditional forest dwellers. The FRA, 2006 as an enactment is in spirit with the international regime that obligates states to secure indigenous peoples' collective rights to land and resources. However, reports by the media, civil society groups and research organizations and the official publications of the government themselves reflect that there is poor implementation of this statute. According to 'MOTA 2010 Status Report', of the 2.9 million claims settled under the FRA, 2006, only 1.6 per cent gave community rights, and most of these did not include rights over MFP. The focus in this regard had been mostly on conferring individual *patta* (for agricultural land and housing). The FRA assessment reports also suggest that exercise of rights over MFP remains a challenge in most of the states.[42]

About 200 million forest dwellers directly depend on forest resources for food and livelihood in India. The FRA, 2006 has extraordinary potential for ensuring livelihood security and poverty alleviation through sustainable and community-based management of forests for these people. However, only 3 per cent of the community forest rights (CFR) (including the MFP rights) have actually been realized.[43] From

---

[40] Section 3 (1) (c)

[41] Section 2(i).

[42] UNICEF, *Nourishing India's Tribal Children.*

[43] Community Forest Rights–Learning and Advocacy Process (CFRLA), Promise and Performance: Ten Years of the Forest Rights Act in India. Citizens' Report on Promise and Performance of The Scheduled Tribes and Other Traditional Forest Dwellers (Recognition of Forest Rights) Act, 2006, after 10 years of its enactment, December 2016. www.cfrla.org.in, accessed 11 May 2017.

the discussions above, there appears to be tardy implementation of a progressive legislation that has the potential to provide food security to millions of forest-dwelling poor and tribal communities in India. A strong political will is needed to achieve the potential of the FRA, 2006 in letter and spirit and secure food and livelihood for India's indigenous people.

CONCLUSION

Indigenous tribal communities are an inherent part of every modern society, including India. Access to food and food security have become precious rights for them because of their constant tussles with modern civilized states. In the course of the development of societies from the perspective of social–cultural–legal–technological developments, rights of the indigenous people have been pushed back. Indigenous communities may not have been able to integrate with the mainstream modern societies because of their ignorance of modern sociocultural norms. They have not received proper education and awareness due to their remoteness. The modern educated societies have taken full advantage of this by depriving the former of their basic rights. Starvation deaths, malnutrition and all forms of exploitations are rampant in indigenous communities. It is the prime duty of the government to take immediate action to protect their rights. The rights of such people may be secured when the modern society at large is made aware about their plights. Common individuals and some of the stakeholders of criminal justice system may not be aware about legislations like the FRA. As a result, they may unnecessarily harass indigenous tribal communities when the latter try to make a living by selling forest products or accessing forest products that may have been legally sanctioned to them by the legislature itself. The author also feels that the government should take more measures to spread education and medical facilities across indigenous communities so that they may be empowered to realize their rights themselves.

Chapter 17

Transgender Human Rights

Identifying the Conflict of Law and Reality

Shrut S. Brahmbhatt

INTRODUCTION

'Transgender' has been considered an umbrella term that includes pre-operative, post-operative and non-operative transsexual people who are strongly opposite to their sex of birth.[1] This means the term includes persons intending to undergo or those who already have undergone sex reassignment surgery and also persons who have not undergone sex reassignment surgery but strongly believe that their gender is opposite to their sex at birth; thus, the term 'transgender' includes lesbian, gay, bisexual, transsexual and cross-dressing people.[2] The word transgender is a combination of two words, 'trans' and 'gender'; 'trans' is a Latin word which means 'beyond'. It means someone who is beyond the identified gender, that is, male or female. This has a wider scope, including even queer, asexual, pansexual or omnisexual, intersexual and polysexual people.

Human rights are rights that are ensured to a person by virtue of their being human. Law is implicated in society, and through rights, people

[1] National Legal Services Authorities v. Union of India, (2014) 5 SCC 438.

[2] Nalsa Judgment, *supra* note 2.

negotiate the fundamental prohibitions and restrictions that are the price of being part of society.[3] Human rights are the rights that are available to all human beings equally without any discrimination on the basis of race, colour, sex, language, religion, political or other opinion, national or social origin, property, birth or other status.[4] Human rights are universal and are beyond the boundaries of nations. The universality of human rights is achieved through various international treaties and agreements that the signatory countries are bound to follow. All *living persons*[5] are considered to have human rights. However, the author opines that even non-living persons have human rights, the reason being that death does not dehumanize anybody. Even after death, the right to be treated equally as other dead persons does exist. A question may arise in any prudent mind as to what right shall be conferred even after death; well, the right to privacy, the right to equality and the right to be treated equally do exist as posthumous rights. The Universal Declaration of Human Rights (hereinafter referred to as UDHR) applies to the living but not to the dead. However, as past human beings, the dead possess posthumous dignity and therefore deserve respect and protection. The UDHR is a powerful source of inspiration for our duties to the dead.[6] A dead body also deserves similar treatment as other dead bodies, such as cremation, burial procedure, etc. In India, *Hijra* or *Kinnar* communities share a historic existence of almost 5,000 years, but despite this, they have not been allotted any special lands to bury the dead members of their communities. A conflict arises when a *Hijra* following a particular religion dies and the crematory grounds of her religion are not open to cremating her. Other members of the community face several problems in cremating her, because religions are open to be followed but crematory grounds of the same religions are not open for *Hijras* because of their being *Hijras*, and also sometimes because of their having a different method of cremating dead bodies.

---

[3] Costas Douzinas, *The End of Human Rights* (Oxford: Hart Publishing, 2000).

[4] Article 2, UDHR; Article 2, ICCPR.

[5] Nickel, James, 'Human Rights', in *The Stanford Encyclopedia of Philosophy*, ed. Edward N. Zalta (Spring 2017 Edition), https://plato.stanford.edu/archives/spr2017/entries/rights-human/.

[6] Antoon de baets, 'The Impact of the Universal Declaration of Human Rights on the Study of History', *History and Theory* 48 (February 2009): 20–43

Hagel's opinion on 'rights' was that rights are institutional expressions of the struggle for mutual recognition, as they contribute towards the creation of identity and are inter-subject rather than individualistic. Humans are constructed by human rights. One is human because others recognizes him/her as human, which in institutional terms mean a bearer of human rights.[7] Transgender people, however, even after decades of their revolutions, have not availed human rights. Their existence in society, once they are known as being transgender, is different from that of others in society despite their being part of society. The views or opinions of a person change once he/she becomes aware of the fact that a person is transgender. This is against the concept of human rights.

This chapter deals with 'transgender human rights', global perspectives or views on and conferment of human rights on transgender people and observations of an empirical research study conducted by the author in the district of Gandhinagar, Gujarat, India. The author opines that 'transgender human rights' shall be the term used to identify what human rights are actually conferred to transgender people. This term, however, does not consider transgender people as different from anybody; as the community is large and exists in society, the term 'transgender human rights' would cater to the need of specifying the rights of transgender people.

TRANSGENDER HUMAN RIGHTS

The UDHR confers human rights on all human beings. All human beings are born free and equal in dignity and rights.[8] The idea of considering human beings equal from the time of birth indeed sounds good, but whether the same has been conceptualized by different legislations and at the end by society needs determination. Transgender people share a history with almost all civilizations. Their recognition has also been unbalanced for centuries. In India, transgender people were endowed with great responsibilities during the times of the Mahabharata and Ramayana. Even during the Mughal era, they were given responsibilities of realizing law and justice. It was with the arrival

---

[7] The End of Human Rights, Article 2, UDHR.

[8] Article I, Universal Declaration of Human Rights.

of the British emperors that transgender people and their activities were controlled in India.

Transgender people were persecuted for their sexual orientation as defective humans, and a large part of their identity and self-esteem was deleted or became the cause of victimization.[9] All human beings have the rights to life, liberty and security without distinction of any kind, such as on the basis of race, colour, sex, language, religion, political opinion, place of origin, property, birth or other status.[10] Though the rights are very well established and conferred on every individual, at the same time, it is very difficult to determine the level of their implementation. Indian courts have been questioned several times through various cases and petitions about the recognition of transgender people. A homosexual man has the same right as does a straight man to live in society with dignity, howsoever different he is from others; a lesbian woman has the same right as does a straight woman; a *Hijra* has the same right as does any other person in society. *Hijras* do have the right to reproduce, they do have the right to be educated, and they do have the right to be treated equally. Indeed, a personality difference is evident from their overall behaviour, but that does not change their human nature. They should be given equal treatment as others. When considering them equal, the consideration should be not only in public but in their private life as well. Their privacy and private rights should also be maintained. The Indian Penal Code, through Section 377, criminalizes even consensual sexual acts between persons of the same sex. Section 377 states:

> Whoever voluntarily has carnal intercourse against the order of nature with any man, woman or animal, shall be punished with [imprisonment for life], or with imprisonment of either description for term which may extend to ten years, and shall also be liable to fine.

This section was considered to violate the fundamental rights guaranteed under the Indian Constitution by Naz Foundation in the case of *Naz Foundation v. Govt. of NCT of Delhi*.[11] Further, it was

---

[9] The End of Human Rights, Article 2, UDHR.

[10] Article II, Universal Declaration of Human Rights.

[11] 160 *Delhi Law Times* 277.

submitted by Naz Foundation that the section is discriminating, results in the denial of fundamental human rights and in abuse, harassment and assault by public authorities, drives the gay community underground and subjects them to great vulnerability in violation of fundamental rights.[12] Section 377, which was enacted in 1860, violates human rights. Any sort of discrimination between humans and by virtue of such discrimination any unequal treatment meted out to a human being goes against human rights. Transgender people are not new in society; their existence is as old as civilization itself. Hence, recognition of them as humans should also be done in a way that there remains no chance of discrimination. The Naz Foundation case judgement is considered a landmark judgement wherein the Delhi High Court considered Section 377 unconstitutional and in violation to Articles 14, 15, 19 and 21 of the Constitution of India. This was however overruled in the case of *Suresh Kaushal v. Naz Foundation*,[13] where the Hon'ble Supreme Court held that Section 377 does not suffer from any constitutional infirmity.

However, the *National Legal Services Authority v. Union of India and Ors.*[14] (herein after referred to as the NALSA judgement) recognized *Hijras* or *Kinnars* as the 'third gender' and, by extension, as citizens of India and conferred the fundamental rights on them. This can be considered as a victory for the *Hijra* community; however, homosexuals, lesbians and bisexuals are yet to be endowed citizenship, and their rights by virtue of being humans are still not conferred on them.

Transgender human rights include the rights to life, liberty and security of a person. Nobody, merely because of their sexual orientation, shall be subjected to deprivation of anything that revokes their rights to life, liberty and security. It shall be the state that is responsible for its citizens, and the rights discussed herein shall be conferred on transgender persons by virtue of their being human.

---

[12] Jarlath Clifford, 'NAZ Foundation v. Govt. of NCT of Delhi and Others', *The Equal Right Review* 4 (2009): 71–74.

[13] Suresh Kaushal v. Naz Foundation, (2014) 1 SCC 1.

[14] National Legal Services Authority v. Union of India and Ors., (2014) 5 SCC 438.

GLOBAL PERSPECTIVES

The UDHR, a declaration adopted by the United Nations General Assembly in 1948, is considered as a milestone document in the history of human rights. However, the declaration belies the human rights for transgender people. The language of the declaration seems to be concentrating on the human rights of men and women only. The marital rights are also conferred only on men and women. The provisions of the UDHR contradict each other, as Article 2 clearly states that human rights shall be conferred without any distinction on the basis of, apart from other aspects, sex. This means that the other provisions of the declaration which talk about the human rights of men and women have not followed Article 2 in totality, as any kind of distinction within the provision would lead to confusion and, at the end, ambiguous implementation, which would be against humans. The declaration protects individuals' rights to equality, education, property, nationality, freedom of speech, movement, employment, non-discrimination, etc.

The International Covenant on Civil and Political Rights (hereinafter referred to as ICCPR), a treaty adopted by the United Nations General Assembly with the objective of recognition of the inherent dignity and the equal and inalienable rights of all members of the human family, through its Article 1 confers the right of self-determination. 'Self-determination', if interpreted literally, means that a human has the right to determine himself/herself, meaning thereby that a person may identify as transgender. The treaty mandates all the signatory states to ensure to all individuals, without any distinction (including on the basis of sex), the rights to life and liberty. However, the treaty also fails like the UDHR when it concentrates on men and women in Article 3. On the one hand, it talks about 'self-determination', and on the other hand, it talks about the rights of men and women.

The universally accepted documents that talk about the protection of human rights themselves fail in their provisions with regard to conferring human rights on transgender people. As documents are men- and women-centric, a document for transgender human rights is also required conferring human rights on transgender people and mandating states to implement the same, after which it can be said that the concept of human rights has been followed in totality.

Otherwise, the rights are not human rights but 'female/male human rights', as for a right to be considered a 'human right' it must concentrate on all human beings and not on any particular gender-based section(s).

OBSERVATIONS FROM AN EMPIRICAL RESEARCH STUDY

The author, along with other faculty members and students of his organization, conducted an empirical research study titled 'Transgender identity: Socio-Legal Position in the District of Gandhinagar'. The study concentrated on the *Hijra* or *Kinnar* community residing in the district of Gandhinagar, Gujarat, India. The report of the study has been published and is also available on the website of the institute with which the author is associated.

The *Hijra* community residing in Gandhinagar mostly comprises followers of the Hindu religion. However, their lifestyle includes rituals of different religions, because the followers in one group belong to different religions. It was observed through the study that equality has not yet been ensured by the state. The community has not received any positive response from not only the society but also governments. The community exists only because of their being considered holy and special by a few sections of the society which consider these people as being equal to god. Unlike other citizens, the community members remain uneducated throughout life because of their gender, their inherent rights over the property of their parents are taken over by other relatives, they have never been considered eligible for any sort of employment by the society and the state, and their access to hospitals, schools and other public places is always prohibited by one or the other person. No member of this community has ever been given love and care by their family after their conversion into a *Kinnar*. Discrimination is still faced by this community even after the passing of the NALSA judgement. Though the status of the 'third gender' has been conferred on *Kinnars*, actual implementation of the same has not yet been manifested.

CONCLUSION

Transgender people, despite existing since the beginning of civilization, have not been conferred human rights. The existence of such people is not endured by other members of society. The reason underlying this is that their existence has always been considered bad in society; their choice of gender has always been criticized and considered a mental illness. Human rights, which are the rights available to a person by virtue of their being human, have never been conferred on a person with the identity of being transgender. This is even reflected in the contradictory provisions of the UDHR and ICCPR which, on the one hand, refrain from distinctions based on sex and give importance to self-determination and, on the other hand, recognize the rights of men and women, leaving the transgender status untouched. When the international declarations and treaties themselves fail at recognizing the human rights of transgender people, it is obvious that the states following the same would fail too, which is why the status of transgender human rights remains untouched. To confer human rights on transgender people, it must be the international declarations and treaties that heed to the need for identifying transgender human rights.

Human rights are the rights that are ensured, without any distinction, to all human beings. Sexual orientations shall not be the reason of prejudice to any individual's human rights as these rights do not follow sexual orientation and are available to every human being. In order to ensure and protect the human rights of transgender people, the state should take essential actions through which even social acceptance of this community can be achieved. Mental trauma and harassment are common elements in the life of a transgender person anywhere across the globe; even the countries that recognize and confer citizenship on transgender people face issues involving discrimination faced by transgender people.

A human if not considered as human remains nothing in the eyes of society, and this may pressurize the existence of such humans despite them being human. The human rights available to men and women should be available to transgender people as well, by virtue of their belonging to the third gender. Their rights to life and liberty should never be taken away or questioned. Peaceful world is the dire need of today and it can be achieved with the implementation of human rights in totality that is inclusive of all humans of society.

Chapter 18

Right to Food

A Critical Socio-legal Analysis from Indian Human Rights Perspectives

Debarati Halder and Esha Maken

INTRODUCTION

The Universal Declaration of Human Rights (UDHR) has observed that the right to live a dignified and meaningful life would be incomplete and meaningless if the right to food is not ensured to every human being.[1] The right to food may necessarily include the right to nutritious food and clean drinking water for all, irrespective of age, gender, caste, creed, race, nationality, economic background, etc. Due to two World Wars, political tensions, famines, man-made and natural calamities and corruption, several countries may have faced food insecurity. Records may show high rates of death due to hunger

[1] See Article 25 of the UDHR which says

1. Everyone has the right to a standard of living adequate for the health and well-being of himself and of his family, including food, clothing, housing and medical care and necessary social services, and the right to security in the event of unemployment, sickness, disability, widowhood, old age or other lack of livelihood in circumstances beyond his control.
2. Motherhood and childhood are entitled to special care and assistance. All children, whether born in or out of wedlock, shall enjoy the same social protection.

and malnutrition due to these phenomena. On the other hand, several countries may have faced excessive production of food that had to be wasted.[2] This may have given rise to unequal distribution of food grains and natural resources worldwide, encouraging the growth of poverty, hunger, malnutrition and starvation deaths. However, it must be noted that food insecurity does not necessarily mean hunger. The latter is a wider term that may include the former and may be caused also due to various other reasons, including poverty, famine, draught, etc. Food insecurity, on the other hand, may indicate a possible shortage of food and food grains due to various reasons, including political tensions, economic recess, rationing of food supply by the government for some particular reason, etc. There may be a possibility of ending food insecurity when the above-mentioned conditions are removed.[3] Nevertheless, both hunger and food insecurity involve the violation of Article 25 of the UDHR, which guarantees the right to food for all. The Covenant on Economic, Social and Cultural Rights[4] therefore

---

[2] For more, see Food Wastage Footprint Impacts on Natural Resources: Summary Report. http://www.fao.org/3/i3347e/i3347e.pdf, accessed 21 January 2020.

[3] For a better understanding, see Cheryl Christensen, 'World Hunger: A Structural Approach', *International Organization* 32, no. 3 (Summer, 1978): 745–74. https://www.jstor.org/stable/2706332, accessed 23 January 2020.

[4] For more, see Article 11 of the Covenant which says as follows:

1. The States Parties to the present Covenant recognize the right of everyone to an adequate standard of living for himself and his family, including adequate food, clothing and housing, and to the continuous improvement of living conditions. The States Parties will take appropriate steps to ensure the realization of this right, recognizing to this effect the essential importance of international co-operation based on free consent.
2. The States Parties to the present Covenant, recognizing the fundamental right of everyone to be free from hunger, shall take, individually and through international co-operation, the measures, including specific programmes, which are needed:
   (a) To improve methods of production, conservation and distribution of food by making full use of technical and scientific knowledge, by disseminating knowledge of the principles of nutrition and by developing or reforming agrarian systems in such a way as to achieve the most efficient development and utilization of natural resources;
   (b) Taking into account the problems of both food-importing and food-exporting countries, to ensure an equitable distribution of world food supplies in relation to need.

has emphasized the role of nation states in ensuring the right to food for every human being through further ensuring cooperation between states for developing methods of cultivation of food, protection of natural resources, including water, proper distribution of food and food grains, etc., for all, irrespective of age, gender, race, class, creed, etc.

The right to food may however also be analysed from the perspectives of the right to nutritious food, the right to have food according to one's own food culture and choice, the right to a certain quality and quantity of food depending on the health and physical maturity of a human being, etc. In several countries, the sociocultural norms and traditions may mandate unequal distribution of food between male and female adults and children. In several jurisdictions, married women may be barred from having nutritious and a proper quantity of food if they fail to produce male heirs. Again, widows, including older widows and senior citizens, may also be prevented access to nutritious food in proper quantities because of the socio-economic culture and norms.[5] People belonging to the third gender and people suffering from physical and mental disability may further be deprived of the right to food as they may suffer social ostracization and negligence by families. As may be seen from the above discussion, the right to food may necessarily be studied in the background of the right to life and the right to equality. The Indian social–legal–economic–cultural set-up may show that while India has adhered to the norms of the UDHR and the covenant for socio-economic and cultural rights in ensuring fundamental and human rights to all individuals residing in India or Indian residents residing abroad, the majority of individuals in India may not enjoy the right to food as promised within the meaning of the right to life. While several studies may have shown the relationship of the right to food with the basic right to life from Indian–food policy perspectives[6] and the right to food from

[5] Esterik, P. V. 'Right to Food; Right to Feed; Right to be Fed. The Intersection of Women's Rights and the Right to Food', *Agriculture and Human Values* 16 (1999): 225–232 https://doi.org/10.1023/A:1007524722792, accessed 21 January 2020.

[6] For example, see Vivek Srinivasan and Sudha Narayanan, 'Food Policy and Social Movements: Reflections on the Right to Food Campaign in India', in *Case Study #11-1 of The Program: Food Policy for Developing Countries: The Role of Government in The Global Food System*, eds. Per Pinstrup–Andersen and Fuzhi Cheng (Cornell University, 2007). https://ecommons.cornell.edu/xmlui/bitstream/handle/1813/52622/dns_gfs_1200428211.pdf?sequence=, accessed 21 January 2020.

the perspective of Indian judicial activism,[7] this chapter aims to study the right to food from a holistic perspective, including gender and right to food, the rights of a child to access nutritious food, the right to food on the basis of traditional food habits, etc. This chapter is divided into four parts, including the introduction. The second part discusses the right to food from the aspect of the right to life and the right to equality under the Indian Constitution. The third chapter throws light on the right to food from the perspective of the food culture in different regions and among different classes in India, and the fourth part contains the conclusion.

RIGHT TO FOOD FROM THE PERSPECTIVES OF RIGHT TO LIFE AND RIGHT TO EQUALITY IN INDIA

In 1943, colonial India witnessed a devastating famine in Bengal province which is infamously known as 'Ponchasher Monnontor',[8] which was a man-made famine caused by British colonial rulers for them to stock food grains for the British army and British people who may be involved in the Second World War directly or indirectly.[9] The impact of this famine was so severe that over a million deaths were reported due to starvation in Calcutta (now Kolkata) itself, and the impact lasted till early 1945.[10] This famine also saw an increase in migratory labourers who sold their lands, travelled to other places and joined other professions as daily wage labourers or even bonded laborers to earn money and food for themselves and their families.[11] Later, in 1947, during the

---

[7] Lauren Birchfield and Jessica Corsi, 'Between Starvation and Globalization: Realizing the Right to Food in India', *Michigan Journal of International Law* 31, no. 1 (Fall 2009). https://heinonline.org/HOL/Page?collection=journals&handle=hein.journals/mjil31&id=701&men_tab=srchresults, accessed 23 January 2020.

[8] For more, see Amartya Sen, 'Starvation and Exchange Entitlements: A General Approach and Its Application to the Great Bengal Famine'. *Cambridge Journal of Economics* 1, no. 1 (March 1977): 33–59. https://www.jstor.org/stable/23596458?casa_token=ghtejOUbirAAAAAA:e1Y6tynNcX4DthT1aTCmLWSlHG0gwAjIGnPAGpGZeTxVeltyf9OjROY6zM_L009AuQOQ450r1f8XFrbcLaMbkc5qC36xJnfniD5t6baiGvWvrqrjVNY&seq=1#metadata_info_tab_contents, accessed 21 January 2020.

[9] ibid.

[10] ibid.

[11] ibid.

partition of India into India and Pakistan (including East Pakistan, now Bangladesh) and the consequential communal riots, food scarcity was again observed among victims of riot and partition who had to leave their homes, jobs and farmlands in haste in the north-western (especially Punjab) and eastern (especially Bengal) regions. Even though after the independence and partition of India several regions saw good cultivation of food grains, questions of hunger and food scarcity persisted.[12] While India had these general issues related to the right to food, the age-old socio-economic and cultural norms and practices yielded another sort of problem: women and girls were reported to be malnourished, suffering from hunger and discriminated against in terms of their right to access nutritious and required quantities of food.[13] This resulted in an increase in infant mortality, health problems in pregnant women and post-delivery health issues for women.[14] Further, the growing nuclear-family system motivated negligence and abuse of older family members, especially old widows who may be retired or may be dependent on the earnings of their children.[15] The framers of the constitution were busy enlisting the essential rights for survival as fundamental and basic human rights post-independence, and hence the rights to food and access to food, as have been enshrined in Articles 25 and 11 of the UDHR and the covenant on socio-economic and cultural rights, were not given special focus but were included within the provisions of the right to life under Article 21, which guarantees the right to life and liberty. This right remained largely inclusive of basic necessities to live a humane life, which loosely included the right to food and clear drinking water, along with the right to shelter and clothes. Human right activists used this provision to explore right to life within the meaning of right against

---

[12] See Gyanesh Kudaisya, 'The Demographic Upheaval of Partition: Refugees and Agricultural Resettlement in India, 1947–67', *Journal of South Asian Studies* 18, no. 001 (1995): 73–94. https://www.tandfonline.com/doi/ref/10.1080/00856409508723245?scroll=top, accessed 21 January 2020.

[13] See Malini Karkal, *Invisibility of The Girl Child in India.* http://ijsw.tiss.edu/greenstone/collect/ijsw/index/assoc/HASH019c/a0bde823.dir/doc.pdf, accessed 21 January 2020.

[14] ibid.

[15] See Saxena N. C. Hunger, 'Under-Nutrition and Food Security in India', in *Poverty, Chronic Poverty and Poverty Dynamics*, eds. A. Mehta, S. Bhide, A. Kumar, and A. Shah (Singapore: Springer, 2018) https://link.springer.com/chapter/10.1007/978-981-13-0677-8_4, accessed 12 February 2020.

solitary confinement and inhuman treatment in the prison,[16] right to privacy,[17] etc. It was only with the case of *People's Union for civil liberties (PUCL) v. Union of India & Others*[18] that the Supreme Court established the understanding that the right to life may necessarily include the right to food and access to food and the right to clean water, without which the right to life would become meaningless. Even though this case emphasized holistic understanding of the right to food, including the state's liability to ensure equal distribution of food, it did not place specific focus on the right to nutritious food for women, girls and senior citizens. The PUCL case touched upon the right to earn for a better livelihood as well, which would ensure the right to access to food. However, the right to food under Article 21 must be seen from the perspective of Article 14 of the Indian Constitution, which guarantees the right to equality, and Article 15(3) of the constitution, which provides the state special power to create laws for women and children. The right to food must also be interpreted in the light of Articles 39 and 47 of the Constitution of India, which place the onus on the state to promote welfare measures and to ensure raising the level of nutrition for the holistic development of public health for the benefits of all, irrespective of gender, caste, creed, etc. Traditionally, India has had problems of food sovereignty, whereby upper castes and males have had better access to food, including nutritious food.[19] Applying the principles of judicial activism, Indian courts have set judicial precedents for the right to food and equal distribution of food. However, it may not fall within the purview of the courts to check for equal consumption of nutritious food by males and females, and especially children, in each household. In several reports, the Food and Agriculture Organization (FAO) and the United Nations Children's Fund (UNICEF) have shown the gender and caste disparity in food consumption[20] in different

[16] For example, see *Sunil Batra v. Delhi Administration.*

[17] For example, see *Kharak Singh v. State of UP.*

[18] People's Union for civil liberties (PUCL) v. Union of India & Others, (2001) WP(Civil) No 196.

[19] For more, see Srinivasan and Narayanan, *Food Policy and Social Movements.*

[20] For more, see The State of The World's Children 2019 Growing Well in a Changing World. *Children, Food and Nutrition.* https://www.unicef.org/media/60806/file/SOWC-2019.pdf, accessed 21 January 2020.

social strata in India.[21] The courts relying on these data had ordered an enquiry and proper execution of the right to food within the meaning of the right to life. In reply to this, several reports have suggested that corrupt practices within the government, especially in the food supply departments, the patriarchal social structure and problems of caste have continued to prevent exercise of the right to equal access to food and clean drinking water.[22]

It has further been observed in recent times that several pockets of India have been affected by natural and man-made calamities, such as the draughts in Kalahandi, Odisha,[23] the 2013 Himalayan tsunami in Kedarnath[24] and the devastating floods in Kerala in 2019.[25] These have also impacted the right to food, including nutritious food and clean drinking water, for all who may have been affected by the said occurrences. Often, such calamities may lead to starvation, diarrhoea, malnutrition, etc.[26] It is therefore essential to ensure the right to digestible and nutritious food for all as well. Corrupt practices in food supply may mar this right. Victims of natural calamity might have to consume rotten or poisonous food, which might further complicate their health problems. The right to food within the meaning of Article 21 and the state's duty to ensure raising the level of nutrition and equal public distribution of food grains, food, etc., within the meaning Article 47 are realized through the establishment

---

[21] See Srinivasan and Narayanan, *Food Policy and Social Movements.*

[22] ibid.

[23] See Jagadish Pradhan, 'Drought in Kalahandi: The Real Story', *Economic and Political Weekly* 28, no. 22 (May 29, 1993): 1084–1088https://www.jstor.org/stable/4399777?seq=1#metadata_info_tab_contents, accessed 21 January 2020.

[24] *The Times of India*, 'Uttarakhand Floods: Epidemic Looms as People Complain of Fever, Diarrhoea', (26 June 2013). https://timesofindia.indiatimes.com/india/Uttarakhand-floods-Epidemic-looms-as-people-complain-of-fever-diarrhoea/articleshow/20770540.cms, accessed 21 February 2020.

[25] See *Business Today*, 'Kerala Flood: Heavy Rains, Landslides Wreak Havoc in State; Red Alert Issued in 4 Districts', 8 August 2019. https://www.businesstoday.in/latest/trends/kerala-rains-heavy-rains-landslides-wreak-havoc-state-red-alert-issued-4-districts/story/371142.html, accessed 21 Janusry 2020.

[26] See B. Fenn, *Malnutrition in Humanitarian Emergencies*, https://www.who.int/diseasecontrol_emergencies/publications/idhe_2009_london_malnutrition_fenn.pdf, accessed 12 February 2020.

of the Food Safety and Standards Authority of India (FSSAI), which ensures safe realization of the right to food through different laws, including the Food Safety and Standards Act, 2006, Food Safety and Standards (Food or Health Supplements, Nutraceuticals, Foods for Special Dietary Uses, Foods for Special Medical Purpose, Functional Foods and Novel Food) Regulations, 2016, Food Safety and Standards (Food Recall Procedure) Regulation, 2017, Food Safety and Standards (Import) Regulation, 2017, Food Safety and Standards (Approval for Non-Specified Food and Food Ingredients) Regulations, 2017 and Food Safety and Standards (Organic Food) Regulation, 2017. These laws, besides laying down basic principles for safe and healthy food preparation, distribution and serving in households, eateries and shops in regular times to the general public, as well as supply of food to victims of malnutrition and natural and man-made calamities, hospitals, etc., also prescribe punishments for violating the food safety norms set by FSSAI.[27] It must be acknowledged that while data and reports may suggest that human beings from different strata, women and girls, senior citizens, etc., may not access food or may be deprived of equal quantities of food as their male counterparts, the above-mentioned laws promise to ensure execution of the right to food in India. The issues of depriving people of the right to access food, right to nutritious food and clean water, etc., are also addressed in the Indian Penal Code. Other statutes also make it a penal offence to deprive people of the right to food: the various ways of deprivation that are shown in such statutes can be—by way of negligence to the child,[28] polluting rivers and water bodies which may be the natural resource for supply of drinking water,[29] refusing to maintain wives, children and old parents,[30] selling noxious food,[31] etc. However, as may be seen in the above paragraph, these laws may be continuously violated due to corruption and the patriarchal mindset of the society, and even due to lack of awareness.

---

[27] For more, see https://www.fssai.gov.in/cms/regulations.php, accessed 21 January 2020.

[28] For more, see Juvenile Justice (Care and Protection of Children) Act, 2015.

[29] See Section 277 IPC, which speaks about polluting river, springs etc.

[30] See Section 125 Criminal Procedure Code, which speaks about maintenance of wives, children etc.

[31] See Section 273 IPC, which speaks about selling of noxious food or drink.

RIGHT TO FOOD FROM THE PERSPECTIVE OF REGION-WISE AND RELIGION-WISE FOOD CULTURE AND FOOD HABITS

India is a country of diversity and multiple cultures that necessarily include multiple food habits. Due to the varied climate and soil characteristics, Indian food habits differ from region to region.[32] Thus, whereas northern and western India may show higher consumption of wheat, dairy products, vegetables, etc., southern and eastern India may show higher rice, milk, meat and fish consumption.[33] Further, southern Indian states may show higher consumption of fermented food because of the hotter climatic conditions. Likewise, eastern and north-eastern regions may show higher consumption of sweets. It may further be noted that these diverse food cultures might directly reflect the religious practices of people as well. While, on the one hand, people from the eastern side may be seen to use meat and fish as part of their religious food,[34] on the other, people from the southern, western and northern sides may not generally accept such food as part of religious food.[35] Again, country liquor may be considered as an integral part of religious and sociocultural food practices in many parts of India, especially among tribal communities. At the same time, consumption of hard liquor may not be considered safe for public health in many states in India. The government has implemented a liquor ban in several states, like

---

[32] Avinash Kishore, Pramod Kumar Joshi, and John F. Hoddinott, *India's Right to Food Act: A Novel Approach to Food Security* (Washington: International Food Policy Research Institute, 2014).

[33] ibid.

[34] See for more understanding in Tim Dyson and Amresh Hanchate, 'India's Demographic and Food Prospects: State-Level Analysis', *Economic and Political Weekly* 35, no. 46 (November 11–17, 2000): 4021–4036 https://www.jstor.org/stable/4409953, accessed 21 January 2020.

[35] Gabriella Eichinger Ferro-Luzzi, 'Ritual as Language: The Case of South Indian Food Offerings', *Current Anthropology* 18, no. 3 (September, 1977): 507–14 https://www.jstor.org/stable/pdf/2741405.pdf?casa_token=64NmPz47yYYAAAAA:DKMIRYy1f8XKT_2FzCekKy2-xGw4Wqnz1f0bkdpahOF1-QepxwqCpKtD4liMQJ1q_mRn3UETOuELivxB_9bVk-KOpO1HyYwvqu_jYB5Aw34K32z9_XE, accessed 12 February 2020.

Gujarat, Bihar, etc., to prevent sale of the same without license to anybody, including children.[36] Several religions in India may also mandate consumption of limited vegetables as a way to *moksha*. There are also instances of fasting for a continuous period of more than a month as part of religious practices.[37] However, it is interesting to note that while religious fasting has been supported by theologists, the said practice is also severely criticized by human rights activists and child rights activists, because this practice is also adopted as a form of passive euthanasia. Consider the case of a 13-year-old Jain girl who had reportedly consented for fasting for 68 days and lived only on boiled water: she died within 2 days of ending her fast, leading the police to arrest her parents for culpable homicide.[38] The question that lurked here was: can a child give consent for fasting? The rights activists opined that while this practice could have been accepted from an adult who may have voluntarily practised *tapasya* that included religious fasting, a child of 13 years may not be expected to withstand fasting for over 2 months.[39] Again, in another incident, the Rajasthan High Court ordered a police investigation of an alleged practice of Santhara (a religious practice of fasting which may lead to death) on an octogenarian by his family members.[40] Later, the Supreme Court stayed the Rajasthan High Court order

---

[36] For more, see Arabinda N. Chowdhury, Jayashree Ramakrishna, Ajoy K. Chakraborty, and Mitchell G. Weiss, 'Cultural Context and Impact of Alcohol Use in the Sundarban Delta, West Bengal, India', *Social Science & Medicine* 63, no. 3 (2006): 722–31, https://dash.harvard.edu/handle/1/35642346, accessed 21 January 2020.

[37] C. K. Chapple, 'A Jain Ethic for the End of Life', in *Death and Dying. Comparative Philosophy of Religion*, eds. T. Knepper, L. Bregman, and M. Gottschalk, vol 2 (Cham: Springer, 2019).

[38] For more, see India parents investigated after Jain girl dies from 68-day fast. Published on 10 October 2016 in *BBC News*https://www.bbc.com/news/world-asia-india-37604951, accessed 21 January 2020.

[39] Ibid.

[40] HT Correspondent, *Jain Woman Dies in Rajasthan After 50 Days of Santhara Fasting* (September 9, 2015). https://www.hindustantimes.com/india/jain-woman-dies-in-rajasthan-after-50-days-of-santhara-fasting/story-Gula2KwNXJVtiMiPBL3acO.html, accessed 21 January 2020.

of declaring the practice of Santhara a criminal offence.[41] However, the question on the supremacy of the right to life over the ancient religious practice of Santhara remains.

There are however instances of food culture–related violence that also hampers the right to life, the right to equality and the right to practise and profess a religion guaranteed under Article 25. Article 29, on the other hand, guarantees the right to enjoy one's own distinct culture. However, in *Ratilal Panachand Gandhi v. State of Bombay*,[42] the courts laid down certain grounds for restricting the right to profess and practise one's religion, which included public order, morality, public health, etc. This indicates that the right to food may not extend to the practices of eating food or feeding food that may harm other people. In this connection, it is essential to discuss the right to consume food as per one's own choice: in several societies with majority vegetarians, people eating non-vegetarian food may be targeted for their food habits. They may be beaten, ousted from the society and prevented from buying or renting properties in societies that may practice consumption of vegetarian food and which may feel that consumption of non-vegetarian food is immoral, unethical and against their religion. In this context, it may be interesting to know that several residential societies and schools have relied on minority rights as enshrined in Article 29[43] without understanding the inherent meaning of Article 29 read with Articles 21 and 14 of the constitution. Wrong interpretation of the provision and lack of awareness regarding the right to food as per cultural demography have also led to violent communal riots in several parts. Consider the cases of beef eating–related violence which erupted in several pockets in India: in 2012, in a university in Hyderabad in India, some students held a beef-eating festival, as they wanted the hostel menu to include beef. Apparently, it led to clashes between

---

[41] For more, see HT Correspondent, *SC Allows Jain Fast Unto Death Ritual, Stays Rajasthan HC Order* (August 31, 2015). https://www.hindustantimes.com/india/sc-allows-jain-fast-unto-death-ritual-stays-rajasthan-hc-order/story-Yn1Ql5mEZ2pAfxQ8zki3rL.html, accessed 21 January 2020.

[42] Ratilal Panachand Gandhi v. State of Bombay, (1954), AIR 388.

[43] For example, see HT Correspondent, *Society Can't Decide Members' Food Habits: Legal Fraternity*. https://www.hindustantimes.com/mumbai/society-can-t-decide-members-food-habits-legal-fraternity/story-4R2UqDddZdXhcRr3BdqgTK.html, accessed 21 January 2020.

upper-caste Hindus who consider the cow as a sacred animal and lower-caste Dalits who wanted to eat beef as part of their daily menu.[44] The situation led to the conduct of more beef festivals in different parts of the country, especially by student and liberal intellectual communities that supported the right to choice of food. This situation took a political turn with specific political parties supporting groups that opposed beef festivals in university campuses or in the vicinity of universities. Soon, there was news about non-political cow protection parties that started getting huge support for their activities against everyone who was supposedly seen or believed to have consumed any meat, irrespective of whether it was beef or not. Villagers, supported by such cow protection groups, murdered and assaulted several persons, including one man in Uttar Pradesh who had beef in his refrigerator and was suspected of consuming it as food,[45] individuals who were transporting bullocks for using them for agricultural work in Haryana,[46] etc. Soon, on 11 July 2016, a cow protection vigilante group was videographed lynching a group of Dalit men who were found skinning the carcasses of dead cows.[47] The victims were beaten with iron rods and were publicly assaulted. The impact of the victimization became graver with the sharing of the clippings through WhatsApp with multiple persons who could identify the victims, which raised the probability of further victimization of them as a group. While the police took steps to prevent any further eruption of violence due to public manifestation of beef eating, there have been reports of campaigns against animal sacrifice and eating of meat and fish during festivals, which may go against the social–religious–cultural practices of a sect of people.[48] A religious

---

[44] For more, see Violence Breaks Out at Indian Beef-eating Festival. https://www.bbc.com/news/world-asia-india-17727379, accessed 21 January 2020.

[45] *The Wire*, 'Dalit Family Stripped, Beaten As "Gau Raksha" Vigilantism Continues'. https://thewire.in/politics/dalit-family-stripped-beaten-as-gau-raksha-vigilantism-continues, accessed 21 January 2020.

[46] Samya Latif, 'Killed Allegedly By "Cow Protectors", Justice Eludes the Family of Mustain Abbas', *The Wire*, 8 July 2016. https://thewire.in/rights/cow-protection-murder, accessed 21 January 2020.

[47] See *The Wire*, 'Dalit Family Stripped'.

[48] For more, see Rakhi Bose, *PSA for All: Durga Puja is Not Navaratri So Please Don't Ask a Bengali to Not Eat Fish* (15 October 2018), https://www.news18.com/news/buzz/psa-for-all-durga-puja-is-not-navaratri-and-please-dont-ask-a-bengali-to-not-eat-fish-1909797.html, accessed 21 January 2020.

festival like Durga Puja in Bengal, India, during autumn is rather seen as a sociocultural festival where Bengalis consume meat, fish, etc., in large quantities. Campaigners for vegetarianism have targeted Durga Puja in recent times because of the food-consuming culture during this festival. However, such campaigns did not get much support in Bengal. It is necessary to know the reason for the same: during the Bengal Renaissance in the 16th, 17th and 18th centuries,[49] educated and intellectual Bengali youths, mostly belonging to economically higher strata, started a vigorous campaign against the caste system and colonial suppression with a liberal mindset to accept a sociocultural–economic renaissance.[50] The religious festivals like Durga Puja were used to break the myth of the Varna system or caste system, and this was mainly executed through the arrangement of feasts including non-vegetarian food by wealthy zamindars and landowners for entire villages or communities, irrespective of class, caste or creed.[51] One of the main purposes of such feasts was to feed poor people who may not be able to access animal proteins, including milk and eggs and tasty food, for the whole year except on such occasions as the festival of Durga Puja.[52] Thus, there may be several debates for and against the understanding of food cultures in India, which may need to be studied within the broader meaning of the rights to life, public health and public welfare.

---

[49] See Pulak Naranyan Dhar, 'Bengal Renaissance: A Study in Social Contradictions', *Social Scientist* (1987): 26–45, https://www.jstor.org/stable/3517400?casa_token=mivTVWBhsgEAAAAA:NXFn0pn6CjvLGBmI9IZX0iBl9TQLXDfyo_QXlwwK8-YyETCXd0Z_TzR1tTjhG9kwLdvAa-_ql6wlOJsGXmvk21hrRk_RufKhvheWfZ8_Mpvb6os9AXg&seq=1#metadata_info_tab_contents, accessed 12 January 2020.

[50] ibid.

[51] Tithi Bhattacharya, 'Tracking the Goddess: Religion, Community, and Identity in the Durga Puja Ceremonies of Nineteenth-century Calcutta', *The Journal of Asian Studies* 66, no. 4 (2007): 919–62. https://www.jstor.org/stable/pdf/20203237.pdf?casa_token=Mu0FEDmiE2YAAAAA:q8kya3JFB92qpXF5XG-q0e5MEwkuxtcWqxW_FiBVKEbvfxyTnOnsBDNvvrKanZn6kuL8RiZywFxam2bivx07-yXJYdABme1_Fjbi5ElECV8XX1LOXBE, accessed 12 February 2020.

[52] Andrew Clinton Willford, *Religious Resurgence in British India: Vivekananda and the Hindu Renaissance* (San Diego: Department of Anthropology, University of California, 1991).

CONCLUSION

The above discussions may suggest that the right to food cannot stand as an exclusive right. While the right to life may necessarily include the right to food and clean and safe drinking water, the right to food should be studied within the meaning of the right to equality and the right to protection against discrimination. India has diverse food cultures. While there are problems of food scarcity, unequal access to food, poverty, etc., this very understanding of the diverse food cultures must not be neglected within the study of the right to food. As evident in the above discussions, courts, on a number of occasions, have recognized the right to consume nutritious food according to one's own food habit as per one's specific culture, and courts and international organizations have also identified the need for more policies and execution of the same for ensuring the right to food and the right to protection against hunger. The existing laws and policies in India may be best utilized to achieve this goal if the government and other stakeholders become more vigilant regarding corrupt practices leading to unequal distribution of food. It is expected that if the stakeholders curb corruption and biased vigilantism, ensuring the right to food, India may overcome the challenges of poverty and food-related human rights violations.

Chapter 19

AFSPA and Human Rights Violation in Jammu and Kashmir

Manish Soni and Darshan Patankar

INTRODUCTION

Jammu and Kashmir (J&K) is the state in which the Union of India spends a massive amount of its revenue for both internal and external security. Compared to other states in India, which have a heavy population, it is less populated, but it has received a good amount of central government funds in view of the everlasting disturbances that exist in the state.[1] Despite this generous approach of the government, peace has eluded J&K ever since independence, and there have been frequent instances of gross human rights violations due to atrocious activities by the Indian armed forces personnel who are deployed in the region for maintaining peace and security against external enemies, including terrorists. Harassment and torture of local protestors (who are against the army activities in

[1] For more, see T. Raghjavan, 'J&K Gets 10% of Central Funds with Only 1% of Population', *The Hindu* (24 July 2016), http://www.thehindu.com/news/national/other-states/JampK-gets-10-of-Central-funds-with-only-1-of-population/article14506264.ece, accessed 26 June 2017.

the region) in the name of mob control, firing of pellet guns, lathi charges without any prior intimation to the local police, etc., by the army personnel have become a daily feature in the state, which result in large-scale violation of human rights. In addition to this, the worsening political situation has also had an adverse impact on tourism in the state, which was considered the main revenue-generating industry in J&K.[2]

The Constitution of India has guaranteed to its citizens the freedom of speech and expression under Article 19(1)(a), and this includes the right to voice peaceful protests against the state.[3] Freedom of speech has no meaning if there is no freedom after speech. This freedom of expression is a hallmark of Indian democracy and separates us from the autocratic regimes of the past. However, this expression through protests has been largely curtailed unlawfully through coercion by the armed forces, which has consequently resulted in abuse of human rights. These violations of human rights bring disgrace to India as the world's largest democracy, and they certainly do not occupy a place of pride in our hearts. Therefore, a solution needs to be arrived at which would ensure peace and stability and at the same time not deprive people of inalienable rights. As news reports suggest, in 2017, army officers in J&K allegedly tied up a local protestor who was protesting against army operations in the state to a moving army jeep in Kashmir region, and he was used as a 'human shield' against other protestors.[4] After this incident was brought to light, it was understood that there have been continuous tussles between the army and police personnel and the local people in recent years, because the former may have used force in searching residences for hiding terror elements and the latter believed that such sorts of violation of rights would best be resisted through

---

[2] For more, see Hakeem Irfan. *Kashmir Sees Sharp Decline in Tourists this Year Due to Political Situation*, https://economictimes.indiatimes.com/news/politics-and-nation/kashmir-sees-sharp-decline-in-tourists-this-year-due-to-political-situation/articleshow/58187469.cms?utm_source=contentofinterest&utm_medium=text&utm_campaign=cppst, accessed 26 June 2017.

[3] Article 19(1) (a) of the Constitution of India states that, 'all citizens shall have the right to freedom of speech and expression'.

[4] PTI, *J&K: Man Seen Tied to Army Jeep in Video Identified* (14 April 2017), http://indianexpress.com/article/india/jammu-kashmir-man-seen-tied-to-army-jeep-in-video-identified-as-farooq-dar-civilian/, accessed 13 January 2018.

creating as much hate as possible against the army and police forces. This mob mindset was allegedly further fuelled by terror organizations that wanted to use the general public to resist any sort of army operations in the valley. This incident was hugely criticized as a gross violation of human rights.[5] There exist several studies on human rights violations in Kashmir perpetrated by the armed forces. Several of these have analysed the issue from the perspectives of biased news reports on behalf of either India on Pakistan, reports that showcased the historical background of the clashes in J&K, etc.[6] The majority of such studies have suggested that violations of human rights do take place in J&K and that these violations may include those against both protestors of army operations, who may support terrorists, and civilians, who may not support terrorism but who may have become victims of the conflict zone because of having resided there for generations.

This chapter analyses the 'human shield' case in the light of the gross abuse of human rights by the armed forces in J&K and seeks to provide a balanced solution to ensure that human rights of the people of J&K are not violated. It also seeks to specifically examine the role of the armed forces and the police forces in the human rights violations in the light of the roles of the legislature, the executive and the judiciary pertaining to the protection of rights of the people. In the conclusion, this chapter offers suggestions for ensuring the proper exercise of human rights in the valley.

HUMAN RIGHTS FROM THE PERSPECTIVES OF THE INDIAN CONSTITUTION AND STATUTES

In the absence of conceptual clarity on the basic concept of human rights, one may infer several aspects in a varied and different context

[5] For example, see Access To Justice in Jammu & Kashmir, https://amnesty.org.in/projects/justice-jammu-kashmir/, accessed 12 December 2019.

[6] For example, see Teresa Joseph Kashmir, 'Human Rights and the Indian Press', *Contemporary South Asia* 9, no. 1 (2000): 41–55, (2000), https://dx.doi.org/10.1080/713658719, accessed 21 January 2020. Shakti Bhatt, 'State Terrorism v. Jihad in Kashmir', *Journal of Contemporary Asia* 33, no. 2 (2003): 215–24, https://dx.doi.org/10.1080/00472330380000131, accessed 21 January 2020.

rather than that intended. In the Indian legal perspective, the concept of human rights is defined by Section 2(d) of the Protection of Human Rights Act, 1993 in the following words: 'Human rights means the rights relating to life, liberty, equality and dignity of the individual guaranteed by the Constitution of India or embodied in the International Covenants and enforceable by Courts in India'.[7] This definition of human rights makes a reference to the Constitution of India and the international covenants that indicate that the concept of human rights is included within the perspectives of constitutional law and international law. This inclusion is certainly conspicuous in the Indian legal framework, if not in other jurisdictions. 'Human rights' is merely a combination of two terms, but these terms include a wide array of rights under various headings. The concept of human rights inter alia includes a wide domain of rights, such as the right to life and liberty guaranteed under Article 21 of the Constitution of India,[8] right to freedom of speech and expression guaranteed under Article 19(1)(a), right to freedom from torture, right to freedom from inhuman treatment, right to nationality within the broader Article 21 of the constitution and equality before law under Articles 14, 15, 16, etc. However, the concept of a right would not be realized unless the concept of duty to ensure proper enjoyment of such rights is established.[9] Therefore, when it is said that an individual possesses a human right, it has the effect of conferring a duty on the state and also on other fellow human beings to ensure that these inalienable rights of the people are not violated or abused.

The concept of human rights is largely accepted by each and every nation in the world and is universal. It received wide recognition because of the traumatic experience and shock the world experienced due to the two World Wars in the first half of the 20th century: these wars violated human rights to an extent that the world had never seen before.[10] Human rights are those basic freedoms that all people are entitled to enjoy irrespective of nationality, gender, ethnicity,

---

[7] Protection of Human Rights Act, 1993, Section 2(d).

[8] Constitution of India, 1950, Article 21.

[9] Salmond on Jurisprudence, Twelfth Edition, PJ Fitzgerald, p. 217.

[10] Justice Palok Basu, *Law Relating to Protection of Human Rights Under the Indian Constitution and Allied Laws* (Allahabad: Modern Law Publications).

religion, etc. The evolution of the modern concept of human rights largely took place in the 20th century. Despite the creation of many landmark instruments, such as *Magna Carta* (1215), the Petition of Right (1628), the United States Declaration of Independence (1776) and the Bill of Rights, the universal concept of human rights could not be established due to several limitations.[11] However, with the creation of the Universal Declaration of Human Rights (UDHR) in 1948, the United Nations ensured that all state parties would adhere to the same to maintain peace and prevent war and war-like situations in the world, as well as within their own territories. The UDHR also ensured that several rights that had remained unrecognized for years and which constitute essential parts for full enjoyment of the right to life should be given proper recognition. The enactment of the UDHR did have much to do with the egregious violations of human rights in the two World Wars, and these infractions certainly did play a significant role. The declaration mandated for the first time universal protection of fundamental human rights.[12] In 1966, the International Covenant on Economic, Social and Cultural Rights, the International Covenant on Civil and Political Rights and the International Convention on the Elimination of All Forms of Racial Discrimination were brought in to establish the formal duties of states to ensure proper execution of human rights as enshrined in the UDHR. In 1948, around the time when the UDHR was enacted, the framers of the Constitution of India were drafting the constitution. Although they did not make a direct reference to the UDHR, an analysis of both the documents would show close resemblances, especially in Part III of the constitution. For instance, Article 7 of the UDHR,[13] which speaks about equality of law and equal protection of laws, is resembled by Article 14 of the Constitution of India. The framers of the constitution relied on the UDHR to a great extent to include provisions securing human rights for the people of India. In the Indian legal perspective, the direct codification of the human rights law occurred with the passing of the Protection of Human Rights Act, 1993 that required the establishment of a National Human

---

[11] Justice Palok Basu, *Law Relating to Protection of Human Rights*, 7.

[12] For more, see http://www.un.org/en/universal-declaration-human-rights/, accessed 4 July 2017.

[13] http://www.un.org/en/universal-declaration-human-rights/, accessed 4 July 2017.

Rights Commission[14] and several State Human Rights Commissions.[15] These institutions were established with the objective of examining and investigating the complaints relating to violation of human rights and also to deal with negligence on the part of any public servant to prevent any such violation.[16] Apart from the Protection of Human Rights Act, 1993, a mention must be made about the procedural laws like the Criminal Procedure Code, 1973, which ensures the rights of victims, as well as those of offenders and accused persons. Further, there are also several specific laws, like the Armed Forces Special Powers Act (AFSPA), 1958 that provides special powers to the armed forces on the basis of human rights protection of the masses. However, the AFSPA has been criticized by human right activists for ignoring the rights jurisprudence in the name of army operations for maintaining peace. Several studies have been conducted on the issues of general human rights violation through armed conflict between militants and the army in J&K, targeting of specific communities in the said region by the armed forces, as well as by militants, rape and mass killing of civilians by the militants, as well as by the armed forces, etc. [17] Each of them shows how human rights may have been violated through the misuse of the special statute that was enacted to be used judiciously within the constitutional limitations.

THE LEETUL GOGOI INCIDENCE: TURF BETWEEN THE CRIMINALIZING ACT OF VIOLATION OF HUMAN RIGHTS AND IMMUNITY TO THE ACCUSED FROM REGULAR CRIMINAL PROSECUTION PROCEDURES

The much-discussed 'human shield' issue in Kashmir occurred on 9 April 2017 when, during the bypolls of the Srinagar Lok Sabha Constituency, an Indian army officer belonging to the Rashtriya

[14] Protection of Human Rights Act, 1993, Section 3.

[15] Protection of Human Rights Act, 1993, Section 21.

[16] Paramjit Kaur v. State of Punjab, AIR 1999 SC 340.

[17] For example, see Ganguly Sumit and Bajpai Kanti, 'India and the Crisis in Kashmir', *Asian Survey* 34, no. 5 (May 1994): 401–416, http://www.jstor.org/stable/2645054; Haley Duschinski, 'Destiny Effects: Militarization, State Power, and Punitive Containment in Kashmir Valley', *Anthropological Quarterly* 82, no. 3 (2009): 691–718.

Rifles, Major Leetul Gogoi, took a drastic step to prevent stone pelting on army officers by protestors: [18] he ordered the tying of one Farooq Ahmed Dar to the bonnet of an army jeep and paraded him through the villages of Kashmir.[19] The army claimed that Dar was one of the stone pelters. Dar vehemently denied the allegations of stone pelting.[20] This act of the army was condemned as violating the basic human rights by human rights activists and organizations. It is pertinent to note that the incident of Dar being tied to the army jeep was recorded by someone, and the recording went viral on the World Wide Web. The said clipping attracted further criticisms on the issues of criminal justice administration in Kashmir, human rights in Kashmir, etc. It further attracted criticisms from the former Chief Minister of J&K, Omar Abdullah, who also condemned the act of Major Gogoi through his Twitter handle. It was only after such expressed condemnation that the Kashmir police initiated criminal proceedings for investigation by filing a First Information Report against Major Gogoi under relevant sections of the Indian Penal Code.[21] However, Major Gogoi did not state whether he saw Farooq Dar pelting stones. Further, he contended that he had to take such steps to control the mob that started protesting violently against the army.[22] Clearly, Dar's right to personal liberty was violated under Article 21 of the Constitution of India. The justification of Major Gogoi pertaining to a *security threat* seemed inconsistent with the laws laid down by the Supreme Court, if we consider some of the landmark judgements by the court where it regarded personal liberty as the most precious possession of mankind and refused to tolerate illegal detention.[23]

---

[18] For more, see Toufiq Rashid, *Major in Kashmir Human Shield Row Says He Did it to Save Local People*, http://www.hindustantimes.com/india-news/major-in-kashmir-human-shield-row-says-he-did-it-to-save-local-people/story-rdXTsP89ylP1rqorkYg90H.html, accessed 3 July 2017.

[19] Ibid.

[20] For more, see the Express Web Desk, Major Nitin Leetul Gogoi awarded for counter insurgency ops: Here is how things unfolded after 'human shield' incident, http://indianexpress.com/article/india/kashmir-budgam-chief-of-army-staff-coas-stone-pelters-major-nitin-leetul-gogoi-awarded-for-counter-insurgency-ops-here-is-how-things-unfolded-after-human-shield-incident-4671502/, accessed 3 July 2017.

[21] See Rashid, *Major in Kashmir Human Shield Row*.

[22] Rashid, *Major in Kashmir Human Shield Row*.

[23] Icchudevi v. Union of India, AIR 1980 SC 1983.

Further, in the case of *Vinay Narain Singh v. State of Bihar,*[24] Justice Chinnappa Reddy opined that those who are responsible for national security and maintenance of public order must not be the sole judges of their arbitrary actions that may violate human rights of the accused, as well as the general public, who should be protected. Major Gogoi's act also violated the international norms of human rights, including Article 3 of the UDHR,[25] which speaks about the right to life, liberty and security of a person irrespective of race, creed, colour, gender, etc., and Article 12,[26] which speaks about the right against arbitrary interference to family, privacy, home or correspondence and the right against attacks upon honour and reputation. These authors argue that the act of Gogoi, whether in order to maintain peace and security or in order to execute arbitrary powers, definitely violated the rights of the person concerned and tarnished his reputation due to the unconfirmed allegations of stone pelting by the army. The act of the army of tying Dar to a jeep was certainly inexplicable and in clear violation of the right to personal liberty guaranteed by the constitution and an established human right. The life and liberty of an individual is sacrosanct, and it should not be interfered by any authority except when such interference is justified and principles of fair and natural justice have been practiced.

Further, these authors argue that the act also violated the right to life with dignity of the concerned individual. It is a well-established principle that life and personal liberty can only be taken away in accordance with the procedure established by law, and such procedure must be just, fair and reasonable.[27] Highlighting the rights of accused persons, in Nilabati Behera's case, the court observed that the right to life cannot be taken away or hampered without exercising due process, even on the pretext of maintenance of law and security by the state or state machinery.[28] Gogoi, however, would not be arrested, because he may be governed by the procedure of a court martial by the army instead of a normal criminal trial, since as per the law laid down in *General Officer Commanding v. CBI & Anr.* by the Supreme Court[29] the army has full discretion to

[24] Vinay Narain Singh v. State of Bihar, AIR 1984 SC 1334.
[25] Universal Declaration on Human Rights, 1948, Article 3.
[26] Universal Declaration on Human Rights, 1948, Article 12.
[27] Maneka Gandhi v. Union of India, AIR 1978 SC 597.
[28] Nilabati Behera alias Lalita Behera v. State of Orissa, AIR 1993 SC 1960.
[29] General Officer Commanding v. CBI & Anr., AIR 2012 SC 1890.

choose between a normal criminal trial and a court martial. This aspect becomes relevant because Major Gogoi might get immunity by virtue of a court martial as there are glaring examples of the army exonerating all its personnel in several encounter cases for want of evidence when allegations of murder, criminal conspiracy and destruction of evidence are made against army officials.[30] However, Dar's case was considered by the State Human Rights Commission of J&K, which directed the J&K government to pay a compensation of ₹10 lakhs to him.[31] The commission reiterated the paramount principle of personal liberty and emphasized the fact that protection of life and personal liberty of a citizen was the basic responsibility of the state government and that the torture and the suffering of Dar necessitated compensation at the very least. However, despite awarding the compensation, the commission could not decide on the guilt of Major Gogoi owing to the limited application of the Protection of Human Rights Act, 1993 in the state of J&K.[32] These authors argue that this particular incident itself may necessitate rethinking the application of the existing laws related to the armed forces, which have been involved in numerous instances of human rights violation cases.

CRITICAL ANALYSIS OF THE ARMED FORCES SPECIAL POWERS ACT

The AFSPA[33] collectively refers to several legislations that have been passed by the Parliament through which certain special powers have

---

[30] For more, see ET Bureau, *Pathribal Fake Encounter Case: Indian Army's Acquittal of Accused Soldiers a Blot on Democracy* (24 January 2014), https://economictimes.indiatimes.com/opinion/et-editorial/pathribal-fake-encounter-case-indian-armys-acquittal-of-accused-soldiers-a-blot-on-democracy/articleshow/29431106.cms?utm_source=contentofinterest&utm_medium=text&utm_campaign=cppst, accessed 18 July 2017.

[31] For more, see Farooq Ahmad Dar, *PTI, Rights Body Tells J&K to Pay Rs 10 Lakh to 'Human Shield'*, https://economictimes.indiatimes.com/news/politics-and-nation/rights-body-tells-jk-to-pay-rs-10-lakh-to-human-shield-farooq-ahmad-dar/articleshow/59528585.cms?utm_source=contentofinterest&utm_medium=text&utm_campaign=cppst, accessed 19 September 2017.

[32] For more, see Basharaat Masood, *Pay Rs10 Lakh Compensation to 'Human Shield' Farooq Ahmad Dar: Rights Body to J&K Govt* (10 July 2017) http://indianexpress.com/article/india/pay-rs-10-lakh-compensation-to-human-shield-farooq-ahmad-dar-rights-body-to-jk-govt-4744723/, accessed 12 July 2017.

[33] For more, see http://www.mha.nic.in/hindi/sites/upload_files/mhahindi/files/pdf/Armedforces_J&K_Spl.powersact1990.pdf, accessed 13 July 2017.

been conferred upon the Indian Armed Forces. This statute is applicable to certain disturbed areas of the country. AFSPA is a colonial legacy and was first used by the British as a tool to suppress the Quit India Movement.[34] In independent India, the Act was first made applicable in the states of Assam and Manipur to control the secessionist tendencies in these regions. Thereafter, in the year 1972, the Act was amended and was subsequently extended to all states of the north-eastern region. In 1990, the J&K AFSPA was enacted with a view to prevent the insurgencies and atrocities in the state of J&K.[35] A minute analysis of Section 3 of the J&K AFSPA may show that the said provision can be used as an essential tool to declare J&K as a disturbed area.[36] The same provision may be found in AFSPA. This legislation has been heavily criticized and is considered to be one of the most draconian laws since independence. The National Human Rights Commission has opined

---

[34] http://www.hrln.org/hrln/images/stories/pdf/172_hrln_2016_NorthEast.pdf, accessed 13 July 2017.

[35] For more, see ttp://www.mha.nic.in/hindi/sites/upload_filesmhahindi/files/pdf/Armedforces_J&KSpl.powersact1990.pdf, accessed 13 July 2017.

[36] S.3 of The Armed Forces (Jammu & Kashmir) Special Power Act, 1990 No. 21 of 1990 says as follows:

3. Power to declare areas to be disturbed areas.- If, in relation to the State of Jammu and Kashmir, the Governor of the State or the Central Government, is of opinion that the whole or any part of the State is in such a disturbed and dangerous condition that the use of armed forces in aid of the civil power is necessary to prevent -
   (a) activities involving terrorist acts directed towards overawing the Government as by law established or striking terror in the people or any section of the people of alienating any section of the people or adversely affecting the harmony amongst different sections of the people;
   (b) activities directed towards disclaiming, questioning or disrupting the sovereignty and territorial integrity of India or bringing about cession of a part of the territory of India or secession of a part of the territory of India from the Union or causing insult to the Indian National Flag, the Indian National Anthem and the Constitution of India, the Governor of the State or the Central Government, may, by notification in the Official Gazette, declare the whole or any part of the State to be a disturbed area.

Explanation.- In this section, "terrorist act" has the same meaning as in Explanation to article 248 of the Constitution of India as applicable to the State of Jammu and Kashmir.

that the AFSPA should be repealed.[37] However, in 1997, the Supreme Court of India upheld the constitutional validity of the AFSPA in the case of Naga People[38] and held that that the powers given to the army were not 'arbitrary' or 'unreasonable'. While upholding the constitutional validity of the Act, the court failed to recognize India's global obligations and duties within the scope of international law. However, the court provided a conditional clause that the declaration of a 'disturbed area' should be reviewed every 6 months.[39] The question that arises here is about how to prosecute army personnel who may have misused the law. As may be seen in the case of Naga People,[40] the court ruled that the central government had to divulge reasons for denying sanction, which resulted in the armed personnel escaping scot-free without facing the prospect of a prosecution. In 2005, a committee headed by Justice B. P. Jeevan Reddy was formed to review the AFSPA legislation mainly due to the alleged rape and murder of Thangjam Manorama Devi in Manipur by members of the security forces. The committee stated in its report that the law had become 'a symbol of oppression, an object of hate and an instrument of discrimination and high-handedness'.[41] In 2012, the Justice Verma Committee suggested that sexual offences against women by members of the armed forces or other forces should be brought under the scope of ordinary criminal law.[42] The committee also recommended an amendment to the AFSPA for removing the requirement of sanction of prosecution from the union government for prosecuting security force personnel for offences against women. Despite the criminal law amendment in 2013,[43] the

---

[37] http://nhrc.nic.in/Documents/Reports/NHRC%20Comments%20on%20Press%20Release%20of%20UNSR%20ESAE.pdf, accessed 13 July 2017.

[38] Naga People's Movement of Human Rights v. Union of India, (1998) 2 SCC 109.

[39] Ibid.

[40] Ibid.

[41] Report of the Committee to review the Armed Forces (Special Powers) Act, 1958, submitted to Ministry of Home Affairs, 2005, p. 75.

[42] For more, see Reports of Committee on Amendments to Criminal Law, https://timesofindia.indiatimes.com/realtime/justice_js_verma_committee_report.pdf, accessed 17 July 2017.

[43] For more, see http://indiacode.nic.in/acts-in-pdf/132013.pdf, accessed 13 July 2017.

recommended amendment to the AFSPA was not done, and still the condition precedent of a sanction is required in order to prosecute members of the armed forces. It was further observed by another commission, under the chairmanship of Justice N. Santosh Hegde, in 2013 that the AFSPA continues to be misused by the armed forces in different parts of the country, including the states like Manipur.[44]

Regarding the misuse of the AFSPA in Kashmir, an Amnesty International report observed the following:

> From 1990 to 2011, the Jammu and Kashmir state government reportedly recorded a total of over 43,000 people killed. Of those killed, 21,323 were said to be "militants",10 13,226 "civilians" (those not directly involved in the hostilities) killed by armed groups, 5,369 security force personnel killed by armed groups, and 3,642 "civilians" killed by security forces. 11 Armed groups have committed thousands of abuses. 12 In general, victims of human rights abuses in the state have been unable to secure justice, regardless of whether the perpetrator is a state or non-state actor.[45]

[46] It is unfortunate to note that till today, not a single member of the armed personnel deployed in J&K for the past 25 years has been tried and prosecuted for alleged human rights violations in a civilian court. Legal proceedings under military courts have remained largely unknown to the common masses. Despite repeated assurances by both the government and the army, more than 96 per cent of all complaints brought against the army in J&K have been dismissed as 'false and baseless' or have been regarded as cases deliberately made to malign the image of the armed forces.[47] The miniscule number of

---

[44] See http://mha1.nic.in/par2013/par2013-pdfs/ls-270813/2926.pdf, accessed 13 July 2017.

[45] See 'DENIED' Failures in Accountability in Jammu and Kashmir (2015), https://www.amnesty.org/download/Documents/ASA2018742015ENGLISH.PDF, accessed 12 December 2019.

[46] For more, see https://www.amnesty.org/en/documents/ASA20/001/1995/en/, accessed 11 July 2017.

[47] For more, see Indian Army Web Portal, 'Human Right Cell and Handling of Human Rights Violation Cases in the Army', http://indianarmy.nic.in/Site/FormTemplete/frmTempSimple.aspx, accessed 13 July 2017.

cases in which complaints against personnel have been investigated and military trials have been conducted are closed to public scrutiny and criticism. As such, the AFSPA now has an ever-growing power that on many occasions has been misused to violate basic human rights: for example, consider the extended scope of the AFSPA over Article 21 of the Constitution of India, which guarantees the right to life and personal liberty to all persons. Article 21 says, 'No person shall be deprived of his life or personal liberty except according to procedure established by law'. In Maneka Gandhi's case,[48] the Supreme Court held that the procedure for suspending the right to life and other basic human rights and fundamental rights would have to be 'just, fair and reasonable'. This case formulated this proposition by overruling the judgement rendered for A. K. Gopalan,[49] which had laid down the principle that any law enacted by the Parliament complied with the requirement of 'procedure established by law'. Section 4(a) of the AFSPA[50] has conferred upon army personnel the power to shoot and kill people; the procedure of such killing may not always be fair or reasonable, because it allows the armed forces to use an excessive amount of force. In the case of Indrajit Barua,[51] it was held that the state has the duty to ensure the protection of rights guaranteed under Article 21 to the maximum number of people. It is clear from the above understanding of the court that for the protection of the 'greater good', the court did not consider Article 21 as a fundamental right for the people of Assam, which should have dominated over any other statute. The court, in the above-mentioned case, stated: 'If to save hundred lives one life is put in peril or if a law ensures and protects the greater social interest then such law will be a wholesome and beneficial law although it may infringe the liberty of some individuals'.[52] These authors argue that this judgement directly was

---

[48] Maneka Gandhi v. Union of India, AIR 1978 SC 597.

[49] A. K. Gopalan v. State of Madras, AIR 1950 SC 27.

[50] The listed offenses under Section 4(a) are as follows: "acting in contravention of any law or order for the time being in force in the disturbed area prohibiting the assembly of five or more persons or the carrying of weapons or of things capable of being used as weapons or fire-arms, ammunition or explosive substances". However, neither of the abovementioned offences involve the use of excessive force dangerous to the people at large.

[51] Indrajit Barua v. Election Commission of India, AIR 1986 SC 103.

[52] Ibid.

an infraction of Article 14 of the Constitution of India which guarantees the fundamental right to equality before the law and equal protection of laws within the territory of India. The AFSPA is confined to certain limited parts of India, including certain parts of J&K and north-eastern regions, and the basic rights, including fundamental rights, of residents of such parts of India are curtailed due to the delicate security situation in these areas. Residents in the rest of the Union of India are not obliged to sacrifice their constitutional rights in the name of the 'greater good'.

The AFSPA also breaches Article 22 of the Constitution of India, which provides a safeguard against illegal detention: Article 22 mandates that a detained person must be informed of the charges on which he/she has been detained, he/she must be produced before the magistrate within 24 hours of detention and that he/she must also be provided the right to legal aid and counselling from his/her chosen legal practitioner, if any. A clear analysis of Article 22 may also show that the detainee must be presented before the judicial magistrate within the shortest possible time under '24 hours': this actually may mean that excluding the travel time to the court or to the judicial magistrate, the detainee must be presented before the judicial magistrate within a minimum period so that possibilities of custodial torture in police custody may be avoided. The AFSPA also contains provisions on the lines of Article 22 under Section 5, which states: 'Any person arrested and taken into custody under this Act shall be made over to the officer in charge of the nearest police station with the least possible delay, together with a report of the circumstances occasioning the arrest'.[53]

In spite of this, it may be seen that the detention of people (included suspected terrorists or supporters of separatists and terrorists) by the armed forces has prolonged for extended periods. Considering the case of Nungshitombi Devi,[54] the husband of the petitioner was arrested by the Central Reserve Police Force on 10 January 1981.[55] However, there was no information about his not being produced before the magistrate

[53] See Section 5 of the AFSPA.

[54] Nungshitombi Devi v. Rishang Keishang, CM Manipur, (1982) 1 GLR 756.

[55] For more understanding, see Syed Tazkir Inam, 'Armed Forces (Special Powers) Act, 1958: A Draconian Law' (2009), https://ssrn.com/abstract=1681499 or http://dx.doi.org/10.2139/ssrn.1681499, accessed 12 December 2019.

till the last week of February 1981. Researchers opine that this may signify that he had been detained under the AFSPA.[56] The court held that this long delay was unjustified and not reasonable. A critical analysis of the AFSPA would also suggest that the Act may lead to misuse of arrest laws and basic concepts of human rights and the principle of checks and balances.[57] Further, as Hans and Rajagopalan (2016) observed,

> ...the armed forces are not obliged to communicate the grounds for the arrest. There is also no advisory board in place to review arrests made under the AFSPA. Since the arrests are made without a warrant it violates the preventive detention clauses of Article 22 of the Constitution of India.[58]

This understanding is reflected in many cases where the detainees were detained by the armed forces: consider the case of Luithukla,[59] where the detainee's (who was detained by the army) whereabouts were not known for 5 years. Further, in the case of Bacha Bora,[60] the army repeated the same action of defying Section 5 of the AFSPA[61] (which provides for handing over the detainee to the officer in charge (OC) of the nearest police station to present him to the magistrate 'with least possible delay') when it detained the detainee for more than 5 weeks without following the legal provisions. Nevertheless, this shows that usage of civil society members as a *human shield* by the armed forces is nothing but an extended arbitrary practice of defying the settled law and violating the existing human rights provisions.

CONCLUSION AND SUGGESTION

The people of J&K have been consistently victimized by the armed forces for a long period, in defiance of the existing laws. The armed

---

[56] Inam, 'Armed Forces (Special Powers) Act'.

[57] Under section 4(C) of the AFSPA, a person can be arrested by the armed forces without a warrant and on the mere suspicion that those persons are likely to commit an offence.

[58] Asha Hans and Swarna Rajagopalan, *Openings for Peace: UNSCR 1325, Women and Security in India* (New Delhi: SAGE Publications India, 2016).

[59] Luithukla v. Rishang Keishing, (1988) 2 GLR 159.

[60] Bacha Bora v. State of Assam, (1991) 2 GLR 119.

[61] See Inam, 'Armed Forces (Special Powers) Act'.

forces, in the name of safeguarding the security of the nation, have deliberately misused the laws, including the AFSPA that, despite attracting huge criticism from human rights activists and organizations, provides certain conditions in line with Articles 21 and 22 of the constitution for detention of individuals. Some members of the armed forces have engaged in human rights violations, and they have not been punished. Gogoi's case may be considered as a glaring example. The immunity conferred on the forces allows them to virtually engage in any act without any legal sanction. These authors suggest that the hurdle in prosecuting armed force personnel, contained in the mechanism of 'sanction' under Section 7 of the J&K AFSPA, 1990, should be amended in order to strengthen the system of checks and balances to make the armed forces accountable to the legal system. These authors also opine that the system of court martial should not be used to shield the army personnel who may have violated the laws and basic tenets of human rights. Considering the political status of J&K, it may not be possible for the government to let the local administration deal with security and terrorism problems, and the armed forces may necessarily be allowed to work to prevent terrorism in the valley. However, these authors strongly suggest that if the AFSPA is properly amended, the arbitrary acts of the armed forces may be controlled and terrorism may be prevented in a more organized and fruitful way, which may bring peace to the valley without violating human rights.

Chapter 20

Legal Accountability in Corporate Social Responsibility in India

A Critical Analysis

Meet R. Shah

INTRODUCTION

Anita Roddick[1] opined that 'the business of business should not be about money. It should be about responsibility. It should be about public good, not private greed'.[2] The term 'corporate social responsibility' (CSR) does not find any uniform academic definition.[3] Several researchers have suggested that CSR may indicate social

[1] British businesswomen and human rights activist.

[2] Anita Roddick, Business as Unusual (2000).

[3] IRMA, *Corporate Social Responsibility: Concepts, Methodologies, Tools, and Applications* (IGI Global), https://books.google.co.in/books?id=atJeDwAAQBAJ&pg=PA189&lpg=PA189&dq=csr+has+no+uniform+definition&source=bl&ots=mxgXZqZy2W&sig=ACfU3U18LWWYIYBSYxQ82iOmB2pc2NY5Bw&hl=en&sa=X&ved=2ahUKEwjWppfxp9bpAhXE73MBHQoRCTwQ6AEwAHoECAkQAQ#v=onepage&q=csr%20has%20no%20uniform%20definition&f=false.

responsibilities taken up by corporate houses or corporate bodies.[4] Some researchers have shown that CSR may also include providing certain securities against financial insecurities to people living below the poverty line (BPL), or to people who may have suffered natural and man-made calamities, etc.[5] Howard Bowen (1953) explained the term CSR in the following manner: 'The pursuance of policies, making decisions and following the lines of desirable actions in terms of objectives and values of our society brings up obligation of doing CSR to businessmen'.[6] Bowen emphasized that the obligation of contribution to the objectives and values of society always rests with businessmen. While providing this insightful note, Bowen missed using 'companies or corporate houses' and indicated that 'businessmen' are duty-bound to give back to society. Technically, being a distinct entity, it is a company's responsibility to contribute by way of CSR. In the view of the United Nations Industrial Development Organization (UNIDO), CSR is a 'Managerial Concept wherein the integration of social and environmental concerns, by the companies, is done to assess business operations and interactions with their stakeholders'.[7] Accordingly, UNIDO makes 'CSR' a management concept where the term 'business operations' conveys or implies 'ordinary business transactions'. This contradicts the provisions of The Companies (Corporate Social Responsibility Policy) Rules, 2014, wherein clauses (c) and (e) of Rule 2 provide that the activities undertaken in pursuance of the normal course of business of a company are explicitly excluded. Further, as per

---

[4] Elisabet Garriga and Domènec Melé, 'Corporate Social Responsibility Theories: Mapping the Territory', *Journal of Business Ethics* 53, nos. 1–2 (2004): 51–71, https://www.jstor.org/stable/pdf/25123282.pdf?casa_token=pta3qR0g73AAAAAA:PDx4Bu3CUf5BgCriJWfQtPZ9NVMLhIrRBVVNEoZcjnUxJXtW1FLQa1PpMCKBzzYQH0tW4ySeSeG2jVHFo-ZUVuWPLPSsxAWTsCyKb6Sfw_KWKSe-Duyq, accessed 12 December 2019.

[5] See Archie B. Carroll, 'Corporate Social Responsibility: Evolution of a Definitional Construct', *Business & Society* 38, no. 3 (1999): 268–95, https://journals.sagepub.com/doi/abs/10.1177/000765039903800303, accessed 12 January 2019.

[6] Howard Bowen, *Social Responsibilities of the Businessman* (Iowa City: University of Iowa Press, 1953).

[7] United Nations Industrial Development Organization, *What is CSR* (June 30, 2017), http://www.unido.org/csr/o72054.html.

the International Organization for Standardization's Guidance Standard on Social Responsibility (IOSGSSR), ISO 26000,

> Social Responsibility means the responsibility of any organisation towards society and environment for the impacts suffered due to its decisions and activities, through a transparent and ethical conduct, that:
>
> a) can ensure contribution to sustainable development including health and welfare of society,
> b) can take into consideration the expectations of its stakeholders,
> c) is in consensus and compliance with the applicable laws and the international norms of behaviour, and
> d) is integrated throughout the organisation and practiced through relationships.[8]

As may be seen, IOSGSSR provides an elaborate and wide definition of CSR. It lays down four mandatory conditions that need to be fulfilled altogether. Here, the term 'impact' includes both positive and negative effects on society. The expression 'international norms of behavior' indicates expectations of socially responsible organizational behaviour. Business Dictionary, on the other hand, defines the term to mean that it is a 'company's responsibility towards the community and environment both ecologically and socially in which it operates. Companies express this through their waste and pollution reduction process; by way of contribution to educational and social programs; and by learning adequate returns on the employed resources'.[9]

Business Dictionary attempts to provide a broader definition. Similar to the previous definitions, it emphasizes the duty of the corporate houses towards the public at large. It provides three ways in which a company can perform its CSR obligation. However, prima facie, earning returns on capital/resources employed seems to be contrary. It appears to be profitable for the company and not society. According to Milton Friedman, CSR may be explained as: 'Increasing of its profits is

---

[8] International Organization for Standardization's Guidance Standard on Social Responsibility, ISO 26000, *Guidance on Social Responsibility* (June 30, 2017), http://www.cnis.gov.cn/wzgg/201405/P020140512224950899020.pdf.

[9] Business Dictionary, *Corporate Social Responsibility* (July 1, 2017), http://www.businessdictionary.com/definition/corporate-social-responsibility.html.

the Social Responsibility of business'.[10] Undoubtedly, this explanation is most controversial and debated. According to it, only people have responsibilities towards society and not corporate houses. It makes CSR look like a negative concept and an act not in the interest of employers. The explanation is in derogation and not in addition or in consonance with the concept of CSR. According to the Commission of the European Communities (CEC), 'CSR is a voluntary activity whereby companies integrate social and environmental concerns in their business operations and in their interaction with their stakeholders'.[11] Branco and Rodrigues opined that CSR is an ethical and moral concept.[12] Carroll arranged the concept of CSR in a four-level pyramid starting from philanthropic responsibility at the top, followed by legal, economic and social responsibility at the bottom.[13]

Companies, apart from making profits, are responsible for the impact of their actions on people and the planet in totality. The term 'people' may include but is not limited to a company's stakeholders, such as its employees, consumers, partners, investors, suppliers and vendors, governmental agencies and the community at large. Nowadays, these stakeholders expect companies to be responsible environmentally and socially while conducting their business.[14] Simply stated, the conceptual understanding of CSR rests on the ideology of 'give and take'. Companies utilize and exploit resources of society. Hence, through performing CSR activities, they give something back to society. CSR is the management tool that every company needs to achieve success in a sustainable society while fulfilling its business purpose(s).

---

[10] Milton Friedman, 'The Social Responsibility of Business is to Increase Its Profits', *The New York Times Magazine*, September 13, 1970. https://www.nytimes.com/1970/09/13/archives/a-friedman-doctrine-the-social-responsibility-of-business-is-to.html.

[11] Com (2002) 347 Final.

[12] M. C. Branco and L. L. Rodrigues, 'Corporate Social Responsibility and Resource-Based Perspectives', Journal of Business Ethics 69, no. 2 (2006): 111–32.

[13] A. B. Carroll, 'The Pyramid of Corporate Social Responsibility: Toward the Moral Management of Organizational Stakeholders', *Business Horizons* 34, no. 4 (1991): 39–48.

[14] Catalyst Consortium, *What is Corporate Social Responsibility* (Annual Report 2002), 2.

The present chapter aims to critically understand the concept of CSR, highlight the apparent issues/challenges in India's CSR provisions and make recommendations accordingly. As stated earlier, corporate houses cannot function in isolation. They have to be connected with society. Undoubtedly, it is the concept of CSR that ethically connects corporate houses with society. However, all efforts would be in vain if the legal principles of CSR are not flawless. Hence, the question of paramount importance is whether the existing Indian CSR policy is adequate to achieve the desired objects. Keeping this question in mind, now is the appropriate time to critically analyse the legal accountability for CSR in India. This chapter is doctrinal in nature. Therefore, it employs the historical, descriptive and analytical methods of research. Further, the chapter encompasses both primary and secondary sources. A uniform mode of citation is used throughout the chapter.

HISTORICAL PERSPECTIVE OF CORPORATE SOCIAL RESPONSIBILITY

India, being a secular country, sustains its history along with the different religions followed by its population. The concept of social responsibility is deep-rooted in the Indian scriptures and writings. Although no religious text ever uses the term 'CSR', the practices of religion clearly teach the importance of sharing one's earning with the deprived and vulnerable section of society. Islamic Law follows the principle of zakat. The term 'zakat' literally means 'to be clear, to grow or to increase'. It is levied on particular assets at a particular rate decided by the religious texts and interpreters. It mandates transfer of ownership of a portion of a person's property to poor and needy Muslims. Zakat is a form of obligatory charity.[15] 'Dasvandh' is religiously followed within the Sikh community, which literally means 'tenth part'. It is the practice of contributing a portion of one's earnings in the name of Guru. The principle stands that if you donate to Infinity, Infinity will give back to you.[16] In ancient India, Hindu merchants constructed temples and other forms of night shelters

---

[15] Muhammad ibn al-Hasan Tusi, *Concise Description of Islamic Law and Legal Opinions* (London, UK: ICAS Press, 2015), 131–135.

[16] Dasvandh Wazir Singh (5 July 2017), https://www.allaboutsikhs.com/sikh-principles/dasvandh.

for the poorer sections or classes of society. Also, a Hindu manufacturer or seller charged a specific amount from the purchaser to be used for charity purposes. This practice was famously called *Dharmada*.[17] These practices of different religions, followed in India, clearly indicate that the ideology of social responsibility is deep-rooted among Indians.

LEGAL PROVISIONS RELATED TO CORPORATE SOCIAL RESPONSIBILITY IN INDIA

The repealed Companies Act, 1956 had no explicit provision on CSR. However, by virtue of Section 293(1)(e), companies used to contribute an amount of ₹50,000 or 5 per cent of their average net profits over the three immediately preceding financial years, whichever was greater. The contribution had to be made to charitable and other similar funds. India's new Companies Act, 2013 incorporated the principle of CSR. The Ministry of Corporate Affairs notified that Section 135 and Schedule VII of the 2013 Act, as well as the provisions of The Companies (Corporate Social Responsibility Policy) Rules, 2014, would come into effect from 1 April 2014. The 2014 Rules, last amended in 2016, define the term 'CSR' under Rule 2(c). The rule states:

> 'Corporate Social Responsibly (CSR)' means and includes but is not limited to:
>
> a) Projects or programs relating to activities specified in the Schedule; or
> b) Projects or programs relating to activities undertaken by the Board in pursuance of recommendations of the CSR Committee as per the declared CSR policy subject to the condition that such policy covers subjects enumerated in the Schedule.

These criteria provide an inclusive and open-ended explanation of CSR. The expression 'projects or programs' is wide in its scope and nature. The only condition mandated by The Companies Rules is that the concerned project or programme relating to CSR shall be in pursuance with Schedule VII of the Companies Act, 2013. 'CSR

[17] B. M. Gandhi, *Hindu Law* (Lucknow: Eastern Book Co., 2003).

Committee' refers to the CSR committee of the 'Board' referred to in Section 135 of the 2013 Act. The term 'CSR policy' refers to activities undertaken by a company as specified in Schedule VII of the 2013 Act and the expenditure thereon, excluding activities undertaken in pursuance of the normal course of business of a company. Hence, transactions in the ordinary course of business are excluded. The expression 'normal course of business of a company' is defined neither in the 2013 Act nor in the 1956 Act. Both legislations remain silent on the explanation of the expression. In common parlance, the expression is understood as the usual transactions, customs and practices of a business. In cases of any conflict or overlap between the ordinary course of business and Schedule VII, the concerned activity would be treated as a business transaction and not as a CSR activity. For instance, if a tea plantation company plants trees and shrubs in close proximity, such tea plantation cannot be classified as CSR spending, because it falls within the ambit of 'ordinary course of such business'.[18]

Chapter IX, Section 135 of the Companies Act, 2013 incorporates the substantive provisions relating to CSR. Section 135 has paved the way for the mandatory CSR regime in the country. This section requires every company having a net worth of ₹500 billion or more, or a turnover of ₹1,000 billion or more, or a net profit of ₹5 billion or more during any financial year to constitute a CSR board.[19]

The section applies to every company, including its holdings or subsidiaries, and foreign companies having a branch office or project office in India, and the requirement applies irrespective of the nature of activities carried on by the company.[20] The Ministry of Corporate

---

[18] Corporate Laws and Corporate Governance Committee ICAI, *Frequently Asked Questions on the Provisions of Corporate Social Responsibility Under Section 135 of the Companies Act, 2013 and Rules Thereon* (2 July 2017), http://dhc.co.in/uploadedfile/1/2/FAQs%20on%20provisions%20of%20CSR%20under%20Section%20135%20of%20Companies%20Act%202013%20&%20rules%20thereon.pdf.

[19] D. K. Jain, *Company Law Ready Reckoner* 17 (Delhi: Bharat Law House, 2016), 815.

[20] A Ramaiya, *Guide to the Companies Act* 18 (New York: Lexis Nexis, 2015), 2524.

Affairs clarifies that 'any financial year' referred to in Section 135(1) of the 2013 Act, read with Rule 3(2) of The Companies Rule, 2014, implies any of the three preceding financial years.[21]

In accordance with Section 135(5), the board of every company meeting the threshold limit as stated earlier shall ensure that the company spends, in every financial year, at least 2 per cent of its average net profits made during the three immediately preceding financial years in pursuance of its CSR policy. Experience has shown that since the provisions of Section 135 and Schedule VII came into effect on 1 April 2014, there has been underperformance by, besides general disinterest from, corporate houses.

The concept of CSR is based on the principle of 'comply or explain'. Section 135 does not stipulate any penal provisions in case a company does not comply with the requirement of spending of a particular amount. The second proviso to sub-section (5) of Section 135 provides that if a company fails to spend the desired amount, the board shall in its report specify its reasons for not spending such amount. However, if one refers to Section 134(8), there is a monetary penalty, as well as imprisonment, for failure to disclose the reasons for not spending the said amount. The interpretations of different sections are misleading, and clarification is needed as to what attracts penalization.

Further, Schedule VII of the Companies Act, 2013 lists the activities that may be included by companies in their CSR policy activities. This list has undergone a recent amendment, through a notification, to include the government reforms such as the Swachh Bharat Mission, National Mission for Clean Ganga, etc.

MEANING OF CORPORATE SOCIAL RESPONSIBILITY: ILLUSTRATIVE VERSUS COMPREHENSIVE

The Companies Act, 2013, via Schedule VII, enlists activities that 'may be' included by companies in their CSR policies. The phrase 'may be' used here merely expresses a possibility. As law is a precise endeavour,

[21] General Circular No. 21/2014, 18 June 2014.

the word 'may' includes both 'may' and 'may not'. This demonstrates that the activities listed in the schedule are purely illustrative and not exhaustive. Thus, a bare reading of Schedule VII makes it clear that companies undertaking CSR activities are not obliged to be absolutely bound by the provisions of the said schedule. This is where companies find the window of opportunity to exclude themselves from doing what is required. However, trouble brews when other legislative provisions are referred to. The Companies Act, 2013 and The Companies (Corporate Social Responsibility Policy) Rules, 2014 are not in consonance with the legislative intention of Schedule VII. According to The Companies Rules, CSR projects or programmes shall be 'relating to the activities which are specified in the Schedule', or CSR policy shall be 'subject to a condition that such policy covers subjects that are enumerated in the Schedule'. As mentioned earlier, the condition mandated by The Companies Rules is that the concerned project or programme relating to CSR shall be in compliance with Schedule VII. Similarly, Clause (3)(a) of Section 135 provides that the CSR committee 'shall formulate and recommend a CSR Policy which shall indicate activities to be undertaken by the company as specified in Schedule VII'. Again, the Companies Act, 2013 makes it obligatory on the part of the CSR committee to undertake activities enlisted under Schedule VII.

A contradiction is evident on reading Schedule VII and the provisions of the 2013 Act and the 2014 Rules, as Schedule VII attempts to secure the freedom of corporations to decide on a productive CSR activity, whereas the 2013 Act and 2014 Rules prohibit companies from undertaking any activity other than those listed under the schedule. Restrictions on CSR activities are extremely harmful and detrimental, because CSR is subject to various interpretations and as yet does not have a universally accepted definition. The unclear and unbounded scope of CSR may result in disastrous consequences with respect to its implementation, as well as increased litigation. CSR activities can be effectively strategized only if corporate boards are free to operate and decide on the best activity. Otherwise, companies may not be able to productively contribute to the development of society.

CORPORATE SOCIAL RESPONSIBILITY—ULTRA VIRES TO THE FUNDAMENTAL RIGHTS: A PRIMA FACIE CASE

There has not been any constitutional challenge to Section 135 of the Companies Act, 2013. However, a few scholars have raised their voices against and do doubt the constitutionality of the section. Amudha Murthy asserted that Section 135 violated Article 14 and Article 19 of the Indian Constitution, arguing that it is against the principle of corporate democracy.[22] Similarly, Gyanendra Kumar Sahu opined that the Indian conceptual understanding of CSR seems violative of Article 14 and even some principles ensured under the Directive Principles of State Policy (DPSP) of the Indian Constitution.[23] Section 135 creates a classification among the existing companies in India. It divides companies into two broad categories, namely:

1. Companies having an annual worth of ₹500 billion or more, or a turnover of ₹1,000 billion or more, or a net profit of ₹5 billion or more; and
2. Companies not falling within the first category.

Article 14 of the Constitution of India guarantees 'equality before the law' by affirming that 'The State shall not deny to any person equality before the law and the equal protection of the laws within the territory of India'.[24]

The words 'any person' in Article 14 clearly make the equal protection of laws available to both citizens and non-citizens, and even natural and legal persons. The guarantee of equal protection of laws does not mean that all laws must be general in character. The Hon'ble Supreme Court, in *National Council for Teacher Education v. Shri Shyam Shiksha Prashikshan Sansthan*,[25] has reiterated that the fundamental

---

[22] Amudha Murthy, 'Constitutional Validity of CSR', *Law Mantra Online Journal* 2015 (2 January 2018), http://journal.lawmantra.co.in/?p=141.

[23] Gyanendra Kumar Sahu, 'Corporate Social Responsibility in Perspective of Indian Constitution', *International Journal of Applied Research* 1, no. 10 (2015): 801–803.

[24] Article 14, Constitution of India.

[25] National Council for Teacher Education v. Shri Shyam Shiksha Prashikshan Sansthan, (2011) 3 SCC 238.

right guaranteed under Article 14 forbids class legislation but permits reasonable classification.[26] Now, the question is whether the above-mentioned classification under Section 135 of the Companies Act, 2013 is reasonable.

In the celebrated judgement of In Re: The Special Courts Bill, 1978[27], the Hon'ble Supreme Court stipulated the test of reasonable classification in great detail. Para 7 of the judgement states:

> the classification must not be arbitrary but must be rational, that is to say… those qualities or characteristics must have a reasonable relation to the object of the legislation. In order to pass the test, two conditions must be fulfilled, namely,
>
> 1. That the classification must be founded on an intelligible differentia which distinguishes those that are grouped together from others; and
> 2. That differentia must have a rational relation to the object sought to be achieved by the Act.[28]

Here, the first test is not in dispute. Section 135 of the Companies Act, 2013 clearly satisfies the first test by creating a group that is distinguishable in terms of net worth, turnover or net profit. However, it is the second test where Section 135 fails to rationally connect with the object.

It was noted by the Ministry of Corporate Affairs that the objective of CSR provisions is to involve companies in discharging their social responsibility innovatively and with their efficient managerial skills for greater outcomes.[29] The interpretation of Section 135 clearly indicates its purpose of ensuring that corporate entities contribute meaningfully towards the growth and prosperity of the country.[30] Similarly, various reports also state that the basic objective of CSR is to maximize

---

[26] Ibid.

[27] In Re: The Special Courts Bill, 1978, AIR 1979 SC 478.

[28] Ibid.

[29] Amit Shah, 'CSR Fund Should not be a Source of Funding Government Schemes: MCA', *DNA Daily* (14 June 2016).

[30] The Companies Bill 2009—Twenty First Report, Standing Committee on Finance (2009–2010), Ministry of Corporate Affairs.

a company's overall impact on the society and stakeholders while considering the environment and overall sustainability.[31]

First, nowhere is there a mention of the threshold limits of net worth, turnover and net profit or why only these particular companies should be subjected to an obligation to the society. Such categorization of companies seems arbitrary and discriminatory. Is the Ministry of Corporate Affairs attempting to pursue only 'big fishes' or huge companies? Does it then mean that a company not meeting the threshold limit in terms of net worth, turnover or net profit does not have any obligation towards society and its prosperity? Undoubtedly, huge companies meeting the above threshold limit use a larger portion of resources as compared to micro- or medium-sized companies. However, in return, these corporate bodies also contribute more in the form of employment, revenue, taxes, etc.

Second, the principle of CSR is applicable only to organizations. It is not applicable to a partnership firm, limited liability partnership (LLP) or any other form of business, despite such firm meeting the threshold limit.

Third, the literal understanding of Section 135 means that a loss-making company's obligation to contribute to CSR is the same as that of a profit-making company so long as the threshold criterion is met. For instance, IDBI Bank, while remaining a loss-making body, spent around ₹35 billion over the last few years in order to comply with CSR provisions.[32] The corporate world is the barometer of the Indian economy. Unfortunately, with this provision, multinational/national companies would avoid investing in India. In terms of Article 14 of the constitution, the above rule in no way can be said to be fair and reasonable. In simple terms, a company pays various taxes to the government. The government uses that amount for the betterment of society. If a loss-making company is exempted from paying direct taxes, how is it reasonable and fair to mandate that the company pay for CSR?

---

[31] PHD Chamber, *Corporate Social Responsibility in India: Potential to Contribute Towards Inclusive Social Development* (Global CSR Summit, 2013).

[32] Gautam Dutt and Abhay Kumar, 'Loss-making IDBI's CSR Spend Rs. 35 Crore', *Deccan Chronicle* (23 March 2017).

In terms of the above arguments/contentions, it is clear that prima facie, CSR does not seem to fall within the scope of 'meaningful contribution' or fair and reasonable. To the contrary, it appears to be arbitrary and harsh. The author here desires to convey that the provision requires judicial review. Ultimately, the constitutionality of the provision is to be decided by the Hon'ble Supreme Court and not by a layperson. However, a prima-facie case exists, as the provision gives a broad idea that it is not in consonance with the object sought to be achieved.

THE SHRINKING ROLE OF THE GOVERNMENT IN ACCOMPLISHING MANDATORY LEGISLATIVE SOCIAL OBJECTIVES

History says that governments have not been so successful while delivering social and environmental objectives with an iron fist. The shrinking role of the government has led to the exploration of voluntary and non-regulatory initiatives. The same is the case with CSR implementation.

In the Annual Ease of Doing Business Report of 2016 of the World Bank, based on a survey, India ranked 130th among the 190 nations sampled in the survey.[33] One other survey conducted by a leading Indian accountancy firm, KPMG, indicates that out of the 100 largest companies of India, 52 companies failed to spend the required 2 per cent on CSR.[34] Further, according to an investigation by *The Economic Times*, many companies cheated the system by donating to charitable foundations.[35]

Ratan Tata opines that the phenomenon of CSR is meant to be good but actually is somewhat chaotic. His argument that India lacks

---

[33] The World Bank, *Economy Rankings, 2017.*

[34] KPMG, *India's CSR Reporting Survey, 2016.*

[35] Oliver Balch, 'Indian Law Requires Companies to Give 2% of Profits to Charity: Is It Working?' *The Guardian* (5 April 2016).

the infrastructural or oversight capability to introduce such scheme seems appropriate.[36] This is because the current situation seems to breed fraudulence.

CORPORATE SOCIAL RESPONSIBILITY: A TAX RELIEVER

A recent enactment, namely The Finance Act of 2014, clarifies that a company's expenditure under Section 135 of the Companies Act, 2013 need not be eligible for tax deduction as per Section 37 of the Income Tax Act, 1961. Tragically, the nature of CSR expenditure described in Sections 30–37 of the Income Tax Act, 1961 allows it to be eligible for tax deduction on the fulfilment of certain conditions.

In 2015, the then Finance Minister Mr Arun Jaitley made an announcement that the CSR activities of companies towards the Clean Ganga Fund and Swachh Bharat Kosh would receive 100 per cent tax exemption.

Such provisions and actions defeat the very purpose of the CSR scheme. Corporate houses are tempted to meet their CSR mandates through investing in schemes providing tax exemptions. The provision benefits companies in the place of society. Any contribution towards any such fund does not serve the specified purpose of the CSR scheme; rather, it becomes a source to suppress companies and to generate revenue. These anomalies in the CSR law need to be addressed so as to make it a more workable and friendlier scheme.

LACK OF CONSENSUS

Different companies subject to the CSR principle do not act in consensus with each other. The lack of coordination pertaining to their CSR activities results in duplication and, the majority of the time, activities within the same area. As a majority of companies or

[36] Andrew White, *India CSR Law Could Open Door to Fraud* (5 July 2017), http://www.philanthropyage.org/society/india-csr-law-could-open-door-fraud-says-ratan-tata.

industries in the country are situated within the same area, the similarity in their CSR activities becomes fatal for collaborative development of society in its true sense. This actually happened in a case involving companies located in Jharkhand, as reported by a leading newspaper—*The Pioneer*—wherein the majority of the companies spent their CSR amount on health, sanitation, employment-related vocational skills and education, leaving the remaining causes such as eradication of hunger and poverty, gender equality, women empowerment and environmental sustainability ignored.[37]

The India CSR Outlook Report 2016[38] presents the amounts of CSR money spent in the financial year 2015–2016 by 250 mega companies. It indicates that the majority of companies focus on particular types of sectors, leaving the rest untouched. This results in duplicity and non-development of certain areas that need greater attention for the collective growth of the country.

CONCLUSION

India, despite having a historical background of practices of social responsibility, actually fails to fulfil the objective of CSR.

The CSR policy of India is one of the most ambitious steps towards the welfare of society. The policy could be a game changer and revolutionize the country provided the government is able to overcome the challenges. The principle makes corporate houses realize the importance of giving back to society. Not only society but also the companies truthfully undertaking CSR activities are benefitted. As goodwill is synonymous to the reputation of a company, CSR acts as a means for companies to earn enormous goodwill and respect.

There exists an immense necessity for a concrete definition of the term 'CSR'. Section 135 of the Companies Act, 2013, Schedule VII of the Companies Act, 2013 and Rule 2(c) of The

---

[37] Sunil Kumar Singh, 'Corporate Social Responsibility in Jharkhand', *The Pioneer* (15 May 2015).

[38] Available at http://indiacsr.in/wp-content/uploads/2016/09/CSR-Outlook-Report-2016-India.pdf.

Companies (Corporate Social Responsibility Policy) Rules, 2014 need to be redrafted in consonance with each other and not in derogation of each other. The nature of Schedule VII should be open-ended, and companies should not be restricted by the activities enlisted therein. It is true that the Ministry of Corporate Affairs through a general circular dated 18 June 2014 cleared the air by stating that the entries listed in Schedule VII are broad-based and must be interpreted liberally. However, the said general circular still nowhere guarantees the freedom to operate outside the enlisted items. A solution can be achieved only through an amendment clarifying the requirements to be followed by companies.

Further, Section 135 and its ancillary provisions should be subject to judicial review and scrutiny so as to bring clarity and explanation about the provisions. There, also, is a need for pooling of companies' efforts in order to avoid duplication of CSR activities. The government, with the aid of leading non-governmental organizations (NGOs), may attempt to equally diversify the CSR amount across different sections of society. Corporate houses may actively consider pooling their resources and building synergies to implement CSR best practices, to scale up projects and innovate new ones and to reach out to more beneficiaries.

The CSR policy should be constructed in consonance with the tax regime of the country. Corporate houses may not be allowed to avoid one for the benefit of the other.

The Indian government may implement the CSR policy with an iron fist. To make this possible, it is extremely imperative to introduce penal provisions. Usually, corporate houses in default of the CSR obligation escape by merely providing the reason for the failure in the board report. Hence, changes should be brought such that every company failing in its CSR obligation shall be punished.

There must be a requirement for covering micro- and medium-sized companies within the CSR regime.

Creation of awareness about CSR among the general public is required to make CSR initiatives more effective. This would bring about effective changes in the approach and attitude of the public towards CSR initiatives undertaken by corporate houses. This effort would also motivate other corporate houses to join the league and play an effective role in addressing social issues.

Unfortunately, the old Companies Act of 1956 failed to impose any obligation on corporate houses to contribute towards the development of the society. Thereafter, despite the criticisms, legislators enacted a salutary provision. It is to be noted that even though the chapter threw some light on the challenges/issues vis-à-vis CSR, the author truly acknowledges the effort and success of the lawmakers. Without the huge contributions by national/multinational companies, the development of society would have been at a standstill. In the end, it is always 'better to do something imperfectly than to do nothing perfectly'.

Chapter 21

Paternity Leave

Right of the Father or Discretion of the Employer?

Mansi Chhaya, Shraddha Parekh and Debarati Halder

INTRODUCTION

Society has a role assigned to every kind of person and is also resistant to any change in its structure. According to it, a child's overall development is the mother's responsibility and financing the same is the father's burden. Any change in these roles is criticized in the harshest manner possible. Nowadays, both the mother and father work to share the burden of responsibility. However, while there is a concept of maternity leave, accepted throughout the world and legislated on in India, the leave that a man requires immediately after the birth of his child is neither recognized nor appreciated. Further, there is no legislation to protect the interest of men to take leave, and it is left to the discretion of their employer to decide on the same. It is evident from recent developments that there is a need to address this issue, but neither the Parliament nor the judiciary is receptive to recognizing paternity leave as a legal right enforceable in a court of law and passing a legislation that can make infringement of the same an offence.

This chapter aims to explore whether there is a need for legislation on this issue in India and whether there is sufficient awareness among the public in this regard. The authors rely on an empirical research conducted by them on 50 employees in Electrotherm (India) Ltd. (a private organization in Ahmedabad) to understand the phenomenon in a better manner.

MEANING OF PATERNITY LEAVE

Paternity leave relates to the bond of a father and his child(ren). It can be said that the word 'paternity' comes from the word 'paternal', which means from the father or his lineage. Paternity leave, in lay language, refers to the number of days a father is allowed to take off from work to be with his newborn child. As his salary is not affected by this leave, it can be considered a paid leave. The duration of this leave given is generally 15 days, for the father to be with his child.

Impact of Presence of Father in the Development of the Child During Babyhood: A tremendous difference may be noticed in the development of children whose fathers take an active part in supporting their birthing and initial nurturing compared to that of those children whose fathers do not take an active part in the same. Children whose fathers are involved in and become part of their development show certain positive traits. They are confident, more likely to show an internal locus of control, seem satisfied and do not feel neglected. Further, the parents', especially the father's, involvement makes a child capable mentally, physically, psychologically, spiritually, etc. The child is more likely to become responsible and understanding. These positive effects are seen in a child whose father is present during his/her development in comparison to a child who develops in the absence of the father.[1]

PRESENT-DAY CONDITION OF PATERNITY LEAVE

It was in 2016, when maternity leave was extended, that people also demanded paternity leave, but Women and Child Development Minister Maneka Gandhi said that such legislation would have little

[1] For more, see http://www.fira.ca/cms/documents/29/Effects_of_Father_Involvement.pdf, accessed 21 August 2017.

impact in India, where men do not even avail their existing leave entitlements to share the responsibility of childcare.[2] India will become the most populated country in the world by 2024 (approximate). Not every person in this country is a law-abiding citizen, and some do exploit the loopholes of the law or take advantage of the absence of law, but this does not warrant neglecting a major part of the population.

For central government employment, Central Civil Services (Leave) Rule 551(A) made provisions for paternity leave in 1999. This leave is available to the father after childbirth up to a period of 6 months of delivery of the child for a span of 15 days. The leave, if not taken, would be considered as lapsed. It can be taken for a maximum of two children, and after that, no paternity leave would be available. Since 2009, adoptive fathers have also been considered for this leave. However, for people employed in the private sector, the decision on paternity leave is left to the discretion of the employer. Thus, when an employer, using this discretion, does not provide leave, the father cannot take leave because he is not legally entitled to it.

In 2009, the Delhi High Court recognized the concept of paternity leave in the case of men who were teachers in private schools.[3] However, the need for legislation arises because of the fact that the role of the father in a child's life is important.

PATERNITY RIGHTS

The Indian employment law does not provide any law related to paternity leave for employees. However, there are some organizations in India which provide their employees with paternity leave so that the husband can take care of his wife during the last, crucial stage of pregnancy. This may not only have a huge impact on the spousal

---

[2] For more, see Shalini Nair, 'Paternity Leave Will be Just a Holiday for Men, Says Maneka Gandhi', *The Indian Express* (25 August 2016), http://indianexpress.com/article/india/india-news-india/paternity-leave-will-be-just-a-holiday-for-men-says-maneka-gandhi-2993274/, accessed 12 December 2017.

[3] TNN, 'HC Allows Paternity Leave in Pvt Schools', *The Times of India* (2 September 2009), http://timesofindia.indiatimes.com/city/delhi/HC-allows-paternity-leave-in-pvt-schools/articleshow/4961013.cms, accessed 12 December 2017.

relationship, but it may also create a responsible bond between the father and the newborn child. However, the hard reality of Indian patriarchal society is that companies and people still consider women's job as secondary and thus feel that their stay in the job would be temporary until they get pregnant, subconsciously considering the financial cost of maternity leave. According to the World Economic Forum, Indian ranks 108 out of 148 countries, with only a 0.35 female-to-male ratio in labour force participation.[4]

It is interesting to note that several countries have recognized the need for paternity leave and that the respective governments have also provided paternity leave in specific statues. The periods of paternity leave in different countries is compiled in the table below:

Table 21.1 Paternity Leaves Across the World

Country	Period (Weeks)
Portugal	21.3
South Korea	52.6
France	28
Sweden	10
Italy	13
Norway	14
Canada	35
Japan	52
Netherlands	26.4
Iceland	13
Luxembourg	26.4
India	–

The above table shows that while the countries like Japan, South Korea, etc., provide maximum paternity leave, India does not provide any statutory paternity leave. Further, it may also be seen that

[4] Vikas Gupta, 'Paternity Leave: The New-age Hands-on Fathers' (11 December 2016), http://www.freepressjournal.in/featured-blog/paternity-leave-the-new-age-hands-on-fathers/985296, accessed 12 December 2017.

worldwide, several companies have been providing paternity leaves to their employees. The table below shows the paternity leave periods that are provided by these companies.[5]

Table 21.2 Company Providing Paternity Leave Worldwide

Company	Paternity Period
Netflix	Full year
Spotify	24 Weeks
Facebook	17 Weeks
Pinterest	16 Weeks
Google	12 Weeks
Microsoft	12 Weeks
Bank of America	12 Weeks
LinkedIn	12 Weeks
Twitter	10 Weeks

However, while there is no proper government initiative regarding paternity leave in India, several companies having offices in India do provide paternity leave as a policy. The table below shows the paternity leave periods provided by such companies.[6]

Table 21.3 Company Providing Paternity Leave in India

Indian Companies	Period
Microsoft India	6 Weeks
Facebook India	16 Weeks
Google India	4 Weeks
Star India	4 Weeks
Adobe India	10 Days
Flipkart	10 Days
Airtel	1 Week

[5] The authors have created this table from the information provided in https://www.fatherly.com/love-money/50-best-companies-new-dads-ranking-2017-parental-leave-childcare/, accessed 12 December 2017.

[6] Ibid.

It must be noted that while maternity benefits include maternity leave, paternity leave is necessary not only for the holistic development of the newborn child but also as a supportive mechanism to establish women's right to reproduction and motherhood in a healthy way. The Convention on the Rights of the Child, 1989 has emphasized the holistic development of children right from the womb and parental engagement in such development. The concept of parental engagement can in no way be limited to the mother's engagement in nurturing the newborn child. Similarly, the Juvenile Justice (Care and Protection of Children) Act, 2000 (amended in 2016) also emphasizes parental care, family care and the responsibility of caregivers towards the development and safety of the child. This remotely touches on the aspect of paternity leave, which, however, is not addressed in any law in India. However, the duties of the father towards his children are enshrined in a few legal provisions as follows: while the Constitution of India directs all parents to be equally responsible for their children under Article 14 (which speaks about the right to equality) and Article 15 (which prohibits discrimination on the basis of gender, race, class, caste, etc.), it also emphasizes the duties of the state to monitor the holistic development of children under Article 39(f); the Protection of Children from Sexual Offences Act, 2012 is again a novel provision that emphasizes the parents', especially the father's duty towards a child through prohibiting and penalizing any sort of sexual relationship between a father and his child or assault by the former on the latter, irrespective of the child's gender. But again, these may only highlight the duties of the father after the child is born and not his duties of supporting the wife in pregnancy or taking care of the newborn child. While this chapter was being written, a provision titled Paternity Benefit Bill, 2017 was proposed by Mr Rajiv Satav, Member of Parliament.[7] This bill was proposed with the aim to regulate employment of men in every sector for a certain period before and after having a child. The bill proposes payment of paternity benefits for the days when a new father would be engaged in assisting his wife just before and after the delivery. The bill also suggests provision of maximum 3 months' paternity leave under certain circumstances. However, at the time when this chapter

[7] The bill can be viewed at https://biblehr.com/wp-content/uploads/2017/09/Paternity-Benefits-Bill-2017.pdf, accessed 12 November 2017.

was submitted, no proper information was available regarding whether the bill has been considered by the Parliament and whether any part of the bill has been considered in amending the existing Maternity Benefit Act. It is unfortunate to note that in India, gender stereotyping has prevented social acceptance of paternity leave as well, since the general norm of the society rules that women are supposed to take care of earlier women.

ROLE OF THE FATHER IN A CHILD'S LIFE

Parenting or child rearing is said to be a team effort. Wonderful and fruitful parenting is that which involves both the mother and the father taking an active part in the child's life. The 'task' of raising a child can be divided equally and interchangeably among both parents. Shared parenting may start right from the time of the first trimester of pregnancy, when the would-be father may need to take care of his wife, that is, the would-be mother. The duties should include not only providing medical facilities to the wife but also providing physical comfort to the expecting mother. This shared parenting may also include responsibilities of the new father during birthing and, after delivery, neonatal care of the child.[8] Decades of research and hundreds of studies have proven that the more involved a dad is in his child's development, the more successful his child would be. A father can influence the physical, intellectual, emotional and social development of his child.[9] The role of the father can further be important as a playmate. Playing with their children gives fathers an excellent medium of communication, as most fathers are not good at expressing their feelings through words and long chats. It also would provide them opportunities to teach their child a few life lessons, like sharing and dealing with winning and losing.[10] The father's role as a

[8] For more, see information available at http://www.indiaparenting.com/pregnancy/117_5605/is-paternity-leave-allowed-in-india.html, accessed 12 December 2017.

[9] For more, see information available at http://www.parenting.com/article/why-kids-need-their-dads,' accessed 12 December 2017.

[10] For more, see information available at http://www.beingtheparent.com/role-of-father-in-raising-a-child/, accessed 12 December 2017.

teacher, coach, protector, companion and finally as a role model cannot be ignored either. Studies have shown that such influences on a child may be stronger when the father takes an active part in the child's rearing from the very beginning of the latter's life.

ANALYSIS OF THE DATA COLLECTED

As has been mentioned earlier, the authors conducted an empirical research with 50 employees of Electroherm (India) Ltd. (a private organization in Ahmedabad) to understand the necessity of and awareness regarding paternity leave. Due to paucity of fund and lack of time, this research could not be conducted on a large scale. Hence, the results may indicate a general understanding of only Ahmedabad city. The questionnaire included various questions related to the awareness of the concept of paternity, need for legislation on the same and need of the father in the initial days by a child. There were a total of 50 sample respondents, out of which 11 were women and 39 men. In terms of percentage, 22 per cent of the sample respondents were women and 78 per cent were men, as shown in the pie chart. The sample included not only husbands/fathers but also women who were wives and/or mothers to determine the level of awareness among both genders.

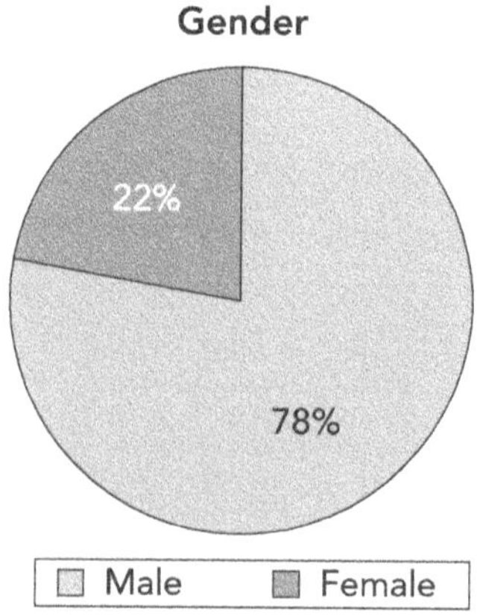

The responses to the questionnaire were further analysed on the basis of gender and also on the basis of the respondents' being married or unmarried, so that their awareness, needs and thoughts could be understood.

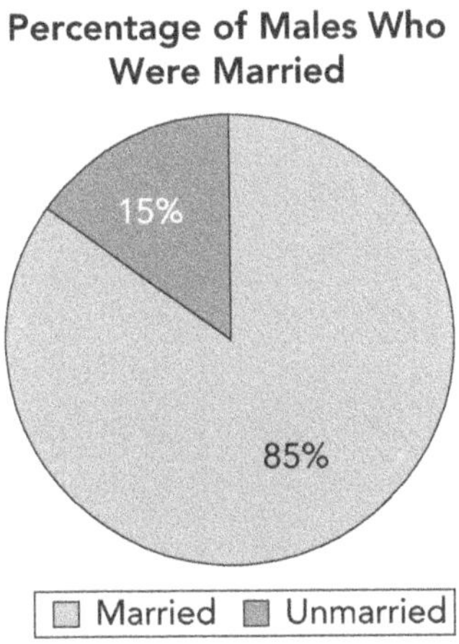

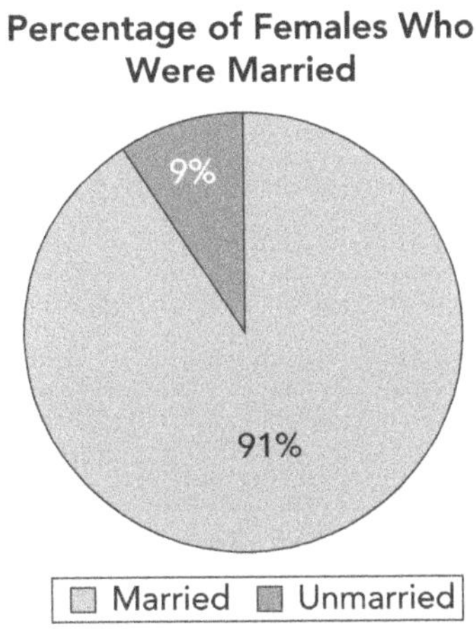

Their awareness about paternity leave was also judged, because if the concept is not known to many, the need for legislation would not be realized.

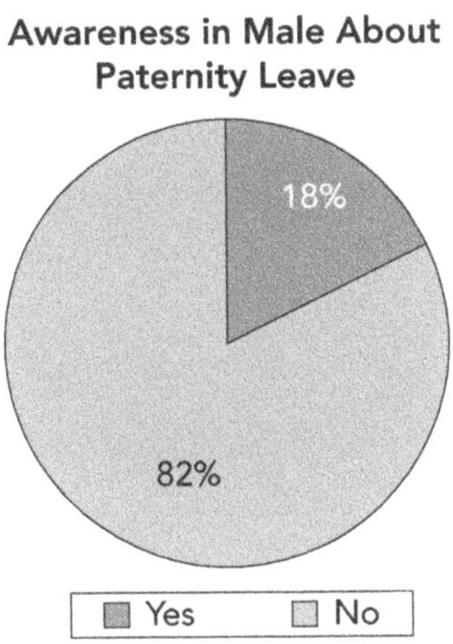

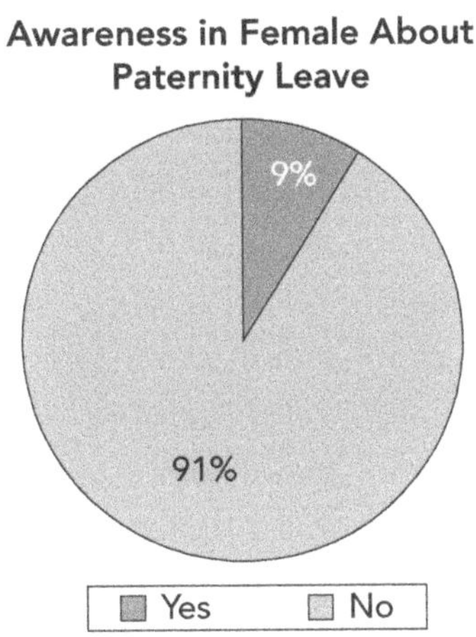

From the above pie chart, it can be easily noticed that among the men, 82 per cent, in comparison to only 9 per cent among the women, were not aware of the concept of paternity leave. Further, even those who were aware of the concept of paternity leave were not aware of the absence or presence of laws that define and protect the concept.

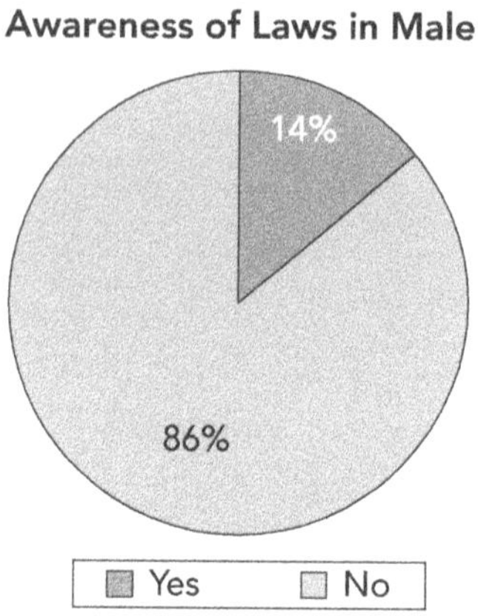

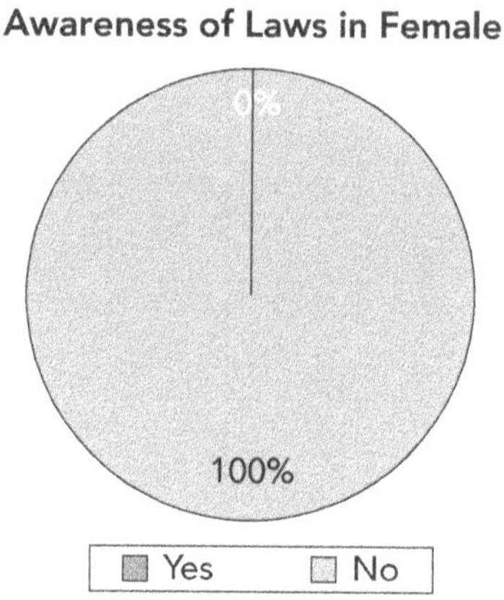

Among the people who were aware of the concept, 100 per cent of the men felt that legislation was required, and more than 60 per cent of the women felt the requirement of a law for men such as that for themselves.

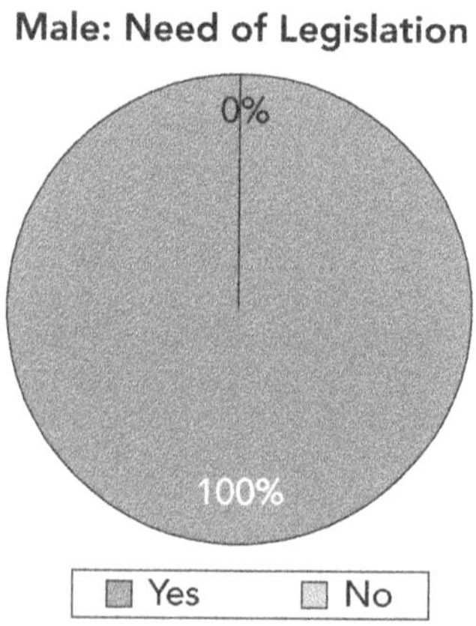

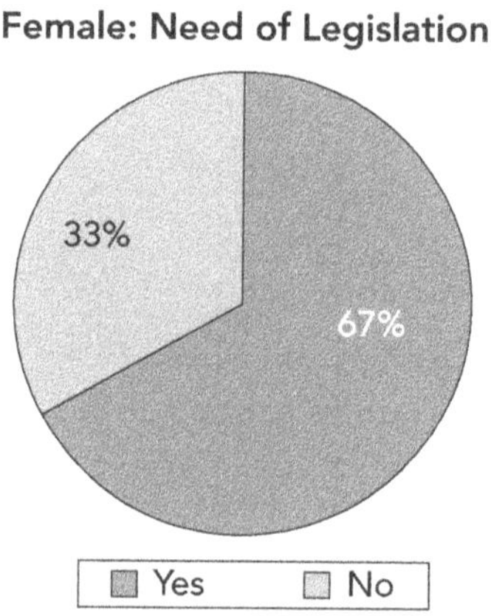

There were also a number of people who thought that absence of the father in the initial days of a newborn child would affect the bond between the father and the child.

Men: Child Needs a Father Initially After His Birth

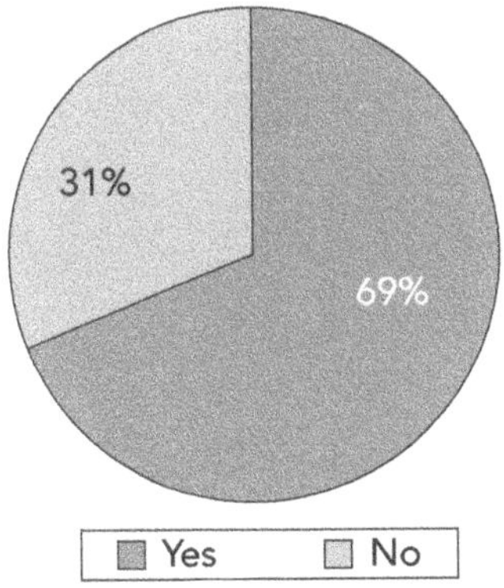

Female: Child Needs a Father Initially After His Birth

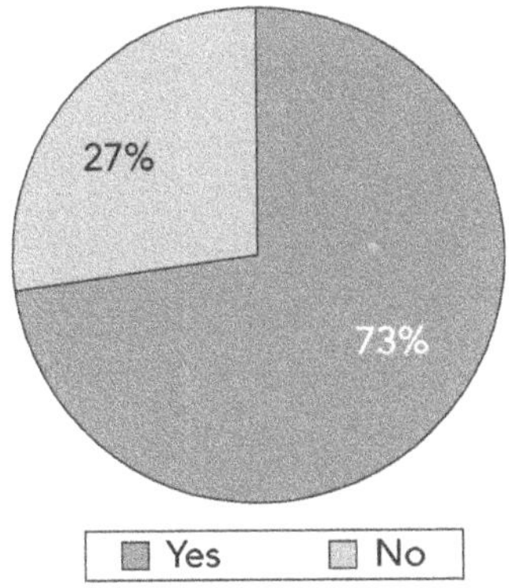

As the data suggest, 82 per cent of the women felt that they would need the support of the husband, and almost 77 per cent of the men felt that the presence of the husband could help in better handling of the situation. These data may suggest that the presence of the husband can really help. A successful pregnancy may be a result of spousal support from the husband to the woman concerned. The period of pregnancy is not a stage during which the whole responsibility lies on the shoulders of the woman; it requires the combined effort of both spouses. The responsibility of the husband is very important, as he has to provide emotional support and an appropriate psychological atmosphere to the wife so that she completes the pregnancy without any complication or problem. The presence and absence of the husband during pregnancy affect the health of the wife and the unborn child positively and negatively, respectively. The husband's emotional and psychological support to his wife during the critical phase of pregnancy results in strengthening the relationship they share, grants the wife security and increases their love for each other. On the other hand, the absence of the husband during pregnancy affects the health of the wife and the unborn child negatively, leading to stress and other complications in the former which also indirectly affect the health of the embryo.

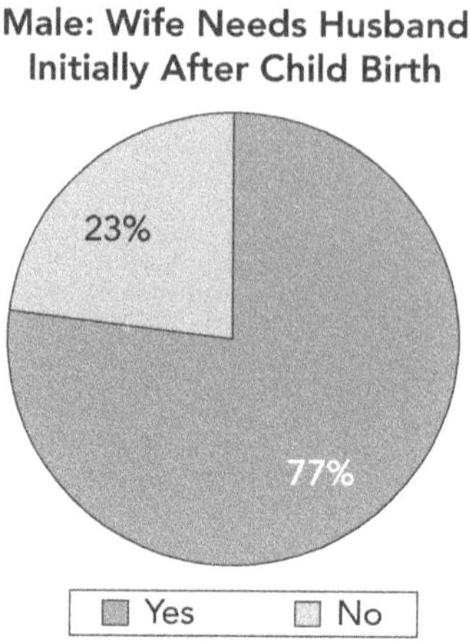

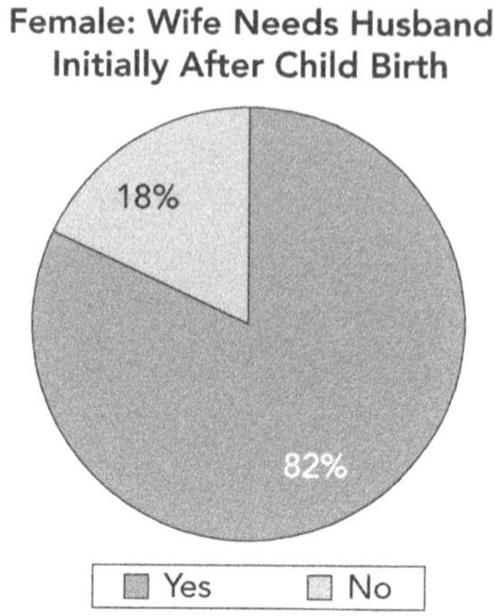

Generally men may consider changing their daily work schedule or even certain life styles after considering the medical and psychological needs of their wives. Data were collected to assess whether a man faces mental stress when burdened with the responsibility of a new life.

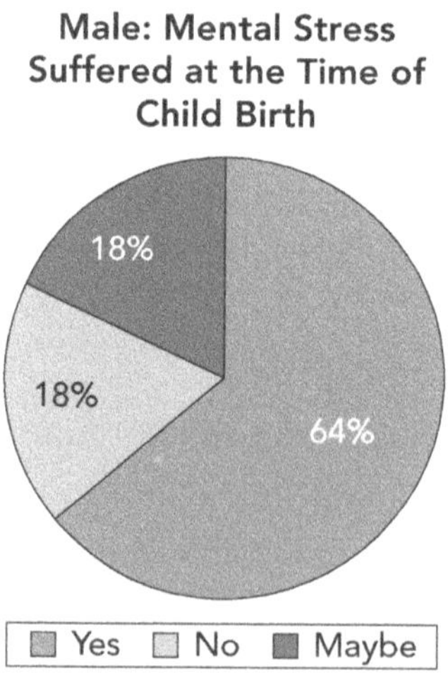

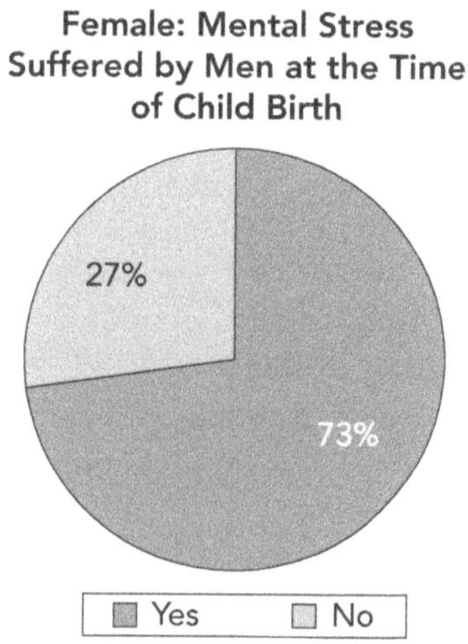

From the data collected and other relevant information, it may be noted that the absence of any focused legislature providing paternity leave and benefits may enhance physical pain and mental stress.

CONCLUSION AND SUGGESTION

The above discussions and empirical research results show that paternity as a concept is not widely accepted and known to people. These authors suggest that the awareness level and perspectives of the top management in organizations should be checked. Further research on a larger scale should be done to determine how the proposed bill can be improved for the benefit of people at large. As seen earlier, many private companies recognize the need of their male employees and provide paternity leave. However, this is by exercise of the discretion they have, and they may change their policies according to their need. Thus, a proper legislation is required to place a mandate on organizations, so that this right to paternity leave becomes enforceable in a court of law. The data in the figures in this chapter clearly show that the presence of a man with his newborn child and wife after childbirth is important not only for the two of them (child and wife) but also for himself, because he might go through many psychological/mental stresses and changes resulting from the burden of responsibility of a new life. Provision for paternity leave would be beneficial not only to employees but also to the organization, since employee satisfaction would increase and, in turn, turnover of human resources also would decrease. These authors suggest that along with legislating a separate Paternity benefit Bill, the Maternity Benefit Act also be amended to make it mandatory for husbands to support wives during and after pregnancy. The Paternity Benefit Act simultaneously must be made more accessible and functional through strengthening the role of the inspectors.

Chapter 22

Land Acquisition Laws in the Light of Eminent Domain Principle

A Socio-Legal Analysis

Bhaumik P. Upadhyay and Debarati Halder

INTRODUCTION

A brief reading into India's sociocultural–economic history would suggest that the Indian economy had been largely dependent on agriculture and agriculture-based industries.[1] Since time immemorial, the growth of Indian civilization (irrespective of geography—northern, southern, eastern or western India), had been connected with agriculture and acquisition of agricultural lands by communities and later by individuals.[2] The ancient codes, including the *Smritis*, indicate that the right to property, including landed property, had been a celebrated right for common individuals in the Indian peninsula. Women, however, did not receive the equal right to own landed property, including agricultural lands, in India due to the patriarchal

[1] Abhijit Banerjee and Lakshmi Iyer, 'History, Institutions, and Economic Performance: The Legacy of Colonial Land Tenure Systems in India', *American Economic Review* 95, no. 4 (2005): 1190–1213, https://pubs.aeaweb.org/doi/pdfplus/10.1257/0002828054825574, accessed 2 February 2020.

[2] Abhijit and Lakshmi, 'History, Institutions, and Economic Performance'.

sociocultural set-up that mandated female children to move to their matrimonial home, leaving behind all sorts of claims on ancestral property, including agricultural lands, except their *Stridhan*.[3] The ancient laws on land ownership by the king or the state and common individuals had given rise to a number of land rights jurisprudences in India.[4] Several studies on the king's patronship for the development of religious institutions, schools, knowledge enhancement establishments, etc., in the ancient and mediaeval periods suggest that kings could hold some land for the purpose of donating to Brahmins for their private use, for cultivation, for the purpose of building temples and schools, etc.[5] However, the ancient codes further suggest that the farmers' community may also get land for cultivation from the state: farmers may also individually own land for agricultural purposes.[6] However, the Sudras, or the lowest caste in the strata, may not necessarily own land. This custom however changed with the social reformation during the mediaeval and colonial periods.[7] However, the studies on land

[3] D. Halder and K. Jaishankar, 'Property Rights of Hindu Women: A Critical Review of Succession Laws of Ancient, Medieval, and Modern India', *Journal of Law and Religion* XXIV, no. 25th Anniversary issue (2008): 101–122.

[4] For more, see Lallanji Gopal, 'Ownership of Agricultural Land in Ancient India', *Journal of the Economic and Social History of the Orient* 4, no. 3 (1961): 240–63.; B. R. Grover, 'The Indian Economic and Social History Review: Nature of Land-Rights in Mughal India', *The Indian Economic & Social History Review* 1, no. 1 (1963): 1–23.; Rob Jenkins, 'Land, Rights and Reform in India', *Pacific Affairs* 86, no. 3 (2013): 591–612.

[5] Benjamin J. Fleming, 'Making Land Sacred: Inscriptional Evidence for Buddhist Kings and Brahman Priests in Medieval Bengal', *Numen* 60, nos. 5–6 (2013): 559–85, https://www.researchgate.net/profile/Jens_Lerche/publication/249764761_Dominant_Castes_Rajas_Brahmins_and_InterCaste_Exchange_Relations_in_Coastal_Orissa_Behind_the_Facade_of_the_Jajmani_System%27/links/5732fa5e08ae298602dc3c59/Dominant-Castes-Rajas-Brahmins-and-InterCaste-Exchange-Relations-in-Coastal-Orissa-Behind-the-Facade-of-the-Jajmani-System.pdf, accessed 2 February 2020.

[6] Bhaskar Majumder, 'Land Acquisition for Industrialization in India: Displacement of People and the Role of the State', *Development and Conflict in the 21st Century* (2010): 27.

[7] For more, see Buddha Prakash, 'A Debated Question: The Genesis and Character of Landed Aristocracy in Ancient India', *Journal of the Economic and Social History of the Orient*[Journal de l'histoire economique et sociale de l'Orient] 14, no. 1 (1971): 196–220.

ownership also suggest that ownership of land could be taken away by the king or the state by way of war, by way of forceful acquisition of land in case of failure of payment of taxes, etc.[8]

Mediaeval Indian history also suggests how landowners, including those who were using their own lands for cultivation by themselves and those who were engaging other people for cultivation in their lands by way of the Bargadari system,[9] may have been provided lands, as well as deprived of their lands, due to various reasons. However, the British colonial system affected the traditional landownership systems and laws in various ways.[10] The various ways of acquisition of land, property and estate by British rulers included use of the doctrine of lapse, which would enable the colonial rulers to include princely states in the growing British empire in India.[11] The colonial rulers also emphasized the principle of *eminent domain*, which signifies that the state has the ultimate power to use the property of its subjects for public purposes or public utility.[12] This principle was particularly used to acquire land from individual landowners by way of the Land Acquisition Act, 1894, which empowered the colonial rulers to acquire lands from common individuals in the name of public utilities. However, the modified, post-independence version of the Land Acquisition Act, 1894[13] states the object of the Act in the following lines:

---

[8] See Abhijit and Lakshmi, 'History, Institutions, and Economic Performance'.

[9] For more, see Arun K. Mukherjee, 'Bargadars of Bengal', *Economic Affairs* (Calcutta) 22, no. 8 (1977): 289.

[10] Sanjoy Chakravorty, 'The Price of Land: Acquisition, Conflict and Consequence', *Indian Journal of Agricultural Economics* 69, no. 902-2016-68358 (2014): 488–93.

[11] Lakshmi Iyer, 'Direct Versus Indirect Colonial Rule in India: Long-term Consequences', *The Review of Economics and Statistics* 92, no. 4 (2010): 693–713, https://www.mitpressjournals.org/doi/pdfplus/10.1162/rest_a_00023, accessed 2 February 2020.

[12] For more, see Abhijit and Lakshmi, 'History, Institutions, and Economic Performance'.

[13] As modified in 1985, as may be seen in the version of the Land Acquisition Act, 1894 at https://dolr.gov.in/sites/default/files/THE%20LAND%20ACQUISITION%20ACT.pdf.

> An Act to amend the law for the Acquisition of Land for public purposes and for the companies. Whereas it is expedient to amend the law for the Acquisition of Land needed for public purposes and for companies and for claiming the amount of compensation to be made on account of such acquisitions.[14]

Section 3(f) of this Act provides a detailed understanding of what may be considered as 'public purposes' within the meaning of its scope. The definition of 'public purposes' includes the following:

> ...the expression "public purpose" includes: (i) the provision of village-sites, or the extension, planned development or improvement of existing village-sites; (ii) the provision of land for town or rural planning; (iii) the provision of land for planned development of land from public funds in pursuance of any scheme or policy of Government and subsequent disposal thereof in whole or in part by lease, assignment or outright sale with the object of securing further development as planned; (iv) the provision of land for a corporation owned or controlled by the State; (v) the provision of land for residential purposes to the poor or landless or to persons residing in areas affected by natural calamities, or to persons displaced or affected by reason of the implementation of any scheme undertaken by Government, any local authority or a corporation owned or controlled by the State; (vi) the provision of land for carrying out any educational, housing, health or slum clearance scheme sponsored by Government or by any authority established by Government for carrying out any such scheme, or with the prior approval of the appropriate Government, by a local authority, or a society registered under the Societies Registration Act, 1860 (21 of 1860), or under any corresponding law for the time being in force in a state, or a co-operative society within the meaning of any law relating to co-operative societies for the time being in force in any State; (vii) the provision of land for any other scheme of development sponsored by Government or with the prior approval of the appropriate Government, by a local authority; (viii) the provision of any premises or building for locating a public office, but does not include acquisition of land for companies.[15]

---

[14] See Land Acquisition Act, 1894, http://megrevenuedm.gov.in/acts/land-aquisition-act-1894.pdf.

[15] See Section 3 of the Land Acquisition Act, 1894.

However, the definition of 'public purposes', as well as the Act itself, suffered from numerous loopholes and carried on the colonial legacy of grabbing land without proper rehabilitation and compensation and without following a proper legal course. It was for these reasons that the Land Acquisition Act, 1874 was severely criticized and a new version of the earlier statute was introduced. This new version is known as the Right to Fair Compensation and Transparency in Land Acquisition, Rehabilitation and Resettlement Act, 2013 (RFCTLARR Act, 2013).

These authors argue that the said statute also could not meet the expectations of Article 17(2) of the Universal Declaration of Human Rights (UDHR), which signifies that no one shall be arbitrarily denied the right over his/her own property by anyone, including the state. This chapter therefore aims to critically examine the issue of land acquisition in India in the light of the present statute, that is, the RFCTLARR Act, 2013, international instruments and the constitutional rights. The chapter is divided into three segments, including the first part, that is, the introduction. The second part critically discusses the issue of land acquisition by the government in the light of the meaning of 'public purposes' and the principle of eminent domain from the perspective of the RFCTLARR Act, 2013. The third part comprises the conclusion.

CRITICAL ANALYSIS OF THE LAND ACQUISITION LAWS IN INDIA

As various studies may suggest, acquisition of privately owned land by the state may happen necessarily for the welfare of people of the state. As discussed earlier, the erstwhile land acquisition statute provided two broad grounds for land acquisition: for the purpose of public utility and for companies.[16] In this chapter, we concentrate more on the former purpose, that is, the 'public purpose'. The terms 'public purposes' and 'public utility' may be considered synonymous, as the earlier Land Acquisition Act had used the former term to denote the grounds to

[16] See Land Acquisition Act, 1894

satisfy the concept of 'public purposes' on the basis of which land may be acquired. These grounds are explained in Section 3(f) of the Land Acquisition Act, which states:

> (i) the provision of village-sites, or the extension, planned development or improvement of existing village-sites; (ii) the provision of land for town or rural planning; (iii) the provision of land for planned development of land from public funds in pursuance of any scheme or policy of Government and subsequent disposal thereof in whole or in part by lease, assignment or outright sale with the object of securing further development as planned; (iv) the provision of land for a corporation owned or controlled by the State; (v) the provision of land for residential purposes to the poor or landless or to persons residing in areas affected by natural calamities, or to persons displaced or affected by reason of the implementation of any scheme undertaken by Government, any local authority or a corporation owned or controlled by the State; (vi) the provision of land for carrying out any educational, housing, health or slum clearance scheme sponsored by Government or by any authority established by Government for carrying out any such scheme, or with the prior approval of the appropriate Government, by a local authority, or a society registered under the Societies Registration Act, 1860 (21 of 1860), or under any corresponding law for the time being in force in a state, or a co-operative society within the meaning of any law relating to co-operative societies for the time being in force in any State; (vii) the provision of land for any other scheme of development sponsored by Government or with the prior approval of the appropriate Government, by a local authority; (viii) the provision of any premises or building for locating a public office, but does not include acquisition of land for companies.'[17]

The eight above-mentioned grounds may suggest that land acquisition may be done only when the government feels that such acquisition may help the needy. It has been suggested by researchers that the state may acquire land on these grounds especially for extending public facilities and for a smoother growth of industrialization, which

---

[17] Ibid.

would fuel economic growth.[18] However, the state may not acquire land arbitrarily and by using force. As mentioned earlier, Article 17 of the UDHR mandates as follows: '(1) Everyone has the right to own property alone as well as in association with others. (2) No one shall be arbitrarily deprived of his property'.[19] This provision empowers all members of civil society to own property and also provides the right against arbitrary deprivation of property. This provision therefore stipulates a duty on the state to protect the right of individuals to own property. At the same time, it also mandates that the state cannot arbitrarily take away property without rehabilitating the owners and without paying compensation for the same. With the growth of industrialization, many countries have seen a revamp of property ownership laws, which have been hugely impacted by the concept of land acquisition by the government.[20] However, human rights activists have observed that in all such cases, there has remained a question over proper compensation and rehabilitation. India is no exception. The Land Acquisition Act was essentially a colonial law which did not emphasize rehabilitation and compensation. The colonial rulers had emphasized the principle of eminent domain in applying the Land Acquisition Act in India. This 17th-century European principle[21] signifies that privately held property may be taken over by the state for public-utility purposes.[22] While during the colonial period payment of compensation remained a mere promise in many cases, in post-independence India, the principle of eminent domain was used by the newly formed governments of India mainly to expand public-utility measures through using the lands of wealthy landlords,

---

[18] See Sanjoy, 'The Price of Land'. Also see Vishal Narain, 'Growing City, Shrinking Hinterland: Land Acquisition, Transition and Conflict in Peri-urban Gurgaon, India', *Environment and Urbanization* 21, no. 2 (2009): 501–12.

[19] See Article 17 of the Universal Declaration of Human Rights.

[20] For example, see Anuar Alias and M. D. Nasir Daud, 'Payment of Adequate Compensation for Land Acquisition in Malaysia', *Pacific Rim Property Research Journal* 12, no. 3 (2006): 326–49.; Joseph L. Sax, 'Buying Scenery: Land Acquisitions for the National Park Service', *Duke Law Journal* 29, no. 4 (1980): 709.

[21] Preeti Sampat, 'Limits to Absolute Power: Eminent Domain and the Right to Land in India', *Economic and Political Weekly* (2013): 40–52.

[22] Preeti, 'Limits to Absolute Power'.

erstwhile princes, etc.[23] Such use of the law also impacted the creation of a ceiling on landed-property ownership.[24] Researchers have further observed that the Land Acquisition Act, 1894 had remotely affected fundamental rights (including the right to property) and Directive Principles of State Policy, which mandated the state to take up welfare measures for the uplift of the community as a whole. Along the same lines, the framers of the constitution had revamped the understanding of the right to own property as well. Originally, Article 19(1)(f) and Article 31(2) of the Constitution of India considered the right to property as a fundamental right, as well as a constitutional right. The former guaranteed every citizen the right to acquire, hold and dispose of property.[25] This right, however, was limited. Article 31(2) stated that no one shall be deprived of his/her right to property except where such deprivation has been authorized by law.[26] However, with the Constitution (Forty-fourth Amendment) Act, 1978, the right to property lost the nature of fundamental rights and Article 31 stood repealed. The right to property became a mere constitutional right under Article 300A, which states, 'No person shall be deprived of his property save by authority of law'.[27] Courts in India on many occasions have analysed the constitutional right to property in the light of Article 17 of the UDHR, and in the case of *P. T. Munichikkanna Reddy v. Revamma,*[28] the Supreme Court of India held that the right to property must be considered a human right and it cannot be a mere statutory right. However, while the courts did analyse the meaning of deprivation of the right to property from the perspective of authorized act of the state, they still did not consider the Land Acquisition Act as detrimental to Article 300A of the constitution. But soon, the courts realized the loopholes of the Land Acquisition Act, 1894.

---

[23] Preeti, 'Limits to Absolute Power'.

[24] Preeti, 'Limits to Absolute Power'.

[25] Article 19(1)(f) of the Constitution of India. 1949. For more, see Namita Wahi, The Fundamental Right to Property in the Indian Constitution (10 August 2015), https://ssrn.com/abstract=2661212 or http://dx.doi.org/10.2139/ssrn.2661212, accessed 2 February 2020.

[26] Ibid

[27] See Article 300A of the Constitution of India.

[28] P. T. Munichikkanna Reddy v. Revamma, (2007) 6 SCC 59.

One of the biggest lacunae of the Land Acquisition Act had been regarding the restorative features: this Act did not specifically speak about compensation and rehabilitation. It must be noted that no statute, policy or government order may deprive any common individual of their rightful ownership of their property without paying them compensation for the same and rehabilitating the occupier of the property acquired by the government. Such deprivation goes against the very basic tenet of human rights which says that every individual must have the inherent right to a decent life, food and shelter. Notably, the right to property is necessarily connected with the right to life in India as well. Even though the present framework of the Constitution of India does not provide the cloak of fundamental right to the right to property, the same may necessarily be included within the meaning of the ever-broadening scope of the right to life as guaranteed under Article 21 of the constitution. Thus, courts in India, in a number of occasions, have suggested that the right to property must be seen in the light of human rights and that deprivation of the same without proper compensation and rehabilitation would amount to violation of the basic human rights: thus, in the landmark case of *Aflatoon and others v. Lt. Legislative head of Delhi and Others*, the Supreme Court observed that the Land Acquisition Act is a colonial pre-constitutional Act and that it does violate the right to property as enshrined in the Indian Constitution. Further, in the case of *Ramji Veerji Patel v. Revenue Divisional Officer*,[29] the Supreme Court observed that the Land Acquisition Act does not address the interest of the affected landowners, as this statute hardly fulfils the promise of compensation and rehabilitation. The court further observed that the Land Acquisition Act had become a tool for illegal acquisition of lands by the government and government stakeholders.

However, the biggest impact of the Land acquisition Act could be seen in the case of *Kedar Nath Yadav v. State of West Bengal & Ors.*[30] This case involved land acquisition by the government of West Bengal

[29] Ramji Veerji Patel v. Revenue Divisional Officer, (2003) Civil Appeal No. 137.

[30] Kedar Nath Yadav v. State of West Bengal & Ors., (2016) Civil Appeal No. 8438 (Arising out of SLP (C) No. 8463 of 2008).

for the purpose of setting up a factory and related establishments for the Tata Nano project. There were huge protests against such acquisition by the opposition party and by other activists, mainly because the protestors claimed that the issue of compensation had not been met fairly.[31] While the Calcutta High Court had dismissed the writ challenging the land acquisition by the government for the Tata Nano project, the Supreme Court reviewed the entire case, especially in the light of the principle of 'public purposes', and declared the entire process of land acquisition, along with its object, void. The court observed that the concept of 'public purposes' had been interpreted in the light of the purposes of the Tata Nano project. The court further observed that even though the project may have promised employment to many others, the government had failed to understand the interest of the landowners, cultivators of the lands that had been acquired and the compensation that had been paid and had failed to satisfy the purpose of the law: the entire process violated basic human rights.[32] The Supreme Court directed the government to return the land to the owners and, at the same time, not to recover compensation from the landowners, including the cultivators.[33]

Understanding the shortcomings of the Land Acquisition Act, 1894, the government of India finally enacted the RFCTLARR Act, 2013. This Act was essentially enacted to make land acquisition more beneficial for the public, as well as for the landowners. The opening paragraph of this Act states its aims and objectives, which are as follows:

> An Act to ensure, in consultation with institutions of local self-government and Gram Sabhas established under the Constitution, a humane, participative, informed and transparent process for land acquisition for industrialisation, development of essential infrastructural facilities and urbanisation with the least disturbance

---

[31] For more, see Shreeja Sen, *Singur Case: Supreme Court Declares Land Acquisition for Tata Plant Illegal*, https://www.livemint.com/Politics/Yrl5OkSielFvHttnG4AajM/CPM-govts-acquisition-of-land-for-Tata-Motors-in-Singur-ill.html on 01-09-2016, accessed 2 February 2020.

[32] Shreeja Sen, *Singur Case*.

[33] Shreeja Sen, *Singur Case*.

> to the owners of the land and other affected families and provide just and fair compensation to the affected families whose land has been acquired or proposed to be acquired or are affected by such acquisition and make adequate provisions for such affected persons for their rehabilitation and resettlement and for ensuring that the cumulative outcome of compulsory acquisition should be that affected persons become partners in development leading to an improvement in their post-acquisition social and economic status and for matters connected therewith or incidental thereto.[34]

The above-mentioned aims and objectives of the Act clearly show that the new Act promises to keep land acquisition a transparent process after considering the socio-economic impact of the same. They further signify the role of Gram Sabhas, human rights activists and experts in ensuring fair gain of both parties. Further, they also emphasize proper rehabilitation and resettlement of the landowners.

A brief review of the RFCTLARR Act, 2013 further suggests that land acquisition must be done consensually and that the same must be done after getting approval from the relevant Gram Sabha, municipality, etc., which must have a good representation of the landowners, cultivators, etc. Section 4(1) of the RFCTLARR Act, 2013 mentions:

> (1) Whenever the appropriate Government intends to acquire land for a public purpose, it shall consult the concerned Panchayat, Municipality or Municipal Corporation, as the case may be, at village level or ward level, in the affected area and carry out a Social Impact Assessment study in consultation with them, in such manner and from such date as may be specified by such Government by notification. [35]

Further, under Section 2, the Act also provides a clear understanding regarding what should be considered as public purpose and states that the acquisition purpose should not deviate from this very purpose if the acquisition needs to be done solely for public purposes.[36] As Section 2

---

[34] See The Right to Fair Compensation and Transparency in Land Acquisition, Rehabilitation and Resettlement Act, 2013 (RFCTLARR Act), 2013, http://legislative.gov.in/sites/default/files/A2013-30.pdf.

[35] See Section 4 of the RFCTLARR Act, 2013.

[36] See Section 2 of the RFCTLARR Act, 2013.

suggests, such purposes may include usage of the land for creation of infrastructure for water harvesting, cold storage, agri-processing units, etc., creation of schools, higher-education establishments, etc., creation of industrial corridors, housing and residential projects for needy and poor people, including people who may be affected by such land acquisition, etc.[37] The Act further emphasizes ensuring food security while the government considers land acquisition.[38] Chapters IV and V of the RFCTLARR Act, 2013 provide an essential understanding about survey of land and associated issues that may impact the landowners, rehabilitation and resettlement of the affected landowners, etc.[39] This Act also provides for a dedicated national monitoring committee under chapter VII to safeguard the rights of the affected parties. Further, it may be seen that the Act promises better compensation than the market value to the affected landowners, which is far better than the compensation promised under the Land Acquisition Act.

However, the drawbacks of this Act are also noteworthy. The term 'social impact assessment' is not defined anywhere in the Act. Further, while the Act suggests that the assessment must be supported by experts, it does not properly express who may be considered as experts in this regard. This exposes possibilities of misuse of the provisions of this statute for the benefit of corrupt stakeholders, including government stakeholders.[40] Further, the issue of compensation and rehabilitation of the affected parties, including the landowners, cultivators, farmers and dependent family members, needs to be addressed from the perspective of proper execution and implementation.

CONCLUSION

As the above discussion suggests, land acquisition is an unfortunate necessity in modern times to support the growth of industrialization

---

[37] Ibid.

[38] See Section 10 of the RFCTLARR Act, 2013 which speaks about special reference to food security.

[39] See Chapter IV and V of the RFCTLARR Act, 2013.

[40] See Swagato Sarkar, 'The Impossibility of Just Land Acquisition', *Economic and Political Weekly* (2011): 35–38.

and urbanization. However, history suggests that the process of land acquisition has violated different kinds of human rights which are recognized by international instruments. India's colonial Land Acquisition Act may have helped in the growth of industrialization. But simultaneously, it invited bloodbaths, confusion, poverty and lack of employment. As the literature reviewed in this chapter suggests, there is no guarantee that land acquisition may assure employment to the affected parties. If land may be acquired for public purposes, it becomes necessary to monitor how far such purposes are met successfully. The new Act promises a holistic improvement in the situation. However, it needs to be ensured that the statute does not become diluted by corrupt practices. The judiciary must play a significant role in monitoring the entire process and delivering proper justice to the beneficiaries. Only then shall the new provision provide justice to the needy in a better way.

Chapter 23

Right to Consular Assistance

The Jadhav Case—A Human Rights' Analysis

Gunjan Chawla

INTRODUCTION

In 2016, Kulbhushan Jadhav got arrested in Pakistan on charges of spying for the purpose of terrorism.[1] His arrest and detention became a sensational news item all over the world, especially in South Asia when, in the next year, Jadhav was sentenced to death by Pakistan and the International Court of Justice (ICJ) ordered Pakistan to suspend the execution order on a plea made by India.[2] The main question that needed to be answered was whether Jadhav was provided the right to consular assistance while he was detained and before pronouncing the death sentence. When a citizen of any country is arrested or detained by a foreign county, he/she may seek help from his/her home country. This is a lawful and natural right of such person. The home country in turn is also under an obligation to afford as much assistance as may be possible to save its national. This very right, which is an essential part

[1] For more understanding, see ET Online, 'Kulbhushan Jadhav Case: What You Need to Know Before the Verdict', (17 July 2019), https://economictimes.indiatimes.com/news/politics-and-nation/kulbhushan-jadhav-case-what-you-need-to-know-before-the-verdict/articleshow/70256759.cms?utm_source=contentofinterest&utm_medium=text&utm_campaign=cppst, accessed 21 January 2020.

[2] ET Online, 'Kulbhushan Jadhav Case'.

of human rights, can be found in several provisions in the Universal Declaration of Human Rights (UDHR), including Articles 5 (which speaks about the right to protection against torture, cruel, inhuman or degrading treatment and punishment), 7 (which speaks about the right to equality and the right to protection against discrimination), 28 (which speaks about the right to enjoy social and international order in which rights and freedoms of the UDHR can be realized), etc.[3] The principles of international law governing the process of legal assistance by a home country to a detainee in a foreign land were developed over many years. Some of these principles have been recognized in several treaties, and some have contributed to the development of customary international law in regard to the rights of the detainee.[4] There are various principles that have developed a sanguine jurisprudence in relation to the pressing need for enforcing the right to consular assistance. The role of a home country shall not end there and must be followed by facilitation of both consular and diplomatic action for preventing and halting the abuse. Lately, all stakeholders across the globe have accepted the fact that there has been a steep rise in human rights violations all over the world—be it the Syrian crisis,[5] the human rights violation of immigrants in the United States, who have been tagged as 'illegal',[6] the inhuman slaying of army jawans and families in Kashmir[7] or the speculations eyeing the possible

---

[3] See Articles 5, 7 and 28 of the Universal Declaration of Human Rights.

[4] For more, see Ronald L. Hanna, 'Consular Access to Detained Foreign Nationals: An Overview of the Current Application of the Vienna Convention in Criminal Practice', S. Ill. U. L. J. 25 (2000–2001): 163, https://heinonline.org/HOL/LandingPage?handle=hein.journals/siulj25&div=15&id=&page=, accessed 21 January 2020.

[5] Nicholas Idris Erameh, 'Humanitarian Intervention, Syria and the Politics of Human Rights Protection', *The International Journal of Human Rights* 21, no. 5 (2017): 517–30, https://www.sciencedirect.com/science/article/pii/S2214109X17304692, accessed 12 February 2020.

[6] David B. Oppenheimer, Swati Prakash, and Rachel Burns, 'Playing the Trump Card: The Enduring Legacy of Racism in Immigration Law', *Berkeley La Raza Law Journal* 26 (2016): 1, https://heinonline.org/HOL/Page?handle=hein.journals/berklarlj26&div=2&g_sent=1&casa_token=Xeb4Qrth4PYAAAAA:lpUnR_IlRL6_n1fPlU27ZUTjHUE74WlqOBuICqVjzJVImJdplIVPwORgX6crMTe-QhoICRGQAQg&collection=journals, accessed 12 February 2020.

[7] Praveen Swami, 'Terrorism in Jammu and Kashmir in Theory and Practice', *India Review* 2, no. 3 (2003): 55–88.

execution of Jadhav in Pakistan. Coincidently, all these cases fall within the arena of gross violation of the basic human rights endowed upon a human being, that is, the right to life and a life of dignity, which has been enshrined in Article 1 of the UDHR.[8] It must be noted that the right to life and dignity of detainees has been a topic of huge discussions and debates till date all over the world. The state parties can no longer curtail this very right in the name of retributive justice. The ICJ considered the mandates of the UDHR in this regard in the case of India versus Pakistan involving a request by India for immediate suspension of the death sentence of Jadhav, which was considered as arbitrary and violating the norms of the UDHR and that of Article 36 of the Vienna Convention on Consular Relations of 1963 (the Vienna Convention),[9] which provides the right to information about availability of right to consular assistance to detainees detained in foreign countries *without delay*.

The detention of an accused must be lawful detention on reasonable grounds, following due process of the law, and should not arbitrarily suspend the right to liberty of the said detainee.[10] The ability of a foreign defendant in a foreign state to communicate with his home state's consular authorities is recognized as an individual right in international law,[11] and an essential human right.[12] Although the UDHR does not expressly provide for rights of detainees or prisoners' rights, it

---

[8] Article 1, UDHR says as follows: All human beings are born free and equal in dignity and rights. They are endowed with reason and conscience and should act towards one another in a spirit of brotherhood.

[9] For more, see Vienna Convention on Consular Relations (1963), https://legal.un.org/ilc/texts/instruments/english/conventions/9_2_1963.pdf, accessed 21 January 2020.

[10] See 'Human Rights and Arrest, Pre-Trial Detention and Administrative Detention', in *Human Rights in the Administration of Justice: A Manual on Human Rights for Judges, Prosecutors and Lawyers*, https://www.ohchr.org/Documents/Publications/training9chapter5en.pdf, accessed 12 March 2020.

[11] LaGrand (Germany v United States of America) (Judgment) [2001] ICJ Rep 466 ('LaGrand'); Avena and Other Mexican Nationals (Mexico v United States of America) (Judgment) [2004] ICJ Rep 12 ('Avena').

[12] See William J. Aceves, 'The Right of Information on Consular Assistance in the Framework of the Guarantees of the Due Process of Law. Advisory Opinion OC-16-99', *The American Journal of International Law* 94, no. 3 (2000): 555–63, www.jstor.org/stable/2555324, accessed 21 January 2020; see also ET Online, 'Kulbhushan Jadhav Case'.

however provides under Article 4 the right to effective remedy against violation of fundamental rights and basic human rights granted by the constitution or any other law of the competent national tribunal.[13] Further, Article 9 of the UDHR provides for protection against arrest and detention that may be done on arbitrary grounds and illegal trials,[14] followed by Article 10, which lays emphasis on a fair public hearing by an impartial tribunal to determine the rights and obligations as against the criminal charges that may have been levelled against the accused.[15] This is further supported by Article 14 of the International Covenant on Civil and Political Rights,[16] which speaks about the rights of detainees and prisoners to be presumed innocent until proven guilty and the right to defend themselves through legal assistance of their choice in case of determination of criminal charges against them. An analogical deduction based on the Constitution of India shall suggest that when the fundamental rights of a national of a state are under trial and suspension in a foreign state, the said foreign state would be under an obligation to preserve the rights of fair trial and access to legal aid of the accused. This is also accurately applicable in the Jadhav case, as he being an Indian national is endowed with the same rights, and the scope of such rights may extend to the detainee even when he is detained in a foreign state on the accusation of involvement in terrorist and extremist activities. According to orders of the ICJ, detained non-citizens also have the right to contact consular officials, and the receiving state must notify them of this right.[17] According to the decisions of the Inter-American Commission on Human Rights

[13] See Article 8, United Nations Declaration on Human Rights.

[14] See Article 9, United National Declarations on Human Rights.

[15] See Article 10, United National Declarations on Human Rights.

[16] Article 14(2) and Article 14(3)(d), International Covenant on Civil and Political Rights.

[17] See The orders of the International Court of Justice of 9 April 1998 in the Case concerning the Vienna Convention on Consular Relations (Paraguay v. United States of America), https://www.icj-cij.org/en/case/99, accessed 10 December 2019, and of 3 March 1999 in Federal Republic of Germany v. United States of America, https://www.icj-cij.org/en/case/104, accessed 10 December 2019, and Advisory Opinion OC–16/99 of the Inter-American Court of Human Rights on the right to information on consular assistance in the framework of the guarantees of the due process of law of 1 October 1999, https://www.corteidh.or.cr/docs/opiniones/seriea_16_ing.pdf, accessed 10 December 2019.

dated 12 March 2002, states are also obliged to respect the human rights of detainees and ensure legal protection, irrespective of whether or not they are in the territory of the state in question.[18]

As may be seen from the above discussion, all human beings have the right to enjoyment and protection of their human rights. The difference lies in the execution of such rights upon citizens and non-citizens. It is under these circumstances that non-citizens are considered as being in need of the remedy of consular assistance. The home state is responsible for providing assistance to citizens detained in a foreign country; similarly, the foreign state is also obliged to ensure the right to consular assistance and legal assistance to the foreign national detained therein, for the preservation of human rights. However, despite clear guidelines in this regard and voluntary ratification of treaties for international cooperation in this regard by member states, there exists a wide gap between the rights guaranteed by international documents and their execution upon non-citizens. Although the constitutional precepts of equality before the law and equal protection of laws are widely glorified by nation states all across the globe, the ground reality remains that several cases, like that of Kulbhushan Jadhav, are pending in many countries across the world where the detainees are deprived of consular assistance from their home country.[19] Even worse, there are a few cases exemplifying ignorance of the home state in bringing its own national to justice, leaving him/her at the mercy of the foreign state, which evades all humanitarian principles and justifies its atrocities under the garb of 'preserving national security and peace'. Jadhav's case attracts the author's attention for being a unique case on the right to consular assistance for a national of a neighbouring state with which the detaining state does not have friendly diplomatic relations. This chapter, in the next part, critically examines the right to consular assistance as an important human right and then analyses it in the light of Kulbhushan Jadhav's case. In the conclusion, the chapter emphasizes deeper analysis of the consular rights of detainees for better execution of the right to life.

---

[18] For more, see Decision of the Inter-American Commission on Human Rights of 12 March 2002 on the request for precautionary measures (Detainees at Guantanamo Bay, Cuba), https://www.cidh.oas.org/pdf%20files/Resolution%202-11%20Guantanamo.pdf, accessed 10 December 2019.

[19] See Articles 5, 7 and 28 of the Universal Declaration of Human Rights.

CRITICAL ANALYSIS OF THE RIGHT TO CONSULAR ASSISTANCE AND ITS APPLICATION IN THE JADHAV CASE

The concept of 'consular assistance' has been clarified by the UK government in their response to the European Commission's Green Paper on Diplomatic and consular protection of Union citizens in third countries.[20] The concept has been explained as support and assistance in legal matters for the protection of human rights by states to their nationals who are in distress in a foreign land.[21] Further, Amnesty International, in its document titled 'Violation of the Rights of Foreign Nationals under Sentence of Death', has broadened the concept of consular assistance for nationals who may be detained in foreign states and may have been charged with capital punishment by adding the following duties of the consuls of the home state: providing legal assistance; providing services for translation, notifying the immediate family members, transferring documents to the detaining country for legal assistance to the detainee, observing a court hearing and ensuring legal assistance in this regard to the detainee.[22]

While states are duty-bound to provide consular assistance to their nationals detained abroad, the Vienna Convention, which is also known as the Vienna Treaty,[23] indicates that intervening in the matters concerning their national(s) abroad, especially when the said national(s) is/are detained, is a customary right of states. India and Pakistan both

---

[20] See UK response to the [European] Commission's Green Paper on Diplomatic and consular protection of Union citizens in third countries, March 2007, para. 1.5, http://www.careproject.eu/database/upload/UKresponseGP/UKresponseGPText.pdf, accessed 12 February 2020.

[21] Ibid. Also see 'Tortured Abroad: The UK's obligations to British Nationals and Residents', Redress Trust, https://www.refworld.org/pdfid/506c0a6f2.pdf, accessed 12 February 2020.

[22] See in Amnesty International, 'Violation of the Rights of Foreign Nationals Under Sentence of Death', January 1, 1998, AMR/51/01/98, https://www.refworld.org/docid/3ae6a98c27.htm, accessed 12 February 2020.

[23] For more, see U.N.T.S. Nos. 8638–40, vol. 596, pp. 262–512 (24 April 1963), http://untreaty.un.org/ilc/texts/instruments/english/conventions/9_2_1963.pdf, accessed 21 January 2020.

signed and ratified this treaty on 28 November 1977 and 14 April 1969, respectively. The Vienna Convention codified international customary law on consular relations. It also threw light on the rule of *pacta sunt servanda.*[24] The treaty also has an 'Optional Protocol' to the Vienna Convention concerning the Compulsory Settlement of Disputes, 1963 (the protocol).[25] The protocol was entered into force on 19 March 1967. Interestingly, both India and Pakistan are parties to this protocol too, since 28 November 1977 and 29 March 1976, respectively.[26] Among the consular functions described in the Vienna Convention, particular importance is given to consular assistance, which includes providing legal assistance to detainees, protecting the legal rights of a detainee in a foreign state, etc.[27]

Article 36 of the Vienna Convention sets out the rights of consuls to communicate with and assist detained foreign nationals. It also sets out the individual rights of detained or imprisoned nationals.[28]

If a state that is duty-bound to provide consular assistance to its citizen who may have been detained in a foreign state, fails to provide any assistance, including legal assistance, it may amount to a breach of consular rights, which are considered an important right under the Vienna Convention. It may also amount to a serious breach of settled principles of international law.[29] Amnesty International further observed:

---

[24] Sandra J. Weiland, *The Vienna Convention on Consular Relations: Persuasive Force or Binding Law?* (University of Denver Strum College of Law, 2006), http://www.law.du.edu/forms/writing-competitions/documents/winners/1.pdf, accessed 21 January 2020.

[25] For more, see https://treaties.un.org/pages/ViewDetails.aspx?src=TREATY&mtdsg_no=III-8&chapter=3, accessed 12 February 2020.

[26] Abhishek Mishra and Kulbhushan Jadhav, 'Pakistan Stands on the Wrong Side of Law', https://www.thequint.com/blogs/2017/04/11/kulbhushan-jadhav-death-sentence-india-response, accessed 22 January 2020.

[27] For more, seehttps://legal.un.org/ilc/texts/instruments/english/conventions/9_2_1963.pdf, accessed 20 January 2020.

[28] See Vienna Convention, Article 36 (1)

[29] See Chapter I, General Principles, Article 1, 'Responsibility of a State for Its Internationally Wrongful Acts', *International Law Commission* II (Part Two) (2001): 31, in Tortured Abroad: The UK's obligations to British Nationals and Residents, September 2012, http://www.redress.org/downloads/publications/121001tortured_abroad.pdf.

> The rights to consular notification and visits are also reiterated under international human rights standards, including Principle 16(2) of the UN Body of Principles for the Protection of All Persons under Any Form of Detention or Imprisonment and Article 38(1) of the UN Standard Minimum Rules for the Treatment of Prisoners.[30]

As may be understood from the above discussion, the right to a dignified life and its suspension only on reasonable, just and humanitarian grounds is a right that is internationally revered as a basic right for persons accused of an offence.

At this juncture, it is important to outline the evolution and development of the right to consular assistance. Several researchers have observed that the jurisprudence of consular assistance has reached its present position through a variety of cases wherein the hosting country may not have provided access to consular assistance for the foreign national and may have exercised arbitrary power in the arrest, detainment and execution procedures.[31] In the LaGrand case[32] between Germany and the United States, the former approached the ICJ for preventing execution of sentences against the LaGrand brothers on the grounds that the United States had failed to exercise its duty to inform the detainees about their right to consular assistance and meted out arbitrary treatment to the same. The ICJ concluded that the United States had violated the established norm in this regard. It further emphasized the fact that the concept of consular assistance must always be understood from dual perspectives: (a) the state's right to intervene and offer assistance to its national who is detained in a foreign land; and (b) the detainee's right to seek assistance from the home state. Yatesh Begoore summed up the order of the ICJ in the following words:

---

[30] Amnesty International: Violation of the Rights of Foreign Nationals Under Sentence of Death, AMR 51/01/98 (1998), https://deathpenaltyinfo.org/node/802, accessed 21 January 2020.

[31] David Leys, 'Diplomatic Protection and Individual Rights: A Complementary Approach', *Harvard International Law Journal Online* 57, http://www.harvardilj.org/wp-content/uploads/January-2016_Vol-57_Leys1.pdf, accessed 21 January 2020.

[32] Le Grand (Germany v. United States of America), 2001 I.C.J. 466 (June 27).

> As It was ordered that the provision regarding consular assistance is a binding provisional measure against the execution of death sentences during the pendency of consular access disputes before it... The ICJ, in consideration of the "irreparable prejudice" that would be caused to the rights of the parties to the dispute if the sentence were carried out, issued binding provisional measures directing the US to ensure that LaGrand was not executed pending the final decision of the court.[33]

It may be interesting to note that the detaining state's obligation to provide the right to consular assistance to detainees was further recognized in several other landmark cases. Including that of Avena,[34] where Mexico raised similar complaints regarding detention of its nationals and alleged violation of rights to consular assistance by the United States. Further, in the case of *Guinea v. Zaire*[35] (presently known as the Democratic Republic of Congo, hereafter DRC), Guinea claimed that the arrest and detention and consequent expulsion of its national by DRC was a violation of the settled principles of international law, including the International Covenant on Civil and Political Rights and Articles 6 and 12(4) of the African Charter on Human and People's Rights.

As the above discussion may indicate, the ICJ played an important role in establishing human rights as per the international instruments in all the above-mentioned cases.

Kulbhushan Jadhav, a former Indian Navy officer, was arrested and detained in Pakistan on charges of terrorism and extremism in 2016. He was not granted consular assistance and the right to legal assistance as mentioned in the international instruments. By April 2016, Pakistan announced through its Inter-Services Public Relations that Jadhav had been tried before a military court and that the court had pronounced

[33] See Yatesh Begoore, 'How International Law Can Help India in the Kulbhushan Jadhav Case', *The Wire*, April 13, 2017, https://thewire.in/123757/international-law-kulbhushan-jadhav-india-pakistan/, accessed 21 January 2020.

[34] Avena and Other Mexican Nationals (Mexico v. United States of America), 2004 I.C.J. 12 (March 31).

[35] Ahmadou Sadio Diallo (Republic of Guinea v. Democratic Republic of the Congo), 2010 I.C.J. 639 (November 30).

him to be sentenced to death on charges of 'espionage and sabotage activities'.[36] India immediately contended that Jadhav was not guilty of the charges and that he had been abducted in Iran. India further contented that the Pakistani government had denied the right to consular access to him despite repeated requests.[37] India sought for relief in this regard on the basis of Article 36(1) of the Statute of the ICJ relating to compulsory jurisdiction of member states that are parties to the Optional Protocol to the Vienna Convention. India sought for appeal at the ICJ, fearing Jadhav's execution at the hands of the Pakistani military court on the allegations of being a spy without giving him any right for consular assistance. India alleged that trials against him were conducted without informing him about the grounds of his arrest and the charges levelled against him, which would be a gross violation of a prisoner's right under the UDHR and the Vienna Convention.[38] India further alleged that Pakistan had repeatedly denied requests for consular access to Jadhav. The ICJ considered the following issues to stay the execution of Jadhav.

The court considered the rights enshrined in Article 36, paragraph 1, of the Vienna Convention for justifying the pleas by India. The court further considered the validity of measures regarding consular access and observed that the detaining state should have provided rights to consular notification and access between the home state and its national and informed the detainee about his rights without delay, as has been mentioned in Article 36, paragraph 1, of the Vienna Convention. Further, on the issue of execution of Jadhav, the court declared that his right to consular access, as well as his right to a fair trial, had been violated, as claimed by India, as Jadhav had been sentenced to death and there was every possibility that he may be executed. The court emphasized the fact that the violation of the above-mentioned rights could be clearly seen, as Pakistan did not guarantee that the death sentence would be further considered in any national tribunal as per

---

[36] See U.N.T.S. Nos. 8638–40, vol. 596, pp. 262–512 (24 April 1963), http://untreaty.un.org/ilc/texts/instruments/english/conventions/9_2_1963.pdf, accessed 21 January 2020.

[37] Ibid.

[38] Vienna Convention on Consular Relations of 1963, Article 36.

the mandates of the international instruments. Considering the above grounds, the ICJ stayed the execution of Jadhav.[39]

This verdict of the ICJ in relation to consular access and subsequent staying of execution of the death sentence has been applauded by other countries. It has reiterated the understanding that the Vienna Convention rules over any arbitrary decision of states to take action against a foreign national in regard to detention and execution of the death sentence. However, Kulbhushan Jadhav had not yet been returned to India while this chapter was being written. He was still in a Pakistani jail. However, interestingly, Indian Wing Commander Abhinandan Varthaman, who was captured by Pakistan during a fierce air force engagement between Pakistan and India along the Line of Control, was released by Pakistan after vigorous diplomatic communications between Pakistan and other countries, including India, the United States and the United Kingdom.[40]

CONCLUSION

Human rights as enshrined in the UDHR and other international instruments, read with the Vienna Convention, would suggest that no human being should live a life without dignity. The right to life cannot be realized in its true sense if the peripheral rights, including the right to protection against arbitrary arrest, right to a fair trial, right to legal assistance, right to protection against torture and inhuman punishment, etc., are ignored. However, there are several cases of violation of such rights of citizens within their own country and of non-citizens detained in foreign countries. Be it a violation of the rights of a child

[39] For more, see Gopal Baglay, 'Kulbhushan Jadhav case at ICJ highlights', *Firstpost* (27 June 2017), http://www.firstpost.com/india/kulbhushan-jadhav-case-verdict-at-the-hague-live-icj-to-pronounce-judgment-at-3-30-pm-today-death-sentence-put-on-hold-pakistan-india-harish-salve-3454798.html#live-blog-20170518165746, accessed 21 January 2020.

[40] For more, see V. Sudarshan, 'How to Solve a Problem Like Kulbhushan Jadhav?' *The Hindu* (20 July 2019), https://www.thehindu.com/thread/politics-and-policy/how-to-solve-a-problem-like-kulbhushan-jadhav/article28620457.ece, accessed 21 January 2020.

in the form of his/her exploitation and/or abuse or a violation of the right of a woman to protection against being exploited sexually, the threat of gross violations of human rights remains everywhere. There are umpteen cases of racial violence, sexual violence and violations of child rights and rights of non-citizens in foreign countries. In the last case, such countries may have tried to justify the situation in the name of protection of their own culture or domestic legal framework. However, such violations of rights have created several understandings about the right to consular access and legal assistance in foreign lands. Such rights can be impacted by the diplomatic relations between two states or by ignorance about their rights by the detainee themselves, or also by language barriers. In all such cases, when the detaining state refuses to inform the detainee about their rights or neglects its duties towards providing consular access to the detainee, it gives rise to a violation of human rights.

The Kulbhushan Jadhav case might prove to be a turning point in the history of India, but India's history also involves scores of dark episodes that prove the country's inability to safeguard and protect human rights from violation and abuse within its own territorial borders. India's efforts in reinstating the rights of its national at the international front are commendable, but its realization and enforcement of such rights shall only be worthy of appreciation once at the national level too all citizens rise together and raise their voice against any violation concerning the human body, life and dignity. The decision of the ICJ has set an example for all the states across the globe which may be reluctant to abide by the international rules relating to protection of human rights of any being—a national or a foreign national—especially when he/she has been criminally implicated.

Chapter 24

Revitalizing Agriculture for Economic Growth and Food Security

A Critical Review

Viralkumar B. Mandaliya and Mradul Mishra

INTRODUCTION

The right to food is an essential element of the right to life. The two World Wars, famines, ups and downs in the political relationships between nation states, civil wars, internal political crises, etc., have hugely affected the concept of the right to food, which is no more limited to the right to have food for survival. The concept of the right to food has expanded to include the right to nutritious and hygienic food for holistic development of the human body. It has been necessarily included in in the holistic concept of child rights. However, the ever-growing human population on earth and the rapidly changing diet patterns have hugely affected the demand for food.[1] Moreover, climate

---

[1] *Climate-Smart Agriculture: An Address of Climate Change and Food Security*, in Proceeding of 1st Virtual Conference on United Nations Sustainable Development Goals, Mumbai, pp. 89, 15–16 October 2016, http://un.iarc.res.in/conference/wp-content/uploads/2016/08/UNITES-2016-Proceedings-1.pdf, accessed 20 May 2017.

change has also affected the level of crop yields and the availability of water for drinking purposes, as well as for supporting agriculture. This in turn has affected hunger management by stakeholders, including both nation states and the international organizations like the Food and Agricultural Organization (FAO) of the United Nations (UN). Reports from the World Bank[2] show that one out of nine people in the world suffers from chronic hunger. The situation is indeed alarming and challenges food security[3] for the entire world. The best possible way to face this challenge is to revitalize agriculture. It has been shown by several researchers that revitalizing agriculture may not only re-energize the groundwater level, but it may also help reduce poverty and problems related to hunger and health.[4] The Green Revolution has shown marvellous results in the recent past in different parts of India.[5] All studies on the Green Revolution and hunger management, however, indicate that the development goals of international and domestic stakeholders in the area of agriculture and food play an important role in mapping the pathway to tackle the latter issue. This chapter aims to critically analyse these goals and policies from international, as well as Indian, perspectives to understand how revitalization of agriculture may be made stronger to support food security in the contemporary era. This chapter is divided into three sections, including the introduction. The second part critically analyses the goals and policies of international organizations, including

---

[2] World Bank, *Making Climate Finance Work in Agriculture* (Washington, 2016), https://openknowledge.worldbank.org/handle/10986/24686, accessed 22 May 2017.

[3] Food Security is defined by World Food Summit as 'A situation which exists when all people, at all times have physical and economic access to sufficient, safe and nutritious food to meet their dietary needs and food preferences for an active and healthy life'. For more, see Agriculture, Global Alliance for Climate-Smart Agriculture Action Plan, Climate Summit 2014, UN Headquarters, New York, http://www.un.org/climatechange/summit/wp-content/uploads/sites/2/2014/09/AGRICULTURE-Action-Plan.pdf, accessed 22 May 2017.

[4] See G. Ejeta, *Food Security* 1 (2009): 391, https://doi.org/10.1007/s12571-009-0045-8. https://ag.purdue.edu/agry/Documents/Ejeta-Food-Security-Journal.pdf, accessed 12 September 2017.

[5] See Peter Timmer, 'Food Security and Economic Growth: An Asian Perspective (13 December 2004)', Center for Global Development Working Paper No. 51, https://ssrn.com/abstract=1112795 or http://dx.doi.org/10.2139/ssrn.1112795.

the UN FAO, and those of India, with special reference to Gujarat. The third part comprises the conclusion.

BRIEF OVERVIEW OF POLICIES SET FORTH BY INTERNATIONAL STAKEHOLDERS FOR REVITALIZING AGRICULTURE AND FOOD SECURITY

Agriculture had been the most chosen profession since time immemorial. It not only addressed food security but also helped securing the financial position of those engaged in farming. However, socio-economic political changes throughout the world made the agricultural sector shrink. Constant movement of labourers from the agricultural sector to other industrial sectors, financial challenges in continuing farming as the sole profession, climate change, rapid urbanization, etc., caused the slow death of the agricultural sector in many places, including India.[6] This enhanced food security issues. The United Nations in its Climate Summit 2014[7] addressed several such issues in order to revitalize agriculture. The primary issue among these was the execution of climate-smart agriculture (CSA), a concept that was originally developed in 2010 by the UN FAO. CSA is a method to promote agricultural policies to tackle various challenges especially related to climate change and achieve food security. In the current scenario, all states (irrespective of whether their economy is dependent on agriculture or not) are concentrating on climate change to attain food security. In the Climate Summit 2014, about 20 countries participated and agreed to review action plans to address CSA. These countries came up with the 'Global Alliance for Climate-Smart Agriculture' (GACSA), a voluntary, farmer-led, multi-stakeholder, action-oriented coalition committee for incorporating climate-smart technologies in agricultural systems.[8] GACSA seeks to improve food and nutrition security and emphasizes the role of governments, farmers, scientists, entrepreneurs, and civil society members, and that of regional and international

[6] See Timmer, 'Food Security and Economic Growth'.

[7] World Bank. *Making Climate Finance Work in Agriculture.*

[8] For a better understanding, see http://www.fao.org/gacsa/about/en/, accessed 12 September 2017.

organizations in preparing policy guidelines to attain food security. CSA has also been supported by the stakeholders like the Consultative Group on International Agricultural Research (CGIAR), which has emphasized monetary investments in the farming sector to bring in new farmer-friendly and climate-friendly farming technologies.[9] The concept of food security has been deeply analysed and discussed by FAO, which has provided much guidance on attaining food security: this includes discussions on farm management, ecosystem and livestock management, services management and value chain intervention in the whole system, etc. Against this background, it is important to review the UN Sustainable Development Goal of achieving food security.

In 2017, the UN set a 2030 agenda for sustainable development and laid down 17 Sustainable Development Goals,[10] among which the second goal is 'Zero Hunger', which was proposed for achieving universal food security through promotion of the concept of sustainable agriculture.[11] The Zero Hunger goal has not yet been achieved fully when this chapter was being written. However, there have been several positive developments towards achieving this goal, which include worldwide decline in undernourished people and children suffering from chronic malnutrition, increase in preservation of seeds and development of natural fertilization of seeds, positive development in biodiversity growth, improved financial strategy planning for the food and agricultural sector by governments and international stakeholders, etc.[12] The World Bank, too, has played a phenomenal role in revitalizing agriculture and food security worldwide. It has supported CSA in various modes. As a result, a tremendous growth in food sustainability was noticed in different countries, including Uruguay, Zambia, Ethiopia, Morocco, etc., which had a history of being badly affected by draughts, civil wars, international political instability, terrorism, etc.

[9] CGIAR: The Consultative Group on International Agricultural Research, http://www.cgiar.org, accessed 2 June 2017.

[10] Sustainable Development Knowledge Platform, https://sustainabledevelopment.un.org, accessed 12 June 2017.

[11] Sustainable Development Knowledge Platform.

[12] For more, see http://www.undp.org/content/unct/lesotho/en/home/sdgs/goal-2--zero-hunger.html, accessed 10 July 2019.

Apart from the UN organizations and the World Bank, several countries from across the globe have also contributed towards sustainable agricultural development. For instance, the United States has emphasized holistic development of the food and agriculture sector, including more research on the development of new techniques for sustainable agriculture, resolution of financial issues relating to supporting agriculture, food and crop waste management, land management, encouragement of non-agricultural civil society members to contribute to sustainable farming and food security, etc. The United States also started Food Policy Action in collaboration with national food policy leaders in 2012. This has tremendously influenced the role of legislators in securing food security[13] and farming.[14] It has also helped in creating a national dialogue on food policy through educating the public regarding the importance of sustainable farming, the need to avoid food wastage, etc. In 2016, the United States came up with a national food policy that helped connect local farmers with large-scale food buyers and thereby revitalize the American economy as a whole.[15] European Union countries, similarly, have also supported sustainable farming and food security issues through supporting the Common Agricultural Policy (CAP).[16] In 2011, a new CAP was introduced to strengthen the economic and ecological competitiveness of the agricultural sector, to promote innovation, to combat climate change and to support employment and growth in rural areas. The 10-point CAP reform plan proposed by the European Commission at Brussels, on 12 October 2011, included targeted income support to stimulate

---

[13] P. G. Pardey and J. M. Beddow, 'Revitalizing Agricultural Research and Development to Sustain US Competitiveness' (2017), http://www.farmersfeedingtheworld.org/assets/7/6/revitalizingagresearch_print.pdf.

[14] Food Policy Action, http://foodpolicyaction.org, accessed 25 June 2017.

[15] Growing Economies: Connecting Local Farmers and Large-Scale Food Buyers to Create Jobs and Revitalize America's Heartland (2016), http://www.ucsusa.org/sites/default/files/attach/2016/01/ucs-growing-economies-2016.pdf, accessed 25 June 2017.

[16] European Commission The Common Agricultural Policy—A Story to Be Continued (Luxembourg: Publications Office of the European Union), http://ec.europa.eu/agriculture/50-years-of-cap/files/history/history_book_lr_en.pdf, accessed 30 June 2017.

employment possibilities, discussions on crisis management to address new economic challenges, 'green' payment for sustainable development of ecosystems, more investment for research on agricultural techniques and economy, encouragement of young farmers to adopt traditional farming methods, promotion of a balanced food chain, development of agro-environmental initiatives, etc.

Brazil, on the other hand, has strengthened its sustainable-agriculture and food security policies through launching the Agro+ programme, which helps achieve modernization of the agricultural sector, promotes the usage of new techniques for sustainable farming, facilitates access to information, simplifies export and import processes, etc. Brazil has also adopted several other measures towards sustainable agricultural development. These include reducing red-tapism in the plantation of plants and rehabilitation of the same in industrial areas, facilitating public consultation for control of the aging of beverages, wines and grape derivatives in wooden containers, simplifying rules for farm-animal transfers and controlling animal diseases, developing facilities for better production of wheat, rice, ginger, yam, taro, beans, flowers and ornamental plants, and for processing grapes, peanuts and tomatoes, etc.[17] Further, in Africa, the agricultural sector offers major employment at present. Nevertheless, Africa is plagued with poverty. The African economy, however, can be revitalized through raising farm incomes, generating employment and reducing food prices. Several African regions have joined hands to achieve this goal. For instance, the West Africa Agricultural Productivity Program (WAAPP) is working towards sustainable food security.[18] Among other countries in the world, Australia has experienced the worst impact on its agricultural sector due to climate change. This has however been addressed by the Farm Support division of the Department of Agriculture and Water Resources of Australia through several policies and missions. These include investment by the

---

[17] Characteristics of measurements of Agro+ program, http://www.agricultura.gov.br/agromais/principais-medidas.html, accessed 27 March 2018.

[18] West Africa Agricultural Productivity Program, http://www.worldbank.org/en/topic/agriculture/brief/the-west-africa-agricultural-productivity-program, accessed 30 June 2017.

Clean Energy Finance Corporation (CEFC) in agriculture[19]: CEFC is an independent Australian Government agency which works for commercial investment in energy efficiency, renewable energy and low-emission technologies. CEFC works both independently, in cases of bigger projects, and through collaborating with major Australian banks for smaller projects. Emissions Reduction Fund[20] is also another voluntary scheme that provides support for farmers and land managers in emissions reduction and carbon sequestration (capture and storage of carbon) projects. This scheme also supports alternative income methods for farmers, landowners and general citizens. The Carbon Farming Futures[21] (CFF) programme is another progressive scheme that has also supported sustainable food growth in Australia. This scheme advocates for stimulating farm growth through holistically working on farmer-friendly budgeting, climate-adjustable farming techniques and usage of organic soil manures to improve crop production.

India, however, has faced major challenges in the context of sustainable farming and food security for a long time. According to the World Bank Report 2012,[22] India has the largest cultivation area for wheat, rice and cotton and is the largest producer of milk, pulses and spices in the global scenario. About 75 per cent of the Indian population is dependent on rural incomes.[23] However, several major constraints pose challenges for sustainable agriculture in India. These include water shortages, recurrent droughts, environmental degradation, vulnerability to weather-related disasters, etc. Further, India also has the largest number of children and adults who lack basic nutrition.[24] However, the problem is not something that cannot be addressed. Proper

---

[19] Clean Energy Finance Corporation (CEFC) Investment in Agriculture, http://www.agriculture.gov.au/ag-farm-food/climatechange/cefc, accessed 27 March 2018.

[20] Emissions Reduction Fund, http://www.agriculture.gov.au/ag-farm-food/climatechange/cfi, accessed 27 March 2018.

[21] Carbon Farming Futures, http://www.agriculture.gov.au/ag-farm-food/climatechange/carbonfarmingfutures, accessed 27 March 2018.

[22] World Development Report 2012 Gender Equality and Development (Washington: The World Bank). doi: 10.1596/978-0-8213-8810-5.

[23] World Development Report 2012.

[24] United Nation's World Food Program, https://www.wfp.org, accessed 1 July 2017.

execution of laws, like the National Food Security Act, 2013, and government policies addressing proper distribution of seeds, water and fertilizers, regular soil checking, periodic training of farmers in organic farming, training and awareness campaigns regarding proper trading in the agricultural sector, etc., may definitely improve the sustainable agricultural development in India. The Ministry of Agriculture and Farmers' Welfare, Government of India,[25] has also taken several initiatives to support sustainable agricultural development to address food security in India. These include providing training on fisheries and introducing new technologies to improve the fisheries industry. Central Institute of Fisheries Nautical and Engineering Training (CIFNET), Cochin,[26] Central Institute of Coastal Engineering for Fishery, (CICEF), Bangalore,[27] National Institute of Fisheries Post Harvest Technology and Training (NIFPHATT), Cochin, Fishery Survey of India (FSI), Mumbai, etc., are being used as prime training institutes for this purpose, which train fishermen and private stakeholders in the fisheries industry on sustainable food growth and food market management. National Dairy Development Board, National Bank for Agriculture and Rural Development (NABARD), Department of Agriculture Cooperation & Farmers Welfare (DAC&FW), National Initiative on Climate Resilient Agriculture (NICRA), Pradhan Mantri Fasal Bima Yojana, etc., are some of the initiatives taken by the government to ensure improved dairy production, provision of training on climate-friendly, innovative agricultural techniques, financial support for farmers from urban and rural areas, etc. Further, since 2015, the government of India has been vigorously advocating the 'Digital India'[28] and 'Make in India' initiatives. The portals created

---

[25] The Ministry of Agriculture and then renamed to The Ministry of Agriculture and Farmers' Welfare from August 2015, Government of India, http://agriculture.gov.in, accessed 27 March 2018.

[26] Central Institute of Fisheries, Nautical & Engineering Training (CIFNET), Cochin, http://www.cifnet.nic.in, accessed 27 March 2018.

[27] Central Institute of Coastal Engineering for Fishery, (CICEF), Bangalore, http://www.cicef.gov.in, accessed 27 March 2018.

[28] For more understanding on Digital India, see https://www.digitalindia.gov.in/, accessed 12 July 2019. For more understanding on Make In India initiatives, see https://www.pmindia.gov.in/en/major_initiatives/make-in-india/, accessed 12 July 2019.

under these initiatives are now offering platforms for agricultural-sector stakeholders, including farmers, traders, consumers, soil scientists, climate researchers, farming technology developers, etc., to come together, share information, create a knowledge base and carry forward commercial activities.[29] For instance, mKisan Portal, the Soil Health Card portal, Farmer Portal, etc., are portals through which farmers may directly access information by way of using information technology and digital communication technology.

In spite of the efforts from the government stakeholders for encouraging sustainable agricultural development, multiple socio-economic–civil–political reasons play a negative role in achieving complete success. These include the tremendous growth in the real estate industry. This growth has impacted the sustenance of farmers and landowners in the agricultural sector, as there is huge migration of labourers from the agricultural sector to industries.[30] However, as information and digital communication technology has been made easily accessible to civil society members in India, over the last 5 years, there has been a steep growth in the involvement of educated professionals, who are engaged in different industries, in the agricultural sector as 'urban farmers', 'friends of farmers', terrace-garden farmers, etc. These stakeholders are engaged in knowledge sharing and volunteering in the agricultural sector. They offer their volunteering services to agriculture labourers and help them revive the traditional systems of farming, which are cost-effective as well.[31] This has helped agricultural labourers access knowledge from digital platforms in a much more user-friendly way. This has also helped the educated urban sector in India understand the financial challenges of grassroots-level

---

[29] Ibid.

[30] For example, see Hans P. Binswanger-Mkhize, 'The Stunted Structural Transformation of the Indian Economy: Agriculture, Manufacturing and the Rural Non-Farm Sector', *Economic and Political Weekly* 48, no. 26/27 (2013): 5–13. http://www.jstor.org/stable/23527235.

[31] For example, see http://amefound.org/, accessed 12 July 2018. Also see A. Sakaria, 'Mumbai Residents Convert Terrace into Garden, Grow 15 Kinds of Veggies, Herbs Organically', https://www.hindustantimes.com/mumbai-news/mumbai-residents-convert-terrace-into-garden-grow-15-kinds-of-veggies-herbs-organically/story-6Uh7w5pFVSDDEhadnlgkHK.html, accessed 12 July 2018.

farmers and small-scale agricultural traders. Further, this has encouraged people to understand about the necessity of food security and avoid food wastage. It has also encouraged stakeholders to address the issue of water and water resource management.

CONCLUSION

As can be seen from the above discussions, sustainable farming is the key for the development of food security policies and successful execution of the same, but it necessarily involves gross awareness among the various stakeholders. Due to global climate changes, farming technologies need to be accurate enough to address drastic changes in the climate. This may be achieved through creating a network of stakeholders, including technological–legal–socio-economic agro-industry experts who can deal with various aspects of farming technologies, soil technologies, seed development, migration of labourers, fair trade practices in the agricultural sector, water resource management, etc. It is necessary to understand that revitalizing agriculture would ensure food security and generates key opportunities for economic growth. This cannot be achieved unless the global community comes together to help each stakeholder in achieving the collective goal of food security.

About the Editors and Contributors

EDITORS

Prof. (Dr) Debarati Halder, LLB, LLM (International & Constitutional Law), LLM (Critical & Security Laws), PhD (Law) from NLSIU, Bangalore, is a professor of Law at Parul Institute of Law, Parul University, Gujarat, India. She is the founder of Centre for Cyber Victim Counselling, Ahmedabad, Gujarat, and founding secretary of South Asian Society of Criminology and Victimology. She is the India Chapter Head of International Society of Therapeutic Jurisprudence. She has published five books and several research articles on cybercrimes against women and law, child sexual abuse and related laws, therapeutic jurisprudence, etc., in reputed national and international journals, including *British Journal of Criminology*, *International Annals of Criminology*, *National Law School of India University Journal*, etc., with reputed publishers. She is a resourceful person for governmental and other international stakeholders, including National Commission for Women, national and state commissions for protection of child rights, UNICEF, Facebook, etc.

Dr Shrut S. Brahmbhatt is a Professor of Law, Business and Project Management with over nine years of experience in post-secondary education across India and Canada. He holds a PhD in Law and is currently affiliated with Seneca Polytechnic, Durham College and Georgian College. A prolific researcher and editor, Dr Brahmbhatt is recognized for his leadership and significant contributions to academia, research and higher education. His scholarly work spans various areas, including transgender rights, animal rights, intellectual property rights and human rights. Dr Brahmbhatt has published numerous articles in national and international journals and conducted several empirical studies. He has also organized national-level seminars and workshops focused on human rights, further solidifying his commitment to advancing knowledge and advocacy in these critical fields.

CONTRIBUTORS

Rubel Bareja is a law graduate and is presently engaged as an associate in a law firm. Her areas of interest include human rights, criminal laws, child rights, etc.

Priju Bhaskar T. is working as Assistant Professor in Siddharth Law College, Gandhinagar, Gujarat, India. She holds a PhD in the field of disability laws. Her research interests include constitutional law, administrative law and disability laws.

Anshuman Mohit Chaturvedi is a practitioner in Noida. He is President of a not-for-profit organization, Yuva Dharti, Noida. He has been teaching 80 underprivileged students who used to beg in the streets near his college. He is working on various issues, such as women empowerment, traffic awareness, plantation, anti-corruption programmes and child education.

Gunjan Chawla is presently working as an Assistant Professor in the Institute of Law, Nirma University, Gandhinagar, Gujarat. She has received her LLM degree from the National Law University, Jodhpur, in intellectual property rights. Several of her articles have been published in national and international peer-reviewed journals. She has also participated and presented papers in national- and international-level seminars, workshops, etc. Her areas of interest are privacy laws, intellectual property rights, international relations, criminal law, human rights, etc.

Mansi Chhaya received her BBA LLB degree from the Unitedworld School of Law, Karnavati University, Gandhinagar, Gujarat. Presently, she is engaged as an associate in the Academic Resource Team, Redbricks Education Foundation, Ahmedabad, Gujrat. Her areas of interest are gender and law, human rights, cyber law, child rights, etc.

Badri Sankar Das is pursuing his PhD in political science and international relations from the Centre for Political Studies, School of Social Sciences, of Central University of South Bihar, Gaya, Bihar. He holds an MA degree in political science and mass communication and an MPhil degree in mass communications. His areas of interest are political science, gender studies, human rights, tribal rights, social exclusion, new media journalism, etc.

Pallavi Dey is pursuing her MSc degree in forensic odontology from Gujarat Forensic Science University, Gandhinagar. Her areas of interest are forensic science, odontology and child rights.

Dipa Dube has been pursuing her career as an academic for almost two decades. Having completed her LLM and PhD degrees from the University of Pune and University of Calcutta, respectively, Dr Dube has been involved in teaching courses in criminal law, criminology, penology, evidence, victim justice, etc., in eminent law schools and universities of India. Presently, she is working as Associate Professor at Rajiv Gandhi School of Intellectual Property Law, Indian Institute of Technology, Kharagpur. She has many books to her credit, including *Rape Laws in India* and *Laws on Domestic Violence*. Her forthcoming publication includes R. Deb's seminal work *Principles of Criminology, Criminal Law and Investigation*, co-authored with Professor N. K. Chakrabarti. Her works have been published extensively in national and international journals in the fields of criminal law, criminology, victimology, forensic sciences, etc. Her latest publication is in *Annual Review of Interdisciplinary Justice Research* published by the University of Winnipeg, Canada. She has delivered lectures in several institutes of repute, including National Judicial Academy, Bhopal and West Bengal State Judicial Academy, Kolkata. She has undertaken research projects in diverse areas of criminal law, disability, gender rights, etc., funded by government agencies.

Dhriti Gupta is a law practitioner. She joined a not-for-profit organization, Yuva Dharti, in 2014 and now serves as the general manager of the said organization. She has been actively participating in women empowerment, traffic awareness, plantation, anti-corruption programmes and child education on behalf of Yuva Dharti.

Smit Hingu is an Advocate and is presently pursuing his LLM degree (specialization in intellectual property rights) from Gujarat National Law University, Gandhinagar. He did his graduation in BA LLB (Hons.) from Maharaja Sayajirao University of Baroda. He also holds a diploma in cyber laws from Asian School of Cyber Laws, Pune, Maharashtra. His areas of interest are intellectual property rights, child rights, human rights and cyber law.

Janardhana Rao Killi completed his LLM and PhD degrees from Andhra University, Visakhapatnam, where he also received his MA (Politics) and MCom degrees. Professor Killi is presently working as Principal at PDEA's Law College, Pune (approved by Savitribai Phule Pune University). He has a rich experience of more than 29 years in teaching. He has participated as a resource person and chairperson in several seminars, conferences and workshops conducted by different organizations. He has published several articles in reputed national and international journals on different topics, such as judicial activism in environmental protection, violence against women, personal laws, rights and status of women in India, corporate social responsibility and the role of the judiciary, and food adulteration and food safety.

V. Kolappan has done his PhD in mathematics from Vellore Institute of Technology, Tamil Nadu. He is working as a Lecturer in the Department of Information Technology, Higher College of Technology, Muscat, Oman.

Esha Maken is pursuing her BBA LLB course from the Unitedworld School of Law, Karnavati University, Gandhinagar, Gujarat. She is a blogger besides being a student. Her areas of interest are human rights, food safety, child rights, violence against women and laws, media law, etc.

Viralkumar B. Mandaliya has done his PhD in biotechnology. He has worked as Assistant Professor (Research) in Gujarat National Law University, Gandhinagar, Gujarat. He has authored books, book chapters and articles in reputed national and international journals on biotechnology, science and law, legal aid, legal awareness, etc.

Mradul Mishra has done his LLM and LLB and worked as Assistant Professor (Research) in Gujarat National Law University, Gandhinagar, Gujarat. He is currently a practitioner. His research interests include criminal law, constitutional law and human rights.

Shraddha Parekh is a practising Lawyer at the Gujarat High Court. She finished her BBA LLB from Unitedworld School of Law, Karnavati University, Gandhinagar, Gujarat. Her areas of interest are human rights, media law, women's rights, company law, etc.

Darshan Patankar is a practitioner and researcher in law. He is a former student of Gujarat National Law University, Gandhinagar. His areas of interest are human rights law and constitutional and administrative law.

Dhwani Patel has done her BDS, LLB and MSc in forensic odontology. She is presently working as Assistant Professor in Gujarat Forensic Science University. She specializes in forensic odontology and medico-legal issues. Her areas of interest are bite marks, human identification through dental structures and tooth DNA analysis.

Vishwa Patel is presently pursuing her LLM from Gujarat National Law University, Gandhinagar, Gujarat. Several of her articles have been published in national and international journals. Her areas of interest are human rights, child rights, women's rights, etc.

M. B. Pavithra has done her MA in criminology and PhD in criminology from University of Madras. She is presently working as an Assistant Professor in the Department of Human Rights and Duties Education, Ethiraj College for Women, Chennai. Her areas of interest are child rights, environmental crimes, crimes against women and laws, etc.

Zeel Raval is a practising lawyer at the Gujarat High Court. She finished her BBA LLB from Unitedworld School of Law, Karnavati University, Gandhinagar, Gujarat. Her areas of interest are human rights, women's rights, intellectual properties and media laws.

Heli Shah is a practising lawyer at the Gujarat High Court. She finished her BBA LLB from Unitedworld School of Law, Karnavati University, Gandhinagar, Gujarat. Her areas of interest are company law, intellectual property rights, human rights, violence against women and laws and media law.

Meet R. Shah is presently pursuing his LLM from Gujarat National Law University, Gandhinagar. His areas of interest are human rights, company law, corporate liability and developmental studies.

Vihasi Shah is pursuing her LLM from Gujarat National Law University, Gandhinagar, Gujarat. Several of her articles have been published in national and international journals. She is also a company secretary. Her areas of interest are women's rights, child rights, human rights, etc.

Vishwajeet Singh Shekhawat has graduated from Rajiv Gandhi National Law University, Punjab. His areas of interest are child rights, human rights, labour-related laws, etc.

Gauri Singh is an LLB graduate from the Faculty of Law, University of Delhi. Prior to this, she completed her graduation in business economics from the University of Delhi. She is the co-founder of *SpeakOut*, an initiative for underprivileged school students to imbibe legal awareness and speaking skills. Currently, she is working at the Supreme Court in New Delhi.

Manish Soni is a practitioner and researcher in law. He has done his LLB from Gujarat National Law University, Gandhinagar. He is interested in constitutional and administrative law.

Anamika Tyagi is a practitioner and an independent researcher. She finished her LLM from Nirma University, Gujarat. Her areas of interest are transgender rights, human rights, violence against women and laws, media law, etc.

Bhaumik P. Upadhyay holds a PhD from Department of Law, Madhav University, Rajasthan. He is working as a faculty in Shree PM

Patel College of Law & Human Rights in Anand, Gujarat. His areas of interest include human rights, land laws, constitutional law, etc.

Nadisha N. Vazirani, LLM, NET, is an Assistant Professor of law in SVKM's Pravin Gandhi College of Law, one of the leading educational institutes in Mumbai, imparting legal education. She graduated from the Government Law College, Mumbai, did her master's (LLM) programme in environment & legal order from the University of Mumbai, where she is currently pursuing her doctorate degree in environmental law. She has actively participated in national seminars on issues of environment law. Additionally, she has worked with eminent legal professionals in the field of corporate, commercial and personal law. Being academically inclined, she has also served with leading academic institutions over the last 5 years, including the esteemed Vivekanand Education Society's College of Law and SVKM's NMIMS (deemed-to-be) University's School of Law, and strives to contribute to the growth and development of the legal profession through academics and her association with leading educational institutes.

Namita Yadav is currently pursuing her LLB course from the University of Delhi. Prior to this, she did an undergraduate course in English literature. She has worked on child rights, disability rights and refugee rights. She is also an active member of various student groups, such as Queer Collective and a group on gender sensitization, and is also in the process of completing her diploma in Human Rights, Humanitarian and Refugee law.

Index

www.ingramcontent.com/pod-product-compliance
Lightning Source LLC
Chambersburg PA
CBHW041303210926
51850CB00001B/2
9788126943067